S0-BNU-755

YOU DECIDE!

Current Debates in American Government

JOHN T. ROURKE

University of Connecticut

PEARSON
Longman

New York   Boston   San Francisco
London   Toronto   Sydney   Tokyo   Singapore   Madrid
Mexico City   Munich   Paris   Cape Town   Hong Kong   Montreal

Executive Editor: Eric Stano
Supplements Editor: Kristi Olson
Senior Marketing Manager: Megan Galvin-Fak
Cover Designer: John Callahan
Cover image courtesy of Getty Images, Inc.
Manufacturing Manager: Dennis J. Para
Manufacturing Buyer: Roy Pickering
Printer and Binder: Phoenix Color
Cover Printer: Phoenix Color

You Decide! Current Debates in American Government by John T. Rourke

For permission to use copyrighted material, grateful acknowledgment is made to the copyright holders on pp. 267–269, which are hereby made part of this copyright page.

Copyright © 2004 by Pearson Education, Inc.

All rights reserved. No part of this publication may be reproduced, stored in a retrieval system, or transmitted, in any form or by any means, electronic, mechanical, photocopying, recording, or otherwise, without the prior written permission of the publisher. Printed in the United States.

Please visit our website at http://www.ablongman.com

ISBN 0-321-24163-0

1 2 3 4 5 6 7 8 9 10 - PBT - 06 05 04 03

TABLE OF CONTENTS

14. JUDICIARY   188

LEGAL PHILOSOPHY AS A QUALIFICATION FOR THE BENCH: JUDICIOUS STANDARD *OR* OBSTRUCTIONIST BARRIER?

Legal Philosophy as a Qualification for the Bench: Judicious Standard

ADVOCATE: Laurence H. Tribe, Professor, Harvard Law School

SOURCE: Testimony during hearings on "Judicial Nominations, Filibusters, and the Constitution: When a Majority Is Denied Its Right to Consent," before U.S. Senate Committee on the Judiciary, May 6, 2002

Legal Philosophy as a Qualification for the Bench: Obstructionist Barrier

ADVOCATE: Todd F. Gaziano, Senior Fellow in Legal Studies and Director, Center for Legal and Judicial Studies, The Heritage Foundation

SOURCE: Testimony during hearings on "A Judiciary Diminished Is Justice Denied: The Constitution, the Senate, and the Vacancy Crisis in the Federal Judiciary" before U.S. House of Representatives, Committee on the Judiciary, Subcommittee on the Constitution, October 10, 2002

Also suitable for chapters on Constitution, Congress

15. ECONOMIC POLICY   216

CONSTITUTIONALLY REQUIRE A BALANCED BUDGET: FISCAL SANITY *OR* FISCAL IRRESPONSIBILITY?

Constitutionally Require a Balanced Budget: Fiscal Sanity

ADVOCATE: William Beach, Director, Center for Data Analysis, Heritage Foundation

SOURCE: Testimony during hearings on the "Balanced Budget Amendment" before the U.S. House of Representatives Committee on the Judiciary, Subcommittee on the Constitution, March 6, 2003

Constitutionally Require a Balanced Budget: Fiscal Irresponsibility

ADVOCATE: Richard Kogan, Senior Fellow, Center on Budget and Policy Priorities

SOURCE: Testimony during hearings on the "Balanced Budget Amendment" before the U.S. House of Representatives Committee on the Judiciary, Subcommittee on the Constitution, March 6, 2003

Also suitable for chapters on Constitution, Policy

16. CRIMINAL JUSTICE POLICY   228

THE DEATH PENALTY: RACIALLY BIASED *OR* JUSTICE SERVED?

The Death Penalty: Racially Biased

ADVOCATE: Julian Bond, Professor of History, University of Virginia and Distinguished Professor-in-Residence, American University

EXTENDED TABLE OF CONTENTS

WEB ISSUES

The following topics are available on the Web at:
http://www.ablongman.com/YouDecide/

---

19. DECIDING POLICY

ADOPT DIRECT DEMOCRACY *OR* REMAIN A REPUBLIC?

Deciding Policy: Adopt Direct Democracy

ADVOCATE: Harlan Hahn, Professor of Political Science, University of Southern California

SOURCE: Testimony during hearings, "Voter Initiative Constitutional Amendment," before the U.S. Senate Committee on the Judiciary, Subcommittee on the Constitution, December 13, 1977

Deciding Policy: Remain a Republic

ADVOCATE: Peter G. Fish, Professor of Political Science, Duke University

SOURCE: Testimony during hearings, "Voter Initiative Constitutional Amendment," before the U.S. Senate Committee on the Judiciary, Subcommittee on the Constitution, December 13, 1977

Suitable for chapters on Introduction, Constitution, Political Participation, Policymaking

---

20. CONSTITUTIONAL AMENDMENTS

LET STATES INITIATE *OR* KEEP CURRENT PROCESS?

Constitutional Amendments: Let States Initiate

ADVOCATE: Nelson Lund, Professor, George Mason University School of Law

SOURCE: Testimony during hearings, "Procedures for State Initiation of Constitutional Amendments," before the U.S. House of Representatives, Committee on the Judiciary, Subcommittee on the Constitution, March 28, 1988

Constitutional Amendments: Keep Current Process

ADVOCATE: Representative Mickey Edwards (R-MA) and Louis Michael Seidman, Professor, Georgetown University Law Center, on behalf of Citizens for the Constitution, nonpartisan organization devoted to fostering public discussion concerning amendments to the Constitution

SOURCE: Testimony during hearings, "Procedures for State Initiation of Constitutional Amendments," before the U.S. House of Representatives, Committee on the Judiciary, Subcommittee on the Constitution, March 28, 1988

Suitable for chapters on Constitution, Federalism

PREFACE

To the Students

This book is founded on two firm convictions. The first is that each of you who read this book is profoundly affected by politics, probably in more ways than you know. The second "truth" is that it is important that everyone be attentive to and active in politics.

POLITICS AFFECTS YOU

The outcome of many of the 18 debates in this printed volume and the 6 supplemental debates on the Web will impact your life directly. If you play college sports, for example, the controversy over Title IX in **Debate 13** helps determine what teams and athletic scholarship support are available at your school. Similarly, the issue of affirmative action in **Debate 17** may influence your admission to graduate school, if that is the course you take. More generally, **Debate 15** over whether there should be a balanced budget amendment to the U.S. Constitution will play a role in what taxes you pay and what services you receive from the government. Such an amendment might, for example, reduce the availability of Pell Grants and other financial support for college students. It is also college-age students who are most likely to be sent to and to die in wars. There has not been a military draft since the Vietnam War era, and U.S. casualties have been relatively light in wars since then. But in that war, 61% of the more than the 58,000 Americans killed were between the ages of 17 and 21. There are some critics who argue that the Bush Doctrine, featured in **Debate 18**, could lead to more wars that would put American young adults in peril. On a related topic, **Debate 12** addresses who gets to decide if Americans will be sent to war. Under current political and constitutional realities, the answer is, "usually the president." Are you comfortable with that, personally or as a citizen in a democracy? **Debate 22** also address presidential powers, and would enhance them if the suggestion of one advocate that the president be giving a line-time veto were to be adopted.

PAY ATTENTION TO THE POLICY PROCESS

Process may seem less interesting than policy to many people, but you do not have to study politics very long to learn that *who* decides something very often determines *what* the policy will be. Process does not always determine which policy is adopted, but plays a large role. Therefore, there are a number of debates in this volume whose outcome does not directly affect a specific policy, but which could have a profound impact on the policy process. For example **Debate 2** on Federalism may seem abstract, but one of the cases on which the debate turns involved the failed attempt of a Virginia woman to use U.S. civil rights law to sue an individual whom she alleged had raped her while she was a student at a public university in Virginia. The Supreme Court rejected her attempt on the grounds that the federal law on which the suit rested violated the division of power between the Washington, D.C. and the state governments in the federal system. **Debate 20** also addresses federalism, and one advocate proposes to strengthen the states by allowing the Constitution to be amended without the involvement of Congress.

Policy is also a reflection, in part, of who serves, and Debates 10, 11, and 21 all focus on that issue. If the Electoral College had been earlier abolished, which is the topic of **Debate 10**, then Al Gore, not George Bush, would have won the presidency in 2000.

Both advocates in **Debate 11** argue that they want to give you more choice as to who will represent you in Congress but they disagree about how. One advocate says the way to do it is to limit the term of federal legislators so that there will be regular turnover. The other advocate replies that doing so will limit your ability to be represented for many terms by an effective legislator whom you support. **Debate 21** takes up changing to a proportional representation system of elections. If adopted that would loosen, if not break the seeming strangle-hold that the Republicans and Democrats have on who gets elected. Indeed, such a change might make **Debate 9** on whether the Democrats or Republicans are likely to be the dominant party in the foreseeable future a moot point.

YOU CAN AND SHOULD AFFECT POLITICS

The second thing that this volume preaches is that you can and should take part in politics. One prerequisite for good participation is good information. Much of that comes through the new media, and, focusing on the Iraq War in 2003, **Debate 7** asks whether the coverage of the war was innovative journalism or voyeuristic reality TV.

Armed with knowledge, you should strive to become involved in the policy process. Anti-terrorist legislation is the subject of **Debate 4**, and many critics think that the freedoms of Americans are threatened by the Patriot Act enacted soon after the 9/11 terror attacks and by Patriot Act II, which the Bush administration has proposed. Others reply that such fears are overblown and that the minor restrictions on civil liberties in the bills help keep Americans safer from terrorism. Whatever your view, your liberties and life are involved, and you can become active in defeating or promoting the necessary renewal of Patriot Act I and the enactment of Patriot Act II.

Other debates may influence your ability to be active. Some people criticize those Americans who feel a strong tie to the land of their heritage and who favor U.S. policies that favor that land. Whether doing so is misplaced allegiance or an all-American tradition is taken up in **Debate 8** on ethnic lobbying. Another line of criticism is leveled at those who dissent from announced policy, especially during time of foreign policy crisis. The advocates in **Debate 6** differ on whether such dissent is un-American or patriotic.

Debate 23 about campaign finance reform also addresses participation. Those who argue that there should be strict limits on how much people and organizations can give to political candidates claim that the impact of money on politics makes a mockery of the idea that all citizens should have an equal say. Opponents rejoin that the proposed restrictions violate their freedom of speech. This issue is followed by a discussion in **Debate 24** about who can participate in perhaps the ultimate way: seeking the country's highest office, the presidency. Arnold Schwarzenegger may have been able to get elected as governor of California in October 2003, but as a foreign-born citizen he is constitutionally barred from becoming president. Should that barrier be eliminated? Perhaps more than any other issue, **Debate 19** relates to the idea that would most radically change participation in this country. That is instituting direct democracy by allowing the people as a whole to make law directly through processes called initiatives and referendums.

THERE ARE OFTEN MORE THAN TWO SIDES TO A QUESTION

Often public policy questions are put in terms of "pro and con," "favor or oppose," or some other such stark choice. This approach is sometimes called a Manichean approach, a reference to Manicheanism, a religion founded by the Persian prophet Mani (c. 216—

276). It taught "dualism," the idea the universe is divided into opposite, struggling, and equally powerful realities, light (good) and darkness (evil).

The view here is that many policy issues are more a matter of degree, and the opinion of people is better represented as a place along a range of possibilities rather than an up or down Manichean choice. Numerous debates herein are like that. For example, surveys of the American people about abortion, the subject of **Debate 3**, find that only a small minority of people is staunchly pro-choice or pro-life. The majority have a nuanced view that, on the one hand, supports women being able to terminate their pregnancies but that, on the other hand, reflects reservations based on timing and circumstances. Opinion is also something like that about the death penalty, the focus of **Debate 16**. A large majority of Americans favor it, but surveys also show that people are troubled by a range of possible injustices such as the relationship of wealth to the ability to mount a top notch defense, the ability to execute people for crimes committed while a juvenile, and claims of racial injustice.

MANY ISSUES HAVE MULTIPLE ASPECTS

Often political issues are sort of like matryoshkas, the Russian nested dolls in which a doll comes apart revealing a smaller doll inside, inside in which there is another doll, and so on. **Debate 1** is about "the right to bear arms." At its most specific, the issue is whether individuals have such a right. But deciding that involves the larger question of how to decide what those who wrote the Second Amendment meant. That matter, in turn, takes us to an even larger debate about whether we should follow the literal intent of those who wrote constitutional language, most of which is more than two centuries old, or apply the language of the Constitution within the context of the 21st century. In much the same way, **Debate 14**, on qualifications for the bench, has some specific and historical aspects, such what the phrase "advice and consent" of the Senate means. There are also matters of narrow constitutional controversy over whether the Senate parliamentary tactic called a filibuster is permissible as a way for a minority of senators to block the judicial nominees of the president. These smaller, albeit important, matters fall within the larger question of ideology and partisan politics in the selection and confirmation or rejection of judges by the Senate.

The discussion in **Debate 5** over whether English should be made the national language is also multifaceted. The language issue is just part of a larger question about what being an American means. The idea of the "melting pot" is not attractive to everyone because, to them, melting into the culture means giving up their own and adopting the largely European-based culture that has so far defined Americans.

SOME CONCLUDING THOUGHTS

The points with which we began are important enough to reiterate. Whether you care about politics or not, it affects you every day in many ways. As the legendary heavyweight boxer Joe Louis put it after knocking out Billy Conn, a more agile but less powerful opponent, in their 1941 championship fight, "You can run, but you can't hide."

Simply paying attention is a good start, but taking action is even better. Everyone should be politically active, at least to the level of voting. Doing so is in your self-interest because decisions made by the federal, state, and local governments in the U.S. political system provide each of us with both tangible benefits (such as roads and schools) and intangible benefits (such as civil liberties and security). Also, for good or ill, the government takes things away from each of us (such as taxes) and restricts our actions (such as speed limits). It is also the case in politics that, as the old saying goes, squeaky wheels get the grease. Those who participate actively are more likely to be influential. Those who do not, and young adults are by far the age group least likely to even vote, are consigned to grumbling impotently on the sideline.

As an absolute last thought (really!), let me encourage you to contact me with questions or comments. My e-mail address is john.rourke@uconn.edu. Compliments are always great, but if you disagree with anything I have written or my choice of topics or have a suggestion for the next edition, let me know. Thanks!

To the Faculty

Having plied the podium, so to speak, for three decades, I have some well-formed ideas of what a good reader should do. It is from that perspective that I have organized this reader to work for the students who read it and the faculty members who adopt it for use in their classes. Below are what I look for in a reader and how I have constructed this one to meet those standards.

PROVOKE CLASS DISCUSSION

The classes I have enjoyed the most over the years have been the ones that have been the liveliest, with students participating enthusiastically in a give and take among themselves and with me. Many of the debates herein have been selected to engender such participation in your classes by focusing on hot-button topics that provoke heated debate even among those who are not heavily involved in politics and who do not have a lot of background on the topic. The very first topic, gun laws, in Debate 1, is just such a subject. More than once I have had students get into spirited exchanges over the "right to bear arms," so I thought it would be a great debate to open the volume. Just a few of the other hot-button topics are abortion (Debate 3), English as the official language (Debate 5), the impact of Title IX on college athletics (Debate 13), and the death penalty (Debate 16). I hope they rev up your classes as much as they have energized mine.

Another point about class discussion as I point out in the Preface section "To the Students," is that while the debate titles imply two sides, many policy topics are not a Manichean choice between yes and no. Instead, I have tried to include many issues on which opinion ranges along a scale. From that perspective, I often urge students to try to formulate a policy that can gain majority support if not a consensus. You will also find that many of the issues herein are multifaceted, and I try to point that out to the students. For instance, the debate about gun control is more than about weapons, it is also about how we interpret and apply the Constitution.

PROVIDE A GOOD RANGE OF TOPICS

I always look for a reader that "covers the waterfront," and have tried to put together this reader to do that. There are numerous debates on specific policy issues and others on process. All the major institutions are covered in one or more debates, and there are also debates touching on such "input" elements as parties, campaigns, interest groups, and the media. The primary focus of the reader is on the national government, but federalism also receives attention in Debates 2 and 20. I have also included several debates that are at the intersection of domestic and foreign affairs, including Debate 4 (anti-terrorist legislation), Debate 6 (the acceptability of dissent during foreign crises), Debate 7 (media coverage of the war with Iraq), Debate 12 (presidential war powers), and Debate 18 (the Bush Doctrine).

My sense of a good range of topics also means balancing hot-button topics with others that, while they will draw less of an emotional response, are important to debate because they give insight about how the system works and might work differently. Debate 2 on federalism is an example, and hopefully it will get students to think about the federal system, which my experience tells me they mostly take as an unchanging given. Another example is the idea presented in Debate 21 of going from a single-member district, plurality electoral system to a proportional representation system.

GIVE THE STUDENTS SOME BACKGROUND FOR THE READING

Readers that work well provide the students with some background material that is located just before the reading. This debate volume follows that scheme. There is a two-page introduction to each debate that establishes its context. As part of this set up, each introduction provides the students with several "points to ponder" as they read the debates.

Moreover, the introductions do more than just address the topic per se. Instead they try to connect it to the chapter of the text for which it is designed. For example, the introduction to Debate 14 on the tensions between President Bush and the Senate Democrats over judicial nominations begins with the power of the judiciary in the U.S. political system and how that makes judicial appointments such a high-stakes issue.

PROVIDE FOLLOW-UP POSSIBILITIES

One of the rewards of our profession is seeing students get excited about a field that intrigues us, and the reader provides a "continuing debate" section after each of the reading pairs. This section has three parts. "What Is New" provides an update of what has occurred since the date(s) of the two articles. "Where to Find More" points students to places to explore the topic further. I have particularly emphasized resources that can be accessed on the Internet on the theory that students are more likely to pursue a topic if they can do so via computer than by walking to the library. Needless to say, I think libraries are great and students should have to use them, so there are also numerous references to books and academic journals. Finally, the continuing debate section has a "What More to Do" part. This segment presents topics for discussion, suggests projects (like finding out how well your school is doing by Title IX standards), and advises how to get active on a topic.

FIT WITH THE COURSE

I favor readers that fit the course I am teaching. I prefer a book with readings that supplement all or most of the major topics on the syllabus and that also allows me to spread the reading out so that it is evenly distributed throughout the semester. To that end, this book is organized to parallel the outline of the major introduction to American politics texts in use today. For those who favor the foundations-politics-institutions-policy approach, the table of contents of this volume should match almost exactly with their text and syllabus. For those who use a foundations-institutions-politics-policy scheme, a little, but not much, adjustment will synchronize the debates herein with their plans. Moreover to help with that, I have labeled each debate in the Table of Contents with the syllabus topic that fits with the debate. Additionally, for the 18 debates in the printed edition, I have indicated alternative syllabus topic for each. I have also made suggestions about how each of the six debates on the Web might fit with various text chapters and syllabus topics.

FLEXIBILITY

While there is a fair amount of similarity in the organization of the major introduction to American politics texts, I suspect that the syllabi of faculty members are a good deal more individualistic. With that in mind, I have provided flexibility in the reader. First, there are 18 debates in the printed edition, each which is related to a topic, but each of which has suggestions in the table of contents for alternative assignment. Then there are 6 additional readings on the Longman Web site associated with *You Decide!* Each of these also has multiple uses and my suggestions about how to work them into your syllabus. Thus, you can use all 24 debates or many fewer, you can substitute some on the Web for some in the printed edition, you can follow the order in the book fairly closely with most texts or you can rearrange the order at will. As the Burger King slogan goes, "Have it Your Way!"

As a final note, let me solicit your feedback. The first edition of any text or reader is always a bit of a prototype, and I consider *You Decide!* to be a work in progress. My e-mail address is john.rourke@uconn.edu. Of course I will be pleased to hear about the things you like, but I and the next edition of the reader will surely benefit more from hearing how I could have done better and what topics (and/or readings) would be good in the next edition. Thanks!

YOU DECIDE!

Current Debates in American Government

1

CONSTITUTION

GUNS, SAFETY, AND THE CONSTITUTION:
Individual Right *or* Subject to Regulation?

INDIVIDUAL RIGHT

ADVOCATE: Joyce Malcolm, Professor, Department of History, Bentley
College and Senior Fellow, MIT Security Studies Program

SOURCE: "Infringement," *Common Place*, July 2002

SUBJECT TO REGULATION

ADVOCATE: Daniel A. Farber, Henry J. Fletcher Professor of Law and
Associate Dean of Faculty and Research, University of Minnesota

SOURCE: "Disarmed by Time: The Second Amendment and the Failure of
Originalism," *Chicago-Kent Law Review*, 2000

In the early days of World War II, British Prime Minister Winston S. Churchill famously described the Soviet Union as a "riddle wrapped in a mystery inside an enigma." Had he been commenting on the current debate in the United States over gun control, Churchill might have used the same words to describe it.

The riddle, so to speak, is the meaning of the words of the Second Amendment to the U.S. Constitution: "A well regulated Militia, being necessary to the security of a free State, the right of the people to keep and bear Arms, shall not be infringed." Ask yourself, for example, Does "people" mean individuals, or does it refer to the collective citizenry, as in "We the people"?

The mystery is what, if anything, the framers of the U.S. Constitution and the Bill of Rights intended the amendment to accomplish. Scholars disagree mightily about this issue.

The enigma is whether the lawmakers of the late 1700s would argue that 21st century Americans should be bound by the literal meaning of words written more than 200 years ago, or should interpret them in the light of modern circumstances.

We might look to the courts to unravel these issues, but they have not been crystal clear. Generally, they have upheld the authority of government to regulate the ownership of weapons, but the Supreme Court has never ruled directly on the essence of the Second Amendment. To date, the most important case has been *United States v. Miller* (1939), in which the Supreme Court upheld a provision of the National Firearms Act (1934) requiring registration of sawed-off shotguns. The majority opinion held that "in the absence of any evidence…that possession [of a sawed-off] shotgun…has some reasonable relationship to…a well-regulated militia, we cannot say that the Second Amendment guarantees the right to keep and bear such an instrument." Notice that the opinion neither denies nor affirms a right to bear arms. It only rules that sawed-off shotguns are not protected, leaving it unclear if other weapons might be.

Most recently, gun control opponents were buoyed by the decision of the Fifth U.S. Circuit Court of Appeals in *United States v. Emerson* (2001). The majority opinion construed the word "people" in the Second Amendment to mean individuals, and said that the clause, "necessary to a well regulated militia," served merely to explain why individuals had the right to keep and bear arms. Still, it was a mixed case, because the judges also upheld the specific federal law that barred Timothy Emerson from owning a firearm based on his history of domestic violence. When the Supreme Court declined to hear Emerson's appeal, as it does in most cases, the major constitutional issues were left largely unresolved. In essence, no Supreme Court decision, including *Miller*, has definitively ruled either that there is an unrestricted right of individuals to keep and bear arms or that government has the unchecked authority to regulate, or even abolish, gun ownership and use.

What would you decide? Considering weapons is one way to start thinking about these policy and constitutional issues. There can be no doubt that weapons have changed. Flintlock pistols and rifles were the personal firearms when the amendment was written in 1789. Today's weapons have much faster firing rates and higher muzzle velocities and, therefore, vastly greater killing power than did their forerunners.

The presence and role of weapons in America is another piece of the puzzle. The latest data indicate that approximately 4.9 million firearms (including 1.7 million handguns) are manufactured or imported for the domestic U.S. market annually. In all, there are about 200 million privately and legally owned firearms in the United States, about 30% of which are handguns. Between 40% and 50% of all households have a legal gun. The uncertain but significant number of illegal weapons adds to these totals.

As for the yearly use of firearms, most are either never fired or are used for target shooting or hunting. But statistics also indicate that 28,633 people died in the United States in 2000 as a result of a gunshot. Most (58%) were suicides. Of the remaining gunshot deaths, 38% were homicides, 3% were accidents, and about 1% each was for unknown causes or by "legal intervention" of law enforcement officers. Left unclear in the government data is what percentage of the "homicides" was committed by individuals exercising their lawful right of self-defense.

POINTS TO PONDER

➤ The most specific debate is about gun control policy and whether widespread gun ownership provides greater or less safety. Given your views on this issue, would you vote for a bill in Congress to ban the manufacture, importation, sale, and possession of all handguns?

➤ At a second level, the debate is about the specifics of the Second Amendment and the intent of those who drafted and ratified it. What do the two advocates claim that those who wrote the language of the Second Amendment intended it to mean?

➤ The third, most general, and most important dispute is over whether the Constitution is a fixed document whose meaning should be derived by "strict construction" of its words and the original intention of those wrote it, or whether the Constitution is a "living document" that it should be interpreted in light of modern realities. What is your view? Should we be bound in the first decade of the 21st century by what people meant in the last decade of the 19th century when the Second Amendment was added to the Constitution?

Guns, Safety, and the Constitution:
Individual Right

JOYCE MALCOLM

In April 1995, I joined three other scholars testifying before the U.S. House Judiciary Committee's Subcommittee on Crime about our research into the meaning of the Second Amendment. As we gave evidence that the Second Amendment guaranteed an individual right to be armed and why the Founders believed it essential, the Republican members of the committee listened politely and with interest. Every Democrat on the committee, however, turned upon us with outrage and disdain. I felt startled and dismayed. The meaning of the amendment, at least for these representatives, seemed less a matter of evidence than of party politics. Sitting opposite us, arguing against an individual right, Dennis Henigan, general counsel for Handgun Control, Inc., presented the committee with a full-page advertisement from the *New York Times* signed by scores of scholars denying that a right to be armed existed. At this juncture one of my co-panelists, Daniel Polsby, then a professor at Northwestern School of Law, pointed out that one signer, a colleague of his, was no expert on constitutional law, let alone the Second Amendment, and that to his knowledge none of the other signers had ever conducted research into the issue. For the scholars who put their names to that testimonial, the conviction that there was no individual right to be armed was an article of faith. The attitudes of both the politicians and the scholars are regrettable. We are all the losers when constitutional interpretation becomes so politicized that otherwise reasonable people are neither willing to accept, nor interested in historical truth.

Political wrangles over the limits of constitutional guarantees are common, proper, and even necessary. The battle over the Second Amendment, however, is being waged at a more basic level, the very meaning of the amendment. This too is understandable where there is doubt about the Framers' intent. But once evidence of that intent is clear, as it now is, further argument, even in the service of a worthy political agenda, is reprehensible. It becomes an attempt to revise the Constitution by misreading, rather than amending it, a precedent that puts all our rights at risk. The argument over the Second Amendment has now reached that stage. But first, some background.

Two important points should be kept in mind as we briefly review this history. First, the debate over the meaning of the Second Amendment is surprisingly recent. Second, many of those who question or disparage the right do so because they believe that guns, in and of themselves, cause crime. Until the end of the nineteenth century, few Americans doubted their right to be armed. The Founders believed privately owned weapons were necessary to protect the three great and primary rights, "personal security, personal liberty, and private property." An armed people could protect themselves and their neighbors against crime and their liberties against tyranny. [James] Madison and his colleagues converted their English right to "have Armes for their defence Suitable to their Condition, and as allowed by Law," into a broader protection that took no account of status and forbade "infringement." "As civil rulers, not having their duty to the people duly before them, may attempt to tyrannize," the *Philadelphia Federal Gazette* explained when the proposed amendment was first publicized, "and as the military forces which must be occasionally raised to defend our country, might pervert their power to the injury of their fellow citizens, the people are confirmed...in their right to keep and bear their private arms." In the 1820s William Rawle, who had been offered the post of attorney general by George Washington, found, "No clause in the constitution could by any rule of construction be conceived to give Congress a power to disarm the people. Such a flagitious attempt could only be made under some general pretense by a state legislature. But if in any blind pursuit of inordinate power, either should attempt it, this amendment may be appealed to as a restraint on both." Supreme Court Justice Joseph Story, writing in 1840, agreed that the right of the people to keep and bear arms had "justly been considered, as the palladium of the liberties of a republic." And after the Civil War, the charge Southern whites were depriving blacks of their right to be armed was instrumental in convincing Congress to pass the Fourteenth Amendment.

Then politics intervened. Early in the twentieth century when American whites, fearful of blacks in the South and the millions of foreign immigrants in the North, wanted to restrict access to firearms, alternative reading of the amendment gained credence. In the absence of serious scholarship, constructions that reduced or eliminated the individual right to be armed seemed plausible, especially in light of the awkward construction of the Second Amendment and the sparse congressional debates during its drafting, both of which relied upon common understandings of the value of a society of armed individuals

that had faded over time. These new interpretations emphasized the dependent clause referring to the militia, to the neglect of the main clause's guarantee to the people. The theory developed that the Second Amendment was merely intended to enhance state control over state militia; that it embodied a "collective right" for members of a "well-regulated" militia—today's National Guard—to be armed, not a personal right for members of a militia of the whole people, let alone for any individual. Even when an individual right was conceded, the amendment was proclaimed a useless anachronism. After all, twentieth-century Americans had the police to protect them while armed individuals would be helpless against a government bent on oppression.

Beset by fears and armed with alternative readings of the Second Amendment, restrictive gun legislation followed. In 1911 New York State passed the Sullivan Law that made it a felony to carry a concealed weapon without a license, or to own or purchase a handgun without obtaining a certificate. Discriminatory laws in the South kept blacks disarmed. The first federal gun legislation, the National Firearms Act of 1934, introduced controls on automatic weapons, sawed-off rifles and shotguns, and silencers, weapons popular with gangsters. It was more than thirty years before rising crime-rates, urban riots, and three political assassinations again led to demands for stricter federal firearms legislation. The resulting Gun Control Act of 1968 limited mail-order sales, the purchase of firearms by felons, and the importation of military weapons. Professor Robert Cottrol [historian and legal scholar] finds this statute "something of a watershed" for, since its passage, the debate over gun control and the right to be armed have become "semi-permanent features" of late twentieth century American life. And "semi-permanent" the debate remains as we enter the twenty-first century.

The argument over the Second Amendment became and remains intense and highly political because the stakes are so great. Americans suffer from a high rate of armed crime that many insist is caused, or made worse, by easy access to firearms. Eliminate these, the thinking goes, and streets will be safer. Thousands of federal, state, and local firearms regulations adorn statute books, but a Second Amendment guarantee of the right to be armed blocks the dramatic reduction or banning of firearms that gun-control groups seek. There is a deep desire on their part to believe no individual right exists. On the other side, the traditional belief that guns protect the innocent and deter offenders is even more widely accepted. Studies show the majority of Americans have always believed the Constitution guarantees them a right to be armed. Approximately half of America's households have at least one gun, an estimated arsenal of some 200–240 million weapons, kept for sport and, more crucially, for personal protection. Every new threat to regulate weapons provokes thousands of additional purchases.

Both sides seek a safer nation. But whether one believes guns cause crime or prevent it, the Second Amendment figures in political solution at every level. National elections turn on a candidate's position on the right to be armed. A small Illinois town bans handguns completely; a small Georgia town requires a gun in every home. The state of Vermont, with no gun restrictions at all, boasts the lowest crime rate in the nation. In the name of public safety, the cities of New York, Chicago, Boston, and Washington, D.C., impose ever tighter gun restrictions. In the name of public safety, thirty-three states—some two thirds—now allow every law-abiding citizen to carry a concealed weapon. Is an

individual right to be armed an anachronism? Not in their opinion. Other states are considering this option.

In this clash of strategies, political gestures and competing claims abound. The Clinton administration allocated millions of dollars for gun buy-back programs, knowing a Justice Department study found this approach ineffective. Flushed with the success of lawsuits against tobacco companies, public officials in thirty-one municipalities sued gun manufacturers claiming millions in damages for gun crimes. In response, twenty-six states passed legislation forbidding such suits. Philanthropic foundations finance research that favors gun control, some even establishing whole institutes for "the prevention of violence." Notwithstanding plummeting rates of gun homicides, leading medical journals publish articles that proclaim guns a health emergency. They print seriously flawed research that purports to demonstrate that the presence of a firearm transforms peaceful citizens into killers, although studies of police records show the great majority of murderers are individuals with a long history of violence.

Nor has the popular press been shy in broadcasting its preferences. For seventy-seven consecutive days in the fall of 1989, the *Washington Post* published editorials calling for stricter gun controls. This was something of a record, but it is indicative of a national media in which three-quarters of the newspapers and most of the periodical press have advocated severe curbs on gun ownership and have denied a right to be armed exists. The press is entitled to its opinions, but unfortunately this bias has often affected and distorted news coverage. Every gun accident or shooting, every study that supports gun restrictions, is intensively reported, while defensive uses of firearms are downplayed along with scholarly investigations that tabulate these or that call into question the notion that legally owned firearms increase violent crime.

As a result, much conventional wisdom about the use and abuse of guns is simply wrong. Such reporting, for example, gives the impression that gun accidents involving young children are common and increasing when, in fact, they are happily rare and declining. The same is true of gun violence in schools. Do guns cause violence? In the thirty-year period from 1968 through 1997 as the stock of civilian firearms rose by 262%, fatal gun accidents dropped by 68.9%. Numerous surveys have shown that far more lives are saved than lost by privately owned guns. And John Lott's meticulous study of the impact of statutes permitting citizens to carry concealed weapons found them of value in reducing armed crime. Yet, convinced advocates are unwilling to examine the evidence of the constitutional protection or studies that contradict their view of the danger of private gun use.

All this has taken its toll. Alone among the articles comprising the Bill of Rights, the Second Amendment has, in recent years, come very near to being eliminated from the Constitution, not through the prescribed process of amendment, but through interpretations that reduced it to a meaningless anachronism. The low point came in 1975 when a committee of the American Bar Association was so befuddled by competing interpretations that members concluded, "It is doubtful that the Founding Fathers had any intent in mind with regard to the meaning of this Amendment." Leading textbooks on constitutional law, such as that by Lawrence Tribe, had literally relegated the Second Amendment to a footnote. Yet the American people remained convinced of their right to be armed despite textbooks and newspaper advertisements to the contrary.

Now scholarship has come to the rescue. The past twenty-five years have witnessed a growing number of studies of the Second Amendment, and these have found overwhelming evidence that it was meant to guarantee an individual right to be armed. In 1997, Supreme Court Justice Clarence Thomas in *Printz v. United States,* noting that the Court "has not had recent occasion to consider the nature of the substantive right safeguarded by the Second Amendment," hoped, "Perhaps, at some future date, this Court will have the opportunity to determine whether Justice Story was correct when he wrote that the right to bear arms 'has justly been considered, as the palladium of the liberties of a republic.'" Thomas added, "[A]n impressive array of historical evidence, a growing body of scholarly commentary indicates that the 'right to keep and bear arms' is, as the Amendment's text suggests, a personal right." Such evidence includes the individual right to be armed inherited from England; Madison's intent to list the right to be armed with other individual rights, rather than in the article dealing with the militia; his reference to his proposed rights as "guards for private rights"; the Senate's rejection of an amendment to tack the phrase "for the common defense" to the "right of the people to keep and bear arms"; and numerous contemporary comments. By contrast, no contemporary evidence has been found that only a collective right for members of a militia was intended. The evidence has convinced our leading constitutional scholars, among them Lawrence Tribe, Akhil Amar, and Leonard Levy, that the Second Amendment protects an individual right. In March 1999, Judge Sam Cummings of the Fifth Circuit [of the U.S. Court of Appeals], in the case of *United States v. Timothy Joe Emerson,* found a federal statute violated an individual's Second Amendment rights. The Fifth Circuit Court of Appeals, in a meticulously researched opinion, agreed that the Second Amendment protected an individual right to keep arms. As the [state] Court of Appeals in Ohio pointed out when, in April 2002, it found Ohio's prohibition against carrying a concealed weapon unconstitutional, "We are not a country where power is maintained by people with guns over people without guns."

Since the evidence clearly shows an individual right was intended, we should now move on to discuss the prudent limits of that right. Yet that discussion can't take place because denials of that right continue along with ever more tenuous theories to refute it, claims that the phrase "bear arms" was used exclusively in a military context; that the amendment resulted from a conspiracy between Northern and Southern states to control slaves; and that since the phrase "the right of the people to keep and bear arms" is set off by a comma it can be eliminated. But in early American discourse, as today, "bear arms" often meant simply carrying a weapon; there is no direct evidence of any conspiracy; and the elimination of every phrase set off by commas would play havoc with constitutional inter-pretation. [Historian] Michael Bellesiles claimed to have evidence there were few guns in early America, Americans were uninterested in owning them, and therefore no individual right to be armed could have been intended. However, his results seriously underestimate numbers of weapons and distort the attitudes toward them. Other scholars looking through some of the same evidence have found widespread ownership of guns.

Why does debate over original intent continue? Lawrence Tribe, who concluded there is an individual right after considering the new evidence, points to the "true poignancy," "the inescapable tension, for many people on both sides of this policy divide, between the reading of the Second Amendment that would advance the policies they favor and the reading of the Second Amendment to which intellectual honesty, and their own theories of constitutional interpretation, would drive them if they could bring themselves to set their policy convictions aside." The time has come for those who deny an individual right exists to set policy convictions aside in favor of intellectual honesty—and a more productive discussion.

Guns, Safety, and the Constitution: Subject to Regulation

Daniel A. Farber

INTRODUCTION

[The prevailing] wisdom [is that] the Second Amendment is little more than a footnote to Militia Clauses of the Constitution, themselves virtually irrelevant to today's military. But this conventional view has been challenged by revisionist scholars [who] contend that the framers had a far more sweeping vision of the right "to keep and bear Arms." In their view, the Constitution protects the individual's right to own guns for self-defense, hunting, and resistance to tyranny. These scholars find no room for uncertainty about the historical meaning of constitutional language. "The Second Amendment," we are told by one scholar, "is thus not mysterious. Nor is it equivocal. Least of all is it opaque." The meaning of the "right to bear arms," says another, "seems no longer open to dispute," and "an intellectually viable response…has yet to be made."

The revisionists' confidence about the original understanding is the foundation for their reinterpretation of the Second Amendment. Yet, the appropriate role of original intent in constitutional law has been debated for the past two decades. That debate should, if nothing else, caution against this sense of certainty about the implications of historical materials for present-day constitutional issues such as gun control….

Reading the historical record on the right to bear arms turns out to be a difficult exercise, full of perplexities. And even if we had a definitive answer that turned out to favor the revisionists, the claim that original

intent should always trump contemporary legislative decisions is itself problematic….

Thus, history cannot provide the kind of unshakable foundation for gun rights. that some scholars have sought. Indeed, there is something profoundly amiss about the notion that the Constitution's meaning today should be settled first and foremost by a trip to the archives. The effort to apply this notion to an issue as contemporary and hotly contested as gun control only serves to underline the fundamental peculiarity of the originalist approach to constitutional law.

Given the deep flaws in originalism, its continuing appeal may seem mysterious. For its more sophisticated adherents, it may appeal as a value-neutral method of decision and as a solution to the counter-majoritarian difficulty—perhaps a solution they would admit to be flawed, yet better than the alternatives. These arguments are ultimately unsatisfactory.

For less sophisticated adherents, however, originalism may have another, more visceral appeal. It harkens back to an earlier, purer age, when today's petty political concerns and squalid politicians were replaced with great statesmen devoted to high principle. This implicit appeal to a nobler, more heroic past may have particular resonance in the context of the Second Amendment, where it brings to mind visions of minutemen and frontier lawmen valiantly defending justice and freedom with their guns. These mythic versions of the past, however, can only obscure the all-too-real issues facing our society today. Being inspired by myth is healthy; being ruled by it is unsafe.

[There are] doubts [about] whether originalism provides a workable methodology for judges in deciding Second Amendment cases. Originalism requires them to make difficult historical judgments with little training in doing so; it gives no guidance about how concretely or abstractly to define the original understanding or about how to distinguish the framers' understanding of the text from their expectations about its implementation; and it leaves open the difficult problem of when to relinquish original understandings in favor of precedent or tradition. Furthermore, as practiced today, originalism may not even correspond with the methods used by the framers themselves to understand the text. Consequently, the so-called "original understanding" may not reflect the understanding of the original framers of how the provision would be applied under new circumstances. In short, with the best will in the world, judges who practice originalism will find themselves in vast disagreement over the meaning of the Second Amendment. Thus, if originalism is intended to constrain judges, it is a failure.

But even apart from these difficulties of implementation, the question remains whether we would want to implement originalism even if we could. The Second Amendment is a good illustration of why we should not want to be bound by the original understanding. Originalists claim that only originalism can reconcile judicial review with majority rule and make the Supreme Court something other than a super-legislature. But in reality, the Justices do not need to give up their bar memberships and join the American Historical Society in order to do their jobs properly. The conventional methods of constitutional law are completely legitimate and adequate to the task at hand. Originalism's greatest failing—in contrast to the conventional process of Common-law decision—is its inability to confront historical change. We should reject the originalist's invitation to ignore all of the history that has transpired since 1790 when we interpret the Constitution.

The Second Amendment once again provides an apt illustration of the defects of originalism. If the original understanding is to constrain judicial discretion, it must be possible to ascertain that understanding in a reasonably indisputable way. But, it is not even possible to give a clear-cut definition of what constitutes the original "understanding," as opposed to the original "expectation" or the original "applications" associated with a constitutional provision. And having cleared that hurdle, formidable difficulties confront the originalist judge, including a historical record that combines enormous volume with frustrating holes in key places, a complex intellectual and social context, and a host of interpretative disputes. If we do not trust judges to correctly interpret and apply their own precedents—a skill which they were supposedly taught in law school and have practiced throughout their professional lives—it is hard to see why we should trust them to interpret and apply a mass of eighteenth-century archival documents.

FIDELITY AND CHANGE

Originalism is an effort to fix of the Constitution once and for all at its birth. But there is an opposing view, one most eloquently expressed by Justice [Oliver Wendell] Holmes:

> [W]hen we are dealing with words that also are a constituent act, like the Constitution of the United States, we must realize that they have called into life a being the development of which could not have been foreseen completely by the most gifted of its begetters. It

was enough for them to realize or to hope that they had created an organism; it has taken a century and has cost their successors much sweat and blood to prove that they created a nation. The case before us must be considered in the light of our whole experience and not in that of what was said a hundred years ago.

The Second Amendment is among the provisions of the Constitution that seem most to call out for Holmes's approach—for the historical changes relating to the right to bear arms have been far-reaching indeed.

Some of those changes relate directly to the two subjects of the Second Amendment: firearms and and the militia. There is first of all the disappearance of the kind of militia contemplated by the framers. As [legal scholar] Akhil Amar explains, perhaps with some regret:

> [T]he legal and social structure on which the amendment is built no longer exists. The Founders' juries— grand, petit, and civil—are still around today, but the Founders' militia is not. America is not Switzerland. Voters no longer muster for militia practice in the town square.

Another relevant change is the development of professional police departments, which limit the need for individuals and groups to engage in self-help. Because these changes, unanticipated by the framers, undermined the asserted original purpose of the Second Amendment, its application today becomes problematic.

Apart from these changes relating directly to the Second Amendment's subject matter, broad changes in the constitutional landscape are also relevant. One watershed is the Civil War, which undermines the insurrectionist argument that armed revolt is a constitutionally sanctioned check on federal power....

Perhaps there may be those who reject the validity of the decision at Appomattox even today. What cannot be disputed as a lesson of the Civil War, however, is that insurrection is not an acceptable practical check on the federal government. Quite apart from the question of whether insurgents could defeat a modern army, the Civil War suggests that the costs of exercising this option would simply be unbearable: if a similar percentage of the current population died during such an insurgency today, we would be talking about five million deaths. Brave talk about insurrection is one thing; "paying the butcher's bill" is quite another. Perhaps the framers can be forgiven for failing to appreciate this reality; it is harder to excuse similar romanticism today.

The Civil War also transformed our concept of the relationship between the state and federal government. The Second Amendment, at least if revisionist scholars are to be believed, was based on the threat a powerful national government posed to liberty. But one effect of the Civil War was to cement the federal government's role as a guarantor of liberty. Since the time of the Fourteenth Amendment, rather than state and local communities being seen as bulwarks of freedom against the federal leviathan, the federal government has been pressed into service to defend liberty. The Fourteenth Amendment arose in part out of a sense of the obligation of the federal government to protect the rights of its citizens, by force if necessary, whether the threat came from a foreign nation or a state or local government.

Thus, rather than entrusting liberty to the "locals," the Fourteenth Amendment calls into play federal judicial and legislative power to ensure that the states respect individual rights. This realignment of the federal government as friend rather than threat to liberty underlies much of our modern Supreme Court jurisprudence and a plethora of twentieth-century civil rights legislation. This fundamental reassessment of the relationship between federal power and liberty would make independent state and local militias as much a threat to liberty as a protector.

If the insurrectionist argument is at odds with the lessons of the Civil War, the self-defense argument for constitutional protection clashes with the modern regulatory state. It is a commonplace that the New Deal [beginning in 1933] was a "watershed" in the development of the regulatory state, enough so to lead one prominent theorist to build a whole theory of constitutional interpretation around this shift. But the New Deal was only the beginning. In the 1960s and 1970s came a new wave of legislation covering matters such as consumer protection, discrimination law, and the environment. As a result, we live in a world where citizens routinely rely on the federal government rather than self-help to protect them against a host of threats.

Today, we expect federal protection against everything from potentially dangerous traces of pesticides in our foods to unwanted sexual overtures in the workplace. In this context, the notion that the government cannot protect us from the dangers of firearms seems like an odd relic of an earlier laissez-faire period. Indeed, it seems peculiar at best to say that the government can constitutionally protect us from one kind of hostile environment—coworkers displaying lewd pictures—but not from a more dramatic kind of hostile environment—neighbors carrying Uzis.

The point here is not that the Second Amendment is an anachronistic text that ought to be ignored, or that its interpretation should necessarily be narrowed in light of these later developments. It is not even that these later developments are fundamentally correct. What is wrong with originalism is that it seeks to block judges from even considering these later developments, which on their face seem so clearly relevant to the legitimacy of federal gun control efforts. But try as they may, it seems unlikely that judges can avoid being influenced by these realities.

CONCLUSION

What do we learn about originalism from the Second Amendment debate? What do we learn about the Second Amendment from the originalism debate?

One set of lessons relates to constitutional interpretation. The Second Amendment shows how the standard academic criticisms of originalism are not just academic quibbles: they identify real and troubling flaws. The debate about the Second Amendment vividly illustrates critical problems with originalism:

- The historical record concerning the right to bear arms is difficult for non-historians such as judges to evaluate, requiring a high level of historical expertise to evaluate the credibility and import of the evidence.

- Originalism might not accurately reflect the way in which contemporary readers understood the document; in particular, it may underestimate their willingness to contemplate limiting the "right to bear arms" clause in light of the purpose clause.

- The original understanding of the Second Amendment can be defined at different levels of generality, and the interpretation will depend on the choice of level as well as on how we distinguish the original "understanding" from mere original "expectations."

- Originalism, to be a realistic option, must acknowledge stare decisis, yet it does not provide us with clear guidance about whether the current Second Amendment case law should stand.

- Although originalism claims simply to be enforcing the will of "We the People," the Second Amendment shows how originalism can undermine majority rule.

- Because of the difficulties judges would face in basing their decisions on purely historical grounds, originalism would not eliminate the role of personal values in judging.

- Originalism forces us to ignore the ways our world has changed since the eighteenth century: the Civil War and its aftermath have cut the ground away from the notion of insurrection as a protection of liberty against federal power; and the New Deal and *its* aftermath have created a world in which we customarily turn to the regulatory state rather than to self-help to protect ourselves from threats.

It would, in short, be a serious mistake for judges to use originalism as their recipe for interpreting the Second Amendment or other ambiguous constitutional language. The fact that the arguments against this approach are familiar does not make them any less damaging.

At a more fundamental level, however, the lesson is not simply that originalists are wrong about how judges should read the Constitution. More importantly, they are wrong about the nature of the Constitution itself. In general, disputed constitutional provisions cannot simply be applied on the basis of whatever examples were discussed at the time, and so it is natural for originalists to attempt, instead, to reconstruct the theories underlying those provisions. This effort to theorize constitutional provisions is quite evident with the Second Amendment originalists we have discussed, but it is equally clear in the efforts of other originalists to find in the original understanding some unified theory of executive power or of federalism. But to look for an underlying theory is to misconceive the nature of the constitutional enterprise. Unlike physics, law does not lend itself to a "standard model" or a grand unified theory.

While the framers were indeed "concerned with such fundamental questions as the nature of representation and executive power," they were also engaged in "a cumulative process of bargaining and compromise in which a rigid adherence to principle yielded to the pragmatic tests of reaching agreement and building coalitions." In short, they were doing their best to create a viable set of democratic institutions, a task that required the utmost attention to both principle and pragmatism. Their task was not to agree on a theory but to create the basis for a working democracy. We hardly do justice to the spirit of their undertaking if we treat the resulting document as *their* Constitution alone rather than being ours as well. The last thing they would want would be for us to be ruled by false certainties about their intentions. Unfortunately, that is an invitation we have received all too often with respect to the Second Amendment.

THE CONTINUING DEBATE:
Guns, Safety, and the Constitution

What Is New

For now, the struggle between the pro- and anti-gun control forces is a stand-off. With the Republicans in control of Congress and the White House, increased gun control is unlikely. But because the issue has not been a top priority for President George W. Bush, GOP dominance in Washington D.C. has not resulted in major relaxations of existing gun control laws. As for the courts, there have been mixed messages. Gun control opponents hailed a 2003 decision in a federal district court in New York City that dismissed a suit brought by the NCAAP against gun manufacturers claiming they were partly responsible for violence in urban areas. But that was soon followed by a case in a Tacoma, Washington federal district court in which a the judge allowed a suit by the families of several of the victims in the sniper shooting in the Washington, D.C. area against the manufacturers of the rifle allegedly used by Allen Muhammad and John Lee Malvo in their December, 2002 killing rampage.

Where to Find More

For data on firearms, see the U.S. Bureau of Alcohol, Tobacco and Firearms report, *Firearms Commerce in the United States—2001/2002,* at http://www.atf.treas.gov/pub/, listed under Firearms Publications. The most recent data on firearms deaths in the United States is available from the U.S. Public Health Service's Centers for Disease Control Web site at: http://www.cdc.gov/nchs/fastats/firearms.htm.

The anti-gun control forces are represented by the National Rifle Association's Web site at http://www.nra.org/. For the opposing view, the URL http://www.bradycampaign.org/ will take you to the Web site of the pro-gun control Brady Campaign to Prevent Violence (named after James Brady, a former White House press secretary, who was shot in the head and disabled during the assassination attempt on President Ronald Reagan on March 30, 1981).

Scholarly legal arguments in favor of a strict constructionist reading of the Second Amendment include Sanford Levinson, "The Embarrassing Second Amendment," *Yale Law Journal* (1989) and Eugene Volokh, "The Amazing Vanishing Second Amendment," *New York University Law Review* (1998). Taking the opposite view is David C. Williams, *The Mythic Meanings of the Second Amendment* (Yale University Press, 2003) and Jack N. Rakove, "The Second Amendment: The Highest Stage of Originalism," *Chicago-Kent Law Review* (2000).

What More to Do

One constant suggestion for this and every debate in this book is to get involved no matter which side you are on. The issue is important, and you can make a difference if you try. Also keep the larger constitutional questions in your mind as you read other debates in this book. Like this debate, some will involve questions about the meaning of words or phrases, such as "due process of law" in the Fourteenth Amendment. Other debates will also include the ongoing dispute over strict construction versus contemporary interpretation of the Constitution by the courts. Perhaps before any of this, though, think about and discuss with others the policy and constitutional issues presented in this debate. Then, as this book's title urges, You Decide!

2

FEDERALISM

THE REHNQUIST COURT AND FEDERALISM:
Hobbling Congress *or* Defending the States?

HOBBLING CONGRESS

ADVOCATE: Leon Friedman, Professor, Hofstra University School of Law

SOURCE: "Overruling the Court," *American Prospect*, August 27, 2001

DEFENDING THE STATES

ADVOCATE: Marci A. Hamilton, Paul R. Verkuil Chair in Public Law,
Benjamin N. Cardozo School of Law, Yeshiva University

SOURCE: Testimony during hearings on "Narrowing the Nation's Power: The
Supreme Court Sides with the States," before the U.S. Senate
Committee on the Judiciary, October 1, 2002

About the time they are in middle school, students taught that one way the delegates to the Constitutional Convention of 1787 in Philadelphia sought to safeguard democracy was by creating a federal system of government that divides powers
between the central government and the states. It would be more accurate to say that
the most important goal of James Madison, Alexander Hamilton, and most of the
other framers, was to change the state-dominant system that then existed under the
Articles of Confederation. Therefore, they wrote a constitution that shifted considerable power from the states to the central government.

There was, however, strong opposition from the Antifederalists. One reason is that
they feared a dominant central government. To counter their argument, Madison and
Hamilton, along with John Jay, wrote a series of published essays. Both Madison and
Hamilton, who is quoted in the following testimony by Marci Hamilton, considerably, some would argue disingenuously, downplayed the authority of the central government under the new Constitution. For example, Madison wrote in *Federalist* No.
45, "The powers delegated by the proposed Constitution to the Federal Government,
are few and defined. Those which are to remain in the State Governments are numerous and indefinite." The new constitution's advocates also agreed to add a bill of rights,
including the Tenth Amendment, which on the face of it, seems to reserve to the states
all government authority not given to the federal government nor denied to the states.

Whatever anyone thought or intended, the imprecise language of the
Constitution left the boundaries between the authority of Washington and the
state capitals neither clear nor fixed. As such, the division of powers has been the
subject of legal, political, and occasionally physical struggle. It has not, however,
been an even contest. Even if one begins in 1789 with the new constitution,
authority has flowed away from the states and toward Washington since then. If
one begins the chronicle of the ebbing of state power earlier, with what existed
under the Articles of Confederation, then the diminution of exclusive state power
has been even more dramatic.

The reasons for this shift are many and complex, but a few are especially pertinent to this debate. Under its *implied powers*, the Constitution permits Congress to make laws "necessary and proper" to carrying out powers specified in the document. What is necessary and proper is subjective. But Congress has taken, and the court's have generally allowed, an expansive interpretation. The *Fourteenth Amendment* has also curbed the states. The courts have used its language about "due process" of law and the "privileges and immunities of citizens" to expand most of the Bill of Rights to apply to the states, as well as the federal government.

Fiscal federalism has also played a role. Over the last century, the federal government has tied numerous regulations to the grants-in-aid that it gives to states. Many of these regulations, such as the drinking age of 18, have created national rules in areas in which the federal government could not legislate directly. Finally, the *Tenth Amendment* has been virtually ignored. The Supreme Court has variously described it as adding "nothing to the instrument as originally ratified" (*U.S. v. Sprague*, 1931) and a "truism" (*U.S. v. Darby*, 1941).

The debate here has been sparked by a series of decisions by the Supreme Court under Chief Justice William Rehnquist that have restrained federal laws enacted under the logic of implied powers and the Fourteen Amendment and have reasserted, at least a bit, the spirit if not the letter of the Tenth Amendment. Some of these decisions have reversed congressional attempts to legislate in such worthy areas as creating "gun-free school zones," and strengthening the laws protecting women against violence. This has led Leon Friedman and others to charge the Rehnquist Court with hobbling Congress by resurrecting outmoded and long-abandoned constitutional theories about federalism. Marci Hamilton and others welcome the court's newfound concern with federalism. The Supreme Court's defenders contend that federalism is a key strength of the U.S. political system, and that the courts should not permit it to be further undermined by Congress, even if its legislative goals are otherwise laudable.

POINTS TO PONDER

➤ As you read, think about how well Madison's portrayal of the federal government's powers as "few and defined" and those of the states as "numerous and indefinite" corresponds to federalism's current reality. Is the change/lack of change positive or regrettable?

➤ Arguably, there is a "do the ends justify the means?" dilemma in this debate. For example, the case of *U.S. v. Morrison* (2000) involved the attempt of a woman who charged that she had been raped to sue the alleged assailant in federal court. In ruling that she could not do so, Chief Justice Rehnquist wrote that while, "no civilized system of justice could fail to provide her a remedy for the conduct," it was also the case that, "Under our federal system that remedy must be provided by the [state], and not by the United States." For the majority of justices, the positive social ends did not justify what to them were unconstitutional means. Do you agree?

➤ Not too far below the surface of some critics' position on federalism is the view that it is an outdated system. The argument is that the United States has become a single country economically and socially and, therefore, should also be unified politically. The defenders of federalism argue that it still, as it did in 1789, protects freedom, promotes diversity, and permits policy experimentation. What do you think? Does federalism make sense any more?

The Rehnquist Court and Federalism: Hobbling Congress

LEON FRIEDMAN

One of the myths of our political system is that the Supreme Court has the last word on the scope and meaning of federal law. But time and time again, Congress has shown its dissatisfaction with Supreme Court interpretations of laws it passes—by amending or re-enacting the legislation to clarify its original intent and overrule a contrary Court construction.

The Supreme Court often insists that Congress cannot really "overrule" its decisions on what a law means: The justices' interpretation has to be correct since the Constitution gives final say to the highest court in the land. But Congress certainly has the power to pass a new or revised law that "changes" or "reverses" the meaning or scope of the law as interpreted by the Court, and the legislative history of the new law usually states that it was intended to "overrule" a specific Court decision.

Often the reversal is in highly technical areas, such as the statute of limitations in securities-fraud cases, the jurisdiction of tribal courts on Indian reservations, or the power of state courts to order denaturalization of citizens. But in the last 20 years, a main target of congressional "overruling" has been the Supreme Court's decisions in the area of civil rights.

In 1982, for example, Congress amended the Voting Rights Act of 1965 to overrule a narrow Supreme Court holding in *Mobile v. Bolden*, a 1980 decision that addressed whether intentional discrimination must be shown before the act could be invoked. In 1988, Congress overruled another Supreme Court decision (in the 1984 case *Grove City College v. Bell*) by pass-

ing the Civil Rights Restoration Act, which broadened the coverage of Title VI of the Civil Rights Act of 1964. The legislative history of that law specifically recited that "certain aspects of recent decisions and opinions of the Supreme Court have unduly narrowed or cast doubt upon" a number of federal civil rights statutes and that "legislative action is necessary to restore the prior consistent and long-standing executive branch interpretations" of those laws.

And in 1991, Congress passed a broad, new Civil Rights Act that specifically reversed no fewer than five Supreme Court cases decided in 1989—decisions that severely restricted and limited workers' rights under federal antidiscrimination laws. Led by Massachusetts Democrat Edward Kennedy in the Senate and New York Republican Hamilton Fish, Jr., in the House, Congress acted to undo those rulings, as well as make other changes to federal law that strengthened the weapons available to workers against discrimination. Despite partisan contention over the language of certain provisions (which led to last-minute-compromise language), President George Bush the elder supported the changes. The new law recited in its preamble that its purpose was "to respond to recent decisions of the Supreme Court by expanding the scope of relevant civil rights statutes in order to provide adequate protection to victims of discrimination." Given the current Supreme Court's track record in civil rights cases, there can be no doubt that congressional remediation is again necessary. In a series of cases over the past two years, the Court has been giving narrow readings to various federal civil rights laws. And once again, an attentive Congress can and should overrule the Court's decisions if the legislators care about fairness in the operation of government and in the workplace.

The recent cases were decided by identical 5–4 votes: Three conservative justices (William Rehnquist, Antonin Scalia, and Clarence Thomas) were joined by two centrists (Sandra Day O'Connor and Anthony Kennedy) to narrow the reach of the laws at issue. Four liberal justices (John Paul Stevens, David Souter, Ruth Bader Ginsburg, and Stephen Breyer) dissented in all of the cases, four of which are described below.

[The four cases:]

- [In 2000], on the grounds of federalism, the Supreme Court held in *Kimel v. Florida Board of Regents* that persons working for state governments cannot sue in federal court under the Age Discrimination in Employment Act, which Congress adopted in 1967. Such suits, the high court said, were constitutionally barred by the 11th Amendment's prohibition of suits against states in federal court. This ruling removed 3.4 percent of the nation's total workforce from the federal law's protections against age bias—some 5 million state employees across country.

- On the same basis as the age-discrimination case, the Court held in February [2001] that state employees cannot sue in federal court under the Americans with Disabilities Act. In this ruling, *Board of Trustees of the University of Alabama v. Garrett*, state workers who alleged disabilities discrimination were relegated to seeking recourse through state courts, where the available remedies are often much weaker than those provided under federal law.

- In April [2001], the Supreme Court narrowed the reach of Title VI, the 1964

provision that prohibits recipients of federal financial assistance from discriminating on the basis of race, color, or national origin. In *Alexander v. Sandoval,* the Court held that Title VI is violated only if a plaintiff proves that the funded party *intentionally* discriminated on the basis of race—an interpretation that runs contrary to the rule for other civil rights laws (such as Title VII), which require only a showing of a discriminatory impact to trigger enforcement. At the same time, the justices held that neither public nor private recipients of federal financial aid who violate the nation's antidiscrimination regulations can be sued in federal court. Thus the state of Alabama was not vulnerable to suit when it established an "English only" requirement for taking a driver's license exam, even though federal regulations prohibit such restrictions. The only remedy, the Court held, was termination of federal funding to the state entity that violated the regulations (a sanction that entails a complicated administrative process).

- [In] May [2001] the Court decided that civil rights litigants who bring suit against the government or an employer cannot collect attorney fees if the defendant voluntarily ceases the practice complained of or settles the claim before going to trial (the case was *Buckhannon Board and Care Home, Inc., v. West Virginia Department of Health and Human Services*). In 1976, Congress passed the Civil Rights Attorney Fees Award Act to encourage lawyers to take civil rights cases as "private attorney generals." Such cases "vindicate public policies of the highest order," Congress explained when it passed the law. The act specified that the legal fees of "prevailing parties" would be paid by the losing party—generally a government that violated the plaintiffs' constitutional rights. As Justice Ginsburg pointed out in her dissent in the *Buckhannon* case, Congress enacted the law to "ensure that nonaffluent plaintiffs would have effective access to the Nation's courts to enforce...civil rights laws." The effect of the Buckhannon decision is that a government body can tenaciously litigate a case until the last minute, then throw in the towel and evade the requirement of paying attorney fees. Since lawyers can no longer be sure that they'll be paid if they file civil rights suits, this ruling will certainly discourage them from taking on such cases, even those that clearly have merit.

Two of these cases are quite easy to correct. Congress can reverse the Supreme Court's decision about attorney fees by simply amending the Civil rights law to provide that a litigant is considered a prevailing party entitled to fees if the lawsuit "was a substantial factor" in remedial action taken by the government and the suit brought by the plaintiff had a "substantial basis in fact and law." That was the rule generally applied by the lower courts before the Supreme Court decision.

The *Sandoval* rule can also be corrected by legislation. Congress could amend Title VI to provide that "any person aggrieved by the violation of any regulation issued pursuant to this act may bring a civil action in an appropriate federal court. Such actions may include suits challenging any discriminatory practice or policy that would be deemed unlawful if it has a disparate impact upon persons protected by this title."

The *Kimel and Garrett* decisions are more difficult to attack. The Supreme Court held that the 11th Amendment to the Constitution protects states against suits in federal court for age or disabilities discrimination by their employees. Although Congress cannot overrule a constitutional determination made by the Court, it can condition federal financial assistance on state adherence to federal requirements. In 1987 the Supreme Court held in *South Dakota v. Dole* (a 7–2 decision written by Chief Justice Rehnquist, in which Justice Scalia joined) that Congress could insist that South Dakota increase the minimum drinking age to 21 as a condition of obtaining federal highway funds. In other words, while Congress cannot force states to do its bidding, it in effect may bribe them to follow federal requirements.

Thus Congress could condition federal grants under Medicaid, Medicare, or the Social Security Act on the states' surrendering their 11th Amendment immunity under the federal acts banning discrimination based on age and disability. If a state wished to obtain federal funds under various social-welfare provisions, it would have to accede to the U.S. antidiscrimination laws and waive its immunity from being sued by its employees in federal court. Indeed, the 1986 Civil Rights Remedies Equalization Amendment specifically declared that Congress intended for states to waive their 11th Amendment immunity in order to receive federal financial assistance.

Congress could use the same device to overrule another recent Supreme Court decision: [the] 5–4 holding in *United States v. Morrison* [2001] that the civil-remedy provisions of the Violence Against Women Act of 1994 are unconstitutional. The majority held that the law exceeded congressional power under the Constitution's commerce clause—the first time a federal law had been invalidated on that basis since 1936. But Congress can counter the Court's action by ensuring that such civil remedies are available to victims of gender-motivated acts of violence through state courts. How? By making the federal funds that are available through Medicare or Social Security programs contingent on a state's provision of such remedies.

In 1991, Congress and the first President Bush acted courageously to overrule manifestly narrow decisions of the Supreme Court that violated a national consensus against discrimination by government or by employers. Now that the Democrats have control of the Senate, they should make similar corrective legislation one of their first objectives. And who knows? This President Bush might even follow the lead of his father and endorse the changes.

The Rehnquist Court and Federalism: Defending the States

MARCI A. HAMILTON

I am grateful to be [able]...to explain why I believe...the Supreme Court has not sided with the states, though this is a popular misconception, but rather with the Constitution....The good faith of the Justices implementing the Constitution's explicit and inherent federalism limits cannot and should not be questioned.

There are some relevant principles on which there is no disagreement.

(1) It is the province of the Supreme Court to say what the law—including the Constitution—is. [A principle decided in] *Marbury v. Madison*...(1803).

(2) The Supreme Court is charged with drawing the lines of power set out by the Constitution.

(3) The federal courts routinely determine the constitutional boundaries between the federal branches (through separation of powers doctrine) and between church and state.

(4) One of the Constitution's fundamentals is that governing power is divided between the federal government and the states.

(5) From 1936 to 1995, the Supreme Court did not police the boundary between the federal and state governments, but rather gave the federal government carte blanche to enact any law at will.

(6) Since 1995, the Supreme Court has clarified the boundaries of power between the federal government and the states.

(7) The Tenth Amendment is a limit on congressional power: [The amendment says:] "The powers not delegated to the United States by the Constitution, nor prohibited by it to the States, are reserved to the states respectively, or to the people."

(8) The Congress is properly limited by the Constitution.

(9) The states are properly limited by the Constitution.

Taken together, these principles fully support the Supreme Court's federalism jurisprudence. [Critics of the Rehnquist court] apparently believe the Constitution places no meaningful limits on Congress's capacity to regulate the states. [One critic] Judge [John] Noonan begins his book [*Narrowing the Nation's Power: The Supreme Court Sides with the States:* University of California Press, 2002] with reference to Alexander Hamilton writing to George Washington that "[t]here are some things the General Government has clearly a right to do—there are others which it has clearly no rights to meddle with, and there is a good deal of middle ground." This is a very odd quote for his purpose, which is to prove that Congress should have plenary power over all subject areas, as it shows that there was clear intent at the time of the framing, even among the most ardent Federalist, that the states would retain certain core areas of power.

Until 1995, there was virtually no middle ground left and there was precious little ground reserved exclusively to the states; rather, Congress (and the policy elites) assumed it had unlimited power. The Supreme Court's refusal to take up federalism principles for most of the twentieth century and Congress's willingness to move in where no limits existed almost eliminated those arenas where Congress "clearly [has] no right to meddle with." Rather, we reached a moment in history where Congress had persuaded itself it had plenary power over any policy item a lobbyist could conjecture. It is that sense of entitlement to plenary power that appears to motivate [critics of the Rehnquist court] and leads...to erroneous conclusions about the proper role of federalism.

Judge Noonan does not quote another passage by Alexander Hamilton, though it is relevant to his task. [In *Federalist* No. 17] Hamilton mistakenly believed that Congress would not have the desire to encroach on the arenas controlled by the states, but rather would only be attracted to the new powers given to the federal legislature:

> It may be said that [the constitutional design] would tend to render the government of the Union too powerful, and to enable it to absorb those residuary authorities, which it might be judged proper to leave with the States for local purposes. Allowing the utmost latitude to the love of power which any reasonable man can require, I confess I am at a loss to discover what temptation the persons entrusted with the administration of the general government could ever feel to divest the States of the authorities of that description. The regulation of the mere domestic police of a State appears to me to hold out slender allurements to ambition. Commerce, finance, negotiation, and war seem to comprehend all the objects which have charms for minds governed by that passion; and all the powers necessary to those objects ought in the first instance to be lodged in the national depository. The administration of private justice

> between the citizens of the same State, the supervision of agriculture and of other concerns of a similar nature, all those things, in short, which are proper to be provided for by local legislation, can never be desirable cares of a general jurisdiction. It is therefore improbable that there should exist a disposition in the federal councils to usurp the powers with which they are connected; because the attempt to exercise those powers would be as troublesome as it would be nugatory; and that possession of them, for that reason, would contribute nothing to the dignity, to the importance, or to the splendor of the national government.

How wrong [Hamilton] was. The innate pride in national issues in which Hamilton placed his faith has not been a check on the "love of power." To the contrary, there is no local arena into which Congress has been unwilling to venture. Indeed, the situation is so bad that the debate has become whether there is any identifiable arena of local control left. Land use? Education? Crime?

The federalism cases unfortunately show Congress at its worst—grabbing for power as it imposed fewer and fewer restraints on itself, vis-à-vis the states. For example, when Congress enacted the Gun-free School Zones Act, it did not even consider the constitutional basis of its action. *U.S. v. Lopez* (1995). When Congress enacted the Religious Freedom Restoration Act, it did not consult with the state and local governments on the likely impact of a law that would apply strict scrutiny to every general law that affected religious claimants.

The Court is not imposing its policies on the nation. Despite Judge Noonan's charges, the Court has not usurped policymaking power and has not aggrandized its own power. It is doing nothing different in the federalism cases than the courts do routinely in separation of powers and church-state cases. The burden of proof lies with those who would disable the courts vis-à-vis federalism to explain why the federal/state divide is off-limits, but the courts properly demarcate the boundaries between federal branches and between church and state. There is nothing in Judge Noonan's work or in the work of others criticizing the Court that satisfactorily explains why the Court should stand down when it comes to federalism but continue to arbitrate the separation of powers and church-state separation.

The federalism cases do not leave civil rights out in the cold. Although this would be hard to decipher if one were to read [Noonan's book] *Narrowing the Nation's Power* and not the cases, the pragmatic result of the federalism decisions is not to shut down any particular policy, but rather to send the lobbyists to the states on particular issues. There is no constitutional guarantee that lobbyists need have offices in Washington only.

In fact, in two civil rights arenas—prohibiting age and disability discrimination—the Court made a point of noting that the states had already enacted laws prohibiting such discrimination (*Kimel v. Florida Board of Regents*, 2000; *Board of Trustees v. Garrett*, 2001). Thus, the heat and light Judge Noonan trains on these decisions is odd, to say the least.

[The book] *Narrowing the Nation's Power* explains the Supreme Court's Eleventh Amendment cases. One of the means the Court has used to bring Congress back within reasonable constitutional boundaries and to give the states some room

within which to act as sovereigns, is to strengthen the Eleventh Amendment doctrine. The Eleventh Amendment is one of the constitutional features that reinforces the Framers' clear intent to set up a federal republic, one wherein the states retained significant power to serve the public good alongside the federal government.

Under the doctrine, the states are protected from suits for damages, unless they abrogate their immunity. Yet, there are still ample means of forcing the states to obey the federal law (assuming the law was enacted within Congress's enumerated powers). As the Court explained in *Garrett* [2001], a holding that the Eleventh Amendment prohibits a suit against a state for monetary damages still leaves open suits brought by the United States for monetary damages, private actions for injunctive relief, and state laws providing "independent avenues of redress."

It is my view that the recent federalism cases do not invalidate the vast majority of congressional lawmaking and certainly do not impede any civil rights agenda. Rather, the [Rehnquist] Court's decisions have called on the Congress to ask whether the states might already have acted on a particular issue, to engage in a dialogue with the states, and to respect the states. That seems hardly worthy of the disapprobation heaped upon it by Judge Noonan, but rather worthy of the high praise earned when a court pursues fundamental constitutional principles.

In sum, it is my view that Judge Noonan has misjudged the Supreme Court's federalism decisions, and the strong constitutional bases for them. The Court should be praised for its wisdom and perseverance in the federalism cases, not castigated.

THE CONTINUING DEBATE:
The Rehnquist Court and Federalism

What Is New

The most recent federalism case to come before the Supreme Court was *Nevada v. Hibbs* (2003). It involved the U.S. Family and Medical Leave Act (FMLA) of 1993, which permits many employees, including state and municipal workers, to annually take up to 12 weeks of unpaid leave for such reasons as a serious health problem of a spouse, child, or parent. The law also allows federal lawsuits for damages against employers who violate the act. Somewhat confounding its critics, the Rehnquist court upheld the FMLA's applicability to states. Indeed, Chief Justice Rehnquist wrote the opinion. Almost certainly, this does not herald a change of heart by the chief justice. Therefore, predicting the decision of the court is always difficult.

Where to Find More

David Walker has a fine study of the evolution of federalism in *The Rebirth of Federalism* (Chatham House, 2000). Walker is mildly optimistic about the future of federalism, in stark contrast to Robert F. Nagel's pessimism in *The Implosion of American Federalism* (Oxford University Press, 2003). Discussion of whether the decisions of the Rehnquist court and other policy changes at the federal level mark a long-term devolution of power back to the states or a rearguard action is in Martha Derthick, *Keeping the Compound Republic: Essays on American Federalism* (Brookings Institution, 2001). Another fine resource is *Publius: The Journal of Federalism*, which can be found in many academic libraries and at: http://ww2.lafayette.edu/~publius/. Along with *Publius*, which explores federal systems globally, information about comparative federalism available in the Comparative Federalism Newsletter of the International Political Science Association's Comparative Federalism and Federation Research Committee, located at: http://www.indiana.edu/~speaweb/IPSA/index.html.

Those who agree with Leon Friedman are not openly opposed to federalism as such, so one does not find "pro-centralization" organizations and Web sites. There are, however, numerous articles, such as Richard Briffault, "A Fickle Federalism," *The American Prospect* (March 2003), that support Friedman's view. By contrast, there is a strong "pro-devolution" presence on the Web, including the Federalism Project of the American Enterprise Institute at: http://www.federalismproject.org/.

What More to Do

In her testimony, Marci Hamilton comments that the erosion of federalism is "so bad that the debate has become whether there is any identifiable arena of local control left. Land use? Education? Crime?" Try to answer her question. Pick a policy area that you think should be an area of exclusive jurisdiction for state and local government and should not be subject to federal law under your concept of how federalism should work. Spend a little time finding out if these are federal laws and regulations governing policy in this area. A group or an entire class can also do this project together, with each person taking a separate policy area.

The Tenth Amendment is another good topic of conversation. What do you think it means? Would you agree with the Supreme Court that it is a "truism"?

CIVIL RIGHTS

BANNING D&X (PARTIAL-BIRTH) ABORTIONS:
Violating Women's Rights *or* Protecting Fetal Rights?

VIOLATING WOMEN'S RIGHTS

ADVOCATE: Center for Reproductive Rights

SOURCE: Position paper, "Unconstitutional Assault on the Right to Choose: 'Partial-Birth Abortion' Ban Is an Affront to Women and to the U.S. Supreme Court," February 2003

PROTECTING FETAL RIGHTS

ADVOCATE: Kathi A. Aultman, MD, board certified obstetrician gynecologist, and Fellow, American College of Obstetricians and Gynecologists

SOURCE: Testimony during hearings on "Partial-Birth Abortion Ban Act of 2002" before the U.S. Senate Committee on the Judiciary, Subcommittee on the Constitution, July 9, 2002

January 22, 1973, was a pivotal day in one of the most contentious legal and social debates in U.S. history. On that date the U.S. Supreme Court handed down its decision in *Roe v. Wade*. By a 7–2 vote, the justices, in effect, invalidated state restrictions on the ability of women to medically abort their pregnancies. At that time, four states permitted abortion "on demand" (for any reason), 15 allowed abortions if continuing the pregnancy endangered a woman's health, and 31 banned abortions unless the woman's life was endangered.

The court based its decision on a "right to privacy." In the majority opinion, Justice Harry Blackmun conceded, "the Constitution does not explicitly mention any right of privacy." Nevertheless, he continued, "The Constitution recognizes that rights exist beyond those specified in that document…this right of privacy…is broad enough to encompass a woman's decision whether or not to terminate her pregnancy."

Supporters of *Roe v. Wade* often claim it secured the right of women to have to an abortion and to control their bodies. However, Blackmun said otherwise. In his words, "Some argue that the woman's right is absolute and that she is entitled to terminate her pregnancy at whatever time, in whatever way, and for whatever reason she alone chooses. With this we [justices] do not agree." Blackmun continued, "The privacy right…cannot be said to be absolute," and he indicated, "It is not clear to us [the justices] that the claim…that one has an unlimited right to do with one's body as one pleases bears a close relationship to the right of privacy."

Thus, instead of unrestricted right, the court outlined a limited right with different standards for each trimester of a normal pregnancy. In Blackmun's words, during the first trimester, "the abortion decision…must be left to the medical judgment of the pregnant woman's attending physician." Abortion could only be regulated during the second trimester in "ways that are reasonably related to maternal health." And during the third trimester, a state "may, if it chooses, regulate, and even proscribe, abortion except where it is necessary…for the preservation of the life or health of the mother."

The Court's decision changed the law, but the debate continues. Indeed, it is hard for many of those who differ on abortion to discuss the subject calmly. They do not even agree on what the fundamental issue is. Abortion rights advocates view the issue as about a woman's right to choose and thus label themselves "pro-choice." Foes of abortion say they are "pro-life" based on their view that human life begins at conception—or at least much sooner than the beginning of the third trimester.

Since *Roe v. Wade*, those oppose abortions altogether or who want to limit them have made numerous attempts to overturn the decision by amending the Constitution. They have also sought to pass state or federal laws that regulate abortion within the parameters set down by the Supreme Court in *Roe v. Wade* and subsequent court decisions.

This debate, for example, centers on efforts in Congress to ban an abortion procedure termed "intact dilation and extraction" (DX), the term favored by pro-choice advocates, and also commonly called "partial-birth abortion," the term favored by anti-abortion advocates. However termed, its implications are far-reaching.

From a narrow perspective, the debate in Congress over whether to ban the DX procedure addresses far less than 1% of the approximately 1.2 million abortions performed annually in the United States. Opponents of banning the procedure make many arguments about its necessity and safety, but from a wider perspective, they also worry that it is a step down the "slippery slope" to even further restrictions. Most proponents of the ban hope that, indeed, the slope does prove slippery.

POINTS TO PONDER

➤ This debate exists at multiple levels. One involves the DX procedure and the specifics of the legislation. On a broader level, the debate is about abortion as such. Do you think the Center for Reproductive Rights would accept any restrictions on the DX procedure, no matter what the law specified? Do you think Kathi Aultman and other abortion opponents would agree to narrowly define the DX procedure and provide exemptions from the ban?

➤ Watch for terminology differences. They can be critical. For example, what does "maternal health" mean? Aultman argues that physicians often find health problems where none really exist. How should mental and physical health be defined?

➤ This debate primarily focuses on the second trimester, particularly the later stage as a fetus achieves reasonable odds of viability outside the womb. Are "viability" and "life" synonymous? Think about how, if at all, you would regulate abortions during the second trimester.

Banning D&X (Partial-Birth) Abortions:
Violating Women's Rights

CENTER FOR REPRODUCTIVE RIGHTS

I. THE HISTORY OF SO-CALLED "PARTIAL-BIRTH ABORTION" BANS

Since 1995, anti-choice fringe groups have waged a campaign to eliminate the right to abortion, as established in the landmark Supreme Court case, *Roe v. Wade* [1973]. As part of their campaign, these organizations have worked to enact so-called "partial-birth abortion" bans throughout the country on both the state and federal level. These bans are unconstitutional, deceptive and extreme measures aimed at making abortion virtually unattainable for women. Falsely touted as a ban on one particular method of post-viability abortion used late in pregnancy, these laws actually represent an attempt to criminalize numerous abortion procedures including the safest and most commonly used pre-viability abortion methods—even early in pregnancy.

In June 2000 in *Stenberg v. Carhart*, a case brought by Center for Reproductive Rights, the U.S. Supreme Court struck down Nebraska's abortion ban, which was similar to laws that had been enacted in 30 other states. The Court ruled that Nebraska's ban was unconstitutional because it failed to contain a health exception and posed an "undue burden" on a woman's right to choose. The Court's ruling had the effect of rendering invalid similar laws throughout the country and exposed these bans for what they are: deceptive and extreme attempts to outlaw the safest and most common methods of pre-viability abortion.

[In] 2002, however, anti-choice forces ignored this crucial Supreme Court ruling and introduced a new federal abortion ban in Congress. [It passed in] the House of Representatives…but was not considered in the Senate. Undeterred,…anti-choice forces reintroduced this bill…, known as the so-called "Partial-Birth Abortion Ban Act of 2003." This new ban suffers from the same fatal flaws and constitutional defects as the earlier versions. Nevertheless, the anti-choice congressional leadership and President Bush are determined to enact this legislation criminalizing numerous pre-viability abortion methods. It is now more important than ever to fight against this unconstitutional bill and protect women's right to choose.

The Mounting Campaign to Pass a Federal Abortion Ban

1996—The U.S. Congress passed the first nationwide ban on abortion, which was vetoed by President Clinton. Although abortion foes were able to override the President's veto in the House, the Senate sustained the President's action and prevented the act from becoming law.

1997—Congress passed a slightly amended version of the law, which was immediately vetoed by President Clinton.

1998—Once again, the House overrode the President's veto and the Senate sustained the President's action.

1999–2000—The Senate and House passed the 1997 version of the ban. However, the bill died with the end of the congressional session.

June 2000—In *Stenberg v. Carhart*, a case brought by Center for Reproductive Rights, the U.S. Supreme Court struck down a Nebraska abortion ban, which had been modeled on the federal ban.

July 2002—The House passed a new abortion ban that failed to remedy the flaws in the statute found unconstitutional in *Stenberg v. Carhart*. With the end of the congressional session, the bill died.

February 2003—The new federal abortion ban was reintroduced in both the House and Senate.

II. THE ABORTION BANS ARE UNCONSTITUTIONAL

A woman's right to terminate her pregnancy is firmly rooted in the Constitution, as recognized by *Roe v. Wade* and its progeny [subsequent cases based on that precedent]. *Roe*'s essential holding that a woman may terminate her pregnancy prior to viability, and that her health must prevail throughout pregnancy, even after the point of viability, has been repeatedly reaffirmed by the Supreme Court. For example, in *Planned Parenthood v. Casey* [1992], the Supreme Court held that "[t]he woman's right to terminate her pregnancy before viability is the most central principle of *Roe v. Wade*. It is a rule of law and a component of liberty we cannot renounce." So-called "partial-birth abortion" statutes are a direct attack on this firmly established right.

A. Two Grounds for Unconstitutionality: Undue Burden and Lack of Health Exception

Like the new federal abortion ban, the statute under consideration in *Stenberg v. Carhart* was a broadly worded abortion ban that would have criminalized numerous abortion procedures, including the most common method of abortion used early in the second trimester. In striking down the law, the Court's majority relied on "established principles" of Supreme Court jurisprudence affirming a woman's right to choose, finding that the law violated the U.S. Constitution "for at least two independent reasons":

- The abortion ban posed an undue burden on the right to choose an abortion in the second trimester because it banned several procedures including the safest and most common method; and

- The abortion ban failed to contain a health exception.

1. The Nebraska Law Posed an Undue Burden on the Right to Choose Pre-viability Abortion in the Second Trimester

The Court found that the Nebraska law would criminalize more than one abortion procedure, including the safest and most commonly used method of second-trimester abortion, and therefore constituted an undue burden on women's right to obtain an abortion. The proponents of the Nebraska law claimed that it banned a particular second trimester abortion procedure known as dilation and extraction (D & X). However, the Court found that Nebraska's law outlawed not only the D & X technique, it also prohibited the commonly used pre-viability second-trimester abortion method, dilation and evacuation (D & E), of which D & X is a variant. The Court found that "even if the statute's basic aim is to ban D & X, its language makes clear that it also covers a much broader category of procedures."

Under *Casey*, states are free to regulate a woman's decision to terminate a pregnancy unless the regulation poses an "undue burden" on her right to choose. The Court held that the Nebraska law would impose "'an undue burden on a woman's ability' to choose a D & E abortion, thereby unduly burdening the right to choose itself." The Court concluded by stating the following:

In sum, using this law some present prosecutors and future Attorneys General may choose to pursue physicians who use D & E procedures, the most commonly used method for performing pre-viability second trimester abortions. All those who perform abortion procedures using that method must fear prosecution, conviction, and imprisonment. The result is an undue burden upon a woman's right to make an abortion decision. We must consequently find the statute unconstitutional.

Because the abortion ban would criminalize not just one limited abortion procedure, but also covers a much broader category of procedures, the U.S. Supreme Court struck down the ban as unconstitutional.

As Justice [Stephen] Breyer states in the majority opinion [in *Stenberg v. Carhart*], "Even if the statute's basic aim is to ban D & X, its language makes clear that it also covers a much broader category of procedures." As Justice [Ruth Bader] Ginsburg states in her concurrence, "A state regulation that 'has the purpose or effect of placing a substantial obstacle in the path of a woman seeking an abortion of a nonviable fetus' violates the Constitution. Such an obstacle exists if the State stops a woman from choosing the procedure her doctor 'reasonably believes will best protect the woman in [the] exercise of [her] constitutional liberty.'"

2. Any Abortion Method Ban Must Contain a Health Exception

The Court also struck down Nebraska's law because it failed to contain a health exception. In Carhart, the Court reaffirmed the importance of the health exception in abortion jurisprudence, emphasizing that the government "may promote but not endanger a woman's health when it regulates the methods of abortion." The Court noted that both *Roe* and *Casey* "make clear that a risk to a woman's health is the same

whether it happens to arise from regulating a particular method of abortion, or from barring abortion entirely," and that "the absence of a health exception will place women at an unnecessary risk of tragic health consequences." The Court noted that earlier decisions "have repeatedly invalidated statutes that in the process of regulating the methods of abortion, imposed significant health risks," and found that "where substantial medical authority supports the proposition that banning a particular abortion procedure could endanger women's health, *Casey* requires the statute to include a health exception." It therefore struck the law down on the basis of this constitutional defect.

For any abortion ban to be constitutional, it must contain a health exception. For example, the Court found that because D & X may be the safest abortion method available to some women, even a ban that was limited to the D & X procedure must contain an exception when the procedure is "necessary, in appropriate medical judgment, for the preservation of the life or health of the mother." The Court stated "a statute that altogether forbids D & X creates a significant health risk. The statute consequently must contain a health exception." Consequently, since the Nebraska ban contained no health exception for the abortion methods it prohibited, it was stuck down as unconstitutional.

As Justice Breyer stated in his majority opinion [in *Stenberg v. Carhart*], "where substantial medical authority supports the proposition that banning a particular abortion procedure could endanger women's health, *Casey* requires the statute to include a health exception."

B. The New Federal Abortion Ban Has the Same Old Flaws

Any restriction on abortion must satisfy these two requirements set forth by the Supreme Court. Yet the new federal abortion ban flagrantly defies the Court's ruling.

1. The Federal Bill Is Similar to the Nebraska Law

The new federal bill is similar to the Nebraska law struck down in *Carhart*. The federal bill states in part:

Partial-birth abortions prohibited

(a) Any physician who, in or affecting interstate or foreign commerce, knowingly performs a partial-birth abortion and thereby kills a human fetus shall be fined under this title or imprisoned not more than 2 years, or both. This subsection does not apply to a partial-birth abortion that is necessary to save the life of a mother whose life is endangered by a physical disorder, physical illness, or physical injury, including a life-endangering physical condition caused by or arising from the pregnancy itself....

(b) As used in this section—

(1) the term 'partial-birth abortion' means an abortion in which—

    (A) the person performing the abortion deliberately and intentionally vaginally delivers a living fetus until, in the case of a head-first presentation, the entire fetal head is outside the body of the mother, or, in the case of breech presentation, any part of the fetal trunk past the navel is outside the body of the mother for the purpose of performing an overt act that the person knows will kill the partially delivered living fetus; and

    (B) performs the overt act, other than completion of delivery, that kills the partially delivered living fetus;

Like the Nebraska law, the federal bill fails to limit the stage of pregnancy to which the bill's provisions apply, so the ban could criminalize abortions through-out pregnancy (not just post-viability or "late term" abortions, as the bill's sponsors often claim). Like the Nebraska law, the federal bill fails to limit its prohibitions to abortions involving an "intact" fetus, fails to explicitly exclude the D & E technique or the suction curettage abortion method from the law's prohibitions, and fails to include definitions of key terms such as "living" or "completion of delivery"; therefore, it is broad enough to criminalize numerous safe abortion procedures (not just one abortion procedure, as the bill's sponsors misleadingly imply). Like the Nebraska law, the federal bill also fails to include the constitutionally mandated health exception. For these reasons, as discussed in greater detail below, the federal bill must be struck down as unconstitutional for the same reasons as the Nebraska law in *Carhart*.

2. The Federal Bill Poses an Undue Burden

In addition to banning the D & X method of abortion, the definition of "partial-birth abortion" in the federal bill, like that contained in the Nebraska bill, is broad enough also to encompass, at the very least, the D & E procedure, which is the safest and most common method of abortion used in the second trimester. Indeed, the language used in the federal bill is substantially similar to the language that was struck down in *Carhart* for posing an undue burden. As the Court held in *Carhart*, "we can find no difference, in terms of this statute, between the D & X procedure as described and the D & E procedure as it might be performed." Furthermore, under the revised wording of the new federal bill, other safe methods of abortion may also be banned.

Moreover, the sponsors of the federal bill ignored clear instructions from the Supreme Court showing how a statute could be written to exclude the D & E from its reach. They neither provided a clear exception for

D & E, nor "tracked the medical differences between D & E and D & X," as suggested by the Court. One of the witnesses supporting the 2002 federal bill confirmed in her testimony at the House Judiciary Subcommittee on the Constitution hearing that the legislation is not limited to a ban on only one procedure, but is intended to cover others as well.

Like the Nebraska bill, the federal bill imposes severe criminal penalties on doctors for performing D & E's, including fines and imprisonment. Enactment of a federal abortion ban could effectively result in a national ban on D & E's due to doctors' justifiable fears of prosecution and imprisonment. Moreover, the statute's broad reach as well as the vagueness of key statutory terms could also have a significant chilling effect even beyond the reach of the statute. Therefore, in addition to creating an unprecedented intrusion into medical practice, the federal bill imposes an undue burden on a woman's right to choose to terminate her pregnancy.

3. The Federal Bill Lacks a Constitutionally Mandated Health Exception

As explained above, the Supreme Court has consistently held that any ban on abortion methods must contain an exception to preserve women's health. Even Attorney General John Ashcroft recently conceded in a brief filed by the Justice Department that some type of health exception is required for legislation banning abortions. The new federal bill, in a direct challenge to this most fundamental principle of abortion jurisprudence, fails to provide any health exception.

Substituting the political will of Congress in place of the medical judgment of doctors, the sponsors acknowledge in the text of the federal bill that it does not include a health exception, claiming that the abor-

tion methods banned by the legislation are "never necessary to preserve the health of a woman." Furthermore, in the 2002 markup of the bill, the committee rejected two amendments that would have permitted women whose health was at risk to undergo the banned procedures. Instead, the bill contains only a limited life exception, allowing an abortion when it is necessary to save a woman's life, but even then only when the woman's life is endangered by a physical condition (which also calls into question the constitutionality of the life exception as written in the bill):

> This subsection does not apply to a partial-birth abortion that is necessary to save the life of a mother whose life is endangered by a physical disorder, physical illness, or physical injury, including a life-endangering physical condition caused by or arising from the pregnancy itself.

In refusing to include a health exception, the sponsors of the federal abortion ban inaccurately argue that Congress is not bound to follow the Supreme Court's ruling in *Carhart*. They claim that the *Carhart* decision was based on "very questionable findings," asserting that Congress is better equipped to assess the evidence since it held "extensive" hearings on the subject. Claiming that congressional findings demonstrate that a health exception is unnecessary, they argue that the Supreme Court should accord "great deference" to these findings. However, as demonstrated in the next section, Congress does not have the power to overturn decisions of the Supreme Court by passing a bill that contains contrary Congressional findings.

4. A Renegade Congress Flouts the U.S. Supreme Court

The sponsors claim that the Supreme Court must defer to Congress's legal conclusion that a health exception is unnecessary in the proposed bill. Not only is this untrue, but such a rule would violate the principle of separation of powers underlying our tripartite system of government. As the Supreme Court noted recently in *United States v. Morrison* [2000]:

> Many decisions of this Court, however, have unequivocally reaffirmed the holding of *Marbury* [*v. Madison*, 1803], that 'It is emphatically the province and duty of the judicial department to say what the law is.'

In *Morrison*, the Court held that Congress's legal conclusions—based on substantial congressional findings—were unsupportable, and struck down portions of the law at issue as a result. Similarly, Congress is now attempting to hide behind legislative "findings" to support a law that is clearly contrary to Supreme Court precedent. Congress cannot simply ignore a legal ruling it dislikes by adopting conflicting legislative "findings."

a. Federal Courts Do Not Blindly Defer to Congressional Fact Findings, But Must Conduct an Independent Review of Facts Bearing on an Issue of Constitutional Law

The Court has repeatedly held...that whatever deference is accorded legislative findings does not "insulate [those findings] from judicial review," nor does it "'foreclose [the judiciary's] independent judgment of the facts bearing on an issue of constitutional law.'" Rather, "[i]t is...a 'permanent and indispensable feature of our constitutional system' that 'the federal judiciary is supreme in the exposition of the law of the Constitution.'" As Chief Justice [Warren] Burger [1969–1986] has explained:

> A legislature appropriately inquires into and may declare the reasons impelling legislative action but the judicial function commands analysis of whether the specific conduct charged

falls within the reach of the statute and if so whether the legislation is consonant with the Constitution.

b. The Supreme Court Has Rejected Congressional Fact Findings

The Supreme Court has rejected congressional findings or found them inadequate to inform a constitutional inquiry in many cases. For example, in...*Morrison*, the Court rejected congressional findings outright. The Violence Against Women Act (VAWA) was enacted after Congress held hearings over a four-year period on the impact of domestic violence on interstate commerce. Despite the "numerous" Congressional findings that domestic violence impacted interstate commerce, the Court struck down the civil remedy provision of VAWA, noting that "'[s]imply because Congress may conclude that a particular activity substantially affects interstate commerce does not necessarily make it so.'"

As these cases demonstrate, the courts have the power and the duty to independently assess evidence and have no obligation to defer to congressional findings. As Justice Clarence Thomas has noted,

> We know of no support...for the proposition that if the constitutionality of a statute depends in part on the existence of certain facts, a court may not review Congress's judgment that the facts exist. If [Congress] could make a statute constitutional simply by 'finding' that black is white or freedom, slavery, judicial review would be an elaborate farce. At least since *Marbury v. Madison*, that has not been the law.

Thus, the sponsors of the federal abortion ban are clearly wrong in their assertion that the courts will adjudicate the bill differently because it contains congressional findings.

c. Similar Attempts by Congress to Overturn Supreme Court Precedents Have Failed

There have been several instances in the past where congressional attempts to overturn Supreme Court precedents have failed. For example, Congress passed the Religious Freedom Restoration Act (RFRA) [1993] in response to an earlier Supreme Court decision. As in the case with the new federal abortion ban, Congress held separate hearings to assess the issues and made independent findings prior to enacting the law. In striking down RFRA, the Supreme Court [in *Boerne v. Flores*, 1997] held that Congress "has been given the power 'to enforce,' not the power to determine what constitutes a constitutional violation." The Court further held that "The power to interpret the Constitution in a case or controversy remains in the Judiciary" and "RFRA contradicts vital principles necessary to maintain separation of powers and the federal balance."

Similarly, Congress attempted to overturn the requirements set out by the Supreme Court in *Miranda v. Arizona* [1966] by enacting a new "voluntariness" standard in their place. In *Dickerson v. United States* [2000], the Supreme Court reviewed the law, and in striking it down held that "Miranda, being a constitutional decision of this Court, may not be in effect overruled by an Act of Congress," and "Congress may not legislatively supersede our decisions interpreting and applying the Constitution."

Here, again, Congress is attempting to overturn Supreme Court precedent on a matter of constitutional law by enacting a law that clearly violates the Supreme Court's ruling. As in those cases, Congress has overstepped its bounds—the federal abortion ban does not pass constitutional muster.

III. THE ABORTION BANS ARE DECEPTIVE

Anti-choice extremists have propagated numerous myths about the abortion bans. The new federal statute is part of a deceptive nationwide campaign to eviscerate the key protections guaranteed to American women by *Roe*, *Casey*, and *Carhart*. Contrary to the way its proponents characterize the legislation, its prohibitions are limited neither to one medical procedure nor to post-viability abortions late in pregnancy.

A. The Abortion Bans Are Not Limited to Only One Procedure

First, despite a deceptive public strategy that has propagated the myth that these bans target a single, specific abortion procedure, the federal bill is not limited to one specific procedure. "Partial-birth abortion" is a fabricated term that anti-choice activists concocted in an attempt to make almost all abortions illegal. There is no medical procedure known as a "partial-birth abortion." Anti-choice extremists created the term as a smoke screen to divert the public's attention away from the true scope of the bill, which would make most current second trimester abortions illegal.

In the case of Nebraska, proponents of the statute attempted to convince the Supreme Court that the ban was limited to D & X. But the Court noted in *Carhart* "there is no language in the statute that supports it." In fact, the Nebraska legislature rejected an amendment that would have limited the law to only one narrowly defined procedure. As discussed above, the federal bill similarly fails to limit the ban to the D & X procedure and exacerbates the vagueness of the bill's proscriptions by including no less than two different descriptions of what is banned.

B. The Abortion Bans Are Not Limited to Post-Viability Abortions Late in Pregnancy

Another myth is that these laws ban post-viability abortions late in pregnancy. However, neither the state laws nor the federal bill contain any reference to the stage of pregnancy to which they apply. The vast majority of states already have laws prohibiting most post-viability abortions, and most of them have been in place since the early 1970s. These laws generally adhere to fundamental constitutional principles establishing that women have the right to chose abortion pre-viability, but that states may more strictly regulate and even forbid abortions after viability, except where necessary to preserve the woman's health or life. Therefore, the new federal abortion ban primarily impacts the legality of pre-viability abortions—although proponents of the bill deliberately confuse this issue.

IV. THE ABORTION BANS ARE EXTREME

The abortion bans are extreme measures promoted by anti-choice politicians and advocacy groups to eliminate a woman's access to the safest methods of abortion. Because the bans are so extreme, medical organizations and the American public oppose them.

A. The Abortion Bans Would Prohibit the Safest Methods for Many Women

The nationwide legalization of abortions after *Roe* lead to dramatic health advances for women and substantial decreases in the total number of abortion-related deaths and complications. Between 1973 (the year that *Roe* was decided) and 1985, the number of abortion-related deaths dropped eight-fold: from 3.3 deaths per 100,000 in 1973 to 0.4 deaths per 100,000 in 1985. Similarly, abortion-related complications resulting in hospitalization fell sharply during the 1970s, with the steepest drop following *Roe* in 1973. The federal bill, if enacted, would produce a significant rollback of these health gains.

As noted earlier, the federal bill would ban D & E—the safest second-trimester abortion method for many women that accounts for nearly all abortions performed

from 12 to 20 weeks. The D & X technique, which would also be prohibited under the federal bill, is the safest abortion method for some women, and the U.S. Supreme Court has recognized the body of medical opinion supporting this fact. In fact, in *Carhart*, the only expert witness testifying in favor of Nebraska's law and deemed credible by the District Court, conceded that D & X could well be safer than other D & E variants.

Furthermore, lower courts throughout the country have reviewed a wide range of medical evidence and concluded that D & X is safe. The factual records in Carhart and many other cases demonstrate that D & X is in fact the safest and best abortion technique in some cases. Though acknowledging the lack of statistical studies comparing the safety of the D & X technique with other abortion methods, every federal court in the country, with the exception of one, has agreed that D & X is a safe procedure that may well be safer for women in certain situations.

A ban on D & E abortions, including the D & X variant, would force women to undergo riskier and unnecessary medical procedures and deprive many women of access to the method of abortion that would be safest in their own individual circumstances. The federal ban would harm women's health, render abortions more dangerous, and infringe upon women's right to privacy.

B. The Proposed Federal Abortion Ban Reflects the Sponsors' Extremism

In addition to drafting the extreme language contained within the federal bill that disregards women's safety, the sponsors also pushed the bill through the U.S. House of Representatives in an extreme fashion.... The House Judiciary Committee considered and rejected numerous amendments that would have made the legislation less severe, including proposals that would:

- provide an exception for abortions "performed before fetal viability, or ...performed after fetal viability where necessary, in appropriate medical judgment, for the preservation of the life or health of the mother";
- provide an exception for abortions "performed before viability where necessary, in appropriate medical judgment, for the preservation of the life or health of the mother, or to such a procedure performed after fetal viability if it is to protect the mother from serious, adverse physical health consequences";
- strike the civil cause of action against physicians and women undergoing an abortion that falls within the bill's definition;
- strike the congressional findings of fact as unsubstantiated;
- ban all post-viability abortions except those abortions that in the medical judgment of the attending physician were necessary to preserve the life of the woman or to avert serious adverse health consequences to the woman; and
- strike the penalties for performing an abortion that falls within the bill's definition.

By rejecting these amendments, the bill's proponents demonstrated a complete disregard for women's health, as well as a desire to supplant the sound medical judgment of doctors with the will of politicians in Congress.

The bill's legislative history demonstrates that its sponsors are intent on adopting a broad ban on pre-viability abortion methods with little, if any, regard for the health of pregnant women. Representative Steve Chabot (R-OH), a primary sponsor of the bill, acknowledged the bill's impact on pre-viability abortions during the markup when he claimed that "limiting the prohibition to only viable fetuses would exempt the vast majority" of abortions that would be criminalized under this legislation.

Furthermore, proponents of the bill maintained that once a woman has decided to have an abortion, politicians in Congress can dictate to a woman what medical procedures she can and cannot undergo, regardless of the medical judgment of her doctor. Representative Randy Forbes (R-VA) acknowledged that the bill would not prevent any abortions from occurring, but instead that its intent is to limit the types of abortion methods that are available to women and their physicians: "This bill is not about having an abortion. It's about whether or not you can have a partial-birth abortion"—a fictitious term invented by anti-choice forces. Moreover, Representative Mike Pence (R-IN) suggested that abortions should be performed by caesarean section instead less invasive techniques. These statements clearly indicate that the intent of the bill is to force women to have more risky procedures by criminalizing the safest abortion methods for many women, and demonstrates the sponsors' contempt for women who have abortions.

C. Medical Organizations Oppose the Abortion Bans

Abortion bans interfere with doctors' medical discretion, create severe health risks for women and impose strict penalties on doctors, including imprisonment and fines. For these reasons, major U.S. medical organizations have publicly opposed these bills.

The American College of Obstetricians and Gynecologists (ACOG), representing over 90 percent of all ob-gyn specialists, has rejected the abortion bans as "an inappropriate, ill-advised and dangerous intervention into medical decision making."

...The American Medical Women's Association (AMWA) also opposes the abortion bans, stating that it is "gravely concerned with governmental attempts to legislate medical decision-making through measures that do not protect a woman's physical and mental health, including future fertility, or fail to consider other pertinent issues, such as fetal abnormalities."

…The American Medical Association (AMA) initially lent support to a 1997 federal bill that was defeated; however, an internal audit indicated that the organization "blundered" and that this support was politically, not medically, motivated. The AMA has declined to support subsequent abortion bans.

Finally, five medical groups, the American College of Obstetricians and Gynecologists, the American Nurses Association, the American Medical Women's Association, Physicians for Reproductive Choice and Health, and the National Abortion Federation, signed onto an amicus curie [friend of the court] brief in *Carhart* arguing against the Nebraska ban. The Supreme Court relied on their medical expertise when rendering the *Carhart* decision.…

V. CONCLUSION

The U.S. Supreme Court has already struck down legislation containing the exact same constitutional flaws contained in the federal version of the abortion ban. It is a violation of the public trust for elected officials to pass laws that are known to be unconstitutional. Through this bill, Congress is also violating fundamental principals of separation of powers upon which this nation was founded, in unabashedly contravening direct U.S. Supreme Court precedent. The federal abortion ban legislation is the latest attempt to attack a woman's basic right to choose, and would force women to undergo abortion procedures that are more dangerous. This ploy must be recognized as an unconstitutional, deceptive and extreme attempt to violate women's constitutional rights.

Members of Congress should heed the Supreme Court's clear message in *Carhart*: sweeping abortion bans that attempt to prohibit numerous pre-viability abortion methods and fail to protect women's health are unconstitutional.

Banning D&X (Partial-Birth) Abortions: Protecting Fetal Rights

Kathi A. Aultman

I have spent my entire career as a women's advocate and have a keen interest in issues that impact women's health. I was the co-founder and co-director of the first Rape Treatment Center of Jacksonville, Florida and performed sexual assault exams as a medical examiner for Duval and Clay Counties. I also served as the Medical Director for Planned Parenthood of Jacksonville from 1981 to 1983.

After mastering first trimester and early second trimester dilation and curettage with suction (D&C with suction) procedures I was able to "moonlight" at an abortion clinic in Gainesville, FL. I sought out special training with a local abortionist in order to learn mid second trimester dilation and evacuation (D&E) procedures. Although I do not currently perform abortions, I have continued to dialogue with abortion providers regarding current practices and have studied the medical literature on abortion. I continue to perform D&C with suction and rarely D&E and inductions in cases of incomplete abortion and fetal demise.

I see and treat women with medical and psychological complications from abortion and have managed and delivered women with pregnancies complicated by fetal anomalies, and medical, obstetrical, and psychological problems. I have personally had an abortion and I have a delightful adopted cousin who survived after her mother aborted her.

I have first hand knowledge and familiarity with the partial-birth abortion issue, having testified before legislative bodies in Florida and Vermont. I also testified in court as an expert witness in Arkansas and Virginia and assisted Florida and several other states in designing and/or defending their bans.

I support HR4965 [a U.S. House of Representatives bill number], the "Partial-Birth Abortion Ban Act of 2002," for the following reasons:

1) This bill clearly distinguishes Partial-Birth Abortion from other abortion procedures.
2) This bill will not endanger women's health.
3) It protects women from being subjected to a dangerous unproven experimental procedure.
4) Partial-Birth Abortion has blurred the line between abortion and infanticide.
5) It bans a procedure that is abhorrent to the vast majority of Americans.

1) HR 4965 clearly distinguishes Partial-Birth Abortion from other abortion procedures.

Partial-Birth Abortion is a legal term that covers a set of circumstances that culminate in the physician intentionally killing the fetus after it has been partially born.

As defined in the act:

> "the term 'partial-birth abortion' means an abortion in which (A) the person performing the abortion deliberately and intentional vaginally delivers a living fetus until, in the case of a head-first presentation, the entire fetal head is outside the body of the mother, or, in the case of breech presentation, any part of the fetal trunk past

the navel is outside the body of the mother for the purpose of performing an overt act that the person knows will kill the partially delivered living fetus: and (B) performs the overt act, other than completion of delivery, that kills the partially delivered living fetus;"

(In the rest of the text the term "partially born" will be defined as the position of the fetus as described in HR 4965.)

Partial-Birth Abortion includes but is not limited to D&X performed on live fetuses. It would also include a procedure used in China where formaldehyde is injected into the baby's brain through its fontanel (soft spot), after the head has been delivered, in order to kill it prior to completing the delivery. It does not prohibit medical abortions, D&C with suction, or D&E procedures. It would not cover Induction unless the physician intentionally intervened during the delivery portion of the procedure and killed the fetus after it had been "partially born." It would not cover a D&X on a dead fetus nor would it cover the accidental death of baby during the normal birth process. Under HR 4965 a Partial-Birth Abortion is allowed if it is "necessary to save the life of a mother whose life is endangered by a physical disorder, illness, or injury."

The **"Partial-Birth Abortion Ban Act of 2002" eliminates the concern that D&E is prohibited under the act by more precisely defining what is meant by a Partial-Birth Abortion.**

According to the Supreme Court in *Stenberg v. Carhart*, the Nebraska statute banning Partial-Birth Abortion was unconstitutional because it applied to **dilation and evacuation (D&E)** as well as to **dilation and extraction (D&X).** The court held that the statute was unconstitutional because it imposed an undue burden on a woman's ability to choose

D&E (the most common 2nd trimester abortion procedure), thereby unduly burdening her right to choose abortion itself. The Court commented, however, that if the definition were more narrowly defined to clearly differentiate D&E, a ban might be constitutional.

Despite assertions to the contrary by some abortionists, both the American Medical Association (AMA) and the American College of Obstetricians and Gynecologists (ACOG) clearly distinguish between D&X and D&E.

D&X (dilation and extraction or intact dilation and evacuation) is generally performed from about 20–22 weeks gestation and beyond and has been done as late as 40 weeks (full term). It is prohibited by HR 4965 if it is performed on a live fetus. In D&X the fetus is delivered intact except for the decompressed head. In order to accomplish this, Laminaria (dried seaweed) or a synthetic substitute, is inserted into the cervix over the course of several days. The goal is to dilate the cervix just enough to allow the body, but not the head, to be pulled through the cervix. The membranes are ruptured and the lower extremities are grasped under ultrasound guidance. If the fetus is not already breech (feet or bottom first) the baby is converted to that position using forceps. The fetus is then delivered except for its head by a method called breech extraction. The abortionist then thrusts a scissors into the base of the skull, suctions out the brains, and then completes the delivery. The placenta is then extracted using forceps and the cavity is curetted to remove any additional tissue. Prostaglandins and/or oxytocin may be used to help "ripen" the cervix and/or help the uterus contract. (There are times when the head may be pulled through the cervix as the abortionist is extracting the body. In that circumstance, if the abortionist isn't careful to hold the fetus in the vagina prior to killing it, he will be faced with the complication of an unwanted live baby.)

D&E (dilation and evacuation) is generally used from about 13–15 weeks up until 20–22 weeks and occasionally 24 weeks gestation (early to mid second trimester) and is not prohibited under HR 4965 because the fetus is removed in pieces.

In D&E the cervix is dilated usually using Laminaria over the course of 1–2 days. It is dilated just enough to allow the forceps to be inserted into the uterine cavity and for body parts to be removed. The membranes are ruptured and the fluid is generally suctioned. The forceps are inserted into the uterine cavity with or without ultrasound guidance. Usually an extremity is grasped first and brought down into the vagina. The rest of the body cannot pass through the cervix so the abortionist is able to detach it by continuing to pull on it. After the smaller parts have been removed, the thorax and head would be crushed and removed from the uterine cavity. The ability to dismember the fetus is based on not over-dilating the cervix. Prostaglandins and/or oxytocin may be used to help "ripen" the cervix and/or help the uterus contract. D&E is not prohibited under the act because fetus dies as a result of being dismembered or crushed while the majority of the body is still within the uterus and not after it has been "partially born."

D&C with Suction (dilation and curettage with suction) is generally used from 6 weeks up until 14–16 weeks gestation (first and early second trimester). It is not prohibited by HR 4965.

In this procedure the cervix is generally dilated with metal or plastic rods at the time of the procedure, but occasionally Laminaria are inserted the night before for the later gestations. A suction curette is then inserted and the contents of the uterus are suctioned into a bottle. The cavity is then usually checked with a sharp curette to make sure all the tissue has been removed. At times forceps are needed to remove some of the fetal parts in the later gestations. Prostaglandins and/or oxytocin may be used to help "ripen" the cervix and/or help the uterus contract. It would not be prohibited under this act because the fetus or fetal parts pass from the uterus through the suction tubing directly into a suction bottle. The fetus is therefore not intentionally killed while it is "partially born." The fetus is usually killed as it is pulled through the tip of the suction curette or on impact in the suction bottle.

Medical Induction is generally performed from 16 weeks gestation to term. This method induces labor and subsequent delivery of an intact fetus and would not be prohibited by HR 4965.

Labor may be induced in several ways. The older methods are termed "Instillation Methods" because they involve injecting something into the uterus. Saline (a salt solution) injected into the amniotic cavity generally kills the fetus and then causes the woman to go into labor but is associated with significant risk. Urea may also be instilled and appears safer than saline but there is a higher incidence of delivering a live baby. It may also need to be augmented with prostaglandins. In another method a prostaglandin called carboprost (Hemabate) is injected into the amniotic cavity or given IM to stimulate labor but may not always kill the fetus. An intra-fetal injection of KCL or Digoxin may be necessary to prevent a live birth.

Newer methods employ the use of prostaglandins. PGE1 (misoprostol) and PGE2 are generally used vaginally, often in conjunction with oxytocin. These methods generally result in the delivery of a live baby so if an abortion is intended an intra-fetal injection of KCL or Digoxin is generally utilized. PGE2 and oxytocin may be used in cases of previous C-section or uterine surgery. HR 4965 would not prohibit a Medical Induction unless the abortionist purposely halted the birth process in order to intentionally kill a still living "partially born" fetus.

Some of the concerns expressed about Inductions, as opposed to surgical methods (D&E and D&X), include 1) the psychological and physical pain of labor, 2) the time involved, and 3) the fact that they are often done in a hospital and are therefore more costly.

Especially if an abortion is the goal, the pain and even the memory of labor can be eliminated with medication. All three procedures generally require more than one day except perhaps in the case of an early D&E. The mean Induction time with vaginal prostaglandins is 13.4 hours and 90% are delivered by 24 hours. All of these methods have been performed in both inpatient and outpatient settings, however, as the gestational age and therefore the risk increases, the inpatient setting generally becomes safer.

Cephalocentesis is a medical procedure during which a needle is inserted into the head of a fetus with hydrocephalus (water on the brain) in order to drain the fluid. It would not be prohibited by HR4965.

This procedure can be lifesaving for the fetus and may prevent brain damage by taking pressure off the brain. The needle is usually inserted through the abdomen but may also be inserted vaginally if the fetus is in the head first position. This is done while the fetus is still inside the womb. This would not be prohibited even if the fetus had been delivered breech if were done to draw off fluid (not brain tissue) in order to shrink the head to allow delivery of an entrapped hydrocephalic head.

Death during the birth process would not be prosecuted under HR 4965, whether or not labor was induced, as long as the fetus was not intentionally killed while it was partially born.

Passage of RH 4965 will not create an undue burden on a woman seeking an abortion because its narrow definition of Partial-Birth Abortion excludes the commonly used methods of abortion which provide alternatives at every gestational level.

Some abortionists have begun to use parts of the D&X technique on earlier gestations. The mere fact that it is possible to use this procedure on pre-viable fetuses should not prevent it from being banned.

2) HR 4965 would not endanger woman's health.

Obstetricians regularly handle medical complications of pregnancy that may threaten a woman's health or life without having to resort to using a Partial-birth Abortion.

When the baby is wanted and the pregnancy must be terminated after or near viability, Induction and C-section are commonly used in an attempt to save both the mother and the baby. Destructive procedures are only considered pre-viability or if the pregnancy is unwanted. Standard procedures such as D&C with suction, D&E, and Induction may be used to terminate an unwanted pregnancy. In an emergency situation, when immediate delivery is necessary D&X would not be used because of the length of time required to dilate the cervix. In it's report on Late Term Pregnancy Termination Techniques, the AMA stated, "Except in extraordinary circumstances, maternal health factors which demand termination of the pregnancy can be accommodated without sacrifice of the fetus, and the near certainty of the independent viability of the fetus argues for ending the pregnancy by appropriate delivery.

Although a Partial-Birth Abortion is never necessary to safeguard the health of the mother, HR 4965 provides an exception just in case "it is necessary to save the life of a mother whose life is endangered by a physical disorder, illness or injury."

The AMA report on Late Term Pregnancy Termination Techniques states that, "According to the scientific literature, there does not appear to be any identified situation in which intact D&X is the only appropriate procedure to induce abortion and ethical concerns have been raised about intact D&X." Even if there were such a situation, however, the fetus could be injected with Digoxin or KCL, or the cord could be cut at the start of the procedure, in order to kill the fetus so that the procedure could be performed without risking prosecution.

In my opinion the health exception required under current case law is so broad that it basically allows elective abortion through term.

3) It protects women from being subjected to a dangerous unproven experimental procedure.

D&X is an experimental procedure that has not been adequately evaluated. There have been no peer reviewed controlled studies that have looked at the benefits and risks of D&X as compared to D&E, Induction, Delivery, or C-Section. We do not have adequate data on its mortality or morbidity. The complications of D&X include hemorrhage, infection, DIC, embolus, retained tissue, injury to the pelvic organs including the bowel and bladder, as well as an increased risk of cervical incompetence. These risks are the similar to those associated with D&E, however, these risks increase with increasing gestational age and D&X may be done at much later gestational ages. There was some suggestion in earlier studies

that greater artificial cervical dilation increases the risk of cervical incompetence. With D&X the cervix must be dilated significantly more than with D&E.

One of the problems in determining both the frequency and mortality and morbidity of the various abortion procedures is that the reporting of the numbers and types of abortion procedures at various gestational ages is grossly inadequate. Four states including California don't report their statistics to the CDC and many don't record the necessary details. D&X is not reported separately nor is it clear which category it should be reported under. There is also inadequate reporting of the complications of abortion.

At times I am called to see women in the ER with complications of abortions. I had always assumed that when I wrote the diagnosis on the hospital face sheet that those cases would be reported to the state. I was shocked when I found out that they aren't reported to anyone and that there is no requirement to report them. In light of that, how can we determine what the true complication rate is for any of these procedures since many never return to their abortion provider?

D&X is often done in outpatient settings. The abortionist may not have hospital privileges or know how to handle the complications of the procedure especially if he is not an OB/GYN.

Although previous C-section has been cited as a reason why D&X might be preferred over Induction, Dr. Haskell, the originator of the procedure, excluded those cases. It is now accepted practice to use prostaglandin E2 and/or oxytocin for Induction after previous C-section.

4) Partial-Birth Abortion has blurred the line between abortion and infanticide.

When I first heard the term I thought it strange that it would called Partial-Birth

Abortion and not Partial-Birth Infanticide. I didn't understand why Drs. Haskell and McMahon weren't charged with murder, or at least lose their license to practice medicine, once they revealed what they were doing in a D&X. The fact that the babies weren't 100% born when they were killed seemed to me like an awfully flimsy technicality.

Who decided that just because a fetus was within the birth canal, the abortionist could still kill it?

Does this mean that the abortionist may kill a baby that has just one foot still in the vagina? Can a woman request, even demand, that the physician attending her delivery, kill her child once it's head has been delivered if she finds it is the wrong race or has a cleft lip? Currently, her claim would be valid if she stated that the birth would damage her psychologically and might actually place her life at risk if her abusive husband found out.

We already have had cases where an infant was not treated with the same care because the mother had intended to abort it. We had several cases where teens killed their babies after delivery and we were horrified. What hypocrites we are. Had they been smart enough to leave a foot in the vagina prior to killing the baby they could only have been charged with practicing medicine without a license.

When my daughter was working on a paper on the Holocaust for school, I became particularly interested in one of her sources. It discussed the mindset of the medical community in Germany right before the holocaust. I was saddened and concerned when I considered where we are as well. Not only are we killing babies during the process of birth, but there are also those in the medical community who are advocating euthanizing babies up to 3 months at the request of the parent. In Nazi Germany defective babies were the first to be eliminated.

In light of current case law, the passage of HR 4965 is necessary in order to re-establish a bright line between abortion and infanticide.

5) HR 4965 bans a procedure that is abhorrent to the vast majority of Americans.

Even though I had done mid 2nd trimester D&Es, I was appalled when I heard about D&X and really didn't believe it was being done. The majority of Americans also [has] found Partial Birth Abortion abhorrent and have supported legislation in numerous states banning its use.

When Nebraska's Partial-birth Abortion Ban was ruled unconstitutional several things happened:

(1) The line between abortion and infanticide was blurred,
(2) The State's ability to regulate abortion at any gestation even in the case of a procedure as repugnant as PBA was effectively blocked and
(3) The State's ability to promote any interest in the potentiality of human life, even post viability, was lost.

For these reasons I feel that this committee is justified in sponsoring legislation to once again attempt ban partial-birth abortion.

Both *Roe* and *Casey* stated that the State has an interest in potential life and could even proscribe certain techniques as long as it did not create an undue burden for women obtaining abortions.

The court emphasizes that "By no means must a State grant physicians unfettered discretion in their selection of abortion methods," and yet with this decision they have done just that. The fact that a D&X can be done on a nonviable fetus does not mean that it cannot be banned as long as the prohibition does not unduly burden a woman's ability to obtain an abortion. Since there are other more acceptable procedures available this is not an issue.

As a former abortionist I can tell you that the worst complication for an abortionist is a live baby at the end of the procedure. The goal is a dead baby.

At our hospital a fetal death before 20 weeks it is considered a spontaneous abortion or miscarriage. After that time it is considered a stillbirth and a death certificate must be filled out and the baby must be sent to the funeral home. If a baby of any gestation is born alive and exhibits definite signs of life, it is considered a birth and a birth certificate is filled out.

Unlike D&E, which is limited to about 20–22 weeks by the toughness of the tissue, D&X allows a surgical delivery of the fetus through term. Unlike induction and C-section, however, the fetus has no possibility of survival with D&X.

Even ACOG, a staunch supporter of abortion rights states in its *Abortion Statement of Policy*, "The College continues to affirm the legal right of a woman to obtain an abortion prior to fetal viability. ACOG is opposed to abortion of the healthy fetus that has attained viability in a healthy woman."

When I reviewed Dr. McMahon's testimony given to the House Subcommittee on the Constitution June 23,1995 I found that the maternal indications he listed for D&Xs he had performed were generally not serious and the vast majority were actually done for fetal indications, many of which were minor. Depression accounted for 39, Induction failure 14, Sexual Assault 19, Down's Syndrome 175, and cleft lip 9.

Dr. Haskell admitted that he did the vast majority of his D&Xs on normal fetuses and pregnancies. During the course of this debate I received a letter from an abortionist in Orlando offering termination of pregnancy up to 28 weeks

for fetal indications. He went on to say that, "To obtain a pregnancy termination beyond 24 weeks gestation, Florida State Law requires that a patient receive a written statement from her personal physician indicating it would be a threat to her health to continue her pregnancy." As the court currently defines health, even continuing a normal pregnancy threatens a woman's health.

I am concerned that some of the effort to preserve this technique is being fueled by the fetal organ trade in addition to the abortion industries desire to have no restrictions on abortion.

As a moral people there are some things that just should not be allowed and the killing of an infant in the process of birth is one of them.

Although the courts have given a woman the right to empty her womb they have not given her the right to a dead child. As technology and Induction techniques improve we will hopefully be able to give a woman the right to terminate her pregnancy without the necessity of terminating her child.

When Dr. McMahon first testified regarding D&X he claimed that the fetus was killed by the anesthetic given the mother. That was soundly refuted by several prominent anesthesiologists. We also now know that the fetus feels pain, which makes this procedure even more ghastly.

I have been accused of being anti-abortion because of my religious beliefs but actually I stopped doing abortions while I was an atheist.

When I started my OB/GYN Residency I was very pro-abortion. I felt no woman should have go through a pregnancy she didn't want. I felt abortion was a necessary evil and I was determined to provide women with the best abortion care possible. I perfected my D&C with suction technique and then convinced one of our local abortionists to teach me to do D&Es. I moonlighted at an abortion clinic in Gainesville as much as I could. The only time I felt uneasy was when I was on my neonatal rotation and I realized that the babies I was trying to save were the same size as the babies I had been aborting.

I continued to do abortions almost the entire time I was pregnant (with my eldest daughter) without it bothering me. It wasn't until I delivered my daughter and made the connection between fetus and baby that I stopped doing abortions. I found out later that few doctors are able to do abortions for very long. OB/GYNs especially, often experience a conflict of interest because they normally are concerned about the welfare of both their patients but in an abortion they are killing one of them. It's hard for most doctors to deliver babies and do abortions. It also has to do with the fact that to almost everyone else the pregnancy is just a blob of tissue, but the abortionist knows exactly what he is doing because he has to count all the parts after each abortion. I never had any doubt that I was killing little people but somehow I was able to justify and compartmentalize that.

Even though I later became a Christian, I continued to be a staunch supporter of abortion rights. I just couldn't stomach doing them myself anymore....I had dehumanized the fetus and therefore felt no moral responsibility towards it.

I joined the fight to ban this procedure only because I felt we were no longer really dealing with abortion but rather a form of infanticide. This bill safeguards women and does not unduly interfere with their ability to obtain an abortion. It clearly does not cover D&E or other commonly performed abortion techniques. It reestablishes a bright line between abortion and infanticide and it bans a procedure that is abhorrent to most Americans.

I urge you to pass "The Partial-Birth Abortion Act of 2002."

THE CONTINUING DEBATE:
Banning D&X (Partial-Birth) Abortions

What Is New

Congress passed a ban on DX/partial birth abortions in October 2003 by votes of 281 to 142 in the House and 64 to 34 in the Senate. President George Bush signed the bill, making it law. It is probable, almost certain, that opponents of the ban will have launched court challenges to its constitutionality by the time you read this volume.

Thus, the debate continues. Public opinion is very divided on abortion, as it has been since *Roe v. Wade* in 1973. Soon after that decision, one poll recorded 47% in favor of the ruling, 44% opposed to it, and 9% uncertain. A strikingly similar result came in a 2003 poll that asked Americans if they were "more pro-life or more pro-choice." Each position was chosen by an identical 44%, with 6% each volunteering "both" or "not sure." Questions about DX/partial birth abortion also reveal a divided public. When a 2003 poll that asked if and when the procedure should be legal, 20% replied "legal in all cases," 41% said legal only if the woman's health was "threatened," 33% answered "illegal," and 3% each said "it depends" or had no opinion.

Where to Find More

For a review of the abortion debate, which dates back even beyond Connecticut's enactment of the first anti-abortion law in 1821, see Rosemary Nossiff, *Before Roe: Abortion Policy in the States* (Temple University Press, 2002). A study of more contemporary policy is Donald T. Critchlow, *Intended Consequences: Birth Control, Abortion, and the Federal Government in Modern America* (Oxford University Press, 2001).

Current information on the abortion debate and its politics can be found on the Web sites of those representing both points of view. That of the Center for Reproductive Rights, author of the first reading is at: http://www.crlp.org/. Representing the pro-life point of view is the National Right to Life Committee at http://www.nrlc.org/. A site that claims to be balanced and seems to strive for that can be found at: http://www.religioustolerance.org/abortion1.htm.

What More to Do

The greatest challenge is to try to reach an agreement on this emotionally charged issue. Certainly it will not be possible to reconcile everyone. There are ardent voices that see no middle ground between the right to choose and the right to life. But polls show that most Americans are less doctrinaire. A 2003 poll recorded 21% of its respondents thinking abortion should be legal in all cases, 33% saying legal in most cases, 24% arguing it should be illegal in most cases, 17% wanting abortion to be illegal in all cases, and 6% uncertain. Somewhere in that majority of 63% Americans who are in the "most cases" or "uncertain" middle there may be a place that takes into account fetal/infant viability, maternal health, and other factors and creates a policy that most Americans can accept. Can your class craft a statement of standards that would receive a majority vote in the class?

4

CIVIL LIBERTIES

ANTI-TERRORIST LEGISLATION:
Threat to Civil Liberties *or* Constitutional Shield?

THREAT TO CIVIL LIBERTIES

ADVOCATE: Timothy Lynch, Director of the Cato Institute's Project on Criminal Justice

SOURCE: "Breaking the Vicious Cycle: Preserving Our Liberties While Fighting Terrorism," Cato Policy Analysis No. 443, June 26, 2002

CONSTITUTIONAL SHIELD

ADVOCATE: Ramesh Ponnuru, Senior Editor, *National Review*

SOURCE: "1984 in 2003? Fears about the Patriot Act Are Misguided," *National Review*, June 2, 2003

For most Americans, September 11, 2001, began well. It was sunny and 66°F at 8:00 A.M. in New York City. On the East Coast, people were arriving at work and otherwise beginning their days. Around the rest of the country, most folks were getting up or enjoying that last hour or two of sleep. All was normal.

Then at 8:45 A.M. an airliner smashed into the north tower of the World Trade Center. Within little more than an hour, a another jet liner crashed into the south tower, a third dove into the Pentagon, and a fourth went down in a field near Pittsburgh. All tolled, 19 terrorists, 33 crewmembers, 219 passengers, and more than 3,000 people on the ground died that morning.

The impact on the Americans was profound. The attacks marked the "End of Illusion," as columnist Robert J. Samuelson entitled a *Washington Post* essay. In addition to the physical damage, he wrote, "What was destroyed...[was] Americans' dreamlike feeling [of being] insulated from the rest of the world."

The U.S. reaction was dramatic. President George W. Bush soon ordered U.S. forces into Afghanistan to attack al-Qaeda and the Taliban regime. Congress quickly approved military action, and polls found nearly 90% of Americans agreed. The impact of 9/11 on U.S. foreign policy also included the formulation of the Bush Doctrine (see Debate 18) and the subsequent invasion of Iraq.

The political shock waves from 9/11 also rippled inward. Amid their shattered sense of security, Americans sought safety and were willing, at least temporarily, to surrender some of their civil liberties to get it. When asked less than a week after the attack, "Would you support new laws to strengthen security measures against terrorism, even if that meant reducing privacy protections?" 78% said yes, 14% replied no, and 8% were unsure.

Americans soon got what they wanted. Bush proposed legislation to greatly increase the ability of government agencies to conduct wiretaps and other covert operations and to ease the barriers to U.S. intelligence agencies conducting investigations within the country. In an anxiety-ridden atmosphere, the USA Patriot Act ("The

Uniting and Strengthening America by Providing Appropriate Tools Required to Intercept and Obstruct Terrorism Act of 2001") quickly passed both houses of Congress by huge margins and was signed into law. Among other things, it:

DEBATE 4

- Eases the authorization process for wiretaps, searches, and other covert activity. Standards for judicially authorized actions are lower; in limited circumstances action can be taken on authorization of the U.S. Attorney General.
- Permits surveillance of electronic communications, including e-mail and voice-mail and of communications records, such as Web sites visited.
- Eases barriers to domestic operations by intelligence agencies. This can now occur when foreign intelligence is a significant, no longer the only, concern.
- Permits "roving" surveillance of whatever communications device a subject is using, rather than being restricted to a single device.
- Allows access to information such as library records, book store purchases, student records (of foreign students) and also many tangible item controlled by rental companies, such as automobiles previously rented by a suspect.
- Expands the use of searches conducted without an individual's knowledge or a requirement that the government reveal what it seized during the search.

The following readings by advocates Timothy Lynch and Ramesh Ponnuru provide more detail on the Patriot Act. But you may want to see it in its entirety at: http://www.fincen.gov/pa_main.html. Detailed knowledge will help you evaluate the worries of some that without the act the country stands virtually defenseless before terrorism and the voices of others who claim that under the act, CIA agents will soon be bugging your home. Neither extreme is likely. So proceed with caution in your evaluation.

POINTS TO PONDER

➤ Read the following debates with almost two contradictory thoughts in mind. One is that it is healthy for citizens in a democracy to be leery of any form of covert government intrusion. At the same time, though, bear in mind that most of these methods are not new, only expanded, and the process for agencies to use them has been made less restrictive, not eliminated. This is an issue of balance, not right or wrong.
➤ One of the oft-quoted remarks of Benjamin Franklin is, "They that can give up essential liberty to obtain a little temporary safety deserve neither liberty nor safety." Is this a bit of enduring wisdom from the "sage of Philadelphia," or is it a shibboleth from the man who also recommended the turkey become the national symbol? Would the maxim, "an ounce of prevention is worth a pound of cure," be more appropriate?
➤ The ability of the government under the Patriot Act to monitor non-citizens, such as foreign students, is much greater than for citizens. Is this appropriate, or should most or all of the same civil liberties enjoyed by citizens also be extended for visiting foreign nationals?

Anti-Terrorist Legislation: Threat to Civil Liberties

TIMOTHY LYNCH

EXECUTIVE SUMMARY

President Bush and his lawyers maintain that terrorists are "unlawful combatants" and that unlawful combatants are not entitled to the protections of the Bill of Rights. The defect in the president's claim is circularity. A primary function of the trial process is to sort through conflicting evidence in order to find the truth. Anyone who *assumes* that a person who has merely been accused of being an unlawful combatant is, in fact, an unlawful combatant, can understandably maintain that such a person is not entitled to the protection of our constitutional safeguards. The flaw, however, is that that argument begs the very question under consideration....

Bush Seeks to Expand the Power to Eavesdrop. In November, 2001, Attorney General Ashcroft announced that the Department of Justice would begin to monitor the conversations of lawyers with their clients in federal custody....

Although the Bush-Ashcroft eavesdropping initiative has a laudable purpose—to stop terrorists from using their attorneys to pass useful information to their confederates outside of the prison walls—the policy is disturbing nonetheless....

Bush and Congress Seek to Expand the Power to Compel Cooperation. Justice Louis Brandeis once described the right to be let alone as "the most comprehensive of rights and the right most valued by civilized men." However, the men and women who serve in the federal government hold the opposite point of view. The federal government takes the position that it can coerce innocent people into cooperating with its investigations. Since September 11, the federal government has threatened more than 4,000 business firms, organizations, and individuals with fines and jail if they do not give the Department of Justice the information it demands. What is worse is that the federal government is compelling every sector of American industry to assist police investigations by systemic surveillance of customers and employees. The American tradition of voluntary cooperation with law enforcement is being perverted into a system of compulsory cooperation....

INTRODUCTION

When thousands of innocent civilians were murdered in a terrorist attack on September 11, 2001, President Bush declared, "Freedom has been attacked, but freedom will be defended." Within a matter of weeks, American military forces were hunting down the culprits by attacking terrorist base camps in Afghanistan. That decisive military action was a perfectly appropriate move to defend the lives, liberties, and property of the American people.

Here at home, however, President Bush and Attorney General John Ashcroft have done a poor job of "defending freedom." The Bush administration has supported measures that are antithetical to freedom, such as secretive subpoenas, secretive arrests, secretive trials, and secretive deportations. A vigorous investigation into the worst attack on American civilians was necessary, but the administration, with the acquiescence of Congress, has disregarded vital constitutional principles....

THE CYCLE: TERRORIST ATTACK AND "ANTITERRORISM" LEGISLATION

Recent experience has shown that the policymakers in America invariably respond to terrorist incidents by proposing and enacting "antiterrorism" legislation. Even though every sort of harmful behavior—murder, attempted murder, bodily injury, destruction of property—is already prohibited by law and carries severe criminal penalties, antiterrorism proposals have proven to be very alluring. After all, the very fact that an atrocity has occurred is irrefutable proof that the police were not able to thwart the attack. Thus, policymakers reason that they must take action and "alter the balance between liberty and security." With their newly acquired "tools," the argument runs, the police will be able to stop the terrorists before they can kill again. This cycle of terrorist attack followed by consideration of antiterrorism legislation has repeated itself many times in recent years....

[Most recently,] President Bush and Attorney General John Ashcroft proposed the "Antiterrorism Act of 2001" [two weeks after the September 11, 2001 terrorist attack]. Among other things, the bill would give the government a freer hand to conduct searches, detain or deport suspects, eavesdrop on internet communication, and monitor financial transactions. When President Bush signed the bill into law in October, he said the legislation would enable the police "to identify, to dismantle, to disrupt, and to punish terrorists before they strike."

In a matter of weeks, however, it became clear that the new antiterrorism law could not alter reality. On December 22, 2001, al-Qaeda terrorist Richard Reid boarded an American Airlines flight from Paris to Miami. In mid-flight, Reid tried to ignite explosives that were hidden in his shoes....

The Reid incident and the anthrax-laden letters that have killed several people are the most powerful recent evidence that the president and his police agents are not capable of stopping terrorists attacks.

BREAKING THE CYCLE

Defense and intelligence experts know that it is only a matter of time before the next terrorist attack. In fact, Secretary Rumsfeld warns that Americans should brace themselves for attacks "vastly more deadly" than the September 11 calamity. If recent experience is any guide, policymakers will respond to any such an attack by rushing to enact more antiterrorism legislation in a desperate attempt to give police and intelligence agencies additional powers to stop the killing. That would be a profound mistake. It is vitally important for policymakers to break the recurring cycle of enacting antiterrorism legislation before the pillars of our constitutional republic are completely undermined....

Deliberate Accountability before Legislating

Before policymakers come to the conclusion that there is too much freedom and privacy in America and that the police and intelligence agencies do not have enough power, they ought to thoroughly examine the question of how well the government has utilized the powers that it already wields. Here are just a couple of the issues that Congress should have investigated before it acquiesced to the president's demand for antiterrorism legislation following the September 11 attack.

- Federal officials in both the intelligence and law enforcement community were repeatedly warned that terrorist attacks in the United States were likely....
- The Department of Justice and the FBI want to access and monitor the

checking account activity and e-mail traffic of 200 million American citizens, but federal investigators inexcusably failed to monitor U.S. flight schools for potential terrorists....

Columnist George Will once observed that when failures are not punished, failures proliferate. If our policymakers evade the issues mentioned above, the future of America seems quite bleak. It is noteworthy that not a single employee in the federal government has lost his or her job in the wake of September 11. While it is possible that no one was truly at fault, a much more plausible explanation is that there is a general unwillingness to hold government officials accountable for failure.

Deliberate History before Legislation

History should matter. Before policymakers come to the conclusion that there is too much freedom and privacy in America and that the police and intelligence agencies do not have enough power, they should pause to consider how much respect the federal government has shown for individual American citizens, the law, and the Constitution. Here are just a few events that should not be soon forgotten.

- The FBI has used its surveillance powers to interfere in domestic politics. During the 1960s and 1970s, the bureau tried to undermine and disrupt the civil rights movement and the movement against the Vietnam war. In 1964, the bureau went so far as to attempt to blackmail Martin Luther King in the weeks preceding his ceremony to receive the Nobel Peace Prize. To thwart King's rising stature, the FBI threatened to give the news media evidence of King's adulterous affairs if he did not commit suicide.
- The FBI has given some of its informers a license to commit crime. The bureau has looked the other way while

sociopaths committed murders and innocent people were jailed for those crimes....

- In 2000, the Department of Justice maintained that the Second Amendment to the U.S. Constitution does not really guarantee the right of citizens to keep and bear arms. The government can, in its discretion, take guns away from the citizenry.
- The Tenth Amendment to the U.S. Constitution says that the powers that are not delegated to the federal government are reserved to the states, or to the people. The Department of Justice, however, has maintained that the federal government's powers are essentially unlimited or "plenary."

Lord Acton was correct when he observed that power tends to corrupt. All too often, government officials come to disdain any limitations on their power. Policymakers should carefully consider the lessons of history before they decide to confer more power on the government.

Deliberate Reality before Legislating

In a free society, the police maintain law and order primarily by reacting to citizen complaints, investigating crimes that have already occurred, and then apprehending the culprit. In America, the government is only rarely able to "prevent" a crime before the fact....

Because terrorists enjoy this same key advantage against our intelligence and law enforcement agencies, policymakers must pause before they rush to the conclusion that more government power is the "solution."...

When Attorney General John Ashcroft testified before Congress after September 11, he was asked whether the expanded powers that he was seeking would have given the FBI the ability to prevent the attack on the World Trade Center. Ashcroft conceded that it would be misleading for him to offer that kind of assurance....

It would be a grave disservice to the American people to curtail their privacy and liberties for nothing more than the illusion of increased security....

Deliberate Liberty before Legislating

Freedom is the essence of America. Many people, including President Bush, believe that the al-Qaeda terrorists attacked America because of their disdain for our free society. Unfortunately, in the days and weeks following the September 11 calamity, President Bush pushed several initiatives that severely undermined freedom in America....

One must first recognize both the short-term politics and the long-term legal implications that are at work here. When terrorists are able to perpetrate a dramatic, surprise attack, elected officials spring into action because they want to help to solve the problem or, at the least, be seen as helping to solve the problem. As noted earlier, altering the "balance between liberty and security" is invariably viewed as the "solution" to the terrorist problem....

Whatever their motivations, it is the responsibility of elected officials to defend Americans from foreign aggressors without violating the safeguards set forth in the Constitution. Thus, President Bush's antiterrorism initiatives must be closely examined for their necessity, wisdom, and constitutionality.

Bush Seeks to Expand the Power to Arrest. President Bush and his subordinates have undermined the Fourth Amendment's protections [against unreasonable search and seizure] in two distinct ways. First, President Bush has asserted the authority to exclude the judiciary from the warrant application process by issuing his own arrest warrants. According to the controversial "military order" that Bush issued on November 13, 2001, once the president makes a determination that a noncitizen may be involved in certain illegal activities, federal police agents "shall" detain that person "at an appropriate location designated by the secretary of defense outside or within the United States. According to the order, the person arrested cannot get into a court of law to challenge the legality of the arrest. The prisoner can only file appeals with the official who ordered his arrest in the first instance, namely, the president. The whole purpose of the Fourth Amendment is to make such a procedure impossible in America....

Second, President Bush and the FBI have tried to dilute the "probable cause" standard for citizens and noncitizens alike. The Supreme Court has repeatedly noted that a person cannot be hauled out of his home on the mere suspicion of police agents—since that would place the liberty of every individual into the hands of any petty official. But in the days and weeks following September 11, the FBI arrested hundreds of people and euphemistically referred to the group as "detainees."...

At bottom, this is an attempt to effect what Judge Richard Posner has aptly called "imprisonment on suspicion while the police look for evidence to confirm their suspicion." Since the Supreme Court has repeatedly rebuffed police and prosecutorial attempts to dilute the constitutional standard of probable cause, that gambit should not be tolerated....

Bush Seeks to Expand the Power to Prosecute and Imprison. President Bush would like to be able to deny the benefit of trial by jury to noncitizens accused of terrorist activities on U.S. soil. Under Bush's military order, he will decide who can be tried before a jury and who can be tried before a military commission....

The new eavesdropping policy bypasses the judiciary. The primary "check" on the power to wiretap is the warrant application process. By requiring the police to seek advance approval from a judicial officer, the process allows wiretap applications to be vetted by an impartial judge. In this way, meritorious applications can be separated from fishing expeditions. Under the president's initiative, however, the attorney general retains exclusive decision making authority to conduct monitoring....

The most recent antiterrorism legislation will allow the police to compel records from any business regarding any person—including medical records from hospitals, educational records from universities, and even records of books that have been checked out from the local library or purchased from the bookstore....

THE ROAD AHEAD

Policymakers cannot guarantee the safety of Americans from terrorist attacks because they cannot control the actions of terrorists....Because additional attacks on the American homeland are virtually certain, a fundamental choice lies ahead with respect to how the ongoing terrorism problem is going to be addressed on the home front....

If policymakers continue to respond to terrorist atrocities by "enhancing" the power of government, it is not terribly difficult to discern the trend lines for the next 20 years. Power has been flowing and will continue to flow, to the federal government and executive branch in particular. If present trends continue, it is likely that America will drift toward national identification cards, a national police force, and more extensive military involvement in domestic affairs. That ought to give pause to people of goodwill from all across the political spectrum—since those are the telltale signs of societies that are unfree....

CONCLUSION

The president of the United States wields enormous power, but it is sheer folly for anyone to think that he can stop terrorists from attacking the American homeland. Since intelligence and defense experts fully expect more atrocities in the foreseeable future, it is clear that Americans have a stark choice: We can either retain our freedom or we can throw it away in an attempt to make ourselves safe.

This choice must be confronted and not evaded. No one can deny the fact that if the cycle of terrorist attack followed by government curtailment of civil liberties continues, America will eventually lose the key attribute that has made it great, namely, freedom. As Secretary Rumsfeld has warned, we should be careful not to "allow terrorism to alter our way of life." It is therefore both wise and imperative to address the terrorist threat within the framework of a free society. That means taking the battle overseas to the terrorist base camps and killing the terrorist leadership. Here at home, it means resisting the implementation of a surveillance state. This course of action is, admittedly, fraught with danger. Innocent people at home and brave soldiers abroad will lose their lives to the barbaric forces of terrorism, but they will at least have died honorably as free people. Everyone wants to be safe, secure, and free, but such a desire denies the reality of our circumstances. In this dangerous world, freedom is a precious thing that must be vigorously defended. Anyone who is not prepared to face down the enemies of freedom with steely determination should seek shelter in the wilderness or outside of America completely. Freedom is not, was not, and will never be, a free good. Anyone who wants it must be prepared to defend it. And defending it necessarily carries the risk of serious bodily injury or death. A free and independent people must take responsibility for their own safety and deal with their vulnerability in a mature fashion. A free and independent people should not expect supernatural powers from their president.

Anti-Terrorist Legislation:
Constitutional Shield

RAMESH PONNURU

Has the war on terrorism become a war on Americans' civil liberties? A coalition of left- and right-wing groups fears so, and has been working hard to restrain the law-and-order impulses of the Bush administration. It's a coalition that includes the ACLU and the American Conservative Union, [columnists] Nat Hentoff and William Safire, John Conyers [(D-MI)] and [congressman] Dick Armey.

The coalition started to form in 1996, when Congress passed an anti-terrorism bill. But it really took off after September 11. Members of the coalition believe that Washington's legislative response—called, rather ludicrously, the "USA Patriot Act," an acronym for "Uniting and Strengthening America by Providing Appropriate Tools to Intercept and Obstruct Terrorism"—was a too-hastily conceived, excessive reaction to the atrocities.

Since then, the coalition has regularly found new cause for alarm. It has protested the administration's plans for military tribunals, the president's designation of "enemy combatants," and the Pentagon's attempts to consolidate data under a program called "Total Information Awareness." This spring, the civil libertarians of left and right worked together again to block Sen. Orrin Hatch's [(R-UT)] attempt to make permanent those provisions of the Patriot Act which are set to expire next year. They have organized, as well, against the possibility that the Justice Department will propose another dangerous anti-terror bill ("Patriot II").

The civil libertarians have had some success. They forced modifications in the Pa-triot Act before its enactment. They have inspired some cities to pass resolutions banning their employees from cooperating with federal authorities to implement provisions of the act that violate the Constitution. (Officials in other cities are, presumably, free to violate the Constitution at will.) They imposed legislative restrictions on Total Information Awareness. They have inhibited the administration from proposing anti-terror measures that would generate adverse publicity.

They themselves have gotten favorable publicity. It's an irresistible story for the press: the lion and the lamb lying down together. The press has tended to marvel at the mere existence of the coalition. They have not been quick to note that there is a larger bipartisan coalition on the other side, which is why the civil libertarians have been losing most of the battles. The Patriot Act passed 357–66 in the House and 98–1 in the Senate. In early May, the Senate voted 90–4 to approve another anti-terror provision—making it easier to investigate "lone wolf" terrorists with no proven connection to larger organizations—that the civil libertarians oppose.

More important, the press has not adequately scrutinized the civil libertarians' claims. This has kept the debate mired in platitudes about liberty and security. It has also reduced the incentive for the civil libertarians to do their homework, which has in turn made their case both weaker and more hysterical than it might otherwise have been.

Take the attack on TIPS, the Terrorist Information and Prevention System. This abortive plan would have encouraged truckers, delivery men, and the like to report suspicious behavior they observed in the course of their work. How effective this idea would have been is open to question. Most of the criticism, however, echoed former Republican congressman Bob Barr [of Georgia], who said that TIPS "smacks of the very type of fascist or communist government we fought so hard to eradicate in other countries in decades past."

But of all the measures the administration has adopted, it's the Patriot Act (along with the possible Patriot II) that has inspired the most overheated criticisms. When it was passed, the Electronic Frontier Foundation wrote that "the civil liberties of ordinary Americans have taken a tremendous blow with this law." The ACLU says the law "gives the Executive Branch sweeping new powers that undermine the Bill of Rights." But most of the concerns about Patriot are misguided or based on premises that are just plain wrong.

Roving wiretaps. Thanks to the Patriot Act, terrorism investigations can use roving wiretaps. Instead of having to get new judicial authorization for each phone number tapped, investigators can tap any phone their target uses. This is important when fighting terrorists whose MO includes frequently switching hotel rooms and cell phones. It's a common-sense measure. It's also nothing new: Congress authorized roving wiretaps in ordinary criminal cases back in 1986. It's hard to see Patriot as a blow to civil liberties on this score.

Internet surveillance. Libertarians have been particularly exercised about Patriot's green light for "spying on the Web browsers of people who are not even criminal suspects"—to quote *Reason* editor Nick Gillespie. This is a misunderstanding of Patriot, as George Washington University law professor Orin Kerr has demon-

strated in a law-review article. Before Patriot, it wasn't clear that any statute limited the government's, or even a private party's, ability to obtain basic information about electronic communications (e.g., to whom you're sending e-mails). Patriot required a court order to get that information, and made it a federal crime to get it without one.

Kerr believes that the bar for getting a court order should be raised. But he notes that Patriot made the privacy protections for the Internet as strong as those for phone calls and stronger than for mail. Patriot's Internet provisions, he concludes, "updated the surveillance laws without substantially shifting the balance between privacy and security."

James Bovard traffics in another Patriot myth in a recent cover story for *The American Conservative*: that it "empowers federal agents to cannibalize Americans' e-mail with Carnivore wiretaps." Carnivore is an Internet surveillance tool designed by the FBI. Don't be scared by the name. The FBI's previous tool was dubbed "Omnivore," and this new one was so named because it would be more selective in acquiring information, getting only what was covered by a court order and leaving other information private. But even if Carnivore is a menace, it's not the fault of Patriot. As Kerr points out, "The only provisions of the Patriot Act that directly address Carnivore are pro-privacy provisions that actually restrict the use of Carnivore."

Hacking. Also in *Reason*, Jesse Walker writes that Patriot "expands the definition of terrorist to include such non-lethal acts as computer hacking." That's misleading. Pre-Patriot, an al-Qaeda member who hacked the electric company's computers to take out the grid could not be judged guilty of terrorism, even if he would be so judged if he accomplished the same result with a bomb. Hacking per se isn't terrorism, and Patriot doesn't treat it as such.

Sneak and peek. The ACLU is running ads that say that Patriot lets the government "secretly enter your home while you're away…rifle through your personal belongings…download your computer files…and seize any items at will." Worst of all, "you may never know what the government has done." Reality check: You will be notified if a sneak-and-peek search has been done, just after the fact—usually within a few days. The feds had the authority to conduct these searches before Patriot. A federal judge has to authorize such a search warrant, and the warrant has to specify what's to be seized.

Library records. Bovard is appalled that Patriot allows "federal agents to commandeer library records," and the American Library Association shares his sentiment. Patriot doesn't mention libraries specifically, but does authorize terrorism investigators to collect tangible records generally. Law enforcement has, however, traditionally been able to obtain library records with a subpoena. Prof. Kerr suggests that because of Patriot, the privacy of library records may be better protected in terrorism investigations than it is in ordinary criminal ones.

The civil libertarians deserve some credit. Their objections helped to rid Patriot of some provisions—such as a crackdown on Internet gambling—that didn't belong in an anti-terrorism bill. Armey added the Carnivore protections to the bill. The law, as finally enacted, places limits on how much officials may disclose of the information they gain from Internet and phone surveillance. Moreover, the civil libertarians make a reasonable demand

when they ask that Patriot be subject to periodic re-authorizations, so that Congress can regularly consider modifications.

The civil libertarians rarely acknowledge the costs of legal laxity: Restrictions on intelligence gathering may well have impeded the investigation of Zacarias Moussaoui, the "twentieth hijacker," before 9/11. David Cole [Georgetown University], one of the movement's favorite law professors, goes so far as to lament that U.S. law makes "mere membership in a terrorist group grounds for exclusion and deportation."

And while civil libertarians may scant the value of Patriot, terrorists do not. Jeffrey Battle, an accused member of a terrorist cell in Portland, complained about Patriot in a recorded phone call that was recently released in court. People were less willing to provide financial support, he said, now that they were more likely to be punished for it.

Speaking of the administration's civil liberties record, Al Gore said last year that President Bush has "taken the most fateful step in the direction of [a] Big Brother nightmare that any president has ever allowed to occur." Dick Armey worries about "the lust for power that these people in the Department of Justice have." The civil-liberties debate could use a lot less rhetoric of this sort—and a lot more attention to detail.

A calm look at the Patriot Act shows that it's less of a threat to civil liberties than, say, campaign-finance reform. A lot of the controversy is the result of confusion. Opponents of the Patriot Act are fond of complaining that few people have bothered to read it. No kidding.

THE CONTINUING DEBATE:
Anti-Terrorist Legislation

What Is New

In 2003, the Bush administration proposed the Domestic Security Enhancement Act of 2003 (dubbed Patriot Act II) in Congress. An analysis of the act, which further expands the surveillance possibilities of Patriot Act I, has been done by David Cole of Georgetown University and is on the Web at: http://www.cdt.org/security/usapatriot/030210cole.pdf. As of this writing in the fall of 2003, the legislation was mired in Congress, which had become much more reticent about expanding covert operations than two years earlier.

Part of the reason that resistance to Patriot Act II is much higher than it was to Patriot Act I is that the public has reverted to its more traditional wariness of government surveillance. That was evident in a 2003 poll that asked, "Which comes closer to your view—the government should take all steps necessary to prevent additional acts of terrorism in the U.S. even if it means your basic civil liberties would be violated, or the government should take steps to prevent additional acts of terrorism but not if those steps would violate your basic civil liberties?" Of the respondents, 33% were willing to see civil liberties violated, 64% were unwilling to see that occur, and 3% were unsure.

Where to Find More

There are numerous Web sites lauding and decrying the Patriot Act. For a supportive view, go to the U.S. Department of Justice Web site at: http://www.usdoj.gov/. Select search and keyboard in "patriot act." For a critical perspective, visit the site of the American Civil Liberties Union at: http://www.aclu.org/SafeandFree/. Finally, for a balanced analysis of the Patriot Act, including an exposition of the surveillance possibilities prior to it, read Nathan C. Henderson, "Impact on the Government's Ability to Conduct Electronic Surveillance of Ongoing Domestic Communications," *Duke Law Journal*, October 2002. The article is available on the Web at: http://www.law.duke.edu/journals/.

What More to Do

One key thing to do is to get involved. The Patriot II Act is pending before Congress. Decide what you think, and act on that conviction by telling your three representatives in Congress what your position is and why.

Also, Patriot Act I is "up for grabs." To the dismay of the Bush administration in 2001, Congress inserted a "sunset provision" in the law. Under this clause, the act will expire at the end of 2005 unless Congress renews it. So the struggle over Patriot Act II in 2003 and 2004 will flow into what promises to be a monumental political fight over Patriot I in 2005.

Finally, do not just be "for" or "against" things. How would you simultaneously give the government the tools it needs to guard against terrorists and preserve the civil liberties the citizenry needs to guard against the government. Perhaps you and others in your class could write an act to Protect American's Traditional Rights while Investigating and Obstructing Terrorism, Patriot III.

5

AMERICAN PEOPLE/ POLITICAL CULTURE

ENGLISH AS THE NATIONAL LANGUAGE:
Make It Official *or* Accept Linguistic Diversity?

MAKE IT OFFICIAL

ADVOCATE: Mauro E. Mujica, Chairman of the Board and CEO, U.S. ENGLISH

SOURCE: "Statement from the Chairman," Web site of U.S. ENGLISH at http://www.us-english.org

ACCEPT LINGUISTIC DIVERSITY

ADVOCATE: Edward M. Chen, Staff Counsel, American Civil Liberties Union of Northern California

SOURCE: Testimony during hearings on "Implications of 'Official English' Legislation," before the U.S. House of Representatives Committee on Economic and Educational Opportunities, Subcommittee on Early Childhood, Youth and Families, November 1, 1995

About half the world's countries have an official language. Some, such as France, have one language. Others are officially multilingual. Canada has two official languages (English and French). Switzerland has four (French, German, Italian, and Romash). There are also many variations on the pattern of official language use. For example, Spain and some other countries have an official national language but designate other languages as co-official in regions where there are many people for whom another language is their first language.

More than half the U.S. states have official English language laws. Almost all of these have been enacted since the 1970s. There have also been repeated attempts in Congress to make English the official U.S. language. None has been successful so far, though, despite the fact that the idea is popular among Americans. A poll conducted in 2000 on the question of English as the official language found 73% in favor the idea, 21% opposed and 6% unsure.

Why the upsurge of official-English state laws beginning in the 1970s? One explanation is the increase in immigration. The traditional massive inflow of immigrants dropped precipitously after World War I to an annual average of just 50,000 in the 1930s. Then, after World War II, immigration rose again. It had sextupled by the 1960s and continued to rise quickly to about 1 million per year in the 1990s. This brought many new non-English speakers into the country.

A second factor prompting official-English laws was the changing cultural and legal climate in the 1960s and beyond. Part of what occurred was a growing sense that being American did not necessarily mean abandoning one's cultural heritage, including language. This sense among some people sparked several issues, such as whether non-English speaking children had a right to bilingual education and whether

English-only practices denied equal opportunity to people with limited or no English language facility. In turn, those who disagreed with the pressure for greater bilingualism pressed for official-English legislation.

A third possibility, in the view of some, is that the shift from primarily European-origin immigrants to newcomers from a much more diverse geographical background intensified a traditionalist reaction in some Americans. As late as the 1950s, more than 70% of immigrants were coming from Europe and other European-heritage countries. This changed when the Immigration and Nationality Act of 1965 ended the bias in favor of immigrants from Europe, and made entry from other regions easier. For example, the changes quintupled the percentage authorized immigrants arriving from Latin America, especially Mexico, and the Caribbean. By the late 1990s, European immigration accounted for only 16% of newcomers, compared to 32% from Asia and 49% from Latin America and the Caribbean. Africans still only make up 4 percent of immigrants, but that is 5 times the percentage in the 1960s.

Puerto Ricans are another group of Americans to whom the debate over whether to make English the U.S. official language is important. There are 3.4 million Puerto Ricans living in the United States, and another 3.8 million who reside in Puerto Rico. Their home island was annexed by the United States after the Spanish-American War in 1898. In 1917 all Puerto Ricans were granted U.S. citizenship, and they, like all citizens are free to live anywhere in the United States and its territories.

Of all Americans who are age five or over, the 2000 census found that 47 million, or 18% of that population, speak a language other than English. Of this 47 million people, 25.7 million rate themselves as fluent ("speak English very well") in English, and 21.5 million characterize themselves as being less than fluent or as not speaking English. The number of these permanent residents who do not English well or at all grew by 36% in the 1990s. Most these people are not citizens, but even some naturalized citizens speak only limited English based on the standard that naturalized citizenship requires only a "basic understanding of English."

Adding to the number of people with limited or no English language ability, the U.S. government estimates that in 2000 there were about 8.5 million undocumented (unauthorized/illegal) immigrants in the United States. As much as 75% of this group is from Mexico and Central America. It is misleading to view these immigrants as transients. Analysts estimate that about half of them have been in the United States for a decade or more, with another quarter residing in the country for between 5 and 9 years.

POINTS TO PONDER

➤ The idea of the United States as a "melting pot" is a persistent idea and is represented on The Great Seal of the United States, which features an eagle with a banner reading, E PLURIBUS UNUM (out of many, one) in its beak. Is this a worthy goal, or does it constitute cultural imperialism given the mostly white, European origins of American culture?

➤ Take note of the very different impacts the two advocates claim that an official English law would have. Is Mauro Mujica guilty of "pie-in-the-sky" optimism or is Edward Chen fear mongering?

➤ If states can designate English as an official language, would it be acceptable if a state, say Arizona, in which Latinos became a majority (a real possibility) enacted a law making Spanish the state's single official language?

English as the National Language: Make it Official

Mauro E. Mujica

I immigrated to the United States from Chile in 1965 to study architecture at Columbia University. While English was not my first language, I am perfectly bilingual today. Learning English was never an option nor was it something to which I objected or feared. It was required for success if I wanted to enjoy a prosperous life in the U.S.

Now, I am chairman of U.S.ENGLISH, the nation's oldest and largest organization fighting to make our common language, English, the official language of government at the federal and state levels.

Why? The high, uncontrolled rate of immigration to the U.S. is rapidly changing the face of our great country. From culture to politics, the way we function as a society is under stress. According to U.S. Census 2000 data, the U.S. is experiencing the highest rate of immigration since 1850—with 31.1 million newly arrived immigrants living here today (a 57 percent increase since 1990). Of these newcomers, it is reported that 21.3 million, or 8.1 percent of our total population, do not speak English very well.

Even so, English, the greatest unifier in our nation's history, is under assault in our schools, in our courts and by bureaucrats. Using scare tactics and divisive rhetoric, self-appointed leaders of immigrant groups are trying to prevent newcomers from learning our shared language. This vocal minority wrongly claims that an immigrant's culture and heritage will be lost if he or she agrees to have English as the official language.

Let me be clear: Encouraging immigrants to learn English is not about bigotry or exclusion. On the contrary, teaching newcomers English is one of the strongest acts of inclusion to our society our government can provide. The whole notion of a melting pot culture is threatened if immigrants aren't encouraged to adopt the common language of this country.

We're not suggesting that people give up their native languages. Bilingualism and multilingualism are quite advantageous in our fast-paced global economy. I, in fact, speak four languages.

While using a multitude of languages in business, at home or in worship is valuable, it is burdensome, needlessly expensive and inappropriate in government. What's more, it only serves as a disincentive to immigrants to learn English; the language 97 percent of our country speaks. We believe it makes far more sense to funnel the money spent on translation services to providing newcomers with the most important instrument in their life's toolbox—the knowledge of English so they can go as far as their dreams take them.

ABOUT THE ISSUE

Declaring English the official language means that official government business at all levels must be conducted solely in English. This includes all public documents, records, legislation and regulations, as well as hearings, official ceremonies and public meetings.

Official English legislation contains common-sense exceptions permitting the use of languages other than English for such things as public health and safety services, judicial proceedings (although actual trials would be conducted in English), foreign language instruction and the promotion of tourism.

In 1996, U.S.ENGLISH was instrumental in passing H.R. 123, "The Bill Emerson English Language Empowerment Act of 1996." That bill, making English the official language of the U.S. government, passed in the House of Representatives with a bipartisan vote of 259–169. Unfortunately, the Senate did not act on the bill before the end of the session. Currently, U.S.ENGLISH is working with Rep. Steve King of Iowa to help pass an official English bill in the 108th Congress. H.R. 997 is pending in the U.S. House of Representatives.

Twenty-seven states have some form of official English law. Most recently, Iowa passed official English legislation in 2002. U.S.ENGLISH is currently working in several additional states to pass official English bills.

WHY IS OFFICIAL ENGLISH NECESSARY?

Declaring English the official language is essential and beneficial for the U.S. government and its citizens. Official English unites Americans, who speak more than 329 languages (1990, U.S. Census), by providing a common means of communication; it encourages immigrants to learn English in order to use government services and participate in the democratic process; and it defines a much-needed common sense language policy.

Official English promotes unity. Our national motto is *E pluribus unum*—out of many, one. Immigrants of many nationalities built our nation, but the "melting pot" melded us into one people. This long tradition of assimilation has always included the adoption of English as the common means of communication. Unfortunately, the proliferation of multilingual govern-ment sends the opposite message to non-English speakers: it is not necessary to learn English because the government will accommodate them in other languages. A study published by the U.S. Department of Labor found that immigrants are slower to learn English when they receive a lot of native language support. (*Monthly Labor Review*, December 1992.) Thus, multilingual government services actually encourage the growth of linguistic enclaves. This division of the United States into separate language groups contributes to racial and ethnic conflicts. Designating English as the official language will help reverse this harmful process.

Official English empowers immigrants. Immigrants will benefit from the elevation of English to official status. Instead of the mixed message government sends by making it possible to file tax returns, vote, become U.S. citizens and receive a host of other services in a variety of languages, immigrants will understand that they must know English to fully participate in the process of government. Providing multi-lingual services creates dependence on "linguistic welfare." Life without English proficiency in the United States is a life of low-skilled, low-paying jobs. Studies of Census data show that an immigrant's income rises about 30% as a result of learning English. Knowledge of English leads to the realization of the American dream of increased economic opportunity and the ability to become a more productive member of society, which benefits everyone.

Official English is common sense government. The designation of official English will eliminate the needless duplication of government services in multiple languages. It is not the responsibility of the government to provide services in the 329 different languages spoken in the United States. It is the responsibility of each individual to either learn English or to find a friend or family member to translate. The money formerly spent on multi-lingual services can instead provide immigrants with the assistance they really need—classes to teach them English.

Official English legislation recognizes the need for common sense exceptions permitting the use of other languages for emergency, safety and health services; judicial proceedings; foreign language instruction and tourism promotion. Of course, because official English is only a limitation on government, it does not affect the languages spoken in private businesses, religious services or private conversations.

FREQUENTLY ASKED QUESTIONS

Isn't English already our official language? No, despite the fact that most Americans speak English, it is not the official language of the United States. Contrary to popular myth, English did not win out over German by one vote to become our official language. The Founding Fathers never really discussed this issue because over 90 percent of the voting population was of British ancestry. It was not until the 1960s that the U.S. began its current multilingual policies and the need for English to be the official language became evident.

Why is it necessary to declare English our official language? Official English promotes unity, and empowers immigrants by encouraging them to learn English, the language of opportunity in this country.

What happens when English is declared the official language? All official documents, records, legislation and regulations, as well as hearings, ceremonies and public meetings are conducted solely in English, with some common sense exceptions.

When are languages other than English permitted in government under official English legislation? Official English legislation allows a variety of common sense exceptions permitting the use of languages other than English: public health and safety, international relations and national security, judicial proceedings (although actual trials would be conducted in English), tourism, foreign language instruction, terms of art or phrases from other languages, etc.

How does official English affect private businesses and private citizens' daily lives? Official English legislation only applies to government functions. Language policies in private business are not affected, and private citizens are still free to use any language they wish in their daily lives.

Is there official English on the state level? Twenty-seven states have official English laws and several more are considering similar legislation. Most recently, Iowa, Alaska, Missouri, New Hampshire, Montana, South Dakota, and Wyoming have declared English their official language.

Does official English legislation affect bilingual education or bilingual ballots? While bilingual education is not directly addressed by official English legislation, U.S.ENGLISH supports the reform of bilingual education to favor programs that are English-intensive, short-term and transitional.

Does official English legislation imply that English is better than other languages or that there is anything wrong with speaking other languages? Official English legislation discourages multilingualism only at the government level. There is no question that being proficient in other languages in addition to English is extremely advantageous to an individual. Multilingualism in government, however, actually discourages immigrants from gaining proficiency English.

Does official English legislation violate "freedom of speech" and has this ever been brought up in the courts? Because official English legislation is a limitation on government, not private individuals, it does not violate the principle of freedom of speech. The courts have usually held that the government is under no general obligation to provide services in a language other than English. The Arizona State Supreme Court did overturn Arizona's official English law on the basis that it was too broad. Other state official English laws are not affected because Arizona's law was unique.

Is official English legislation anti-immigrant? Official English legislation is actually pro-immigrant. A study published by the U.S. Department of Labor found that immigrants learned English more quickly when there was less native language support around them. A "linguistic welfare" system that accommodates immigrants in their native languages lowers the incentive to learn English and restricts them to low-skilled, low-paying jobs. Official English legislation encourages immigrants to learn English so they can truly enjoy the economic opportunities available to them in this country.

MISCONCEPTIONS ABOUT OFFICIAL ENGLISH

Let's clear up some misconceptions about Official English.

Can other languages be used in our day-to-day private lives? Of course!

Can other languages be used by government officials in emergency situations or in the investigation of crimes? Absolutely!

Can other languages be taught and promoted in our society? We encourage it!

Can other languages be used by elected officials to communicate with constituents? You bet!

Can non-English terms of art, names, phrases or expressions be used? Certainly!

Can other languages be used for international trade, tourism and diplomacy? Definitely!

So what's the fuss all about? We don't know.

Official English benefits every resident of this wonderful melting pot called America. The melting pot works—because we have a common language.

English is the key to opportunity in this country. It empowers immigrants and makes us truly united as a people. Common sense says that the government should teach people English rather than provide services in multiple languages. What would happen if our government had to provide services in all 329 languages spoken in the U.S.? Without a common language, how long would we remain the "United" States?

English as the National Language:
Accept Linguistic Diversity

EDWARD M. CHEN

[T]he American Civil Liberties Union (ACLU)…is a membership-based non-profit organization representing more than 275,000 members dedicated to preserving civil rights and liberties protected under our Constitution. Since our founding 75 years ago, the ACLU has defended the rights of all, particularly unpopular and disenfranchised groups against unconstitutional discrimination and restrictions on their liberties. Early in our history, the ACLU represented immigrant workers deported and imprisoned because of their political beliefs. We have long been active in protecting racial minorities from discrimination in connection with their right to vote, to participate in the political process, to equal education and opportunity, and to equal access to important governmental services and benefits.

The ACLU believes that English-only laws—laws that make English the "official" language of government—and particularly those which broadly restrict the government's ability to use languages other than English in communicating and delivering services to non-English speaking Americans, violate civil rights and liberties. They do so in three ways.

First, by restricting the government's ability to communicate with and provide services to non-English speaking Americans, many of whom are children and elderly citizens, English-only laws deny fair and equal access to government. These limits, especially as they apply to such rights and services as voting assistance, education in a comprehensible language, health services and information, financial assistance such as social security and police protection, infringe upon important and fundamental rights.

Second, by prohibiting the government from communicating with its citizens in any language other than English, English-only laws violate the First Amendment rights of elected officials and public employees. They also impair the First Amendment rights of limited English proficient residents to receive vital information and petition the government for redress of grievances.

Third, English-only laws are based on assumptions predicated on false and disparaging stereotypes about today's immigrants. Thus, they foster anti-immigrant bigotry and intolerance and exacerbate ethnic tensions.

English-only laws are unnecessary, patronizing and divisive. They run contrary to the spirit of tolerance and respect of diversity embodied in our Constitution.

"OFFICIAL ENGLISH" LAWS ARE UNNECESSARY

Laws declaring English the "official" language of government are entirely unnecessary. Since the founding of our nation, America has been linguistically diverse. There have been hundreds of Native American and African languages, and substantial population of Spanish-speakers in Florida, Texas, California and the Southwest, French-speakers in Louisiana and in New England, German-speakers in Pennsylvania, the Dutch in New York, and the Swedish in Delaware. Yet, the primacy of English as America's common language has never been in jeopardy.

Nor is it in jeopardy now. U.S. English, the largest organization dedicated to the establishment of English-only laws since 1983, concedes that 97% of Americans already speak English. Even within the largest single language minority, Spanish-speakers, approximately 80% speak English. Just as significantly, studies show that today's immigrants are learning English just as fast as immigrant of prior years. For instance, half of all recent Mexican immigrants in California already speak English. Among first-generation Mexican-Americans, 95% are proficient in English; for second-generation Mexican-Americans the transformation is even more dramatic— more than 50% have lost their mother tongue. The rate of language assimilation of language minorities is just as rapid as it has been in previous generations.

"Official English" laws are not needed to teach immigrants the importance of learning English. Immigrants more than any other Americans fully appreciate the importance of learning English. Each day they must negotiate the daily hardships of surviving in a society that is largely monolingual English, whether it is looking for a job, trying to get information about their children's school, communicating with health providers, law enforcement officers or a bus driver, or even buying groceries or clothing. One need only look to the tens of thousands of immigrants waiting to get into adult English classes in Los Angeles and New York in order to understand their appreciation for the importance of learning English. Indeed, in 1987, immigrants filed a lawsuit in Los Angeles Superior Court to force the County to expand English classes for non-English speaking immigrants.

And immigrant parents know full well that their children cannot fully participate in the economic mainstream of America without becoming proficient in English. That is why a survey taken in Florida in 1985 revealed that 98% of Latinos, as compared to 94% of Anglo and Black parents, felt it was essential to their children to read and write English "perfectly." Immigrants do not need to be "taught" the importance of learning English by the federal government through an act of Congress.

What immigrants need are English classes, not patronizing proclamations. Ironically, "Official" English proposals do nothing to increase resources needed to provide English instruction.

Nor are English-only laws needed to stem excessive bilingualism in government operations as claimed by English-only proponents. In a study done by the GAO [General Accounting Office, an congressional research agency] at the request of Senator Richard C. Shelby (R. AL) and Representatives William F. Clinger (R. PA) and Bill Emerson (R. MO), the GAO found that for the 5–year period from 1990 through 1994, of the 400,000 documents printed by the federal government, only 265—.065%—were printed in languages other than English.

If anything, despite forward-looking efforts to provide minimal language assistance to non-English speakers through bilingual education and the Voting Rights Act, language minorities are vastly under-served. Even in California, which has the most comprehensive set of laws in the nation aimed at providing language assistance by governmental agencies. It is not uncommon for a Vietnamese cancer patient to wait for hours in a Bay Area county hospital waiting room until a translator is available, for a five-year old son of a Chinese-speaking couple to choke and lapse into a coma because emergency dispatchers could not understand their calls for help, for Latino earthquake victims to receive no assistance from relief workers who do not speak Spanish, for a Cuban immigrant to be shot and killed by the police because no officer was available to command him to stop in Spanish, for Spanish-speaking workers to be disproportionately injured by workplace toxic hazards because of the lack of Spanish speaking OSHA [Occupational Safety and Health Administration] inspectors, doctors and warnings, or for more than 50% of limited English proficient students in California to receive no instruction in their native language. The harsh reality is that language minorities remain under-served and the national resources devoted to foreign language assistance, particularly outside of public education, are relatively minuscule.

What few services and publications are provided in multiple languages make government more efficient, not less efficient as English-only proponents contend. Barring the government from choosing in specific circumstances to communicate with its non-English speaking citizenry in languages comprehensible to these communities will result in miscommunications and hinder the implementation of governmental policies such as protecting public health (through multi-lingual notices, counseling, etc.), enhancing water and resource conservation (through foreign language bulletins and educational pamphlets), increasing tax collections (by use of bilingual service representatives and tax forms), and ensuring law compliance (by providing bilingual investigators, interpreters in administrative and criminal proceedings, translations of compliance bulletins issued by OSHA, EPA [Environmental Protection Agency], Dept. of Commerce, etc.).

It makes no sense to have a sweeping rule requiring English-only which serves to straight-jacket executive agencies and other governmental bodies from making particularized judgments about the need to utilize languages in addition to English under appropriate circumstances. Indeed, a recent decision by the Ninth Circuit Court of Appeals striking down Arizona's "Official English" law, the Court found that government's use of languages other than English in communicating with limited English proficient residents increased rather than decreased efficiency, and that a law broadly prohibiting the use of different languages served no significant governmental interest.

"OFFICIAL ENGLISH" LAWS DENY IMPORTANT AND FUNDAMENTAL SERVICES TO LANGUAGE MINORITIES

The actual effect of English-only laws on the provision of services depends upon their text. Most of the laws which have been passed at the state and local levels, as well as the federal proposals pending in Congress contain broad and ambiguous terms. For instance, what does it mean for the government to have "an affirmative obligation to preserve and enhance the role of English as the official language" of government? What is the scope of the injunction that "[t]he Government shall conduct its official business in English"? Do these provisions mean that a social security counselor cannot convey important information to a Chinese-speaking applicant or recipient otherwise entitled to benefits? Would they overturn existing requirements that federal funded migrant and community health centers and alcohol abuse and treatment programs provide language assistance where there is a substantial number of non-English speakers? Do these provisions bar a Member of Congress from communicating with his or her constituents in Spanish, Russian or Navajo? Do they prohibit the INS [Immigration and Naturalization Service] from employing interpreters to interview asylum applicants, speak with witnesses in an investigation, or translate in deportation proceedings? Would the EPA be barred from issuing or requiring the issuance of a Spanish language summary of an environmental impact report on a proposed toxic waste site where the affected residents are primarily

Spanish-speaking migrant workers? Will these laws affect the issuance of FCC [Federal communications Commission] licenses to foreign language television and radio broadcast stations?

The potential mischief of "Official English" laws cannot be overestimated. Other English-only laws have been interpreted to impose severe restrictions on the use by government and its employees and officials of languages other than English. The first of such laws passed in recent times was enacted by Dade County, Florida in 1980. Its effect was to bar distribution of bilingual materials on fire prevention, publication of Metrorail schedules in foreign languages, Spanish language consumer information, prenatal advice by the county hospital in Creole, and funding for ethnic festivals. An "Official English" constitutional initiative passed by 51% of the voters in Arizona in 1988 has been held to bar legislatures from communicating with the constituents in Spanish or Navajo and public employees generally from communicating with the public in a language other than English.

Some current congressional proposals are explicit about the termination of specific language assistance programs. H.R. 739, for instance, would expressly require that "[c]ommunications by officers and employees of the Government of the United States with United States citizens shall be in English" and repeals provisions of the Elementary and Secondary Education Act of 1965 and the Voting Rights Act of 1965 which provide for bilingual education and voting assistance. H.R. 1005 requires the federal government "to conduct its official business in English, including publications, income tax forms and informational materials."

English-only laws which ban the provision of governmental services to non-English speakers unjustly target and disenfranchise language minorities. Such deliberate withdrawal of and ban on services to this already disadvantaged and insular sector of the American public is callous and mean-spirited. It is also unconstitutional.

THE RIGHT TO VOTE

The right to vote is a fundamental and inalienable constitutional right. Laws and devices, such as literacy tests, designed to impose burdens on minority groups in the exercise of their franchise violate that right. A broad ban requiring the withdrawal of bilingual assistance to limited English proficient citizens (many of whom are elderly have limited English speaking proficiency, but whose English reading ability is insufficient to comprehend complex and lengthy ballots and voting materials) imposes such a burden. That burden will fall most heavily on older Americans, who are the least likely to learn English as a second language and who also have the greatest need for bilingual assistance. The injurious impact upon ethnic minority bilingual voters of such a ban cannot be overstated. A 1982 study for the Mexican American Legal Defense and Educational Fund found that 70% of monolingual Spanish-speaking citizens would be less likely to register to vote if bilingual assistance were eliminated. If bilingual ballots were unavailable, 72% of the monolingual Spanish-speakers would be less likely to cast a vote.

EDUCATION

Although not currently recognized as a "fundamental" constitutional right, education is nonetheless an important right affecting the futures and destinies of millions of school children. As the Supreme Court stated in *Brown v. B[oar]d. of Education* [1957] forty years ago:

> Today, education is perhaps the most important function of state and local governments....In these days, it is doubtful that any child may reasonably be expected to suc-

ceed in life if he is denied the opportunity of an education. Such an opportunity, where the state has undertaken to provide it, is a right which must be made available to all on equal terms.

Denying immigrant children who do not yet speak English a meaningful education in a language comprehensible to them during the period in which they are learning English—the primary purpose of bilingual education—denies them an equal educational opportunity. In holding that the failure to provide language assistance to non-English speaking immigrant students violates Title VI of the Civil Rights Act of 1964, the Supreme Court stated [in *Lau v. Nichol*, 1974]:

> [T]here is no equality of treatment merely by providing students with the same facilities, textbooks, teachers and curriculum; for students who do not understand English are effectively foreclosed from any meaningful education. 414 U.S. at 566. While there has been a longstanding debate about the effectiveness of different pedagogical techniques, it would be premature and inappropriate to permit a politically driven agenda to end bilingual education.

"OFFICIAL ENGLISH" LAWS VIOLATE EQUAL PROTECTION PRINCIPLES BECAUSE THEY DISCRIMINATE AGAINST AN ALREADY DISADVANTAGED AND POWERLESS MINORITY

In addition to infringing upon voting and educational rights, English-only laws which systematically limit access of language minorities to governmental services are constitutionally suspect because: (1) language discrimination is functionally equivalent to national origin discrimination, and (2) language minorities are a prime example of a

"discrete and insular minority" (*United States v. Carolene Products*, 1938) who deserve heightened judicial protection under the Equal Protection clause. Moreover, English-only laws which impose a sweeping ban on foreign language assistance to language minorities constitute the purposeful disadvantaging of language minorities and are far more insidious than the mere failure to provide such assistance as a result of oversight or lack of funding. These laws disadvantage minorities "because of, not merely in spite of" their limited English proficiency (*Personnel Administrator of Massachusetts v. Feeney*, 1978).

LANGUAGE DISCRIMINATION AS AN ASPECT OF NATIONAL ORIGIN DISCRIMINATION

There is an obvious correlation between a language and its corresponding national origin group. The vast majority of non-English speakers are national origin minorities. 97% of those who usually speak Spanish are of Hispanic origin; approximately 77% of American Hispanics speak Spanish. [There is also a] high correlation between language and national origin among Asian Pacific Islanders. Moreover, language is the prime symbol of ethnicity, a central aspect of the ethnic identity of national origin minorities. To many Americans, speech is a cultural indicator second in importance only to physical appearance. Language is often a proxy for race and ethnicity. The Supreme Court recently observed: It may well be, for certain ethnic groups and in some communities, that proficiency in a particular language, like skin color, should be treated as a surrogate for race under an equal protection analysis (*Hernandez v. New York*, 1991).

National origin discrimination, like race discrimination, is considered inherently suspect under Equal Protection principles. Given the intimate and inextricable relationship between language and ethnicity,

English-only laws which systematically and purposefully disenfranchise language minorities are therefore constitutionally suspect. This is particularly so given the fact that the negative images and arguments advanced by English-only supporters have at times been a thinly disguised attack on Hispanic immigrants in particular. It is no coincidence that blatant anti-Hispanic statements have been attributed to the founder of U.S. English, Dr. John Tanton, or that a former chair of the organization has argued, "We have Hispanic politicians who have an unstated or hidden agenda to turn California into a bilingual, bicultural state."

LANGUAGE MINORITIES ARE A DISCRETE AND INSULAR MINORITY

English-only laws are also constitutionally suspect because language minorities, as a class, are a discrete and insular minority "saddled with such disabilities, or subjected to such a history of purposeful unequal treatment, or relegated to such a position of political powerlessness as to command extraordinary protection from the majoritarian political process." (*San Antonio Independent School District v. Rodriguez*, 1973).

Language minorities are socio-economically disadvantaged. Persons with limited English skills were more than two to three times as likely to have incomes below the poverty line, to have had far fewer years of formal education, and to be more unemployed than their English-speaking counterparts.

They suffer discrimination in practically all aspects of life ranging from the justice system, education, social welfare, and employment. Congress has expressly found: [V]oting discrimination against citizens of language minorities is pervasive and national in scope. Such minority citizens are from environments in which the dominant language is other than English.

In addition, they have been denied equal educational opportunities by State and local governments, resulting in severe disabilities and continuing illiteracy in the English language. The Congress further finds that, where state and local officials conduct elections only in English, language minority citizens are excluded from participating in the electoral process. In many areas of the country, this exclusion is aggravated by acts of physical, economic, and political intimidation.

In addition to voting discrimination, the political powerlessness of non-English speakers is heightened by the simple fact that a disproportionate number of them are not citizens and cannot vote at all.

Like other groups deemed to constitute a "suspect classification," language minorities have also been "subjected to a history of purposeful unequal treatment." (*San Antonio Independent School District v. Rodriguez*, 1973). Until the late 1800's, our nation had a tolerant policy towards linguistic diversity. Bilingualism in government and education was prevalent in many areas. The German language, for instance, was prevalent in schools throughout the mid-West. But the influx of eastern and southern Europeans and Asians gave rise to nativist movements and restrictionist language laws in the late 1800's and early 1900's. The Federal Immigration Commission issued a report in 1911 contrasting the "old" and "new" immigrant. The report argued that the "old" immigrants had mingled quickly with native-born Americans and became assimilated, while "new" immigrants from Italy, Russia, Hungary, and other countries were less intelligent, less willing to learn English, were not assimilating, and were criminally inclined.

In response, English literacy requirements were erected as conditions for public employment, naturalization, immigration, and suffrage in order to "Americanize" these "new" immigrants and exclude those perceived to be lower class and "ignorant of our laws and language." The New York Constitution was amended to disenfranchise over one million Yiddish-speaking citizens by a Republican administration fearful of Jewish voters. The California Constitution was similarly amended to disenfranchise Chinese voters who were seen as a threat to the "purity of the ballot box."

World War I gave rise to intense anti-German sentiment. A number of states, previously tolerant of bilingual schools, enacted extreme English-only laws. For instance, Nebraska and Ohio passed laws in 1919 and 1923 prohibiting the teaching of German until the student passed the eighth grade. The Supreme Court ultimately held the Nebraska statute unconstitutional as violative of due process in *Meyer v. Nebraska* (1923).

Native Americans were also subject to federal English-only policies in the late 1800's and early 1900's. Native American children were separated from their families and forced to attend English language boarding schools where they were punished for speaking their native language.

Thus, English-only laws' discrimination and disenfranchisement of language minorities, a particularly vulnerable group, is profoundly unfair and constitutionally suspect. Moreover, to the extent English-only laws restrict lower, more local levels of government from enacting laws, policies and programs providing for bilingual services, these laws are unconstitutional for yet an additional reason. Such laws deny language minorities the ability of obtain favorable legislation from local political bodies and government agencies. For instance, under the Arizona "Official English" constitutional provision added by the voters in 1988, language minorities cannot obtain an ordinance from the local city council or a policy from the county department of social services to provide for bilingual forms, notices or assistance. Indeed, language minorities could not even seek from the Arizona legislature a statute requiring, funding, or even authorizing language assistance in matters such as voting, job training, or consumer fraud. In short, preemptive laws which disable state and local governments from deciding on their own to provide bilingual assistance, excludes language minorities from equal participation in the normal political process and imposes upon them special burdens not placed on other groups (such as veterans and the disabled) who are free to seek favorable legislation at the local level. Barring such a discrete minority from equal access to the political process violates equal protection.

"OFFICIAL ENGLISH" LAWS VIOLATE THE FIRST AMENDMENT

The prohibition in English-only proposals upon the conduct of government business in any language other than English would bar communication between public employees and the public. The ban on informational materials in other languages significantly and affirmatively interferes with the ability of non-English speakers....It also interferes with public employees' First Amendment interest in communicating with language minority citizenry.

Moreover, those congressional proposals which make no exception for informational materials in languages other than English could even prohibit elected officials from communicating with their non-English speaking constituents. In the 1988 hearing before the House Committee on the Judiciary, Subcommittee on Civil and Constitutional Rights on "Proposed Amendments to the Constitution to establish English as the Official Language of the United States," Representative Stephen Solarz described the value of a Russian language newsletter he sent out to the large community of emigres from the Soviet Union in his district:

My purpose in sending this newsletter were fourfold: I wanted to extend a personal welcome to these special individuals who had endured so much adversity in their lives in their successful quest to find freedom and democracy in this country. Secondly, I sought to explain my positions on issues that are very important to this community—Soviet Jewry and U.S.-Soviet relations. Third, I wanted to share with my constituents a heartwarming story of a family reunification that I was fortunate enough to help facilitate with the help of several hundred Brooklyn junior high school students. Finally, I urged my constituents to contact my office if they wanted me to intercede on behalf of relatives still awaiting permission to emigrate from the Soviet Union. Dozens of Soviet Jewish families responded to this newsletter. In their letters to me—most of them also written in Russian—I learned of many refusenik cases of which I was previously unaware. I was then able to contact Soviet officials in an effort to expedite their emigration requests.

Enjoining elected government officials from communicating with their constituents in languages other than English would violate both the rights of elected officials under the First Amendment as well as the interests of constituents in receiving important information, to communicate with elected officials, and to participate in the political process. In striking down a similar provision of the Arizona Constitution violative of the First Amendment, [federal Appeals Court] Judge Brunetti stated [*Yniguez v. Arizonans for Official English*]:

> [Part of the law] offends the First Amendment not merely because it attempts to regulate ordinary political speech, but because it attempts to manipulate the political process by regulating the speech of elected officials. Freedom of speech is the foundation of our democratic process, and the language restrictions [in the law] stifle informative inquiry and advocacy by elected officials. By restricting the free communication of ideas between elected officials and the people they serve, [part of the law] threatens the very survival of our democratic society

"OFFICIAL ENGLISH" LAWS FOSTER BIGOTRY AND INTOLERANCE

Even if "Official English" laws did not ban the provision of particular services in languages other than English and were merely symbolic, the message that underlies the symbolism is unmistakenly pejorative of immigrants and imbued with fear mongering. The critical question is why do we now need a law declaring English the "official" language when we have lived without such a declaration for 200 years? The answer invariably given by English-only proponents is that for the first time in U.S. history the primacy of the English language, the purported common bond which holds this disparate society together, is being threatened by a new breed of immigrants who do not speak English, who are not learning English they way previous immigrants did, and who do not appreciate the importance of learning English....

The equation of bilingualism and un-Americanism is a more vicious version of the nativist sentiment expressed in Theodore Roosevelt's oft quoted diatribe at the turn of the century: "We have room for but one language here and that is the English language, for we intend to see that the crucible turns our people out as American, of American nationality, and not as dwellers in a polyglot boarding house." It is also a reiteration of the Americanization movement which culminated in the Federal Immigration Commission's report in 1911 contrasting the "old" and "new" immigrants and which led to restrictionist language policies. These arguments are predicated on false negative stereotypes of today's immigrants and inaccurate assumptions about language policy of our government. They portray today's immigrants, largely Latino and Asian, as being more resistant to assimilation, less willing and able to learn English, and more of a threat to the primacy of English and Americanization than European immigrants of past generations. Nothing could be further from the truth. As discussed earlier, today's immigrants are no different from immigrants of the past in their desire to learn English and in the speed with which they are learning English.

These historical episodes should serve as reminders of the dangers of basing policy of false and negative stereotypes. To base legislation regulating language on false assertions not only makes for bad public policy, but by perpetuating false stereotypes, demonizing immigrants an already unpopular segment of the public, and fostering the public perception that the English and American culture are being overrun immigrants unwilling or unable to learn English, "Official English" laws breed prejudice and bigotry. At best, regardless of its stated intent, such legislation is divisive and irresponsible, particularly in the current atmosphere of heightened racial tensions, economic insecurity, and anti-immigrant nativism. At worst, such legislation represents little more than hate mongering.

Immigrant bashing is as popular as ever. Although there are no official reporting mechanisms, the anecdotal evidence that does exist suggests that language discrimination, an aspect of the backlash against immigrants, is on the rise. For instance, after Californians passed Proposition 63 in 1986, making English the State's "official" language, a number of California cities enacted ordinances limited the amount of foreign languages that could appear on private business signs. In a recent case, Latino passengers on a Greyhound bus were threatened with being expelled for refusing to comply with the driver's demand that they stop speaking Spanish to each other. In a much publicized decision, a Texas judge ordered a mother having custody over her 5-year-old child to stop speaking Spanish to her at home, calling it "child abuse." Workplace complaints about discrimination against non-English speakers and accented English speakers and about employees being disciplined for speaking to a co-worker in their native tongue abound particularly in high immigration areas such as California.

Legislation making English the "official" language, which implies that those who do not speak English are somehow less than "official" and thus relegates them to second class status in the eyes of the law. Because these laws are predicated upon false and disparaging assumptions about today's immigrants, they can only fan the flames of prejudice, mistrust and divisiveness. And because the disparaging arguments are directed against today's immigrants who are largely Hispanic and Asian, the racial undercurrents that lay beneath the surface of English-only efforts make these laws doubly dangerous and divisive. Rather than inspiring cohesion and unity, such legislation will, in the end, exacerbate societal discord and ethnic tension.

"ENGLISH-ONLY" LAWS UNDERMINE THE SPIRIT OF TOLERANCE AND PLURALISTIC IDEALS EMBODIED IN OUR CONSTITUTION

Undergirding the proponents' argument in favor of English-only laws is the assertion that the English language is the "common bond" or "social glue" that holds are diverse society together, and that multi-lingualism jeopardizes the fragile social cohesion singularly owed to the English language. The proponents often cite the Quebec secessionist movement and even the conflict between Serbs and Croats as examples of societal discord and disintegration that occurs in the absence of a common tongue. This assertion is wrong both empirically and as a matter of principle. Linguistic diversity need not lead to social conflicts. Switzerland for instance has four official languages. There is no single "official" language for the European Common Market. On the other hand, one need only look to deep conflicts in Northern Ireland and Bosnia to see that a common language does not assure social tranquility.

Indeed, America's own history dispels the notion that an "official" language is needed to preserve national unity. As noted previously, from the founding of this nation, there have been substantial populations of speakers of languages other than English. Indeed, in the early 1800's a greater percentage of Americans spoke German than speak Spanish today. Bilingual education in German and Yiddish was common throughout Eastern cities and the Midwest. Official minutes of many town meetings in the Midwest were printed in German. The presence of language diversity and official bilingualism had no detrimental effect on the nation's social fabric.

A more specific example is New Mexico with its historically large Spanish-speaking population and its proud history of tolerance and acceptance of Spanish heritage. New Mexico, which has been officially bilingual since 1912, has printed all government documents in English and Spanish. Far from ethnic balkanization, Hispanics in New Mexico enjoy one of the highest rates of political participation (and hence integration into the political mainstream) in the nation.

Where social tensions have arisen over language conflicts, language tension are the manifestation, not the cause, of underlying social problems. Historically, language has often been used as a tool of social and political subjugation. It is the suppression of native and ethnic minority languages by a dominant group that most often gives rise to ethnic conflicts, be it the "Russification" of Soviet ethnic minorities, Franco's attempt to suppress the language rights of Basques and Catalans, or South Africa's attempt to impose the Afrikaner language as the language of instruction in the schools of Soweto. Racial and ethnic hostility are fostered not by language diversity, but by the attempts of certain language groups to suppress the use of other languages in political and social discourse.

Most scholars agree that the conflict between French and English speakers in Canada, often cited by English-only proponents as the prime example of the supposed threat posed by multilingualism, is the "result of the withdrawal of, or the failure to recognize, language rights rather than the result of linguistic tolerance and generosity." According to commentators, the Quebec separatist movement is a reaction to perceived economic, political and cultural subordination. If anything, Canada's tension was not caused but was in fact alleviated (at least temporarily) by the recognition of French as a co-official language. There are vast differences in the role of language, religion, political memory, geographic mobility, role of politics and founding myths that make the Canadian/Quebec situation completely different from that of America. One of the most significant differences is the degree of language integration within the two societies. Twenty years ago, the rate of French speakers' acquisition of English was so slight that native born Spanish speakers in the Southwest were thirty times more likely than French-speaking Quebecois to adopt English as their dominant language.

The ACLU does not question the importance of having a common language; obviously a common language (or set of languages) is necessary as a practical matter for government and society to function efficiently. But the predicate assumption of English-only proponents—that English is the "social glue" that holds our society together—is facile. The common bond that unites Americans of all backgrounds, origins, and languages is our shared belief and commitment to freedom, democracy and liberty. That bond runs deeper than the English language.

Domestic tranquility is achieved not through coerced conformity, but through tolerance and mutual respect. In this regard, "Official English" laws ignore the central teaching of the First Amendment. Many of the world's most virulent wars have been based on religious differences; yet, despite the diversity of religious faiths within the United States, our nation has avoided the intense heretical wars and violent theologi-cal conflicts experienced elsewhere. Why? Because the First Amendment guarantees tolerance and teaches mutual respect of different faiths, rather than allowing the imposition of an official orthodoxy. In contrast, "Official English" laws impose an official orthodoxy that breeds intolerance. It is intolerance not diversity which threatens our nation's unity.

CONCLUSION

"Official English" laws are unnecessary. If passed they will impose material hardships, violate constitutional rights, and exacerbate ethnic tensions. We should celebrate not fear our diversity. The rich tapestry of ethnicities and languages that comprise America is one of our greatest strengths. "Official English" laws reflect our worst fears, not our highest ideals. The ACLU urges this Committee to reject "Official English" proposals as unwise, unfair and unconstitutional.

THE CONTINUING DEBATE:
English as the National Language

What Is New

In 2003, as Mauro Mujica mentions, Representative Steve King (R-IA) introduced the English Language Unity Act of 2003 (H.R. 997). Explaining his bill, King told the House, "The English language is the carrier of liberty and freedom throughout history and the world. For centuries, our common tongue, English, has been the uniting force in this great nation, knocking down ethnic and religious barriers to make us truly one nation. Today, as we rally for unity and patriotism a common means of communication propels us toward our goal." As of late August 2003, an additional 94 House members had become signed co-sponsors.

It is also worth noting that among the Advisory Board members of U.S. ENGLISH is Arnold Schwarzenegger, actor of *Terminator* fame, who was elected governor of California in October, 2003 as a result of the recall procedure instituted against the sitting governor, Gray Davis.

One thing to note when you visit the U.S. ENGLISH Web site is the digital counter tallying up the group's estimate of the annual cost of not having English as the official language. At this writing in late 2003, the cost was $3.2 billion. Another important figure is the total $3.5 trillion in federal, state, and local budgetary spending in 2003. Which is more relevant: the amount ($3.2 billion) or it percentage of all spending (one-tenth of one percent)?

Where to Find More

For a site opposed to English as the national language, visit the Web page of James W. Crawford, at http://ourworld.compuserve.com/homepages/JWCRAWFORD/. The opposite perspective is on the site of U.S. English at: http://www.us-english.org/. It would also be good to familiarize yourself with the specific legislation to make English the official language. For the details of H.R. 997, the English Language Unity Act of 2003, go to "Thomas," the Web site of Congress at: http://thomas.loc.gov/. Enter "H.R. 997" in the search window for the 108th Congress (2003–2004). The text of the bill will appear. You will also see hyperlinks to track the status of the legislation. If a new Congress has been seated by the time you read this, go to Thomas and keyboard in "English language" in the search window under the current Congress.

What More to Do

H.R. 997 was referred to two House committees, Education and the Workforce and Judiciary One option for a committee is to "mark up" a bill. This involves debating it and making changes to it before voting on whether to send it to the floor of (in this case) the House. What your class might do is to constitute itself as a congressional committee in order to consider and mark up H.R. 997. Ponder, for instance, whether you would include exceptions, such as for trials of non-English speakers or 911 operators, to the English-only mandate on governments.

If you support the bill, your object is to compromise enough, if necessary, to win majority support, or else the bill will die in committee. If you oppose the bill, you can "just say no," but that carries risks. If it passes, you will have lost the chance to alter it through amendments.

6 PUBLIC OPINION/PARTICIPATION

POST-9/11 CRITICISM OF U.S. FOREIGN POLICY:
Un-American *or* Patriotic?

UN-AMERICAN

ADVOCATE: Victor Davis Hanson, Shifrin Visiting Professor of Military
History, U.S. Naval Academy, Annapolis
SOURCE: "I Love Iraq, Bomb Texas," *Commentary*, December 2002

PATRIOTIC

ADVOCATE: Gore Vidal, novelist, playwright, and essayist
SOURCE: "We Are the Patriots," *The Nation*, June 2003

Americans like to think of themselves as living in the "land of the free," as the national anthem goes. Part of what makes the United States a land of the free is the First Amendment's guarantee of free speech. Polls show that Americans strongly support free speech in the abstract. For example, when a survey asked in 2002 whether people should be allowed to express "unpopular opinions," fully 94% of respondents said they should be; just 6% disagreed.

Americans are less supportive of First Amendments rights when they are applied to specific situations. This is especially apt to occur during times of foreign conflict and other crises. A poll during the war with Iraq in March 2003 found that 57% of its respondents thought it was "okay" for war opponents to hold public protests, while 41% thought protesting was not okay, and 2% were unsure. Certainly it is the case that a majority of the public supported the protestor's constitutional rights, but it is also true that the majority willing to do so was far smaller than the 94% who supported the First Amendment in theory.

Such attitudes often engender the sort of dismay voiced by Victor Davis Hanson in the first reading and also create social and economic pressures on dissenters. For example, the Dixie Chicks paid the price in 2003 when singer Natalie Maines spoke against the war with Iraq and added, "We're ashamed the president of the United States is from Texas." Facing an uproar, she argued, "One of the privileges of being an American is you are free to voice your own point of view." However other people agreed with the Reverend Jerry Fallwell's rebuke, "You don't talk about your own country, especially during war," and the group's sales and concert bookings dropped off, and some radio stations refused to play their songs.

The increased disapproval of dissenters during foreign crises has two causes. One is the "rally effect." Feelings of patriotism, the urge to rally 'round the flag,' usually increase during foreign crises. This emotional response increases the propensity of people to think patriotism demands that everyone agree with the famous toast given in 1816 by Commodore Stephen Decatur, "Our country! In her intercourse with foreign nations, may she always be in the right; but our country, right or wrong." The second reason that disapproval of protesters increases is the belief that they undermine the U.S. position or its war effort. Polls found that this attitude was held by 38% of the public during the Iraq War of 2003 and 43% during the Persian Gulf War in 1991.

Do protesters undermine a country's war effort? Undeniably, such activity is watched closely by leaders of countries confronting the United States, and those leaders sometimes factor American domestic dissent into their decisions. Years after the Vietnam War ended, Bui Tin, a former high-ranking North Vietnamese officer, told a *Wall Street Journal* reporter that North Vietnam's leaders had "follow[ed] the growth of the American antiwar movement," and that it "gave us confidence that we should hold on in the face of battlefield reverses."

It is also true, though, that U.S. leaders try to manipulate opinion by warning that foreign policy divisions create national danger. "The way to do that," former U.S. Secretary of State Dean Acheson once admitted, "is to say politics stops at the seaboard—and anyone who denies that postulate is a son-of-a-bitch or a crook and not a true patriot. Now, if the people will swallow that, then you're off to the races."

Before turning to the two advocates, it is important to note that this issue is a long-standing one. At times, the United States has moved to legally curb dissenters. As early as 1798 amid fears of war with France, Congress passed the Sedition Act specifying fines and imprisonment for "any person [who] shall write, print, utter or publish" anything that would "excite…the hatred of the good people of the United States" against the government. Similarly, in 1917, Congress passed the Espionage Act that, among other things, made it illegal to oppose purchasing war bonds or to interfere with military recruiting.

The courts have validated some such actions. In *Schenck v. United States* (1919), the Supreme Court upheld a conviction under the Espionage Act of 1917 for urging resistance to the military draft. Speaking for the court, Justice Oliver Wendell Holmes held that the legality of curbing free speech rests, "in every case [on] whether the words used are used in such circumstances and are of such a nature as to create a clear and present danger that they will bring about the substantive evils that Congress has a right to prevent. It is a question of…degree."

POINTS TO PONDER

➤ This debate is about boundaries. Think about Justice Holmes's comments as you read the following articles. As for his standard of "degree," do you agree with Vidal that he and other critics are the true patriots or would you characterize them, as Hanson does, as unpatriotic "anti-Americans," whose "creed is really a malady [that] cries out to be confronted and exposed"? Or do you see "a clear and present danger" that should be legally restrained?

➤ Think about the argument that protests in time of crisis weaken the country and encourage its enemies. Do you agree or disagree? And, whichever view you hold, do you think it is acceptable for protestors to demonstrate and take other actions during times of crisis?

➤ Which comes closer to your belief: Commodore Decatur's toast, "Our country, right or wrong" or Albert Einstein's comment, "Heroism on command, senseless violence, and all the loathsome nonsense that goes by the name of patriotism—how passionately I hate them!"?

Post-9/11 Criticism of U.S. Foreign Policy: Un-American

VICTOR DAVIS HANSON

With [the] discussion in Washington over what to do about Iraq there arrived also the season of protests. They were everywhere. In the national newspapers, Common Cause published a full-page letter, backed by "7,000 signatories," demanding (as if it had been outlawed) a "full and open debate" before any American action against Iraq. More radical cries emanated from Not in Our Name, a nationwide "project," spearheaded by [MIT professor] Noam Chomsky and affiliates, which likewise ran full-page advertisements in the major papers decrying America's "war without limit," organized "Days of Resistance" in New York and elsewhere, and in general made known its feeling that the United States rather than Iraq poses the real threat to world peace; at one late-October march in Washington, there were signs proclaiming "I Love Iraq, Bomb Texas," or depicting President Bush wearing a Hitler mustache and giving the Nazi salute. In the dock with America was, of course, Israel: on university campuses, demands circulated to disinvest from companies doing business with that "apartheid state"—on the premise, one supposes, that a democratic society with an elected government and a civilian-controlled military is demonic in a way that an autocratic cabal sponsoring the suicide-murder of civilians is not.

Writers, actors, and athletes revealed their habitual self-absorption. The novelist Philip Roth complained that the United States since September 11 had been indulging itself in "an orgy of national narcissism," although he also conceded, reclaiming his title as the reigning emperor of aesthetic narcissism, that immediately after the fall of the Twin Towers New York "had become interesting again because it was a town in crisis"—a fleeting, final benefit to connoisseurs of literature from the death of thousands. Barbra Streisand, identifying Saddam Hussein as the dictator of Iran, faxed a misspelled and incoherent but characteristically perfervid memos to Congressmen, while Ed Asner, of sit-com fame, threatened publicly to "lose his soul" if we went into Iraq. The Hollywood bad boy Sean Penn, not previously known for harboring a pacifistic streak, demanded that the President cease his bellicosity for the sake of Penn's children. Traveling abroad, the actress Jessica Lange pertly announced: "It makes me feel ashamed to come from the United States—it is humiliating." And the jet-setting tennis celebrity Martina Navratilova, who fled here to escape Communist repression and has earned millions from corporate sponsors, castigated the repressive atmosphere of her adopted homeland, a country whose behavior is based "solely on how much money will come out of it."

And so forth. Harbingers of this sort of derision were, of course, on view a year ago, in the period right after September 11 and well into the campaign against the Taliban in Afghanistan. Thus, Michael Moore, currently making the rounds plugging his movie *Bowling for Columbine* and a sympathizer of Not in Our Name, bemoaned the 9/11 terrorists' lack of discrimination in their choice of target: "If someone did this to get back at Bush, then they did so by killing thousands of people who did not vote for him!" Norman Mailer, engagingly comparing the Twin Towers to "two huge buck teeth," pronounced their ruins "more beautiful" than the buildings themselves. In the *London Times,* the novelist Alice Walker speculated whether Osama bin Laden's "cool armor" might not be pierced by reminding him of "all the good, nonviolent things he had done." There was the well-known poet who forbade her teenage daughter to fly the American flag from their living-room window, the well-known professor who said he was more frightened by the speech of American officials than by the suicide-hijackers of 9/11, and the well known columnist who decried our "belligerently militaristic" reaction to the devastation of that day.

Not all the criticism of the American response to terrorist cells and rogue governments has partaken of this order of irrationality; serious differences, responsibly aired, are also to be found, including in newspaper ads. But in the year since the slaughter of September 11 there has emerged an unpleasant body of sentiment that has little or nothing to do with the issues at hand but instead reflects a profound and blanket dislike of anything the United States does at any time. For a while, the *New Republic* kept track of this growing nonsense by Western intellectuals, professors, media celebrities, and artists under the rubric of "Idiocy Watch," and the talk-show host Bill O'Reilly is still eager to subject exemplars of it to his drill-bit method of interrogation. The phenomenon they represent has been tracked daily by Andrew Sullivan on his weblog, [www.andrewsullivan.com/], and analyzed at greater length by, among others, William J. Bennett (in *Why We Fight*), Norman Podhoretz (in "The Return of the 'Jackal Bins,'" *Commentary*, April 2002), and Keith Windschuttle (in "The Cultural

War on Western Civilization," the *New Criterion*, January 2002), the last-named of whom offers a complete taxonomy of schools and doctrines. And yet the sheer strangeness of the overall enterprise, not to mention its recent proliferation and intensification, would seem to merit another look.

A number of general truths emerge from any survey of anti-American invective in the context of the present world conflict. First, in each major event since September 11, proponents of the idea of American iniquity and/or Cassandras of a richly deserved American doom have proved consistently wrong. Warnings in late September 2001 about the perils of Afghanistan—the peaks, the ice, the warring factions, Ramadan, jihad, and our fated rendezvous with the graveyard of mighty armies gone before us—faded by early November in the face of rapid and overwhelming American victory. Subsequent predictions of "millions" of Afghan children left naked and starving in the snow turned out to be equally fanciful, as did the threat of atomic annihilation from across the border in Kashmir.

No sooner had that theater cooled, however, than we were being hectored with the supposed criminality of our ally [Israeli Prime Minister] Ariel Sharon. Cries of "Jeningrad" followed, to die down only with the publication of Palestinian Authority archives exposing systematic thievery, corruption, and PA-sanctioned slaughter. During the occasional hiatus from gloomy prognostications about the Arab-Israeli conflict, we were kept informed of the new cold war that was slated to erupt on account of our cancellation of the anti-ballistic-missile treaty with the defunct Soviet Union; of catastrophic global waring, caused by us and triggering floods in Germany; and always of the folly of our proposed intervention in Iraq.

That effort to remove a fascist dictator, we are now assured (most tediously by Anthony Lewis in the *New York Review of Books*), is destined to fail, proving instead to be a precursor to nuclear war and/or a permanently inflamed Arab "street." On the other hand, a *successful* campaign in Iraq, it is predicted, will serve only to promote America's worst instincts; its imperial ambition, its cultural chauvinism (a/k/a hatred of Muslims and Arabs), and its drive for economic hegemonism (a synonym for oil). Those who oppose preemption warn on Monday that the Iraqi dictator is too dangerous to attack and shrug on Tuesday that he is not dangerous enough to warrant invasion. Take your pick: easy containment or sure Armageddon.

The striking characteristic of such judgments is that they, too, are wholly at odds with the known facts. Confident forecasts of American defeat take no notice of what is the largest and best-trained military in history, and fly in the face of recent American victories in the Gulf war (where, at the time, Anthony Lewis likewise predicted quagmire and disaster) and Kosovo, both achieved at the cost of scarcely any American casualties. Alleged American hatred of Muslims hardly comports with our record of saving Kuwaitis from fascist Iraqis, Kosovars and Bosnians from Christian Serbs, or Afghans from Russian Communists and then from their own Islamist overlords, all the while providing billions of dollars in aid to Egypt, Jordan, and the Palestinian Authority. It was Jordanians and Kuwaitis, not we and not Israelis, who ethnically cleansed Palestinians; Iraqis and Egyptians, not we, who have gassed Muslim populations. And it is to our shores that Muslims weary of Middle Eastern despotism are desperate to emigrate.

Is there a consistent theme here? We are talking, largely though not exclusively, about a phenomenon of the aging Left of the Vietnam era and of its various progeny and heirs; and once upon a time, indeed, the anti-American reflex could be linked with some rigor to the influence of Marxism. True, that particular religion, at least in its pristine form, is just about gone from the picture these days. Some of its fumes, though, still linger in the doctrines of radical egalitarianism espoused by postmodern relativists and multiculturalists and by now instilled, in suitably diluted and presentable form, in several generations of college and high-school students. Hence, for example, the regular put-down of George W. Bush as a "Manichean" [after the Persian philosopher Mani (A.D. 216–A.D. 276) who saw the cosmos as a dualistic struggle between good and evil]—for could anything be more self-evidently retrograde than a view of our present conflict as a war of good versus evil, or anything more simplistic than relying on such "universal" arbiters of human behavior as freedom, pluralism, and religious tolerance?

Eschewing any reference to truths of this kind, adherents of postmodernist relativism assess morality instead by the sole criterion of power: those without it deserve the ethical high ground by virtue of their very status as underdogs; those with it, at least if they are Westerners, and especially if they are Americans, are ipso facto oppressors. Israel could give over the entire West Bank, suffer 10,000 dead from suicide bombers, and apologize formally for its existence, and it would still be despised by American and European intellectuals for being what it is—Western, prosperous, confident, and successful amid a sea of abject self-induced failure.

One is bound to point out that, as a way of organizing reality, this deterministic view of the world suffers from certain fatal defects, primarily an easy susceptibility to self-contradiction. Thus, a roguish [Chilean dictator Augusto] Pinochet, who executed thousands in the name of "law and order" in Chile, is regarded as an incarnation of the devil purely by dint of his purportedly close association with the United States, while a roguish and anti-American [Fidel] Castro, who butchered tens of thousands in the name of "social justice" in Cuba, is courted by Congressmen and ex-Presidents even as Hollywood celebrities festooned with AIDS ribbons sedulously ignore the thousands of HIV-positive Cubans languishing in his camps. [U.N. Secretary General] Kofi Annan gushes of Saddam Hussein, "He's a man I can do business with," while the ghosts of thousands slain by the Iraqi tyrant, many of them at his own hand, flutter nearby; for this, the soft-spoken internationalist is lionized.

Few have exploited the contradictions of this amoral morality as deftly as Jimmy Carter, who can parlay with some of the world's most odious dictators and still garner praise for "reaching out" to the disadvantaged and the oppressed. As President, Carter evidently was incapable of doing much of anything at all when tens of thousands of Ethiopians were being butchered; but as chief executive emeritus, he has managed to abet the criminal regime of North Korea in its determination to fabricate nuclear bombs and lately, having been rewarded with the Nobel Prize for peace, has brazenly attempted to thwart a sitting President's efforts to save the world from the Iraqi madman.

But all such contradictions are lightly borne. Since, for our postmodern relativists and multiculturalists, there can be no real superiority of Western civilization over the available alternatives, democracy and freedom are themselves to be understood as mere "constructs," to be defined only by shifting criteria that reflect local prejudices and tastes. Like Soviet commissars labeling their closed societies "re-

publics" and their enslaved peoples "democratic," Saudi officials assert that their authoritarian desert monarchy is an "Islamic democracy"—and who are we to say them nay? ("To my ear," the *New York Times* columnist Nicholas Kristof helpfully explains, "the harsh [American] denunciations of Saudi Arabia as a terrorist state sound as unbalanced as the conspiratorial ravings of Saudi fundamentalists themselves.") In Afghanistan, the avatars of multiculturalism and utopian pacifism struggled with the facts of a homophobic, repressive, and icon-destroying Taliban, but emerged triumphant: according to their reigning dialectic, the Taliban still had to be understood on their own terms; only the United States could be judged, and condemned, absolutely.

As for the roots of elite unhappiness with America, this is a subject unto itself. It would hardly do to reduce everything to a matter of psychology: a whole class of unhappy individuals motivated by resentment over the failure of their society to fulfill their own considerable aspirations. Nor does it quite satisfy to say more globally, and theoretically, that they suffer at several removes from the paradoxes of the radical Enlightenment: the unquestioned belief that sweet reason alone, in the hands of its proper acolytes, and yoked to commensurate powers of coercion, can remake the world. But we need not discount other and much simpler factors—like the law of the pack.

As in the medieval church or among Soviet apparatchiks, the pull of groupspeak is always strong among compliant and opportunistic elites. For today's intellectuals, professors, and artists, being on the team pays real dividends when it comes to tenure, promotion, publication, reviews, lecture invitations, social acceptance, and psychic reassurance. And the dividends are compound: one is a lockstep member of one's crowd *and* one enjoys the frisson of dissidence, of being at variance, but always so comfortably at variance, with one's benighted fellow citizens.

Our unprecedented affluence also explains much, although its role as a facilitator has been relatively scanted in most discussions of anti-Americanism that I have seen. The plain fact is that civilization has never witnessed the level of wealth enjoyed by so many contemporary Americans and Europeans. Vast groups are now able to insulate themselves from the age-old struggle to obtain food, shelter, and physical security from enemies both natural and human. Obesity, not starvation, is our chief health problem; we are more worried about our 401(k) [retirement] portfolios than about hostile tribes across the border.

What does this have to do with the spread of anti-Americanism? Home-grown hostility to American society and the American experiment is hardly a new phenomenon, but in the 19th century it tended to be limited to tiny and insulated elite circles (see the writings of Henry Adams). Now, it is a calling card for tens of thousands who share a once rare material splendor. That brilliant trio of Roman imperial writers, Petronius, Suetonius, and Juvenal, warned about such Luxus and its effects upon the elite of their era, among them cynicism, nihilism, and a smug and crippling contempt for one's own.

An ancillary sort of unreality has emerged in modern Western life alongside the reduced need to use our muscles or face physical threats. In a protected world, Saddam Hussein comes to seem little different from a familiar angry dean or a predictably moody editor, someone who can be either reasoned with or, if necessary, censured or sued. In this connection, it is not surprising that those most critical of America are not the purported victims of its supposedly rapacious capitalist system—farm workers,

car mechanics, or welders—but more often those in the arts, universities, media, and government who have the time and leisure to contemplate utopian perfection without first-hand and daily exposure to back-breaking physical labor, unrepentant bullies, or unapologetically violent criminals. For such people, the new prosperity does not bring a greater appreciation of the culture that has produced it but rather enables a fanciful shift from thinking in the immediate and concrete to idle musings of the distant and abstract.

For many, today's affluence is also accompanied by an unprecedented sense of security. Tenure has ensured that tens of thousands of professors who work nine months a year cannot be fired for being unproductive or mediocre scholars, much less for being abject failures in the classroom. In government at every level, job security is the norm. The combination of guarantees and affluence, the joint creation of an enormous upper-middle class, breeds a dangerous unfamiliarity with how human nature really works elsewhere, outside the protected realm.

Such naiveté engenders its own array of contradictory attitudes and emotions, including guilt, hypocrisy, and envy. Among some of our new aristocrats, the realization has dawned that their own good fortune is not shared worldwide, and must therefore exist at the expense of others, if not of the planet itself.

This hurts terribly, at least in theory. It sends some of them to their fax machines, from where they dispatch anguished letters to the *New York Times* about the plight of distant populations. It prompts others, more principled and more honorable, to work in soup kitchens, give money to impoverished school districts, and help out less fortunate friends and family. But local charity is unheralded and also expensive, in terms of both time and money. Far easier for most to exhibit concern by signing an ostentatious petition against Israel or to assemble in Central Park: public demonstrations that cost nothing but seemingly meet the need to show to peers that one is generous, fair, caring, and compassionate.

As if that were not hypocrisy enough, those who protest against global warming, against shedding blood for oil, or against the logging of the world's forests are no less likely than the rest of us to drive SUV's, walk on hardwood floors, and lounge on redwood decks. Try asking someone awash in a sea of materialism to match word with deed and actually disconnect from the opulence that is purportedly killing the world and its inhabitants. Celebrity critics of corporate capitalism neither redistribute their wealth nor separate themselves from their multinational recording companies, film studios, and publication houses—or even insist on lower fees so that the oppressed might enjoy cheaper tickets at the multiplex. Jessica Lange and Alec Baldwin so hate George W. Bush that they threaten to leave our shores—promises, promises.

An even less appetizing quality of the new privileged is their palpable and apparently unassuageable envy. Intellectuals and people in the arts are perennially surprised—no, outraged—to find that corporate managers and Rotary Club businessmen, with far less education and infinitely less taste than they, make even more money. To the guilt they feel over what they have is therefore added fury at those who not only have more but seem to enjoy it without a necessary and concomitant sense of shame. Worse yet, because America is still a plutocracy where riches and not education, ancestral pedigree, or accent bring status, it can be galling for a sensitive professor of Renaissance literature to find himself snubbed at dinner

parties by his own university's president in favor of the generous but (shall we say) less subtle owner of a chain of Taco Bells. From there it is but a step to seeing the face of that same smiling and unapologetic plutocrat before him whenever he gazes upon the likeness of George W. Bush or Richard Cheney.

This brings us to another element of the new anti-Americanism. All of us seek status in accordance with what we feel we have accomplished or think we know. This naturally selfish drive is especially problematic for radical egalitarians, who must suppress their own desire for privilege only to see it pop out in all sorts of strange ways. I do not mean the superficially incongruous manifestations: Hollywood actors in jeans and sneakers piling into limousines, Marxist professors signing their mass mailings with the pompous titles of their chairs, endowed through capitalist largesse, or the posh Volvos that dot the faculty parking lot. Rather, I have in mind the pillorying by National Public Radio of those who say "nucular" for "nuclear," the loud laments in faculty clubs over threats posed to rural France by McDonald's, and all the other increasingly desperate assertions of moral and cultural superiority in a world where meaningful titles like earl, duke, and marquis are long gone and in theory repugnant. "Axis of evil? Totally banal," scoffed Felipe Gonzalez, the former prime minister of Spain, not long before his own country swaggeringly recaptured an uninhabited and rather banal piece of rock that had been briefly snatched by Morocco.

The superciliousness of the educated knows no end, and may even betray a final anxiety. One million bachelor's degrees are awarded in this country each year, but under the new therapeutic curriculum there is little to guarantee that any of the holders of these certificates can spell a moderately difficult English word or knows which dictator belongs to which enslaved state. And what is true of students is too often true as well of their pretentious professors, as can be seen whenever Noam Chomsky pontificates about war ("Let me repeat: the U.S. has demanded that Pakistan kill possibly millions of people…") and in place of references to historical examples or citations from the literature raves on with "as I have written elsewhere," "there are many other illustrations," "as would be expected," "it would be instructive to seek historical precedents," "as leading experts on the Middle East attest," and all the other loopholes and escape clauses that are the mark not of a learned intellectual but of a calcified demagogue.

But who has time to acquire expertise or exhibit patience with human frailty? The innate limitations of mortals matter little tour irritated utopians, nor can moral progress ever be rapid enough to keep up with a definition of perfection that evolves as quickly as the technology of cell phones. That Afghanistan a mere year after the fall of the Taliban is not yet as tranquil and secure as New England proves that our postbellum efforts there are not much better than the Taliban. "No one," asserts [Columbia University professor] Edward Said, "could argue today that Afghanistan, even after the rout of the Taliban, is a much better and more secure place for its citizens." No one? That we once *aided* Saddam Hussein is a supposedly crippling fact of which we are reminded ad nauseam, as if, not before but after the Gulf war, France, Russia, and Germany did not proceed to sell him the components for weapons of mass destruction, or as if we ourselves did not once give the Soviets a third of a million GMC trucks to thwart Hitler, only to see them used in the Gulag. But in the perfect world of America's critics, if Barbra

Streisand can fly to Paris in four hours and fax her scrambled thoughts in seconds, and if Gore Vidal from his Italian villa can parse sentences better than the President of the United States, then surely we are terminally culpable for not having solved the globe's problems right now.

Is it because these elite Americans are so insulated and so well off, and yet feel so troubled by it, that they are prone to embrace with religious fervor ideas that have little connection with reality but that promise a sense of meaning, solidarity with a select and sophisticated group, moral accomplishment, and importance? Is it because of its very freedom and wealth that America has become both the incubator and the target of these most privileged, resentful, and unhappy people? And are their perceptions susceptible of change?

If the answer to the first two questions is yes, as I believe it is, then the reply to the third must be: I doubt it. The necessary correctives, after all, would have to be brutal: an economic depression, a religious revolution, a military catastrophe, or, God forbid, an end to tenure. At least in the near term, and whether we like it or not, the religion of anti-Americanism is as likely to grow as to fade.

But it can also be challenged. The anti-Americans often invoke Rome as a warning and as a model, both of our imperialism and of our foreordained collapse. But the threats to Rome's predominance were more dreadful in 220 B.C.E. than in 400 C.E. The difference over six centuries, the dissimilarity that led to the end, was a result not of imperial overstretch on the outside but of something happening within that was not unlike what we ourselves are now witnessing. Earlier Romans knew what it was to be Roman, why it was at least better than the alternative, and why their culture had to be defended.

Later in ignorance they forgot what they knew, in pride mocked who they were, and in consequence disappeared.

The example of Rome, in short, is an apt one, but in a way unintended by critics who use passing contemporary events as occasions for venting a permanent, irrational, and often visceral distrust of their own society. Their creed is really a malady, and it cries out to be confronted and exposed.

Post-9/11 Criticism of U.S. Foreign Policy: Patriotic

GORE VIDAL

I belong to a minority that is now one of the smallest in the country and, with every day, grows smaller. I am a veteran of World War II. And I can recall thinking, when I got out of the Army in 1946, Well, that's that. We won. And those who come after us will never need to do this again. Then came the two mad wars of imperial vanity—Korea and Vietnam. They were bitter for us, not to mention for the so-called enemy. Next we were enrolled in a perpetual war against what seemed to be the enemy-of-the-month club. This war kept major revenues going to military procurement and secret police, while withholding money from us, the taxpayers, with our petty concerns for life, liberty and the pursuit of happiness.

But no matter how corrupt our system became over the last century—and I lived through three-quarters of it—we still held on to the Constitution and, above all, to the Bill of Rights. No matter how bad things got, I never once believed that I would see a great part of the nation—of we the people, unconsulted and unrepresented in a matter of war and peace—demonstrating in such numbers against an arbitrary and secret government, preparing and conducting wars for us, or at least for an army recruited from the unemployed to fight in. Sensibly, they now leave much of the fighting to the uneducated, to the excluded.

During Vietnam, [President George W.] Bush fled to the Texas Air National Guard. [Vice President Richard] Cheney, when asked why he avoided service in Vietnam, replied, "I had other priorities." Well, so did 12 million of us sixty years ago. Priorities that 290,000 were never able to fulfill.

So who's to blame? Us? Them? Well, we can safely blame certain oil and gas hustlers who have effectively hijacked the government from presidency to Congress to, most ominously, the judiciary. How did they do it? Curiously, the means have always been there. It took the higher greed and other interests to make this coup d'état work.

It was Benjamin Franklin, of all people, who saw our future most clearly back in 1787, when, as a delegate to the Constitutional Convention at Philadelphia, he read for the first time the proposed Constitution. He was old; he was dying; he was not well enough to speak but he had prepared a text that a friend read. It is so dark a statement that most school history books omit his key words.

Franklin urged the convention to accept the Constitution despite what he took to be its great faults, because it might, he said, provide good government in the short term. "There is no form of government but what may be a blessing to the people if well administered, and I believe farther that this is likely to be well administered for a course of years, and can only end in Despotism, as other forms have done before it, when the people shall become so corrupted as to need despotic Government, being incapable of any other." Think of Enron, Merrill Lynch, etc., of chads and butterfly ballots, of [Supreme Court Justice Anthony] Scalia's son arguing before his unrecused father at the Supreme Court while unrecused Thomas sits silently by, his wife already at work for the approaching Bush Administration. Think, finally, of the electoral college, a piece of dubious, antidemocratic machinery that Franklin doubtless saw as a source of deepest corruption and subsequent mischief for the Republic, as happened not only in 1876 but in 2000.

Franklin's prophecy came true in December 2000, when the Supreme Court bulldozed its way through the Constitution in order to select as its President the loser in the election of that year. Despotism is now securely in the saddle. The old Republic is a shadow of itself, and we now stand in the glare of a nuclear world empire with a government that sees as its true enemy "we the people," *deprived* of our electoral franchise. War is the usual aim of despots, and serial warfare is what we are going to get unless—with help from well-wishers in new old Europe and from ourselves, awake at last—we can persuade this peculiar Administration that they are acting entirely on their vicious own, and against all *our* history.

The other night on CNN I brought the admirable Aaron Brown to a full stop, not, this time, with Franklin but with John Quincy Adams, who said in 1821, on the subject of our fighting to liberate Greece from Turkey, the United States, "goes not abroad, in search of monsters, to destroy." If the United States took up all foreign affairs, "she might become the dictatress of the world. She would no longer be the ruler of her own spirit," her own soul.

Should we be allowed in 2004 to hold a presidential election here in the homeland, I suspect we shall realize that the only regime change that need concern our regained spirit—or soul—is in Washington.

President Adams is long since dead. And we have now been in the empire business since [the Spanish-American War in] 1898: We had promised to give the Filipinos their independence from Spain.

Then we changed our mind, killing some 200,000 of them in the process of Americanizing them.

A few years ago there was a significant exchange between then-General Colin Powell [Chairman, Joint Chiefs of Staff] and then-statesperson [Secretary of State] Madeleine Albright. Like so many civilians, she was eager to use our troops against our enemies: What's the point of having all this military and not using it? He said, They are not toy soldiers. But in the interest of fighting Communism for so long, we did spend trillions of dollars, until we are now in danger of sinking beneath the weight of so much weaponry.

Therefore, I suppose it was inevitable that, sooner or later, a new generation would get the bright idea, Why not stop fooling around with diplomacy and treaties and coalitions and just use our military power to give orders to the rest of the world? A year or two ago, a pair of neo-conservatives put forward this exact notion. I responded—in print—that if we did so, we would have perpetual war for perpetual peace. Which is not good for business. Then the Cheney-Bush junta seized power. Although primarily interested in oil reserves, they liked the idea of playing soldiers too.

Last September Congress received from the Administration a document called the National Security Strategy of the United States [aka the Bush Doctrine]. As the historian Joseph Stromberg observed, "It must be read to be believed." The doctrine preaches the desirability of the United States becoming—to use Adam's words—dictatress of the world. It also assumes that the President and his lieutenants are morally entitled to govern the planet. It declares that our "best defense is a good offense." The doctrine of pre-emption is next declared: "As a matter of common sense and self-defense, America will act against such emerging threats *before* they are fully formed." (Emphasis added.) Doubtless, [Attorney] General [John] Ashcroft is now in Utah arresting every Mormon male before he can kidnap eight young girls for potential wives.

Article 1, Section 8 of the Constitution says that only Congress can declare war. But Congress surrendered that great power to the President in 1950 and has never taken it back.

As former [Wyoming] Senator Alan Simpson said so cheerily on TV the other evening, "The Commander in Chief of the military will decide what the cause is. It won't be the American people." So in great matters we are not guided by law but by faith in the President, whose powerful Christian beliefs preach that "faith is the substance of things hoped for, the evidence of things not seen."

In response to things not seen, the USA Patriot Act was rushed through Congress and signed forty-five days after 9/11. We are expected to believe that its carefully crafted 342 pages were written in that short time. Actually, it reads like a continuation of Clinton's post–Oklahoma City antiterrorist act. The Patriot Act makes it possible for government agents to break into anyone's home when they are away, conduct a search and keep the citizen indefinitely from finding out that a warrant was issued. They can oblige librarians to tell them what books anyone has withdrawn. If the librarian refuses, he or she can be criminally charged. They can also collect your credit reports and other sensitive information without judicial approval or the citizen's consent.

Finally, all this unconstitutional activity need not have the slightest connection with terrorism. Early in February, the Justice Department leaked Patriot Act II, known as the Domestic Security Enhancement Act, dated January 9, 2003. A Con-

gress that did not properly debate the first act will doubtless be steamrolled by this lawless expansion.

Some provisions: If an American citizen has been accused of supporting an organization labeled as terrorist by the government, he can be deprived of his citizenship even if he had no idea the organization had a link to terrorists. Provision in Act II is also made for more searches and wiretaps without warrant as well as secret arrests (Section 201). In case a citizen tries to fight back in order to retain the citizenship he or she was born with, those federal agents who conduct illegal surveillance with the blessing of high Administration officials are immune from legal action. A native-born American deprived of citizenship would, presumably, be deported, just as, today, a foreign-born person can be deported. Also, according to a recent ruling of a federal court, this new power of the Attorney General is not susceptible to judicial review. Since the American who has had his citizenship taken away cannot, of course, get a passport, the thoughtful devisers of Domestic Security Enhancement authorize the Attorney General to deport him "to any country or region regardless of whether the country or region has a government." Difficult cases with no possible place to go can be held indefinitely.

Where under Patriot Act I only foreigners were denied due process of law as well as subject to arbitrary deportation, Patriot Act II now includes American citizens in the same category, thus eliminating in one great erasure the Bill of Rights.

Our greatest historian, Charles Beard, wrote in 1939:

> The destiny of Europe and Asia has not been committed, under God, to the keeping of the United States; and only conceit, dreams of grandeur, vain imaginings, lust for power, or a desire to escape from our

domestic perils and obligations could possibly make us suppose that Providence has appointed us his chosen people for the pacification of the earth.

Those Americans who refuse to plunge blindly into the maelstrom of European and Asiatic politics are not defeatist or neurotic. They are giving evidence of sanity, not cowardice, of adult thinking as distinguished from infantilism. *They* intend to preserve and defend the Republic. America is not to be Rome or Britain. It is to be America.

THE CONTINUING DEBATE:
Post-9/11 Criticism of U.S. Foreign Policy

What Is New

The American victory over and occupation of Iraq set off a new round of criticism that the United States was attempting to become a new Rome, imperially dominating the world. The inability to uncover any weapons of mass destruction (WMDs) furthered the suspicions of critics that the war had been one of aggression rather than defensive preemption. The continued resistance within Iraq furthered dissent even more. By late October 2003, more American troops had been killed in ambushes after the fall of Baghdad than had been killed during the war itself. There were early signs that the public was becoming restive with the occupation and that it could turn into a major issue in the 2004 presidential election. At the end of the war, 70% of Americans thought it had been "worth fighting." Four months later, only 57% held that view.

Where to Find More

For a volume that contains a range of views on patriotism, read Martha C. Nussbaum, *For Love of Country?* (Beacon Press, 2002). A review of the origins and nature of patriotism can be found in Daniel Bar-Tal and Ervin Staub, *Patriotism* (Wadsworth, 1999). Insights into earlier anti-war protests can be gained from Melvin Small's, *Antiwarriors: The Vietnam War and the Battle for America's Hearts and Minds* (Scholarly Resources, 2002). A book that argues that freedom of political speech can be carried too far is Walter Berns, *Making Patriots* (University of Chicago Press, 2001).

What More to Do

Discuss the concepts of "degree" of dissent and "clear and present danger" enunciated in *Schenck v. United States*. A one end of a continuum of dissent, opposition to American policy, including foreign policy, is a both healthy for a democracy and a core right of Americans. At the other ends of the continuum lies treason, which the Constitution defines as not only "levying war against" the United States but also "adhering to [its] enemies, giving them aid and comfort." Somewhere in the many degrees of activity between those extremes is the "clear and present danger" point that separates legitimate protest from actions that can lawfully be suppressed.

One way to shape your discussion is to consider the case of Jane Fonda and her opposition to U.S. involvement in Vietnam. In 1972, Fonda travelled to North Vietnam. There she made anti-war speeches over Radio Hanoi, had her picture taken wearing a North Vietnamese helmet while crewing an anti-aircraft gun used to shoot down U.S. planes, and said that American prisoners of war were "U.S. aggressor pilots" who were "healthy and repentant" in captivity. Some anti-war activists hailed her as a heroine of democratic dissent; others labeled her Hanoi Jane. What is your view? Should she have been lauded, chided for bad judgment, or tired for treason?

7

MEDIA

"EMBEDDED" REPORTERS DURING THE WAR WITH IRAQ:
Innovative Coverage *or* Voyeuristic Reality TV?

INNOVATIVE COVERAGE

ADVOCATE: Sherry Ricchiardi, Senior Writer, *American Journalism Review*
SOURCE: "Close to the Action," *American Journalism Review*, May/June 2003

VOYEURISTIC REALITY TV

ADVOCATE: Paul Friedman, former Executive Vice-President, ABC News
SOURCE: "TV: A Missed Opportunity," *Columbia Journalism Review*, May/June 2003

"All the News That's Fit to Print," the front page of The *New York Times* proclaims. This promise to the paper's readers by the legendary publisher Adolph Ochs has appeared in the *Times* since October 25, 1896. The slogan and the paper's early history tell us something about the news media and the pressures it faces. Established in 1851 to appeal to New York's more educated readers, the *Times* prospered. By the 1890s though, the press environment had changed. Yellow journalism, the sensationalistic reporting of human-interest stories and scandal, was selling newspapers. Staid reporting was not. The future of the *Times* was in doubt, while its two rivals that epitomized yellow journalism, Joseph Pulitizer's *New York World* and William Randolph Hearst's *New York Journal*, were flourishing. It was at this point that Ochs bought the *Times* and saved it by dropping its price to a penny and by lightening up its content. For example, one front-page column headline in 1897 read, "OBJECT TO PICKLED TONGUE: The Young Women of the Chicago University in Revolt." The story told of the anger of women students who had fallen ill after being served pickled tongue in their dorm and of the view of "Miss Yeoman, head housekeeper at Kelly Hall" that the real "trouble with the girls is that they have been eating too much molasses candy for their health." The "fit to print" part of Ochs' slogan reflected his determination to avoid yellow journalism, but he also recognized that to a degree he needed to give the public "all the news it wants to read" in order to survive.

Like the *Times*, the rest of the American news media has a dualistic nature. First, it is central to the democratic process, a key role symbolized by the protection afforded it in the First Amendment. Much of what most people know about national and world events is transmitted to them by the news media. Second, almost all news organizations are commercial enterprises that need to generate subscriber and/or advertising revenue. As such, media executives face the same dilemma today as Adolph Ochs did in the 1890s. To prosper financially, how far should the media go to "get the story first," and to meet the public demands for intimate details?

If anything, these questions have intensified in recent decades. Increased competition is one reason. The one-time dominance of ABC, CBS, and NBC has vanished with the coming of CNN, Fox, and other cable networks. All these broadcast networks are in turn feeling pressure from an increasing importance of the Internet as a news source. Falling ratings mean declining advertising revenue. Technology is the second cause of change. The gap between an event occurring and it being reported has narrowed to almost nonexistent. The advent of television began this change. More recently it has been accelerated by lightweight "minicams" that allow reporters great mobility and by the ability to transmit voice and images almost instantaneously around the world via satellite links. Now getting the story first often means transmitting raw images more than sorting out the facts and providing analysis.

Changing social attitudes are a third reason the news environment has changed. For better or worse, society has become open to, even desirous of, stories and images that were once unthinkable, and journalism reflects that change. Not that long ago, for instance, the press knew about but never reported the sexual escapades of President John Kennedy. More recently, the reporting on President Bill Clinton's sexual encounters with intern Monica Lewinsky left little to the imagination. Moreover, what many would consider the voyeuristic bent of the public has spawned a new genre of entertainment, reality TV. Be it *Survivor, Joe Millionaire,* or *The Osbournes,* a substantial segment of the public wants to peer into people's lives.

It is hardly surprising then—given increased competition, technical capabilities, and changing public tastes—that in 2003 the media pressed for greater access to the battlefield than ever before. Responding to those demands, the military agreed to "embed" about 800 journalists by attaching them to various U.S. and British units. Most of these units never saw combat in Iraq, but some and their accompanying journalists did.

The question is where the use of embedded journalists to report of the U.S.-led invasion of Iraq in 2003 fell along the scale between informative journalism and reality TV. This issue is of particular importance because television is the dominant source of news. During the war with Iraq in 2003, one poll found that 89% of Americans were getting most of their war news from television. More than 80% were watching war news more than an hour a day. Thus a great deal of what Americans learned about the war was derived from television, and a significant part of that was entwined with the images and commentary broadcast by embedded journalists.

POINTS TO PONDER

➤ Think about what you saw of the war. Did the minute-to-minute coverage of the war give you better insights into how the war was proceeding than what would have been available without live images from the front?

➤ From another perspective, think about whether the pictures from the war were sanitized or did they convey the grim realities of death and destruction. If not, should they? And if they did, what would be the impact on American and global opinion about future possible wars?

➤ Especially if you agree that the gap between news and entertainment has become too narrow, ask yourself who is responsible: journalists for what and how they report or the public for what it demands.

"Embeded" Reporters During the War with Iraq: Innovative Coverage

SHERRY RICCHIARDI

War reporting will never be the same.

After surviving a hail of bullets en route to Baghdad, *Atlanta Journal-Constitution* reporter Ron Martz cradled the head of a wounded American soldier in his hands, imploring him not to black out before medics could patch the hole in his chest. Later, Martz collapsed against an Army vehicle, drenched in sweat, mouth dry, his clothes sticky with blood.

Newsweek correspondent Rod Nordland stared in disbelief as an Iraqi army officer approached with hands on his head and surrendered to him in southern Iraq. He turned the man over to a British Royal Military Police officer, who bummed a pack of cigarettes. "It's for them, not me," the officer said, referring to a group of prisoners. Later, in an article about the incident, Nordland concluded, "My POW was in good hands."

USA Today photographer Jack Gruber spent weeks huddled alongside dust-caked combat troops in the steel belly of an armored personnel carrier as they blazed through the desert, sharing everything from bags of Skittles and baby wipes to stark terror when rocket-propelled grenades thundered into their path.

"We sleep with our feet in each other's face," said Gruber, who traveled with the Army's 3rd Infantry Division.

That's how it was in Gulf War II. The media had unprecedented access to America's fighting forces. The press credential dangling from Gruber's neck labeled

him "embedded," a Pentagon-sanctioned passport to the front lines.

And despite initial skepticism about how well the system would work, and some dead-on criticism of overly enthusiastic reporting in the war's early stages, the net result was a far more complete mosaic of the fighting—replete with heroism, tragedy and human error—than would have been possible without it.

For military planners, the new approach represented a total about-face. Over the past two decades, journalists have relentlessly pounded the Pentagon about being shut out of Grenada, Panama and, most recently, Afghanistan. During the first Persian Gulf War, correspondents were far from the action thanks to the ill-conceived 1991 Desert Storm press pool. It was only after the fighting had ended that a full picture of what had transpired began to emerge.

Now, correspondents—more than 600 of them—were invited to eat, sleep and ride into battle with combatants under a bold government plan.

Questions swirled after the Bush administration unveiled its radical new approach before the war—hardly a surprise, given the meager media access during recent military campaigns. Would there be military censorship, news blackouts and ethical minefields for embedded journalists? Correspondents, dependent on soldiers for everything, including their own safety, might be vulnerable to emotional bonding that could sway news judg-

Sherry Ricchiardi, from "Close to the Action," *American Journalism Review*, May 2003. Reprinted by permission of American Journalism Review.

ment. Some speculated that embedding was part of a White House strategy to win the propaganda war in the Middle East.

Media experts squared off. Early in the war, Alex S. Jones, director of Harvard's Joan Shorenstein Center on the Press, Politics and Public Policy, called embedding "one magnificent recruitment video" for the Pentagon. He likened the process to salted nuts, "very tasty and almost empty of high-quality nourishment."

Los Angeles Times media critic David Shaw saw it differently: "For now, embedding is giving us a rare window on war. The critics should stop carping."

…In the early stages, it looked as if the skeptics might be right. Breathless television reporters often made themselves the story. On the second day, CNN anchor Aaron Brown cut away to Kyra Phillips, embedded on an aircraft carrier. Phillips blithely announced she had arranged for a squadron of fighter pilots to wave from their aircraft before they took off. "They basically gave me a thumbs-up," she told Brown.

The TV correspondents frequently used the term "we" as they chronicled the American forces' dash through the desert toward Baghdad, almost sounding as if they were fellow soldiers.

But the major dividends paid by the unprecedented access quickly became clear. Sometimes, accounts filed by embeds contradicted the official line delivered at Central Command in Doha, Qatar, or by government spokespeople in Washington.

In early April, the *Washington Post*'s William Branigin, embedded with the Army's 3rd Infantry Division, wrote about a civilian shooting in central Iraq. According to the Pentagon, U.S. troops fired on a Toyota packed with 13 Iraqi civilians at an American-held intersection after the driver ignored shouts and warning shots. Officials placed the death toll at seven.

Branigin, an eyewitness, reported that the Americans had not fired warning shots quickly enough and that 10 people had been killed, five children among them. As proof, he quoted conversations between Capt. Ronny Johnson and his crew. "'Cease fire!' Johnson yelled over the radio. Then, as he peered into his binoculars from the intersection on Highway 9, he roared at the platoon leader: 'You just [expletive] killed a family because you didn't fire a warning shot soon enough!'"

Embedded journalists reported during the trek toward Baghdad that Marines were down to one MRE—Meal Ready to Eat—per day and that the advance had stalled. Pentagon spokeswoman Victoria Clarke, architect of the embedding program, promptly discounted the reports.

Some stories provided raw glimpses of war made possible by the frontline access. Matthew Cox of the Army Times, a newspaper owned by Gannett, wrote of 21-year-old Army private Nicks Boggs gunning down two boys, no older than 10, in Karbala. The children darted out of an alley to retrieve a rocket-propelled grenade dropped by a dead Iraqi soldier.

"'I got my gun up. I had my sights on'" the RPG, said Boggs, who was armed with a machine gun that spits out 600 rounds a minute.

"'I didn't shoot. I didn't shoot,' Boggs said."

Then the child reached down and grabbed the RPG.

"'That's when I took him out,' Boggs said. 'I laid down quite a few bursts,' When the smoke cleared, both small boys lay in the street, clearly dead."

A *New York Times* story by Dexter Filkins told of an American Army sergeant who, along with other members of his unit, opened fire and accidentally killed an Iraqi woman who was standing too close to their target. "I'm sorry. But the chick got in the way," the soldier was quoted as saying.

Embeds also produced upbeat stories and images that showed the best of America's fighting forces as they befriended terrified Iraqis, offered MREs to malnourished children and, in some cases, helped to bury bodies of civilians caught in the crossfire....

From the beginning, there were questions about the ethical consequences of embedding. Some viewed the constant contact as a quagmire.

USA Today's Gruber describes having "zero privacy" while traveling with the Army's 3rd Infantry Division. There were no secrets from the soldiers. They talked about everything, about wives and girlfriends and high school escapades. "These guys are all brothers, and it's like I'm in their family," he says. But Gruber doesn't feel the intimacy compromised his photojournalism.

"I think they understand that I have a job to do here just like they do, and when they screw up and are reprimanded or blasted over the radio, they know I am listening," the photographer said in an interview in April.

The risks that the watchdog could become the lapdog increased as correspondents bonded and became sympathetic to soldiers who provided a place to sleep and food and helped keep them alive. The hedge against this intimacy affecting their performance boiled down to professionalism. "It's going to be hard, but honorable journalists know their responsibility," says Stephen Hess, a media and terrorism expert at the Brookings Institution in Washington, D.C.

It also was a matter of personal credibility—being involved in a cover-up for the military could end up being a humiliating, career-ending experience. "As a whole I wouldn't worry," says Gutman, a veteran war correspondent. "Everybody

expects you to do [your job], including the guys you are covering. They know they've got a reporter along."

Journalists have long treasured their roles as outside observers and endeavored not to become "part of the story." For Martz of the *Atlanta Journal-Constitution*, though, the decision to help save lives transcended his field's ethical boundaries.

"Talk to them! Have them squeeze your hand!" an assistant medic shouted to the reporter as he held a soldier's head while struggling to peel off his flak jacket and shirt so the medic could bandage him. Martz recalls shielding a soldier with his body to keep dust off his wounds.

In a highly emotional first-person account, Martz later wrote about how the two U.S. soldiers wounded that day had helped save his life. "Had they not been there, I most likely would not be typing this now," said Martz.

Earlier, another incident had raised the issue of crossing the line. Martz and *Journal-Constitution* photographer Brant Sanderlin were asked to hold intravenous drip bags of saline solution for wounded civilians. The request came when a medic was pressed into duty as a rifleman to round up enemy prisoners and suppress small-arms fire directed at the unit. "I helped free a soldier to do what he's supposed to," Martz said on NPR.

Did he get too close? "I don't know exactly how you keep that distance when you're drenched in somebody's blood," says Susan Stevenson, a deputy managing editor at the *Journal-Constitution*. "That's something that we, as editors, have to guard against."

Martz, who was still on the move with Charlie Company when he was interviewed by e-mail in mid-April, says he hadn't done much soul-searching. He was more intent on filing daily stories and staying alive.

"I have not had time to sort this all out yet," he wrote from the war zone. He's certain a time will come when the stark reality of his experiences will take a toll. "I just don't know how or when yet."

Embedding represented a stark departure from the past, and media critics placed it under a microscope from the get-go. At times the reporting won applause for providing reality checks on war, such as the Army Times story about Pfc. Boggs. There also were lapses that lent credence to pejorative labels such as "gas mask journalism" and "tunnel vision reporting" coined by pundits.

Often, battlefield stand-ups on the cable news networks, delivered in the fog of sandstorms and in the middle of artillery blasts, lacked context and perspective. Print, it was generally agreed, offered more substance and details. Major newspapers devoted entire sections to the war each day, packed with stories, photographs and graphics as well as the jumps of myriad page-one pieces.

"The war has been reported superbly by newspapers," says Hess. "The stories have been rich in variety, coming at this from so many different angles."

Whatever its shortcomings and pitfalls, embedding emerged as a major plus for the news media—and, more significant, their audiences. The presence of hundreds of journalists in the midst of combat meant a much fuller picture of the war, warts and all. The dramatic snippets that TV provided were supplemented by sophisticated newspaper analysis that helped viewers make sense of what they had seen the night before.

NPR's Bruce Drake, vice president for news, credits embeds with providing important information early on when strong Iraqi resistance entered the picture. "We might not have gotten that same sense from daily military briefings," Drake says. "Whatever downside there might be to this doesn't add up to anywhere near the benefits."

Some early critics of the Pentagon plan have reassessed their opinions. The Shorenstein Center's Jones says of the embedded journalists, "In my opinion, they've done a great job." He remembers the precise moment when he changed his mind. "It was when the embeds reported that the Apache helicopter had gotten shot to pieces when they went after the Republican Guard," Jones says. "That was not the official version coming from headquarters."

Drake feels there's been too much "navel-gazing" over the pros and cons of embedding, a system that many would like to see become part of the Pentagon's permanent war-coverage policy.

Sandy Johnson, the Associated Press' Washington bureau chief, directed coverage of the 1991 Persian Gulf War. Compared with the scant access allowed then, she says, "This system has worked incredibly well.

"The naysayers," she adds, "will be eating their words."

"Embeded" Reporters During the War with Iraq: Voyeuristic Reality TV

PAUL FRIEDMAN

After a week of war, a senior producer at one of the network news divisions was reduced to muttering darkly about a Pentagon conspiracy. Much had been said about unprecedented media access to the front lines, but with descriptions flowing in of bloody pitched battles in Basra and Umm Qasr, the producer complained, "I have yet to see decent video of a firefight."

Very little went as predicted. The war did not open with a bomb attack designed to reduce the enemy to "shock and awe," but with a focused attack aimed at Saddam Hussein and his leadership core. Not all Iraqi soldiers ran away, and not all that many civilians greeted their liberators with open arms. Broadcast networks quickly returned to basketball games and highly rated sitcoms and Oscar ceremonies, and were only mildly criticized. Then they left 24/7 coverage to cable news, and waited for a major battle for Baghdad that never took place. And news coverage of this war—even with the heralded "embedding" of more than 600 journalists in dozens of armed forces units—was less dramatically different than many had expected.

The embedding process was, in a sense, a bold return to the Vietnam War, the last time the government was willing to take its chances with giving reporters the freedom to cover military action up close, with few restrictions. For television, the combination of access and new technology meant the possibility of covering the war live from the battlefield. War meets the small video camera and instant transmission via computer, videophone, and satellite. How much more dramatic could it get? Yet

embedding did not live up to advance billing, at least at the beginning. Still, as time went on, the impact of embedded reporters became very important, and a central part of the debate over the war. Of course, we should not have been surprised.

THE LONG DISTANCE WAR

At first, the embedded television reports had a gee-whiz quality that overwhelmed the fact that very little information was being conveyed. NBC's David Bloom (later, tragically, to die of an embolism) traveled at high speeds across the Iraqi desert, broadcasting live from his customized "Bloommobile," and making other broadcasters drool with envy. The pictures were irresistibly fascinating, though perhaps not crammed with information. ABC's Ted Koppel gave viewers one of the first embedded reports to deliver on the potential of live television; he was able to bring together stunning pictures, information, and vivid descriptions from the scene of a massive column of armored vehicles breaching the berms into Iraq. It was hard for any viewer not to be impressed with the sight of the seemingly endless column of tanks and personnel carriers, unchallenged, starting the long trek toward Baghdad. Never mind that other units not too far away were crossing the berms and coming under fire; we would all soon learn (and some would complain) that the embedded reports, while largely accurate, could only supply small "slices" of reality, and might not reflect the overall picture. Never mind that Koppel's conversation with Peter Jennings, thousands of miles away in a New York studio, clearly showed how impressed they were with what was playing out before them; it may have provided the Pentagon with exactly what it wanted (as some critics predicted the embedding would do). But it was unavoidable, and it was early.

Many of the early reports from the embedded television reporters were of the standing-in-front-of-the-camera, chest-thumping, look-at-where-I-am, and we're-ready-to-go-but-I-can't-tell-you-exactly-where-for-security-reasons variety, followed by the anchors back home warning the reporters to "stay safe" and asking them to relay best wishes to the troops. (Fox's Shepard Smith to correspondent Rick Leventhal, embedded with the Marines: "Rick, Godspeed and our best to the men there.") On the move, the reporters and their cameramen followed a story they usually could not really see; it's the nature of modern warfare that much of it takes place with the enemy a long distance away. The embedded reporter and camera see weapons fired at an unseen enemy and, if they are lucky (or unlucky), they may see tracers of weapons fired back. But there is seldom the time or the mobility needed to reconstruct what happened and tell a complete story. Leventhal described one of the first Marine engagements as a "tremendous pyrotechnics display" of outgoing artillery fire, but "whether they're hitting their targets, we cannot tell you." Later, as American troops closed on Baghdad, there was video of destroyed Iraqi armor, pickup trucks with mounted weapons, and other vehicles. But nothing matched the reports of hundreds of tanks destroyed, and there was certainly no video to document reports of thousands of Iraqi soldiers killed. Either the bodies were removed before the embedded units caught up with the targets they'd attacked from miles away or they were steering around them. Or the reports were off base.

Some of the best live television reports came when the story found the camera:

NBC's Bloom was on camera when a powerful sandstorm brought total darkness at 4:15 in the afternoon; CNN'S Walter Rodgers was doing an otherwise routine live interview with an Army sergeant when the soldier turned and fear crept across his face as he heard incoming fire, and they both ran for cover.

THE TECHNOLOGY TRAP

Most of the pictures were not very special. Even though there was much tougher fighting than predicted, little of it was seen on video. (Anyone who doubts it should have spent an hour or two watching the same few seconds of footage repeated over and over again, often when it bore no relation to what was being discussed.) The reasons for the scarcity of great combat video will not be absolutely clear until the embedded reporters, producers, and cameramen are thoroughly debriefed after the war, but several factors seem to be involved (in addition to the long-distance nature of much of the fighting). The journalists embedded with American units had to stick close to them, both because they were on the move a lot, and because the military was worried about the journalists' safety and restricted their movements. (Several journalists who tried to go it alone got in bad trouble quickly; two died in the first days of the war.) Journalists embedded with British units were given somewhat greater slack; partially because of that and partially because of the close fighting the British forces did in southern Iraq, most of the "good" video in the first stages of the war came from British agencies.

In addition, the American television journalists put enormous emphasis on making frequent live transmissions, which forced them to spend a great deal of time on the logistics and technology—time that could not be spent on gathering pictures and information for more complete stories. It turned out the technology was not quite ready for this war. The small cameras were great until the sand and general wear and tear ruined them; ABC's Mike Cerre took four cameras with him and complained he was down to the last one as his Marine unit neared Baghdad. New, small satellite transmission equipment either failed completely or worked less often than hoped. The "store and forward" technique of transferring video to the laptop and then by telephone to the States did provide excellent quality, but it took too much time—roughly thirty minutes to feed one minute. At least half of what viewers saw on television was transmitted by videophone, a relatively old technique that is fast and simple to use, but produces very rough video and ragged sound. The best pictures from this war were the still photos and, ironically, the video over which American journalists had no control. Until the troops reached Baghdad at the end of the third week, there were many days when the best video came from cameras abandoned by the networks on the roofs of Baghdad but still transmitting, or from the cameras transmitting from U.S. weapons and shown at Pentagon briefings to document direct hits, or from government cameras covering the nighttime rescue of Private Jessica Lynch and the nighttime invasion of a presidential palace.

RUMSFELD'S PROBLEMS

Still, reporters who knew how to report and write and speak were able to use embedding to their advantage and ours. After three decades of tight control by the government, combat news actually was found and reported within minutes of its happening, and well before military briefers confirmed it and doled it out. The most dramatic early example of this, ironically, brought memories of Vietnam: a

"fragging" incident in the headquarters tents of the 101st Airborne. Embedded journalists reported it quickly, and one of them—who said he was listening in on Army radios at the base—almost immediately was able to knock down initial reports of terrorism, and correctly identify the suspect as an American soldier. We are left to guess how soon, or even whether, the Pentagon would have revealed all this if there had been no reporters at the scene.

More important, it was embedded reporters who gave us the first indications that the campaign against Saddam Hussein was not going as predicted. CNN's Rodgers, talking to the camera, unaided by pictures, was able to paint vivid word pictures of the relentless small attacks on units of the Seventh Cavalry as they pushed north and across the Euphrates River—"Seventy-two hours of continuous fighting," he said. ABC's Koppel reported that all thirty-two Apache helicopters returning from a mission had bullet holes in them. CNN's Martin Savidge described a hazardous mission to refuel forward elements running dangerously low on fuel; others reported shortages of food and water, and cases of rationing. The BBC's David Willis, with U.S. Marines in central Iraq, reported that "we've got to the stage where some of the infantry here are down to one meal a day, so it's a pretty difficult situation supplying such a large and high-tech army." John Roberts of CBS was able to feed pictures of marines trying to protect convoys near Nasiriya, and raised questions about whether there were enough troops to protect the long lines of supply.

All of this was quite different from the initial pictures of rapid advances by U.S. forces, and the reaction was swift. After less than a week of war, Defense Secretary Donald Rumsfeld complained that while the "breathtaking" minute-by-minute coverage was generally accurate, the "slices" of reported fighting lacked overall context and made people believe the fighting had been going on for weeks rather than days. The plan, he said repeatedly, was working.

Secretary Rumsfeld's argument had two problems. First, day after day the embedded reporters were gathering evidence at the scene. It turns out, of course, that while embedding runs the risk of some journalists getting too chummy with soldiers, it also means that some soldiers get chummy with journalists—and they talk. They talk about bad decisions, malfunctioning equipment, dwindling supplies, and an enemy that wasn't rolling over the way it was supposed to. (Marine sergeant to reporter, on camera: "The United States was planning on walking in here like it was easy and all....It's not that easy to conquer a country, is it?") That was Rumsfeld's second problem: before the war, when the administration was selling it, most background briefings predicted a relatively quick, easy fight, and minimized worries about troop levels and long supply lines. There were some public pronouncements— like those of some officials predicting a collapsing Iraqi "house of cards"—that helped create an overly optimistic set of expectations.

Still there was merit in the objection raised by Secretary Rumsfeld and others that more context was needed. It got support from disparate members of the media.

CNN's anchor, Aaron Brown, said during one broadcast that the embedded reporters give us "snapshots" of what is going on, "and it's our job here to put it all together." ABC's George Will observed somewhat more elegantly that "today's problem—live television from journalists with units engaged in Iraq—is the problem of context. Up-close combat engagements almost always look confusing and awful because they are." Necessarily, it was up to the anchors, former generals, and other experts to provide context. They did, often ad nauseam.

What was really missing were the kinds of stories that came out of Vietnam: the up-close and detailed stories with beginnings, middles, and ends; the gritty, gripping stories about people and courage and fear and heroism. It did not matter that it took days for those stories to make it back to the States and onto the air. They gave us much more than tiny slices of war and they were, in their way, timeless—just the opposite of what was most prized by news executives who were driven to compete this time on terms dictated by the twenty-four-hour cable networks: put as many people as possible in as many places as possible, and use smaller, lighter gear to get them on the air live. That need dovetailed nicely with the Pentagon's tight restrictions on the number of journalists and the amount of television equipment it could or would accommodate with each unit. But it did not produce the kind of television journalism we deserved. While the embedded journalists were brave, and often endured conditions that well-trained soldiers ten to forty years younger found tough, it was unrealistic to expect two-person television teams working under such conditions with inadequate equipment to do much more than they did. Especially in tough situations, television journalists must be allowed to concentrate on the jobs they do best. It is the old-fashioned (and more expensive) model that allows reporters to report, producers to produce, cameramen to take pictures, and technicians to worry about sound and lights and keeping the gear working. It's not always necessary—different stories require different resources—but it is no coincidence that this war's most memorable pieces were turned in by strong reporters (ABC's Koppel and CBS's Scott Pelley stood out), who—whether embedded or not—had the benefit of working with a producer, an extra crew member, and sometimes a satellite technician. They also had the personal clout or the support from editors back home to take more time on their pieces and less on "live shots."

The ambitious experiment with embedding started to wind down as American troops took over in Baghdad, and embedded journalists began to leave their units to pursue their own stories. The triumph in Baghdad provided the war's most symbolic piece of video: the statue of Saddam being pulled down from its pedestal in Firdos Square. But it was not embedding that produced this demonstration of television's power to define a story. The scene played out in front of the Palestine Hotel, where many journalists rode out the war, and where the cameras waited.

THE CONTINUING DEBATE:
"Embedded" Reporters During the War with Iraq

What Is New

Polls during and after the war with Iraq showed that Americans generally approved of the media's performance. In one poll, 68% of the respondents rated the job done by the press "excellent" or "good," 21% thought it "fair," 8% evaluated it as "poor," and 3% were unsure. In a question that focused on embedded journalists, 57% of those polled believed that the "news reporters...traveling along with the U.S. troops and reporting directly from the battlefield" was a "good idea," 35% disagreed, and 8% were uncertain.

In addition to criticism of embedded reporters for promoting shallow coverage, there was also criticism, mostly from people who opposed the war, of the press for not being objective and, in particular, for overlooking civilian Iraqi casualties. Whatever the truth of this charge, it is important to also understand the pressures on the press to be patriotic. A poll taken shortly after the war that asked Americans what they thought about the news media "taking a strong pro-American point of view," found that 70% replied that doing so was a "good thing," and only 20% thought it a "bad thing." Journalists also have to be careful to avoid seeming to harm the war effort. A poll during the was found that 53% of Americans thought the press was making it "harder for U.S. officials to conduct war", only 42% disagreed, with the rest uncertain.

Where to Find More

Among the early books on the press and the war in Iraq are Todd Purdum, *A Time of Our Choosing* (Times Books, 2004) and Dan Rather, *America at War* (Simon & Schuster, 2003). For a recent study that criticizes the press generally for superficiality and imbalance, see Kathleen Hall Jamieson and Paul Waldman, *The Press Effect* (Oxford University Press, 2002) The Internet has several worthwhile sites. The home page of the American Press Institute at http://www.americanpressinstitute.org/ will allow you to search for the media's own take on the war with Iraq. Also good is Journalism.org at http://www.journalism.org/. To gain insight on how journalists have covered war in the past, go to the Web site of the Newseum project on the history of war journalism at: http://www.newseum.org/warstories.

What More to Do

The issues about the coverage of the war in Iraq extend beyond it. For example, the charge that the news is akin to entertainment includes areas such as political campaigns. Some critics charge that the media is more interested in the contest than the issues. You might follow a newspaper or a television channel for a week and evaluate its focus and depth of coverage. Also debatable is whether the press should interpret or merely transmit information. One study of the reports from embedded journalists found that 94% were primarily factual rather than analytical and 60% were unedited. Is this good journalism or reality TV? Finally, think about whether journalists should transmit grim images of dead bodies and writhing wounded. The coverage from embedded reports was not graphic. One study found "not a single story examined showed pictures of people being hit by fired weapons." Is this sanitization good reporting?

ETHNIC FOREIGN POLICY LOBBYING:
Misplaced Allegiance *or* All-American Tradition?

MISPLACED ALLEGIANCE

Advocate: Geoffrey Wheatcroft, a British journalist
Source: "Hyphenated Americans," *Guardian Unlimited* online, April 25, 2000

ALL-AMERICAN TRADITION

Advocate: Yossi Shain, Aaron and Cecile Goldman Visiting Professor, Georgetown University; Professor of Political Science, Tel Aviv University
Source: "For Ethnic Americans, The Old Country Calls," *Foreign Service Journal*, October 2000

E pluribus unum (out of many, one) reads the banner the eagle holds in its beak on the Great Seal of the United States. These words on the seal, which was adopted by the Congress in 1782, refer to the union of 13 former colonies into one United States. Whatever its initial meaning, *e pluribus unum* has come to symbolize what is sometimes called the "American melting pot." This is the idea that one nation, the American people, have been created by the assimilation of people of diverse national origins. More accurately, it might be said that the blending of foreign immigrants in the melting pot into one puree in which the original makings cannot be distinguished, has never been realized. Instead, Americans are something of a demographic stew, one in which carrots, potatoes, celery, and other ingredients often maintain their identity.

Scholars disagree about why this imperfect amalgamation has occurred. Whatever the cause, though, many Americans tend to think of themselves as not just Americans, but as Irish Americans, Italian Americans, Mexican Americans, African Americans, Jewish Americans, and many other kinds of Americans. The hyphen to denote these groups (as in Irish-American) has gone out of style, but its earlier use has left the term "hyphenated American" to designate the lingering identification of many Americans with the heritage of their immigrant ancestors. Identification with a specific country is the most common link, but there are others. Religion is one, with, for example, many Jewish Americans having a strong sense of community with Israel. Other groups have regional cultural connection. For example, because the history of slavery wiped out the ability of most blacks to trace their heritage to a specific location, what sense of identification that group does have is linked more to sub-Saharan Africa than a single country. Similarly, many Arab Americans identify with that broader cultural identity instead of, or along with, a specific country.

For many the foreign connection is quite recent. Some 12% of all U.S. residents were born elsewhere, and many others are second and third generation Americans. When the U.S. Census Bureau asked people to identify their cultural heritage, 80% did so. The most frequent answers were German (15%), Irish (11%), English (9%), Italian

(6%), Mexican (7%), Chinese (4%), Polish (3%) and French (3%). Another 7% of U.S. residents chose "American" as their ethnic heritage.

Throughout American history, hyphenated American groups have often acted as interest groups dedicated to influencing U.S. foreign policy to be favorable to their homeland and ancestral culture. For one, Jewish Americans who support Israel are represented by such organizations as the American-Israel Public Affairs Committee (AIPAC, http://www.aipac.org/), which declares itself, "America's Pro-Israel Lobby." Among the groups trying in part to counterbalance the efforts of AIPAC is the Arab American Institute (http://www.aaiusa.org/), which lists among its missions, "represent[ing] Arab American interests in government and politics" on such issues as "U.S. Middle East policy." To this list of ethnic lobbies could be added the Cuban American National Foundation, American Latvian Association, the TransAfrica Forum, the Armenian National Committee of America, the American Hellenic Institute (Greek Americans), the Irish National Caucus, the Polish American Congress, and myriad others.

The issue that the activity of these groups raises is the propriety of ethnic foreign policy lobbying. There can be little doubt that the language of the First Amendment guaranteeing the right "to petition the government for a redress of grievances," gives ethnic interests groups, as all interest groups, the right to lobby the U.S. government. Equally certain is that lobbying by groups of every ideological and policy persuasion is a key, and perhaps a necessary, element of the American democratic tradition and process. Some people, however, believe that lobbying for a policy to benefit a foreign government falls outside the boundaries of what is, or should be, acceptable. They charge that such pressures distort U.S. foreign policy in ways that can actually contravene U.S. national interests.

Such concerns are not new. For example former President Theodore Roosevelt was outraged at the opposition of German American groups, Irish American groups, and others to U.S. entry into World War I against Germany and as a British ally. In a 1915 speech, Roosevelt declared, "There is no room in this country for hyphenated Americanism." He asserted that "Our allegiance must be purely to the United States" and he condemned the "tangle of squabbling nationalities,…each at heart feeling more sympathy with Europeans of that nationality, than with the other citizens of the American Republic." Roosevelt even termed it "treason" for "an American citizen to vote as a German-American, an Irish-American, or an English-American."

POINTS TO PONDER

➤ Advocate Yossi Shain writes of a "flexible world of multiple loyalties." Think about this idea. Is it possible to simultaneously be a loyal American and loyal to another country? What if those two countries disagree?

➤ To argue that ethnic lobby groups sometimes advocate policies counter to the national interest necessarily assumes that there is an objective national interest. Is that so, or is the national interest subjective—that is, whatever the American policy process eventually decides it is?

➤ There are foreign policy lobby groups based on economic interests, ideological views, gender, and many other bases, as well as ethnicity. Are your views on the legitimacy of foreign policy lobbying the same for all these groups? If you differentiate, why?

Ethnic Foreign Policy Lobbying:
Misplaced Allegiance

GEOFFREY WHEATCROFT

Although the old saying that hard cases make bad law might seem to apply to the case of Elian Gonzalez, it wasn't really so hard. The law held that he should be reunited with his father, that is what most Americans thought should be done and that is what has now happened. But the case leaves ugly scars, and it raises once again the question of what should be the rights—and responsibilities—of "hyphenated Americans." The boy would have joined his father in Cuba weeks ago if he hadn't become an emblem, or a pawn, for one of the most noisiest and most feared of such groups, the Cuban Americans.

The United States is a land of immigrants, with complicated feelings towards their ancestral lands. It is also a free country where interest-group politics have always flourished, which does not mean that the effects of these groups or lobbies have been benign. To the contrary, the pressure exerted by the "hyphenates" has been almost unfailingly malign, for the American republic and for American people as a whole.

It is made worse by the cravenness of American politicians. In *Of Thee I Sing*, the Gershwin brothers' very funny 1931 musical satire on American politics, the campaign song goes, "He's the man the people choose,/Loves the Irish, loves the Jews." Real-life American polls have all too often taken this jest as a true word.

The US's emergence as a great power dates from the first world war, which the country entered belatedly, and despite the wishes of many Americans. Tens of millions of German Americans obviously didn't want to fight against their fathers' fatherland. Millions of Irish Americans were scarcely keener to fight for the king of England, or millions of Jewish Americans for the tsar of all the Russians whose oppression most of them had fled. And indeed the US did not enter the war until after the 1917 February revolution and the fall of tsardom.

Then the fun began. Irish-American pressure led towards the creation of an Irish Free State. Whatever else may be said of this, it was by no means in the American national interest. During the second world war, the most important war the Americans ever fought, once they, again belatedly, entered it, that Irish state was sullenly neutral.

There has recently been much bitter criticism in America of Swiss neutrality during the war. Apart from the fact that Switzerland was surrounded by the Axis and had no choice between neutrality and annihilation, Swiss neutrality did no military harm to the Allied cause. By contrast, Irish neutrality delayed victory in the battle of the Atlantic and thus the defeat of Hitler, with all that implies.

After the Irish came the Czech Americans' turn. Largely thanks to them President Woodrow Wilson's 14 points included the 10th point: "The peoples of Austria-Hungary...should be accorded the freest opportunity of autonomous development." From this light-hearted undertaking came the destruction of the Habsburg monarchy.

The rights and wrongs of that aren't simple, but it is worth noting that the allegedly national "successor state" of Czechoslovakia thereby called into being no longer exists. Nor does Yugoslavia, the other state invented after the great war.

No other hyphenated group has been as politically powerful as the Jewish-American lobby. Although Washington politicians may tremble at the phrase "the 40m[illion] Irish Americans", they tremble more before the numerically fewer Jewish Americans. The American-Israeli Public Affairs Committee has won a reputation as the most formidable, and often the most ruthless, of all such pressure groups. Having spent some little time looking into this subject, I would merely say that the activities of that lobby will one day come to be seen as not having served the true interests of the United States, of Jewish America, or even, in the end, of Israel.

The behavior of Cuban America over Elian speaks for itself, and the lobby has anyway prevented a necessary rapprochement between the US and Cuba. What has been more shocking than the hysteria of Little Havana in Miami has been the fawning on the Cuban Americans by politicians, including both presidential candidates?

Yet even that is trivial compared with what may prove to be the true "legacy" (in the president's favorite word) of the Clinton administration. The eastward expansion of NATO [North Atlantic Treaty Organization by adding many new countries in Eastern Europe to the alliance] must rank, in a hotly contested field, as the craziest single piece of American statecraft since the invasion of Cambodia 30 years ago this week. After the end of the cold war, it has no good strategic or political justification but can only justifiably inflame Russian suspicions and means, strictly speaking, that we must go to war on behalf of Hungary in a border dispute with Slovakia.

Why has it happened? It was inspired partly by the president's desire to enrich what his wiser predecessor Eisenhower called the military-industrial complex, but more importantly by his ingratiating himself with ethnic lobbies. Historians will date NATO expansion [to include many new countries in Eastern Europe in the alliance] to Clinton's groveling to a Polish-American audience in Chicago.

Even if the politics of hyphenated-America didn't produce such sorry practical consequences, it would be an affront to the "American idea". In direct contrast to European nationalism, the concept of "the American nation" is not based on ethnicity. Unlike European nation states, the American republic is founded not on a people, but on a proposition. This ideal has often been neglected, to put it mildly, and it may not say much to many black Americans, but it is noble in inspiration. If only American politicians remembered that more often.

In between sucking up to Cuban Americans and claiming to have invented the Internet, Vice-President Gore not long ago produced an exquisite howler. The country's motto is *E pluribus unum*, which means, he told his audience, "out of one, many." It was a true Freudian slip. He made a mistake, but in his ludicrous way he expressed a truth, about the fragmentation of America into all too many fractious and competitive components.

What the 18th-century creators of the American republic believed in was "out of many, one." One people would emerge from many different origins, sharing common creeds (that all men are created equal, entitled to life, liberty and the pursuit of happiness), rather than common gene pools. What the 20th century has seen is a regression to the primitive atavistic group loyalties which the new country was meant to avoid.

More than a hundred years ago, a federal judge told an Irish-American agitator that any American was entitled to sentimental sympathies for another country, but that every American's first political duty must be to the United States.

Ethnic Foreign Policy Lobbying:
All-American Traditions

YOSSI SHAIN

American ethnics don't just lobby for their ancestral homelands—they also export American values.

Last March, when Marie Jana Korbelova returned to her birth city, Prague, this time as Madeleine Albright, U.S. secretary of State, Czech President Vaclav Havel declared, "I would personally consider it excellent [if Madeleine Albright could succeed me as President of the Czech Republic] because into this rather staid provincial environment this would bring an international spirit, someone who knows the world well, understands it, and would be able to act." In the Czech Republic, the president must be a Czech citizen over 40 years of age. Albright, a naturalized U.S. citizen, qualifies for Czech citizenship under the law that enables those who fled the communist regime after 1948 to reclaim citizenship. Albright smiled and said "I am not a candidate and will not be a candidate....My heart is in two places, and America is where I belong."

Havel's vision, that transnational allegiance to both an ancestral homeland and to the U.S. can exist without conflict, is quite remarkable. It represents not only his own liberal-humanistic vision of world affairs—where boundaries of state and culture are no longer so rigid—but also the perception that Americans are the best conveyers of this mentality. As members of an open liberal society where multiple ethnic identities are no longer suspect and where, in fact, ancestral identities are welcomed as the cornerstone of multiculturalism, Americans in the post-Cold War world are often perceived as the best representatives of a more flexible concept of citizenship and loyalty.

Havel's extraordinary invitation is just one sign of a changing configuration of national and ethnic loyalties. For the United States, a nation of immigrants, the meaning of ethnic identity is being transformed. Old nativist fears—that Americans with emotional ties to their ancestral homelands cannot be fully loyal to the United States—are rapidly disappearing. Those people once disparagingly called "hyphenated Americans" feel increasingly free to organize and lobby on behalf of the "old country." Even within America's foreign policy establishment, one finds increasing acceptance of the legitimacy of ethnic lobbies and full participation by ethnically identifiable players such as Jews and Cuban-Americans.

But what is arguably the most interesting new development is that the flow of political influence is becoming more of a two-way street. American diasporas—of Arabs, Jews, Armenians, Chinese—are playing significant roles in their ancestral homelands. They bring American ideologies and influence into the politics of the mother country. At times—taking up the challenge that Secretary Albright declined—U.S. citizens have even returned to their countries of origin to play leading political roles.

DIVERSITY AND DIASPORAS

The signs of this more flexible world of multiple loyalties are easy to find. For example, The *Washington Post* reported this year a sharp increase in the number of young Americans who are spending summers in their parents' homeland. These parents apparently no longer fear that their children will be stigmatized; in fact, many now consider their children's bilingual abilities and familiarity with ancestral culture an asset in a globalized world order. Indeed, as America recognizes the value of diversity, homeland countries that previously restricted their kin abroad to single citizenship now permit them dual nationality. These countries have also enabled their kin diasporas to retain broad economic and political rights in their kin states, including absentee voting, even though the individuals have clearly established themselves as loyal citizens in the U.S.

The December 1996 passage of Mexican legislation permitting dual nationality is but one example. That law affects the lives of millions of Mexican-Americans—the fastest-growing voting bloc in American politics. With Mexican politicians now routinely courting support of the Mexican community in the United States, Mexico has laid to rest the image of the "pocho"—a derogatory term that questions the loyalty of diasporic Mexicans seen as having abandoned their roots in order to assimilate into American society.

There are many reasons that Mexico and other countries have reversed course and now encourage rather than prohibit dual nationality. Most importantly, they see numerous advantages in cultivating the continued loyalty of their kin diasporas. For countries such as Colombia, Nicaragua, the Dominican Republic and El Salvador, remittances and investments from kin communities in the United States play an important economic role. Diaspora money also now influences national politics and political campaigns in many countries, so politicians may want to win the approval of their financial backers abroad. More generally, they want to keep their diaspora's loyalty intact, and thus they use citizenship as an incentive for ethnic or national pride.

Many states [countries] also want to use the lobbying power of their kin, especially in the United States. Armenia, for example—which is involved in a bitter territorial struggle with a neighboring state—works hard to maintain the intensity of diasporic involvement in the motherland's cause.

During the past decade, Eastern European countries have evoked kinship ties even more dramatically by inviting expatriates in the U.S. to take leading roles in their countries of origin. Consider Milan Panic, a California pharmaceutical industrialist who became the prime minister of Yugoslavia in 1992; Alexander Eiseln, an American Army colonel who became the defense minister of Estonia in 1993; and Valdas Adamkus, a Lithuanian-American who moved to Lithuania in 1997 and was elected Lithuania's president in 1998. In the words of one Lithuanian voter, "He lived in America for a long time....He knows how the system works there. I think he will bring democracy from America to us." Also, in Armenia, former foreign minister Raffi Hovannisian and energy minister Sebuth Tashjian are both from California. These are of course rather rare cases of ethnically identified Americans taking posts in their countries of origin at a time when American political and business expertise is sought in nascent states or in new democracies emerging from the shadow of communism. Because of their American experience, these individuals with dual attachments are in a special position to help their ancestral homelands.

Leaders in other countries, realizing that ethnic Americans can be a powerful lobbying force, have at times encouraged their kin to become involved in U.S. foreign policy. However, they fail to recognize that in the process of empowerment, these ethnic Americans may become even more American, and in turn bring back unexpected messages and ideas, such as democratic reforms, much to the chagrin of the kin state. Take, for example, Arab-American relations with Saudi Arabia.

In April 1999, Jeddah's conservative newspaper Al-Madina ran an editorial entitled "A Clinton Victory and Arab Americans." Noting that the peace accord in Ulster showed the great political clout of Irish-Americans, the editorial stated, "The Arab minority in the United States must move toward influential centers in a society where domestic politics [is so crucial]." However, when Arab-American lobbyists like Jim Zogby and Khalil Jashan were welcomed by the Clinton administration as harbingers of peace in the Middle East and subsequently began to contemplate advocating greater openness in the Arab world, they were immediately rebuffed by Arab states, including Saudi Arabia.

FEAR OF HYPHENATED AMERICANS

The question of expatriate loyalty has evolved over the years. In the 19th and early 20th centuries, the idea of hyphenated Americans was used by nativists to question the allegiance of immigrants, despite the newcomers' claims that their ancestral identities were not incompatible with their loyalty to America. Even cultural assimilation in America did not shield many immigrants from feeling threatened because of a perceived affinity to their homelands. This was especially the experience of diasporas whose homelands were enemy states at war with the U.S. American fear of transnational allegiance was also behind the exclusionary laws of the late 1910s and the early 1920s. During World War I, the issue of dual loyalties became particularly prominent with the growing suspicion of pan-German organizations, which prompted America's demand for total assimilation and unqualified renunciation of German-American past loyalties. President Woodrow Wilson feared

that American involvement against Germany might unleash "serious domestic clashes inside the U.S."

The most vivid example of misguided fear manifested itself during World War II after the attack on Pearl Harbor. The belief that Japanese-Americans might still be loyal to the ancestral homeland resulted in the relocation and internment of 120,000 Japanese-Americans. As recently as 1991, this animosity surfaced again (albeit in a much milder form), as Arab-Americans became vulnerable to attack during the Gulf War with Iraq.

During the Cold War years, ethnic Americans who sought a voice in foreign policy matters regarding a country of origin could gain access to decision-makers mostly when their views coincided with America's hostility to communism. Richard Allen, Ronald Reagan's first national security adviser, encouraged Cuban-Americans to build up an ethnic lobby that would serve as a tool furthering the administration's effort to delegitimize the Castro regime. Over time, Jorge Mas Canosa and the Cuban-American National Foundation became a major power broker in American foreign policy.

With the changing nature of America's ethnic mix—i.e., with the proliferation of non-European immigrants arriving mostly from Latin America and Asia, and with the growing advancement of minority groups, especially African-Americans—ethnic Americans began to consider a voice in foreign policy an additional form of empowerment. In America today, there are many new ethnic voices making themselves heard. Even groups which are satisfied with their accomplishments in the American economic arena no longer shy away from foreign policy. Thus, in contrast to their historical timidity in American public affairs, the 1.4 million Indian-Americans have found a political voice and are raising the stature of India in Washington.

ETHNIC LOBBIES' GROWING POWER

At a time when global foreign relations are no longer defined in strictly East-West terms [the cold war rivalry between the U.S-led bloc and the Soviet-led bloc] and [when] U.S. foreign policy is characterized by a diminished cohesiveness, ethnic lobbies are becoming more important in influencing foreign policy makers. The fact that American society and politics permit, or even welcome, expressions of ethnic solidarity and no longer discourage preoccupation with motherlands lends itself to special diasporic influences on the U.S. foreign policy agenda. This reality has raised concerns about the ability of the U.S. to develop foreign policy in the "American national interest." Will its foreign policy be tainted and confused by partisan and divisive ethnic voices? On this point, Samuel Huntington says that by accepting the validity of multiculturalism and by heeding ethnic voices, American decision-makers are at risk of compromising American national interests.

Such concerns are usually exaggerated. In my book, *Marketing the American Creed Abroad: Diasporas in the U.S. and Their Homeland*, I document that ethnic Americans who engage in U.S. foreign policy are frequently carriers of American foreign policy messages and values, rather than being agents or fifth columns for their countries of origin.

For example, Iranian radicalism is said to be waning as reformist politicians win elections in Teheran. Even Iranian-Americans now see the possibility of building an ethnic lobby without compromising their American loyalties or without being suspected of treason by their kin in Iran. Especially when a homeland is at odds with America, first-generation exiles may feel compelled to remain silent, lest they be accused of being traitors at home or spies abroad. Over time, however, their offspring become sufficiently comfortable to organize as ethnic Americans, and eventually to act as a liaison between the U.S. and their homeland. In the case of the million-strong and economically thriving Iranian-American community, Negar Akhvi has recently noted that after the revolution of 1979, first-generation immigrants were too timid either to speak against Ayatollah Khomeini or to organize as diasporic Americans. Describing the younger generation of Iranian-Americans in Los Angeles, Akhvi maintains, "the fatigue and the stress that enveloped the generation that fled Iran has not been passed on to my own. My generation is less scared by the Revolution and at greater ease in democratic forums. In short, we are American enough to form a lobby, yet Iranian enough to care about what happens in our homeland."

Other American ethnic communities, both newcomers and those of long standing, have discovered they can unify and mobilize their particular community by pursuing goals related to the homeland as well as domestic issues in the U.S. That was certainly true of African-Americans as they effectively protested apartheid in South Africa in the mid-1980s. When in 1988 a number of American black leaders announced their preference for the appellation "African-American" over "black," the Rev. Jesse Jackson declared, "Every ethnic group in this country has a reference to some land base, some historical cultural base. African-Americans have hit that level of maturity." Indeed, in recent years African-American activists inside and outside Congress have gained high visibility and importance in the foreign policy arena. When in 1994 President Clinton was hesitant about restoring deposed President Jean-Bertrand Aristide in Haiti, it was the Congressional Black Caucus and the hunger strike of Randall Robinson, director of the

African-American lobby TransAfrica, which forced him to act.

The recent case of Elian Gonzalez [a Cuban boy who survived the sinking of the boat in which his mother and others fleeing to the United States died. The father, still in Cuba, and the Cuban government demanded the boy's return. The Cuban-American community strongly opposed his return, but he was eventually taken by U.S. Marshals and sent back to Cuba] is a fascinating example of how diaspora community leaders try to safeguard the exile mentality against the atrophy that would be quite natural for a community of immigrants after 40 years in the United States. It appeared that the Cuban-American community found itself at a critical juncture: Was its identity that of exiles and refugees nurturing their old rhetoric and the hope of return—or were they to become ethnic Americans plain and simple? For Cuban-Americans, the Gonzalez case served as the impetus for reassessing the question of their loyalty, and the community found itself in a precarious dilemma. The difficulty is that if Cuban-Americans are perceived as acting outside the laws of America regarding child custody, or in opposition to congressional tendencies to relax the economic sanctions against Cuba, they endanger the sympathy they enjoy as adherents of American interests and values and opponents of the Castro regime. That struggle over the loyalty and identity of Cuban-Americans is certain to continue.

In today's America it becomes more and more difficult to distinguish between domestic and foreign politics. America's divided government, which empowers single members of Congress and even local municipal leaders in foreign policy, enhances the stature and the clout of well-organized ethnic lobbies. These lobbies also benefit from the declining power of traditional foreign policy elites—the old "Eastern establishment." For example, the highly mobilized and well-funded Armenian-American community has gained its reputation over the past decade as the most important element in shaping U.S. foreign policy posture toward the newly independent states in the Caucasus and especially toward the conflict in Nagorno-Karabakh, a territory claimed by both Armenia and Azerbaijan. While Congress continues to support the lobby's position and prohibits direct U.S. assistance to Azerbaijan under Section 907, the Clinton administration strongly opposes Section 907 and has testified in favor of repeal of these sanctions. In his inaugural address in 1998, Armenian President Robert Kocherian emphasized the importance of "the unification of efforts of all Armenians, and ensuring the Armenian diaspora's active participation in the social, political and economic life of our republic. ...Armenia should be a holy motherland for all Armenians, and its victory should be their victory."

JEWISH AMERICANS AND MIDDLE EAST POLICY

When U.S. foreign policy was determined by traditional professional elites, there was a tendency to perceive Jewish-American affinity with Israel as a liability, especially since the Foreign Service held that America's close ties to Israel could jeopardize its interest in the Arab world or the oil-rich countries. In the 1950s, U.S. foreign policy-makers under Eisenhower viewed Israel as, at best, a benign presence in the Middle East and, more commonly, as an irritant in America's strategic planning in the region. At the height of the Cold War, Jewish Americans were leery about breaking with the American official line. For instance, during the Suez Crisis of 1956, the Jewish-American lobby emphasized its allegiance to American interests and was reluctant to push Israel's case for fear of being labeled disloyal....

The emphasis on American allegiance by Jewish Americans could also be seen in Secretary of State Henry Kissinger's handling of the Middle East conflict. During the Nixon and Ford administrations, Kissinger downplayed his Jewish origin in his work on this policy area. Kissinger was attacked vehemently by the American-Israel Political Action Committee when he attempted to push Israel into a deal with the Arabs. In light of Israel's reluctance to accept an American dictate, AIPAC mobilized the Congress against President Ford's decision to reassess U.S. policy in the Middle East and U.S. relations with Israel. When 76 senators wrote to the president urging him to declare that "the U.S. acting in its own national interest stands firmly with Israel," Kissinger responded angrily. He berated Israeli Ambassador Simcha Dinitz and told him that the letter "will increase anti-Semitism, it will cause people to charge that Jews control Congress." As a result, Kissinger was accused of betrayal and hounded by demonstrators in Israel. His insistent loyalty to the United States thus resulted in his being pulled from both sides of the ethnic bridge.

The allegation that Jews cannot always be both good Americans and good Jews surfaced on various occasions when there was a contest between the White House and the Israel lobby. Today, however, as foreign policy-making in Washington is becoming more dispersed and influenced by, among other things, think tanks, public opinion and the media, ethnic lobbyists are no longer perceived as an inherent threat to the national interest, and the dreaded charge of "divided loyalties" is less and less persuasive. In fact, the end of the Cold War and deep splits within Israel regarding the direction of the Palestinian peace process and the character of the Jewish state have tended to divide the

U.S. Jewish community. Thus, when President Clinton wanted to demonstrate his frustration with former Israeli Prime Minister Benjamin Netanyahu, he could call upon certain Jewish-American community leaders to mobilize their constituencies to reprimand the Israeli government for its behavior.

At times, individuals associated with ethnic lobbies have even established themselves as leading experts in their respective kin states and, as such, are mobilized by the American government as more effective messengers in the United States or in their ancestral homelands. When persons of Jewish origins, such as Aaron Miller, Dennis Ross, or Martin Indyk (who was a member of the pro-Israel lobby before he established the Washington Institute for Near East Policy) are situated at the forefront of American foreign policy in the Middle East, the idea that committed Jews cannot be trusted as brokers in the Arab-Israeli peace process is no longer viable. Even Arab leaders and Arab-Americans have grudgingly accepted this as a fact of life, despite ongoing Arab-Israeli conflicts. Take, for example, Daniel Kurzer, America's current ambassador to Egypt, who is a deeply committed and publicly identified Jew. The prominence of these individuals in Middle East policy-making is a clear indication that in America at least, Jewish identity does not provoke serious suspicions of divided loyalties.

Finally, we should not forget that America's generally benign attitude toward questions of ethnic loyalty does have its limits. After Jonathan Pollard, an Israeli-American, was convicted of spying for Israel, it was not surprising that the Jewish-American community was much less merciful toward Pollard than was the Israeli government, which has been trying for years to secure his release from prison. More recently, Wen Ho Lee, the physicist formerly at Los Alamos National Laboratory who is alleged to have passed nuclear secrets to China, has reportedly caused a cloud of suspicion to be cast over other Chinese-American scientists. Despite these rare cases, the overall trend in the United States has clearly moved in recent decades in a more positive direction. There is an ever greater acceptance of the legitimacy of ethnic Americans in national policy-making, as well as a growing appreciation that in the present period of globalization, America's ethnic groups can strengthen and expand U.S. influence around the world.

THE CONTINUING DEBATE:
Ethnic Foreign Policy Lobbying

What Is New

Ethnic lobbying continues to exert influence on foreign policy. For example, recent studies have shown that foreign aid is connected to ethnic lobbies, not only in the United States, but also in other aid-giving countries. Other recent research has shown that ethnic lobbying groups influence U.S. economic sanctions policy.

In 1915, Theodore Roosevelt condemned lobbying by various European American groups. The changing demographic characteristics of Americans and the rising political activity and strength of non-European heritage groups has diversified ethnic lobbying. The TransAfrica Forum, for one, is a relatively new organization, which, its mission statement says, "focuses on U.S. policy as it affects Africa and the Diaspora in the Caribbean and Latin America" on behalf of "African-American community." Cuban Americans have for decades influenced U.S. foreign policy, and now they are being joined by such other Latino groups, such as the National Council of La Raza, which includes among its missions presenting "an Hispanic perspective on trade, assistance, and other international issues."

Where to Find More

A good place to begin would be Thomas Ambrosio's edited study, *Ethnic Identify Groups and U.S. Foreign Policy* (Praeger, 2002). Additionally, a recent book that frets about ethnic lobbying while also supporting its validity is Tony Smith, *Foreign Attachments: The Power of Ethnic Groups in the Making of American Foreign Policy* (Harvard University Press, 2000). A study that worries that strong multiculturalism, including on foreign policy, is endangering American national unity is Arthur M. Schlesinger Jr., *The Disuniting of America: Reflections on a Multicultural Society* (W. W. Norton, 1998). For an optimistic view of competing identities, read Peter J. Sprio, *Embracing Dual Nationality* (Carnegie Endowment for International Peace, 1998). Also positive toward ethnic lobbying is James M. Lindsay, "Getting Uncle Sam's Ear: Will Ethnic Lobbies Cramp America's Foreign Policy Style?," *Brookings Review*, Winter 2002. It is available on the Web at: http://www.brook.edu. Also worthwhile and available on the Web is a summary of a conference on ethnic foreign policy lobbying. See David J. Vidal, "Defining the National Interest Minorities and U.S. Foreign Policy in the 21st Century: Project for Diversity in International Affairs" at: http://www.ciaonet.org/conf/vid01/.

What More to Do

The view of many people may be that ethnic foreign policy lobbying is neither always good nor always bad. Given that, one thing to do in class is to work with others to come up with a "do's and don'ts" list of such activities.

You will also find it enlightening to keep an eye on the 2004 U.S. presidential race to watch for the influence of various foreign policy lobby groups on that contest. The Middle East, U.S.-Cuba relations, immigration, and numerous other foreign policy or mixed *inter*national/dom*estic* (intermestic) issues of interest to one or another ethnic groups will play a role in who takes the oath of office on January 20, 2005 and who just watches the swearing-in ceremony.

9 POLITICAL PARTIES

THE ODDS-ON FAVORITE IN THE FUTURE:
Democrats *or* Republicans?

DEMOCRATS

ADVOCATES: John B. Judis, Senior Editor, *The New Republic*, and Ruy
  Teixeira, Senior Fellow, the Century Foundation

SOURCE: "America's Changing Political Geography: Where Democrats Can
  Build a Majority," *Blueprint: Ideas for a New Century*,
  September/October 2002

REPUBLICANS

ADVOCATE: Daniel Casse, Senior Director, White House Writers Group

SOURCE: "An Emerging Republican Majority?" *Commentary*, January 2003

This debate brings to mind the classic tune, "The Party's Over," originally made
famous by Judy Holliday in the 1956 Broadway musical *Bells Are Ringing*. The
theme of the lyrics is captured in two lines:

> The party's over, it's time to call it a day,
> They've burst your pretty balloon and taken the moon away.

Judy Holliday was singing about lost love, but the advocates in this debate might
use her words to back up their theme that one of the major parties is destined to fade in
the affections of a majority of American voters. What the advocates disagree about is
which party is destined for loneliness and which is destined for love. John Judis and Ruy
Teixeira contend that the country is entering an age of "a new Democratic majority"
because demographic "growth trends within states favor the Democrats, not the
Republicans." To the contrary, Daniel Casse argues in his essay that the Republican Party
has a good chance of building on the string of successes it had in the presidential and
congressional elections of 2000 and 2002 and turning those victories "into something
more permanent and more meaningful."

There can be little doubt that the immediate picture was looking bright for
Republicans when Casse published his article in early 2003. Not only was a Republican
in the Oval Office, but President George W. Bush's poll number were exceptional. A CBS
poll taken during the first week of January 2003 found 64% of its respondents indicating
they approved of "the way...Bush is handling his job as President," compared to just
28% who disapproved, and 8% who were unsure. Additionally, the GOP (Grand Old
Party) was in control of Congress with majorities in both the House and the Senate.

Recent history clearly shows, however, that current success does not necessarily
translate into positive long-term prospects. Just three decades ago, the Watergate scandal that forced President Richard M. Nixon to resign in August 1974 also tainted his
Republican Party, which lost 48 House seats in that November's elections. When the
new Congress convened in 1975, the Democrats held 291 seats in the House, more

than two-thirds of the total, against only 144 Republicans. The GOP also lost five Senate seats, leaving it was almost nearly as lop-sided, with 60 Democrats, 38 Republicans, and 2 independents. The Democrats made even further gains in both houses in 1976 when their presidential nominee, Jimmy Carter, captured the White House, and the opinion columns and talk-show airwaves around the country were full of predictions about the imminent demise of the Republican Party.

That did not occur. Republicans Ronald Reagan and George H. W. Bush won the presidency in 1980 and 1984 and in 1988 respectively. The GOP also gained in Congress, and even was the majority party in the Senate for six years under Reagan. Then Democrat Bill Clinton won the 1992 presidential election, but the uncertain start his presidency helped cost Democrats 54 House seats in 1994. When the 104th Congress convened in January 1995, the GOP controlled both house of Congress for the first time since 1954. Many pundits touted the so-called "Republican revolution," and opined that new GOP Speaker of the House, Newt Gingrich would be powerful enough to move the center of political gravity in Washington a considerable distance eastward on Constitution Avenue away from the White House and toward the Capitol. Gingrich proved inept as speaker, however, and was soon forced from office. But that GOP setback was overcome when George W. Bush completed the Republican trifecta by edging Al Gore for the presidency in 2000. To make matters even better for the Republicans, they gained seats in Congress in 2002, thereby overcoming the tradition of the president's party losing seats in the off-year elections.

Do these shifts in recent decades mean that one or the other party cannot dominate for a significant period? The answer is no. The Republicans controlled both houses of Congress for all but six years (1913–1919) between 1901 and 1933. During this time, Woodrow Wilson (1913–1921) was the sole Democratic president. Then the Democrats took control with the election of President Franklin Roosevelt. Except for four years (1947–1949, 1953–1955), they then were a majority in the Senate until 1981 and in the House of Representatives until 1995. Furthermore, Democrats served as president for 8 of the 12 presidential terms between 1933 and 1981.

In addition to personalities and issues, another factor that affects the parties' fortunes is the percentage of the electorate that identifies with one of the two parties. Between 1952 and 2000, the percentage of people who either said they were Democrats or "leaned" in that direction declined from 57% to 47%, while Republican partisans or leaners increased marginally from 35% to 37%. True independents increased from 6% to 12% and people describing themselves as apolitical or attached to another party made up the balance.

POINTS TO PONDER

➤ Think about the concept of "ideopolises" in the essay by Judis and Teixeira and the role they think these focuses of political geography will play. Do you find this a helpful analytical approach?

➤ The country is experiencing demographic shifts in voting activity. Women, African Americans, Asia Americans, and Latinos have become a significant part of the voting electorate. What do these changes augur for the parties?

➤ What are the chances that neither Judis and Teixeira nor Casse are correct? What has the best odds: a Democratic majority, a Republican majority, or a shifting political contest in which neither party dominates during the next decade or two?

The Odds-On Favorite in the Future:
Democrats

John B. Judis and Ruy Teixeira

After the 2000 election, political commentators began referring to the Democrats as the "blues" and the Republicans as the "reds"— terms corresponding to the colors used on electoral maps to denote which states each party's presidential ticket carried. So the question of America's political future has become: Who will dominate, the blues or the reds?

The Republicans think it'll be the reds. They look at the 2000 electoral map and see good things. For one thing, there's more red than blue, reflecting the fact that Republican states tend to be physically larger. More important, they figure that if they just hold the states they carried in 2000— which basically means the Solid South, the Mountain States, the Border States, and the more conservative Midwestern states—their electoral vote margin of four (271–267) will go up to 18 (278–260), due to reapportionment. Then, for a safety margin, all they have to do is pick off a few of the states they lost by less than 5 percent—Oregon, New Mexico, Iowa, Wisconsin, Washington, Minnesota, Michigan, Pennsylvania, and Maine—and they're home free.

That was Bush political guru Karl Rove's essential message in his now infamous lost-and-accidentally-found PowerPoint presentation to a group of California Republicans [in] June [2001]. Stick with us, allow us to do a little judicious pandering to workers in states like Wisconsin and Pennsylvania, and the GOP's Reagan coalition—albeit a bit slimmed down—will rise again. And, he might have added, we don't even need California, that current bastion of blue America; we can build our red America without it.

Republicans don't just rest their case on reapportionment. They think that below the state level, the trends favor the GOP. They argue that the pattern of growth within states favors the Republicans since formerly rural counties on the fringes of metropolitan areas are growing the fastest and these counties lean strongly Republican. Political analyst Michael Barone called these fringe areas "edge counties" in his influential "49 percent nation" article in *The Almanac of American Politics 2002*. David Brooks referred to these "fast-growing suburbs mostly in the South and West" as "sprinkler cities" in his recent cover article in *The Weekly Standard*, "Patio Man and the Sprawl People," but his argument is basically the same as Barone's: Demographic trends favor the Republicans.

Fortunately for the Democrats, these arguments don't hold up to scrutiny. The Solid South is unlikely to remain solid; some of the mountain and Midwestern states that are red are likely to go blue; and the blue states that Al Gore carried by small margins in 2000 are likely to get harder, not easier, for the Republicans to pick off. Moreover, and crucially, growth trends within states favor the Democrats, not the Republicans.

As we argue in our new book, *The Emerging Democratic Majority*, the reason for these trends is the emergence of a new American political geography—a geography intimately linked to the spread of a postindustrial economy. Rove, Barone, and Brooks are missing the contours of this new geography as they attempt to resuscitate a California-less Reagan coalition. They're living in the past; they don't see that the same changes that have moved California into the Democratic column over the last decade are moving most of the rest of the country in the same direction. Here's how:

Democrats have been gaining strength in areas where the production of ideas and services has either redefined or replaced an economy dependent on manufacturing, agriculture, and resource extraction. Many of these areas are in the North and West, but they are also in states like Florida and Virginia. Republicans are strongest in areas where the transition to postindustrial society has lagged. Many of these are in the Deep South and Prairie States. As Democratic politics has evolved over the last decade, it has increasingly reflected the socially liberal, fiscally moderate priorities of these new areas—what we call a politics of progressive centrism. Republicans have continued to espouse an anti-government credo closely identified with business and the religious right—a politics that plays well in parts of the Deep South but not in a new postindustrial America.

This new postindustrial politics is not defined by states but by metropolitan regions within states. These postindustrial metropolises, which we call "ideopolises," are the breeding ground for the new Democratic majority. Insofar as these areas are not confined to the Northeast, far West, and upper Midwest but are found also in the South and Southwest, the Democrats have a chance to build a large majority and to rewrite today's political map. By 2008, Democrats could enjoy an electoral base of 332 electoral votes, many more than they need for a majority, while holding a competitive position in a number of additional states that might swell that majority.

The Role of Ideopolises. The transition to a postindustrial society has transformed the economic geography of the country. After World War II, industrial society was divided into three domains: the cities of offices and manufacturing plants, where white ethnics, minorities, and immigrants lived; suburbs, where many of the white middle class were moving; and rural areas of farms, mines, and forests. Postindustrial society is organized around metropolitan areas that include both suburbs and central cities. The production of goods has moved out of the central city into the suburbs, or even into semi-rural areas. And many ethnics and minorities have migrated from the city to the suburbs. The sharpest contrast now is not between city and suburb, but between the new metropolitan areas, taken as a whole, and the rural countryside. The suburbs themselves have become extensions of the city—demarcated artificially on maps—rather than extensions of the countryside housing city workers.

Some of the new postindustrial metropolitan areas like Silicon Valley [near San Francisco] or the Boulder, Colo., metro area contain significant manufacturing facilities, but it is manufacturing—whether of pharmaceuticals or semiconductors—that consists in the application of complex ideas to physical objects. And some of these metro areas specialize in producing what Joel Kotkin and Ross C. DeVol call "soft technology"—entertainment, media, fashion, design, and advertising—and in providing databases, legal counsel, and other business services. New York City and Los Angeles are both premier postindustrial metropolises that specialize in soft technology.

Most of these postindustrial metropolises also include a major university or several major universities that funnel ideas and, more important, people into the hard or soft technology industries. Boston's Route 128 feeds off Harvard and MIT. Silicon Valley is closely linked to Stanford and the University of California at Berkeley. Dane

County's biomedical research is tied to the University of Wisconsin at Madison. And all of them have a flourishing service sector, with ethnic and vegetarian restaurants, multimedia shopping malls, children's museums, book store-coffee shops, and health clubs.

Professionals and technicians are heavily concentrated in the workforces of these postindustrial metropolises. A quarter or so of the jobs in Austin, Texas, Boston, San Francisco, or North Carolina's Research Triangle are held by professionals and technicians. Plentiful, too, are low-level service and information workers, including waiters, hospital orderlies, sales clerks, janitors, and teachers' aides. Many of these jobs have been filled by Hispanics and African-Americans, just as many of the high-professional jobs have been filled by Asian immigrants. It's one reason that the workforces in these areas we call ideopolises tend to be ethnically diverse and more complex in their stratification (various combinations of employers, employees, contract workers, temps, consultants, and the self-employed) than the workforce of the older industrial city.

The ethos and mores of many of these new metropolitan areas tend to be libertarian and bohemian because of the people they attract. Economists Richard Florida and Gary Gates found a close correlation between the concentration of gays and of the foreign-born and the concentration of high technology and information technology within a metropolitan area. They also found a high percentage of people who identified themselves as artists, musicians, and craftspeople. Concluded Florida, "Diversity is a powerful force in the value systems and choices of the new workforce, whose members want to work for companies and live in communities that reflect their openness and tolerance. The number one factor in choosing a place to live and work, they say, is diversity. Talented people

will not move to a place that ostracizes certain groups."

The politics of these ideopolises emphasizes tolerance and openness. It is defined by the professionals, many of whom were deeply shaped by the social movements of the '60s. They worry about clean air and water, and when the market fails to provide them, they call on government. They favor civil rights and liberties and good government. They disdain the intolerance and fundamentalism of the religious right. But they are also leery of the old Democratic politics of "big government" and large-scale social engineering. Some backed Ronald Reagan in 1980 and 1984, but since then, they and the places they have lived have moved steadily into the Democratic column—and in the meantime, they have reshaped the Democratic Party in their own postindustrial image.

Metropolitan areas come in different stages and configurations. In the San Francisco Bay area or the Chicago metro area, the work and culture of the ideopolis pervades the entire metropolitan area. Many of the same people, the same businesses, and the same coffee shops or book stores can be found in the central city and in the suburbs. These are the most advanced and integrated ideopolises. Many of these areas were once Republican but have become extremely Democratic in their politics. Gore won Portland's Multnomah County [in Oregon] 64 percent to 28 percent. Princeton University's Mercer County [New Jersey] went for Gore 61 percent to 34 percent. Seattle's King County was 60 percent to 34 percent for Gore. Other metropolitan areas like Fresno, Calif., or Muncie, Ind., have not yet made the transition to a postindustrial economy. They lag in telecommunications, computers, and high-tech jobs. In some of these areas, which are not yet ideopolises, Republicans continue to have a strong following.

The Democrats' vote in the integrated ideopolises has included three groups that loom large in the emerging Democratic majority: professionals, women (especially single, working, and highly educated women), and minorities. But it has also included relatively strong support from the white working class—white workers who have not graduated from a four-year college and tend not to have credentialed jobs—the very group whose defection from the Democrats allowed conservative Republicans to build a majority. In the most advanced ideopolises, the white working class seems to embrace the same values as professionals and in some of them, white working-class men vote with remarkable similarity to their female counterparts. As a result, Republican appeals to hot-button issues such as race (or resentment against immigrants), guns, and abortion have largely fallen on deaf ears, and these voters have not only rejected Republican social conservatism but also reverted to a preference for Democratic economics. In Seattle's King County, white working-class voters backed Gore 50 percent to 42 percent. In Portland's Multnomah County, it was by 71 percent to 24 percent. By comparison, working-class whites nationwide supported Bush 57 percent to 40 percent.

To gauge the effect of these ideopolises nationally, we looked at 263 counties that are part of metro areas that have the highest concentrations of high-tech economic activity or contain a highly ranked research university. Most of these areas used to be Republican and voted for Republican presidential candidates in 1980 and 1984. In 1984, for instance, they went 55 percent to 44 percent for Reagan. But in 2000, Gore garnered 54.6 percent of the vote in these areas compared to 41.4 percent for Bush. And since Ralph Nader got 3.3 percent in these counties, the total Democratic-leaning vote in America's ideopolises can be reckoned at close to 58 percent.

By contrast, Democrats have continued to lose in rural areas in states like Missouri and Pennsylvania and in many low-tech metropolitan areas like Greenville, S.C., that have not made the postindustrial transition. In all, Gore lost the non-ideopolis counties 52.9 percent to 43.6 percent. Indeed, if you compare 1980, the beginning of the Reagan era, to today, it is clear that almost all of the pro-Democratic change in the country since then has been concentrated in America's ideopolis counties. This is what has happened to the Reagan coalition: It has vanished into the postindustrial economy.

Ideopolises v. Edge Counties and Sprinkler Cities. The changes wrought by this new political geography can be readily seen by looking at three states that voted Republican in the six presidential elections from 1968 to 1988—California, Illinois, and New Jersey—but are now solidly Democratic.

California. In the Reagan era, the Los Angeles area in Southern California, except for minority and Jewish enclaves, backed Republican conservatives, while the Bay area in Northern California was divided between Democratic-leaning San Francisco and the moderate Republicans of San Mateo, Santa Clara, and Contra Costa counties. But in the '90s, the economic and political differences between the Bay area and Los Angeles County suddenly disappeared. The Bay area, of course, became the headquarters for Silicon Valley and one of America's leading ideopolises. But Los Angeles County also changed. In 1983, there had been almost twice as many aerospace workers as workers in the motion picture industry. By 2000, there were almost three times more workers employed in motion pictures than in aerospace. It, too, became an ideopolis and, like the Bay area, began voting about 2-to-1 for Democrats. In the state as a whole, Gore in 2000 won the ideopolis counties but lost the counties that had not yet been transformed by the postindustrial economy. California's 14 ideopolis counties, which made up 69 percent of the overall vote, supported Gore 57 percent to 38 percent, while the 44 non-ideopolis counties supported Bush 49 percent to 46 percent.

Illinois. In 1972, Richard Nixon actually won Chicago and Cook County, and Walter Mondale won the county by only 3 percent in 1984. But Chicago and Cook County were making the transition to a postindustrial metropolitan area. Between 1970 and 1997, Chicago lost 60 percent of its manufacturing jobs. While Chicago still manufactured goods, what it made was often high-technology computer equipment like modems or semiconductor chips. According to a Humphrey Institute study, the Chicago metropolitan area now has the highest number of high-tech jobs of any metropolitan area. All in all, the hog butcher of the world now has twice as many professionals and technicians in the metro area as production workers.

At the same time, Chicago and its suburbs began to move Democratic in 1988, but the most dramatic change came in the 1990s. In the 1992, 1996, and 2000 elections, the Republicans never got more than 30 percent of the vote in Cook County, and the Democratic total rose from 58 percent in 1992 to 69 percent in 2000. With Cook County tallying about 40 percent of the votes in the state, Bush in 2000 would have had to win 65 percent outside of Cook County to carry Illinois. That's an insuperable obstacle in a state that, even outside of Chicago and Cook County, is beginning to trend Democratic. For example, Lake County, one of Chicago's "collar counties" and part of the overall Chicago ideopolis, backed George H. W. Bush against Michael Dukakis in 1988 64 percent to 36 percent; in 2000, it supported his son by just 50 percent to 48 percent, with 2 percent going to Nader. In general, Illinois' ideopolis counties have gone from about a 50–50 split in 1988

to a 59–39 Democratic margin in 2000, while the Democratic disadvantage in the rest of the state—a shrinking share of the electorate—has remained steady at about 7 percentage points.

New Jersey. In the '80s, Reagan and Bush won the first and third biggest counties, Bergen in the North and Middlesex in the center, by comfortable margins. But in the 1990s, the central and northeastern sections of the state became almost a continuous ideopolis. The state's largest occupational group—and fastest growing—consists of professionals, who make up 23.3 percent of the workforce compared to 15.4 percent nationally. Counties like Bergen and Middlesex moved sharply Democratic. Bill Clinton in 1996 and Gore in 2000 took the two counties by identical margins: 14 points in Bergen and 24 points in Middlesex. In Bergen County, Gore won 65 percent of college-educated white voters, including 77 percent of college-educated white women. In the state, he won voters with postgraduate degrees (usually a good indication of professionalism) by 62 percent to 34 percent. At the same time, he won 88 percent of the black vote and 58 percent of the Hispanic vote (which includes pro-Republican Cubans from Union City.)

But what of the Republican Solid South? The changes that have swept through California, Illinois, and New Jersey are affecting politics there. Take Florida, which the Republicans desperately need to keep in their column. As Florida's high-tech and tourist centers have grown dramatically, they have also moved sharply Democratic. For example, Orlando's Orange County, once the center of Florida agriculture, has become a major entertainment center and a home for computer services. Democrats lost Orange County by 37 percent in 1988; in 2000, Gore won it by 2 points.

But the changes are not just in Orange County. As the table shows, since 1988,

Democratic strength has dramatically increased in all five counties of the state that added the most people during the last decade—Fort Lauderdale's Broward County, Miami-Dade, Palm Beach, and Tampa's Hillsborough County, as well as Orange County. It's not hard to see where Florida's political future lies.

As the postindustrial economy grows, change is coming to the rest of the South as well. As North Carolina has moved away from reliance on textiles and tobacco, it has become more receptive to a progressive centrist politics. All the state's postindustrial areas have become more Democratic since 1988. Dukakis lost Charlotte's Mecklenberg County 59 percent to 40 percent in 1988, but Gore lost it only by 51 percent to 48 percent in 2000, even though he did not campaign in the state (Clinton carried it by 3 points in 1996). The Democrats' edge in Durham County in the Research Triangle increased from 54 percent to 45 percent up to 63 percent to 35 percent over the same time period. In the Raleigh metro area as a whole, Gore edged Bush by a point, up from a 5 point Democratic deficit in 1988.

Virginia's premier postindustrial area, the Northern Virginia suburbs of Washington, D.C., where AOL and many of the nation's telecommunications firms are headquartered, has also been moving Democratic. Fairfax has gone from a 61 percent to 38 percent Republican margin in 1988 to a 49 percent to 47 percent Bush margin in 2000, with 3 percent to Nader. Arlington went from a 53 percent to 45 percent Democratic edge to a 60 percent to 34 percent Democratic advantage, with 5 percent to Nader, over the same time period. If these suburban voters keep increasing their proportion of the Virginia vote, and if they continue to trend Democratic, they could very well tilt Virginia back to the Democrats, even in presidential elections. Certainly, Democratic

Gov. Mark Warner's recent victory suggests this is a very real possibility.

But what about all those fast-growing edge counties and sprinkler cities that Barone and Brooks write about? Won't the increasing weight of these pro-Republican counties tilt these states and others back toward the Republicans? That's not likely for two simple reasons. First, most of these counties aren't very big (the 50 fastest growing average 109,000 in population), so their high growth rates translate into only modest increases in actual Republican voters. These modest increases pale in comparison to the additional Democratic voters provided by populous metropolitan counties (the 50 largest growing average 1.46 million) that had the largest increases in population. Al Gore gained a 2.7 million vote advantage from the 50 largest growth counties; George W. Bush gained only a 500,000 vote advantage from the 50 fastest growing counties.

Second, as these edge counties and sprinkler cities get bigger and become more integrated into a metropolitan area, they typically become more Democratic (call it the "ideopolis effect"). Combined with their relatively small size, it means that even Brooks' and Barone's best-case counties are unlikely to have the potent political effects they predict.

Take Loudon County in the Northern Virginia suburbs, the sixth-fastest growing county in the country, cited by Brooks in his article. Even after a decade of very fast growth, Loudon still has only about 170,000 inhabitants. And, as Loudon has grown, it has become less Republican, going from a 66 percent to 33 percent Republican margin in 1988 to a much more modest 56 percent to 41 percent Republican advantage in 2000. The county's modest size and its declining Republican edge mean it can't stop an area-wide pro-Democratic trend (much less start a pro-Republican one): Even as Loudon was growing like topsy, the Northern Virginia suburbs as a whole went from a 20 point Democratic disadvantage to almost even over the same time period.

Or take Douglas County, Colo., outside of Denver, the fastest growing county in the country and lovingly cited by both Brooks and Barone. Douglas still has only 176,000 inhabitants. And, while it went for Bush by 34 points in 2000, that's down from 42 points in 1988 and 60 points in 1984. Reflecting these realities, Douglas' fast growth just hasn't been enough to drive its metro area toward the Republicans. Instead, the Denver metro area has gone from a 3 point Republican margin in 1988 to a 1 point Democratic advantage in 2000.

And Loudon and Douglas are two of the larger, fast-growing counties. The smaller ones, of course, have even less chance of impacting political trends. Contrary to Barone and Brooks, edge counties/sprinkler cities are clearly no antidote for trends in the nation's ideopolises—not in states that still lean Republican and certainly not in states that lean or are solid Democratic.

The new political geography has a powerful logic that should lead, over time, to a Democratic, not Republican, electoral majority. Of course, demography is not destiny—Democrats could fall back into the bad habits of their past, while Republicans could move decisively to the center. But barring unforeseen developments, the trends moving America toward a postindustrial economy should favor Democrats in the decade to come.

The Odds-On Favorite in the Future:
Republicans

DANIEL CASSE

By the time Al Gore conceded the presidency to George W. Bush in December 2000, there was widespread agreement that the razor-close election they had just fought, and the fractious litigation that followed it, had exposed a disturbingly deep fissure in our national politics. In newspapers and magazines and on television, brightly colored maps showed a country divided almost exactly in half into red (Republican) and blue (Democratic) voting patterns. "There are now two distinct Americas," proclaimed *Business Week* in a typical cover story, "split along geographic, social, religious, and racial lines." So disparate were the tastes and attitudes of the people inhabiting those two different Americas, the story continued, as to "demand entirely different things from government."

Not only was the country said to be fractured, it was also said to be, on that account, ungovernable—and certainly ungovernable by George W. Bush. Wherever the new President turned, averred the political scientist Walter Dean Burnham, he was bound to find himself crippled by severely "limited opportunities" to forge a consensus behind his policies.

It was in this very circumstance, indeed, that some in the still-smarting Democratic party saw a sign of hope. Although the Democrats had lost not only the presidency but, as it then seemed, both houses of Congress, opportunity lurked in Bush's irreparable weaknesses. The new President, after all, was woefully inexperienced, especially in foreign affairs. The Republican coalition that had supported him—an unlikely mix of business groups, social conservatives, and libertarians remained as fragile as ever. Only through the tiebreaking vote of the Vice President could the GOP expect to hold its majority in the Senate. And, as if these difficulties were not enough, the new administration was facing the first serious downturn in the national economy after eight years of remarkable prosperity presided over by a Democratic executive.

As the 2000 results were further digested, Democratic strategists took particular comfort in their reading of the red-blue map. The blue metropolitan clusters that had gone for Al Gore were composed disproportionately of educated professionals, women, and minorities—groups that were projected to grow more quickly than the rural and suburban voters who had pulled the lever for Bush. These demographic trends, along with the swooning stock market and other economic woes, suggested that Democrats might be well positioned to mount a fresh challenge to the GOP as early as the mid-term election of 2002. The party's prospects brightened further when, in June 2001, Senator James Jeffords announced that he was bolting the GOP and would henceforth vote as an independent—thus giving Democrats a majority in the Senate. In July, for the first time since Bush's inauguration, a Zogby poll showed a majority of Americans disapproving of his performance. Around Washington, "Re-Elect Gore" bumper stickers began to appear.

But then came September 11, followed by the war in Afghanistan and the budding confrontation with Saddam Hussein—events whose political importance served to boost George W. Bush's popularity to once-unimaginable levels and make the Gore defeat fade into memory. Last year's midterm campaign, on which the Democrats had pinned so much hope, became instead a month's-long exercise in frustration; by November 5, the actual results left in tatters the party's dream of a public backlash against an "accidental" President and of its own quick reemergence in American politics. In fact, its fortunes today are lower than they were in November 2000. Two years after the country seemed split down the middle, it is George W. Bush's Republicans who look to be on the verge of creating a new and wholly unexpected political majority.

To get a sense of the magnitude of the Democratic defeat, it helps to bear in mind that only twice since 1862 has the party not holding the White House failed to gain seats in the House of Representatives in a mid-term election, and seldom has it failed to gain in the Senate. As November 5 approached, however, candid Democratic leaders were already admitting they had little hope of winning the House (though none foresaw the loss of fully seven Democratic seats). As for the Senate, eleven races were still deemed to be toss-ups through the final weekend before the balloting. Stunningly, the Republicans went on to win all but one of them. At the end of the balloting, the President enjoyed larger majorities in both houses of Congress than on the day he took office.

The morning after the voting, the line from the Democratic National Committee (DNC) was that the party's losses in Congress were offset by significant gains in gubernatorial races, including in such former Republican strongholds as Michigan, Pennsylvania, Wisconsin, Kansas, and Arizona. But this was spin. Not a single elected Republican governor lost on November 5. Most of the Democratic victories occurred in states where Republicans had held the governor's mansion for twelve years

or more, making it relatively easy for Democratic candidates to call for a change. Moreover, many of the victorious Democrats had campaigned on explicitly conservative platforms, and in Tennessee, Kansas, and Arizona they had vigorously opposed tax increases. The one notable exception was Mark Fernald in New Hampshire, who advocated an increase in state taxes and lost to the Republican candidate by 21 points.

Democratic gubernatorial victories also have to be seen against even more surprising wins by the GOP. Sonny Perdue became the first Republican governor to be elected in Georgia since Reconstruction. Robert Ehrlich, a graduate of [Speaker of the U.S. House of Representative] Newt Gingrich's congressional class of 1994, defeated Kathleen Kennedy Townsend in Maryland, a state widely viewed as the most Democratic in the nation. And [Florida Governor] Jeb Bush, the President's brother, resoundingly upset the prediction of DNC chairman Terry McAuliffe that he would soon be "gone," defeating his challenger by thirteen points.

There were other significant reverses at the state level as well, where Democrats lost control of seven legislatures. Republicans now control 21 state capitols nationwide, compared with only seventeen still in the hands of Democrats. (Another eleven are split.) This marks the first time since 1952 that Republicans have enjoyed such a majority. In Texas, the state House of Representatives is ruled by Republicans for the first time since 1870; in Missouri, for the first time since 1955.

From one perspective, of course, the results of the November election were not so astonishing. Ever since September 11, President Bush's approval rating had stood at historically high levels, and in most polls a majority of Americans were saying that the country was on the right track. In the new era of patriotism and national unity, the deep political chasms that separated Bush voters and Gore voters had become less meaningful.

The mid-term election reflected this changed mood in more ways than one. Although many Senate races were closely contested, and there were many tight gubernatorial races, none was a pitched ideological battle. In no contest did abortion, the death penalty, gun control, race, or class warfare play a major role. With the exception of the late Paul Wellstone [of Minnesota, who died in a plane crash during his 2002 reelection campaign], no candidate for the U.S. Senate actively argued against disarming Saddam Hussein or removing his regime from power. Even on the economy, which remains worrisome to most voters, the campaigns produced no clear party-line disagreements that might have tipped the balance one way or another in the hundreds of local races.

If the country was no longer so bitterly torn, however, Democratic activists failed to notice it or so their campaign strategy would suggest. Many in the party's leadership appeared to believe that Bush's post-September 11 popularity was ephemeral, and that the lingering wounds of the "stolen" election of 2000 would be enough in themselves to excite the Democratic base. "We must never, ever forget what happened" in 2000, intoned Ralph Neas, president of People for the American Way. Donna Brazile, Gore's former campaign manager, advised activists to "go out and say, 'Remember what happened in Florida.'"

It may well have been this mistaken assumption of a generalized desire for payback that lay behind the failure of the party's elites to present a genuine challenge to Bush's Republicans. That failure, at any rate, was the burden of much post-election analysis. The Democrats, lamented Peter Beinart, the editor of the *New Republic*, had "fought this election from the meek and cynical center." Two former Clinton advisers, Tom Freedman and Bill Knapp, sounded a similar note in the *New York Times*, complaining that the Democrats had "ended up arguing over seemingly esoteric differences [and] let bigger national trends, like the war on terrorism, dominate."

But what all such Monday-morning criticisms ignore is that, from the very start of the election year, Democrats in Congress had in fact tried to seize upon every possible issue by which to create a clear distinction between their own priorities and those of the White House. In every instance, however, they found themselves outmaneuvered by a President who seemed determined not to let them get the upper hand on any contentious matter.

Thus, early in 2002, Democrats proposed a reconsideration of the Bush tax cut, only to be waylaid by a White House gleefully reminding reporters of the many Democrats who had initially supported the cut. When, soon thereafter, congressional Democrats joined Senator John McCain's call to rid election campaigns of soft money, they found the President suddenly willing to sign a campaign-finance bill even if it was patently defective and constitutionally suspect. Democrats hoping to tie a cascade of corporate scandals to Republicans and their business donors came up against a White House that welcomed bipartisan legislation to contain corporate fraud. On government financed prescription-drug benefits—a winning Democratic issue according to every poll—the GOP produced a plan that to the casual eye was indistinguishable from the Democrats'. And so it went.

In short, the Democratic problem in 2002 was not just the failure to win a fight but the inability even to pick one. Politically, the war on terror was off-limits—even John Ashcroft, Bush's attorney general and the Democrats' nemesis, was given a relatively free hand to implement his controversial measures for detaining and investigating suspected terrorists. And in the meantime, again and again, domestic issues that had once seemed the exclusive preserve of the Democratic party were being quietly co-opted by a President riding a crest of popularity and a White House enjoying a unique moment of immunity to complaints from the Right that it was pandering to liberals or selling out its own political base.

So what has happened to the red and blue map, with its supposedly hard-line divisions between Democratic and Republican voters? Few analysts of American politics could have been more confounded by the electoral transformation wrought by Bush than John Judis and Ruy Teixeira. Ever since the 2000 election, these two authors had been arguing tirelessly that the demographic facts signified by that famous map augured well for the Democratic party. In a book bearing the now-embarrassing title *The Emerging Democratic Majority*—a play on Kevin Phillips's prescient book of 1969, *The Emerging Republican Majority*, Judis and Teixeira drew a profile of the new, winning coalition. Its members are the educated professionals, working women, minorities, and middle-class Americans who live in large metropolitan areas— "ideopolises," in the authors' coinage— and are affiliated with the technology sector, universities, social-service organizations, and government.

Today it still seems indisputable that these urban clusters will be increasingly important in national elections—and also that, as Judis and Teixeira demonstrated, they are growing faster than the older suburbs and rural areas in the South and West where Republicans have dominated. But

the core of the Judis-Teixeira argument rests less on shared demographics than on shared ideas. What has drawn this particular group of voters together, they give the collective name "progressive centrism."

If the name sounds somewhat oxymoronic, that is for a reason. On the one hand, the authors write, these voters "do not subscribe to the [Republican] gospel of deregulation and privatization. They want to supplement the market's invisible hand with the visible hand of government. ...They want to strengthen social-insurance programs...[and they] reflect the outlook of the social movements that first arose during the 60's....They oppose government interference in people's private lives...[and] support targeted programs to help minorities that trail the rest of the population in education and income."

But, on the other hand, this is not your father's brand of progressivism. Although these voters may indeed "favor government intervention," they do not, "except in very special circumstances," favor the government's supplanting and replacing the operation of the market....They want incremental, careful reforms that will substantially increase health-care coverage....They want aid to minorities, but they oppose the largescale imposition of quotas or the enactment of racial reparations.

And so forth. Judis and Teixeira are quite deliberate in defining what is to their mind this winning combination of fiery Democratic populism with the tempered incrementalism of "New Democrat" politics a la Bill Clinton. This "new synthesis," they believe, accurately reflects the transformation of America into a post-industrial society characterized by large, diverse metropolitan centers; it speaks to the interests and preferences not only of the blue (Democratic) states but of most denizens of "ideopolises" who are hungering for a new political brew. And it is the natural property of the Democratic party, its two components having been clearly if separately at work in, respectively, Clinton's 1992 centrist appeal and Gore's populist defiance of corporate power in 2000. The successful amalgam of these two strategies is what, in their view, will help usher in the new era of Democratic dominance.

After the divisive election of 2000, it was surely not unreasonable to suggest that a new brand of politics would emerge. But Judis and Teixeira's analysis, shaped by hopes as much as by facts, was out of date even as they were writing it, and is at odds with the current disposition of both political parties.

Concerning the Republicans, Judis and Teixeira are stuck in the year 1994, the year of Newt Gingrich's Contract with America. Their straw man is a GOP supposedly rife with racial hatred, disdainful of single mothers and homosexuals, hostile to all government programs, and eager to infiltrate religious orthodoxy into every nook and cranny of American life. This overheated caricature prevents them from recognizing a lesson that in retrospect can be seen emerging out of their own reading of the 2000 election data. Two years later, not only had major parts of the agenda of "progressive centrism" been seized by a Republican president, but the party he led was no longer, if it ever had been, the party of their imagining.

Judis and Teixeira are hardly the only observers who thought the Republicans were heading for the precipice in the mid-1990's. As Christopher Caldwell wrote in the *Atlantic Monthly* in 1998, the party had allowed itself to be captured by a Southern voting bloc that socially and culturally was far to the right of the rest of the country, and as a result it had lost the confidence of the electorate. But if voters once told pollsters that they trusted Democrats more on everything from education to the

economy to crime and taxes, that is surely not the case today.

In a Gallup survey conducted a few days after November's mid-term elections, respondents consistently held a much more positive image of Republicans than of Democrats, and regarded them as better equipped to lead the country by a margin of 57 to 47 percent. To be sure, those findings reflected the afterglow of a Republican electoral triumph, and would undergo revision in later surveys. But the fact remains that, thanks largely to Bush, Republicans have become more palatable to a majority of Americans, and they have done so by moving away from some of the defining themes of late 20th-century Republicanism.

I have already mentioned a number of signposts from last year, but the shift really goes back to the fall of 2001. It was then, in the weeks immediately following the attacks of September 11, that Bush sent a signal of things to come by adroitly acquiescing in Democratic demands to federalize airport security workers. The shift could be seen again last spring when he announced the imposition of tariffs on imported steel, a stunning retreat from the free trade principles he himself had advocated during his campaign for the presidency. Since then, he has signed a massive expansion of farm subsidies, reversing a market-driven policy instituted just a few years earlier; agreed to a corporate-accounting law that includes a high level of new regulation and a considerable expansion of federal intrusiveness; and created a $37-billion Department of Homeland Security that may augment and consolidate federal power to a breathtaking degree.

One can defend each of these initiatives on its merits, or at least try to explain why it has been politically necessary. But that is beside the point. Nowhere in this list can one find the themes—limited government, reduced spending, local empowerment—that preoccupied Republican leaders only a few election cycles ago.

As those themes have faded, so, too, have the cultural hot buttons that gave the GOP such strength among social and religious conservatives. As the columnist John Podhoretz has pointed out, it was only three years ago that prominent conservative spokesmen, notably including Lynne Cheney, appeared before Congress to condemn the violence purveyed in rap lyrics by stars like Eminem. But when Eminem's semi-autobiographical movie *8 Mile* opened to large crowds recently, not a syllable of conservative criticism was to be heard. Of course, rap singers in general and Eminem in particular have somewhat moderated the raw brutality of their message in recent months; but it is also true that, in the age of terrorism, the battle against the liberal culture has faded as a key component of Republican politics.

If once high-profile conservative causes are losing their punch, the same can be said of certain high-profile conservative spokesmen. Jerry Falwell may have permanently lost his place in acceptable conservative circles when, on the heels of the September 11 attacks, he appeared to place the blame on America's "tolerant" culture. More recently, the Bush White House has distanced itself from both Falwell and his fellow Christian broadcaster Pat Robertson for antagonistic remarks about the Muslim religion.

Nor are conservative Christian activists the only ones out of favor with the White House. In the lead-up to the mid-term elections, it was widely reported that Karl Rove, the President's top political strategist, was discouraging openly ideological candidacies. In California's GOP primaries, Richard Riordan, the former mayor of Los Angeles, known as a moderate, was said to be favored by the White House over the conservative activist Bill Simon.

In Minnesota, the majority leader of the state House of Representatives was reportedly dissuaded by Vice President Richard Cheney from challenging Democrat-turned-Republican Norm Coleman in the primary. Both stories, if true, reflect an effort to shape the public face of GOP challengers, and in retrospect the political judgment involved is hard to fault: Coleman's victory in Minnesota relied in part on his ability to attract Democratic voters, while Bill Simon, who won the Republican primary in California, went on to be trounced by the incumbent Gray Davis in a race that many thought Riordan would have won.

This is hardly to say that George W. Bush is out to create a Republican party in the mold of a James Jeffords or even a John McCain. After all, he pressed for and signed the largest tax-cut package in more than a decade and is now seeking to make those cuts permanent. He has consistently selected bona-fide conservatives as his nominees to the federal bench. He fought, successfully, to keep the new Homeland Security Department exempt from federal-employee union rules. He is a strong opponent of human cloning, and has severely restricted the use of stem cells in federal medical research. His administration has proposed privatizing thousands of government jobs. In his personal style, and in his religious faith, he appears genuinely conservative. And this is not even to mention his vigorous stance in foreign policy, clearly reminiscent of Ronald Reagan and clearly distinct from the typical Democrat of today.

But there is also no mistaking the fact that Bush is prepared to offer voters something different from Reaganism and Gingrichism, something that goes beyond even the "compassionate conservatism" he introduced in his campaign for the presidency. What he and his advisers—and his party appear to have grasped is that mustering the kind of bipartisan support required by a wartime Republican President depends on the ability to stand in or near the center, and so turn to advantage the same demographic and cultural trends that, a mere two years ago, seemed so threatening to the GOP's future. The question is whether the palpable successes of Bush and the new GOP as measured in the mid-term elections are an artifact of the moment, or whether they can be molded into something more permanent, and more meaningful.

That will depend in large measure on the Democrats, and on how they play the hand they have now been dealt. So far—and here again is where Judis and Teixeira go wrong—there are abundant signs that they will play it not by sticking to "progressive centrism" but by moving left. For all the alleged changes that the Democratic party underwent during the Clinton years, it now appears that its congressional wing is retreating to a familiar form of interest-group populism. Despite all the attempts to create a coalition of the center, the party as a whole remains hostage to public-employee unions, trial lawyers, and organized lobbyists of every kind.

The choice of the unreconstructed liberal Nancy Pelosi to lead the minority caucus in the House, together with the emergence of Senator Hillary Rodham Clinton in a leadership role in the Senate, is a clear indication of the left's determination to claim for its own the shreds of the party's fortunes. Similarly not to be ignored is Al Gore, still the most recognizable presidential aspirant in the Democratic field. In the last year, Gore has almost entirely abandoned the "New Democrat" creed by which he was once defined and moved sharply to the left, criticizing the administration's response to al Qaeda, its handling of the economy, and its alleged neglect of the changing American family.

If this pattern continues, one can safely predict that on the road to the next presidential campaign, even as Republicans continue to downplay their "wedge" issues, Democrats will be more and more likely to emphasize theirs—especially in such areas as environmental protection and guaranteed health insurance, already emerging as favored themes. So far, faced with challenges on these or similar issues—the Patient's Bill of Rights, protection of the domestic steel industry—Bush Republicans have tended to respond with their now-standard "me, too." But a more left-wing, populist Democratic party may render this strategy unworkable by robbing Bush of any chance of compromise.

That will be a testing moment for the GOP and, conceivably, an opportunity to define itself for the foreseeable future. If it is to hold on to its edge, the party may be driven to articulate a more consistent and more truly conservative approach to issues of policy, if not to evolve a true conservative philosophy of governance. This does not mean veering sharply right in a move mirroring the Democrats' turn to the left. It does mean, in the broadest terms, developing a constantly reiterated commitment to the virtues of limited government over expanded entitlements, to market incentives over command-and-control regulation, to competition in place of entrenched bureaucratic monopolies, to economic growth over austerity, to conservation over radical environmentalism.

Such an exercise has much to recommend it, and not just in order to reassure doubting conservatives that Republican politics is about more than winning elections from Democrats. There is, in fact, a real danger in the strategy being pursued by the White House. In the hands of a less gifted, or less convincing, politician than Bush, and in circumstances other than wartime, it may represent less a blueprint for future political dominance than a reversion to an older and thoroughly failed Republican role. I am thinking, of course, of the long decades after the New Deal when the GOP was defined primarily by its efforts to slow the inexorable march of liberal ideas—not by substituting better ones but by accommodating them and sanding down their sharper edges. This is essentially a defensive form of politics, and it is a losing proposition. By contrast, making the case for limited government in a consistent and serious and positive manner could actually increase the appeal of the GOP in the eyes of many centrist and/or traditional Democratic voters who have been drawn to it in the months since September 11.

Over the last three decades, the GOP has gone through a number of minor revolutions in an effort to reinvent itself. Kevin Phillips chronicled the start of the process in *The Emerging Republican Majority,* where he forecast a GOP majority based in the new entrepreneurial communities of the South and West rather than in the old WASP business elites. Ronald Reagan transformed the political face of the party, combining supply-side economics and anti-big-government themes at home with internationalism abroad. Fifteen years later, Gingrich shook up the party once again, demanding the reform of Congress and a shifting of power from Washington to state governments.

Today, Bush's mix of aggressive foreign policy, expanded government in the interest of domestic security, and a willingness to find a middle ground on domestic issues long owned by the Democrats has given him strengths that have defied almost every prediction of how his presidency would evolve. To be sure, he is a beneficiary of extraordinary circumstances. Nor do we yet know whether the brand of politics he has practiced is ultimately driven by expediency or by principle. But it is certain to set the terms of political debate for the balance of his first term, inform his reelection bid two years hence, and just possibly determine whether his party will emerge unexpectedly as a new political majority.

THE CONTINUING DEBATE:
The Odds-On Favorite in the Future

What Is New

It is safe to say the political currents in the country had shifted considerably between the time advocate Daniel Casse wrote his essay in early 2003 and this writing in the fall of that year. The problems of governing a defeated Iraq and a sagging economy had undermined George Bush's popularity. As a result, what had earlier seemed would be a hopeless run by a sacrificial Democrat against an unassailable incumbent president showed signs of becoming a real contest. Polls found mixed results. One August 2003 poll found 40% of respondents describing themselves as Democrats or Democratic learners, 38% in those categories for the Republicans, 15% true independents and 8% identifying with another party or unsure. Another poll that month was somewhat better for the GOP. When asked in August 2003, "Overall, which party, the Democrats or the Republicans, do you trust to do a better job in coping with the main problems the nation faces over the next few years?" 40% of the respondents replied the Republicans, 39% said the Democrats, 3% thought they would do an equally good job, 10% thought neither party would perform well, and 7% had no opinion. However, specific issues made a huge difference in party evaluations. When asked which party would do better dealing with the economy, the Democrats bested the Republicans by 47% to 37%. When respondents were asked about terrorism, 54% favored the Republicans compared to only 25% who thought the Democrats would be more successful.

Where to Find More

A good recent study that emphasizes the recent changes in the Democratic and Republican parties and their support and that makes a strong case for parties as a vital part of the American democratic process is Larry J. Sabato and Bruce Larson, *The Party's Just Begun: Shaping Political Parties for America's Future* (Longman, 2002). The full-scale version of the argument by advocates John B. Judis and Roy Teixeira is their *The Emerging Democratic Majority* (Scribner 2002). As a follow up, to learn how one of these two "pro-Democrat" advocates evaluated the impact of the Republican gains in the 2002 elections, read Ruy Teixeira, "Deciphering the Democrats' Debacle," *Washington Monthly Online*, May 2003 at: http://www.washingtonmonthly.com/features/2003/0305/teixeira.htm. A view of the future of party politics that is more optimistic about Republican chances is Lee Edwards, *Conservative Revolution: The Movement That Remade America* (Free Press, 2002). Also worthwhile are the Web sites of the two major parties: the Republican National Committee is at http://www.rnc.org/ and the Democratic National Committee at http://www.democrats.org/.

What More to Do

The most important thing to do is to become a part of the decision. Neither Judis and Teixeira nor Casse argues that the emergence of a Democratic or Republican majority that will dominate politics in the foreseeable future is certain. The party Web sites are a place to start if you identify with one of the two. For a nonpartisan effort aimed especially at young adults, visit the Web site of Rock the Vote at: http://www.rockthevote.com. Project Vote Smart has a good site to learn about candidates and issues at: http://www.vote-smart.org/.

10 VOTING/CAMPAIGNS/ELECTIONS

THE ELECTORAL COLLEGE:
Abolish *or* Preserve?

ABOLISH

ADVOCATE: Becky Cain, President, League of Women Voters

SOURCE: Testimony during hearings on "Proposals for Electoral College Reform: H.J. Res. 28 and H.J. Res. 43" before the U.S. House of Representatives Committee on the Judiciary, Subcommittee on the Constitution, September 4, 1997

PRESERVE

ADVOCATE: Judith A. Best, Professor of Political Science, State University of New York at Cortland

SOURCE: Testimony during hearings on "Proposals for Electoral College Reform: H.J. Res. 28 and H.J. Res. 43" before the U.S. House of Representatives Committee on the Judiciary, Subcommittee on the Constitution, September 4, 1997

Sometimes figuring out your course grade in college can get pretty complicated. Your raw score on tests may not exactly equate to your final "curved" grade. Determining the final score in the Electoral College can be a little like this. The raw score (the popular vote) and the final score (the vote of the electors) never match up. In 1980, for example, Ronald Reagan received 90.1% of the electors' votes, while getting only 51.6% of the popular vote. It is even possible in the Electoral College to have a higher raw score than anyone else yet lose. Al Gore received 51,003,238 popular votes to only 50,459,624 votes for George Bush in the 2000 presidential election. Yet Bush received 50.4% of the electoral vote compared to 49.4% for Gore.

Then, like in some college grading, the Electoral College has other variables. For example, electors selected by the voters in many states can legally vote for someone other than the candidate to whom they are pledged. Such unexpected votes are not common, but they have occurred in 10 elections. For example, a disgruntled elector from Alabama who was supposed to vote for Democratic candidate Adlai Stevenson in 1956 instead cast his ballot for Walter B. Jones, a judge from his hometown who was not even running.

These oddities and other quirks bring up three questions. What is the Electoral College? Where did it come from? Should we keep it? The first two questions are easier. The Electoral College is an indirect process for selecting the U.S. president. Each state selects a number of electors equal to its representation in Congress, and the District of Columbia gets three electors, for a total of 538 electors. The exact process for choosing electors varies by state, but as a general rule each party or candidate selects a slate of electors. It is for one of these slates that the people vote in November. In all states except Maine and Nebraska, there is a "winner-take-all" system in which the slate that receives the most votes wins. Then the individual electors cast their separate ballots for president and vice president in December. The ballots are sent to Congress, where they are counted in early January. It takes a majority of all electoral votes (270) to win. If no individual receives a majority, then the House selects a president from among the candidates with the three highest electoral votes. Each state casts one vote in the House, and it requires a majority of the states (26) to win. The Senate, with each member voting individually, chooses a vice president from among the top two electoral vote recipients. It is not possible to detail here all the possible permutations, but the choice has gone to the House twice (1800 and 1824), and on three occasions (1876, 1888, and 2000) the candidate with the most popular votes has lost the electoral vote.

The Electoral College was established for two reasons. One is that it stressed the role of the states. They can choose electors as they wish and are not even obligated to have popular elections. The second motive for the Electoral College was to insulate the selection of president from the people. As Alexander Hamilton explained in *Federalist* #68 (1788), he and others worried that the "general mass" would not " possess the information and discernment requisite to such complicated investigations," raising the possibility of "tumult and disorder."

The question is whether to abolish or preserve the Electoral College. Throughout its history, the process has been controversial, and it has provoked over 700 proposals in Congress to reform or eliminate it. Yet it survives. The following articles lay out their respective attack on and defense of the Electoral College, but beyond those substantive arguments, the process continues for two additional reasons. One is that changing it would require a constitutional amendment, most probably through a two-thirds vote by each house of Congress and ratification by three-fourths of the state. Obtaining such supermajorities is very difficult. The second procedural reason the Elector College survives is that, for contradictory reasons, it appeals to many states. States with big populations, such as California with its 55 electoral votes (more than 20% of those needed to win), believe they gain political advantage through their hefty share of the electoral votes. States with small populations also see political advantage. Wyoming may have only 55/100ths of one percent of the electoral vote, but that is more than three times the state's 17/100ths of one percent of the U.S. population. States in a middle position come out mathematically about right. For example, New Jersey with 8.1 million people and 15 electoral votes has 2.86% of the population and 2.78% of the electoral votes. Thus the Electoral College seems either politically favorable or neutral to almost every state, making an amendment even more difficult to pass and ratify.

POINTS TO PONDER

➤ Becky Cain, testifying in 1997, predicts a fiasco if, once again, a candidate were to lose the electoral vote while winning the popular vote. Three years later that occurred, yet there were no widespread protest demonstrations. Why not?

➤ Judith Best contends that abolishing the Electoral College would diminish the influence of minority groups. Why might this occur?

➤ Which is more important, the aspect of federalism that is part of the Electoral College vote calculation or the principle of "one person—one vote"?

The Electoral College:
Abolish

BECKY CAIN

Mr. Chairman, members of the subcommittee, I am Becky Cain, president of the League of Women Voters.

I am pleased to be here today to express the support of the League [League of Women Voters of the United States] for a constitutional amendment to abolish the Electoral College and establish the direct election of the President and Vice President of the United States by popular vote of the American people.

The League of Women Voters of the United States is a non-partisan citizen organization with 150,000 members and supporters in all fifty states, the District of Columbia and the Virgin Islands. For over 75 years, Leagues across the country have worked to educate the electorate, register voters and make government at all levels more accessible and responsive to the average citizen.

Since 1970, the League has supported an amendment to the Constitution that would abolish the Electoral College and establish a direct, popular vote for the President and Vice President of the United States. The League arrived at this position through its time-honored study and consensus process. Leagues in over 1,000 communities across the country participated in the study and came to the same conclusion: our method of electing a President must be changed to ensure a more representative government.

Political developments since the 1970s have only underscored the need for the elimination of the Electoral College system. The downward trend in voter participation, coupled with increased cynicism and skepticism amongst the public about the ability of elected leaders to provide meaningful representation are the warning signs of a potential electoral fiasco.

Picture if you will a future national election in which a presidential candidate receives a majority of the popular vote, but is denied the 270 votes necessary for election by the Electoral College. This has already happened once in our nation's history, when, in 1888, Grover Cleveland outpolled Benjamin Harrison in the popular vote but lost the Electoral College vote by 233 to 168. It caused a public furor then, when political office was often gained through back-room deals and closed-door maneuvering. Imagine the public outcry today, after a long primary campaign and a grueling race for the Presidency. Imagine the public's rage at being denied their candidate of choice.

Now go one step further. Consider a close three-way race for President in which no candidate earns the necessary Electoral College votes to win. This has happened twice before in our nation's history, in 1801 and 1825, when the House of Representatives chose Thomas Jefferson and John Quincy Adams, respectively. While the League believes both of these men were great presidents, we are troubled about the potential for a future presidential candidate with the highest number of popular votes to lose the election in a House of Representatives dominated by one or another political party.

In the twentieth century, we have only narrowly avoided a series of constitutional crises in which the Electoral College could have over-ruled the popular vote.

- In the 1916 presidential election, a shift of only 2,000 votes in California would have given Charles Evans Hughes the necessary electoral votes to defeat Woodrow Wilson, despite Wilson's half-million vote nationwide plurality.

- In 1948, a shift of only 30,000 votes in three states would have delivered the White House to Governor [Thomas] Dewey, in spite of the fact that he trailed President Truman by some 2.1 million popular votes.

- In 1960, a shift of only 13,000 votes in five states (5,000 in Illinois, 5,000 in Missouri, 1,200 in New Mexico, 1,300 in Nevada and 200 in Hawaii) would have made Richard Nixon president.

- In 1968, a shift of 42,000 votes in three states (Alaska, Missouri and New Jersey) would have denied Nixon an Electoral College victory and thrown the election into the House of Representatives.

- In 1976, a shift of only 9,300 votes (5,600 from Ohio and 3,700 from Hawaii) would have elected Gerald Ford, even though he trailed Jimmy Carter in the popular vote by 1.6 million ballots.

Apart from the public outcry that would be caused by a circumvention of the popular will, there are a number of other serious flaws in the Electoral College system.

The Electoral College system is fundamentally unfair to voters. In a nation where voting rights are grounded in the one person, one vote principle, the Electoral College is a hopeless anachronism.

The current system is unfair for two reasons.

First, a citizen's individual vote has more weight if he or she lives in a state with a small population than if that citizen lives in a state with a large population. For example, each electoral vote in Alaska is equivalent to approximately 112,000 people. Each electoral vote in New York is equivalent to approximately 404,000 eligible people (based on 1990 census data). And that's if everyone votes!

The system is also unfair because a citizen's individual vote has more weight if the percentage of voter participation in the state is low. For example, if only half of all people in Alaska vote, then each electoral vote is equivalent to roughly 56,000 people.

Moreover, the electoral vote does not reflect the volume of voter participation within a state. If only a few voters go to the polls, all the electoral votes of the state are still cast.

Finally, the Electoral College system is flawed because the constitution does not bind presidential electors to vote for the candidates to whom they have been pledged. For example, in 1948, 1960 and 1976, individual electors pledged to the top two vote getters cast their votes for third place finishers and also-rans. Defecting electors in a close race could cause a crisis of confidence in our electoral system.

For all these reasons, the League believes that the presidential election method should incorporate the one-person, one-vote principle. The President should be directly elected by the people he or she will represent, just as the other federally elected officials are in this country. Direct election is the most representative system. It is the only system that guarantees the President will have received the most popular votes. It also encourages voter participation by giving voters a direct and equal role in the election of the President.

Of course, a direct popular vote does not preclude the possibility of a close three-way race in which no candidate receives a majority, or even a plurality, of the votes. The League believes that if no candidate receives more than 40 percent of the popular vote, then a national run-off election should be held.

Until there is a constitutional amendment to abolish the Electoral College, the League supports the early establishment of clear rules and procedures for the House and Senate to handle their responsibilities in electing the President and Vice President if there is no majority vote in the Electoral College.

Procedures should be established to avoid the last-minute partisan wrangling that would inevitably take place. In addition, we believe any congressional vote for President must take place in full public view, with individual representative's votes entered into the Congressional Record.

When the constitution was first written, our nation was a vastly different kind of democracy than it is today. Only white, male property owners could vote. The 15th Amendment gave black men the right to vote. The 17th Amendment provided for direct popular election of the Senate. The 19th Amendment gave women the vote. The 26th Amendment established the right of citizens 18 years of age and older to vote.

The time has come to take the next step to ensure a broad-based, representative democracy. Fairness argues for it. Retaining the fragile faith of American voters in our representative system demands it. We urge the House and the Senate to pass a constitutional amendment abolishing the Electoral College system and establishing the direct popular election of our President and Vice President.

The Electoral College: Preserve

JUDITH A. BEST

Critics of the electoral vote system believe that the principle of democratic legitimacy is numbers alone, and therefore they think the system is indefensible. On the contrary, the electoral vote system is a paradigm— the very model—of the American democracy, and thus is quite easy to defend. For all practical purposes it is a direct popular federal election. (The Electors are mere ciphers, and the office of elector, but not the electoral votes, can be abolished.) The critics' principle of democratic legitimacy is inadequate because it is apolitical and antifederal. Logically it boils down to: the majority must win and the minority must lose no matter what they lose. It is a formula for majority tyranny. But majority rule is not the principle of our Constitution. Rather it is majority rule with minority consent. The critics, however, think that because the system does not follow an arithmetical model it may produce the "wrong" winner. In fact, I contend, because it is federal it produces the right winner.

The following passage from my recent book, *The Choice of the People? Debating the Electoral College* explains my point:

Politics and mathematics are two very different disciplines. Mathematics seeks accuracy, politics seeks harmony. In mathematics an incorrect count loses all value once it is shown to be wrong. In politics even though some people are out-voted they still have value and must be respected in defeat. Efforts must be made to be considerate and even generous to those who lost the vote, to make then feel they are part of the community, for if they feel alienated they may riot in the streets. Further, mathematical questions, like those in all the sciences, deal with truth and falsehood. But politics is an art, not a science. Political questions do not deal primarily with truth and falsehood, but with good and bad. We do not ask whether a political decision on war or taxation or welfare or agricultural subsidies is true. We ask, is the policy good for the country? And, will it actually achieve its purpose?

Those who confuse politics and mathematics, the head counters, operate on an unstated assumption that the will of the people is out there like some unsurveyed land, and all we need do is send out the surveyors with accurately calibrated instruments to record what is there. They also assume that our democratic republic is a ship without a specific destination. Whatever most of the people want, most of the people must get, and the minority be damned. Mathematical accuracy being their sole criterion for legitimacy, they make a great fuss about politically imposed devices, intermediary institutions like the electoral vote system with its federal principle and its winner-take-all rule. From their perspective, such majority building and structuring devices complicate their self-assigned task, distort the accuracy of their count and possibly produce the "wrong" result.

If their assumptions were correct they would have a point. But their assumptions are false. Ours is a ship of state bound for a port called Liberty. On such a ship majority rule doesn't suffice without the consent of the minority. Their assumption about the will of the people is particularly false in this vast and varied country, in a continental republic populated by a people who do not share a common religion, race, or ethnic heritage, in a commercial republic populated by people with diverse and competing economic interests. In such a country the will of the people and the will of the majority can be two very different things. Therefore, the will of the people—that one thing which all can share, which is the goal of liberty for all—must be constructed and periodically reconstructed. This requires a political, not a mathematical process.

In this country, it requires a federal political process. The federal principle is one of the two fundamental structural principles of our Constitution (the other being the separation of powers). The proposals to abolish the Electoral College are proposals to abolish the federal principle in presidential elections. All of our national elective offices are based on the federal principle—they are state based elections for we are a nation of states. Thus our national motto: *E Pluribus Unum*.

The federal principle in presidential elections forces presidential candidates to build broad cross-national political coalitions. Thereby it produces presidents who can govern because of their broad cross-national support. In politics as well as in physics there is such a thing as a critical mass. In presidential elections numbers of votes are necessary but not sufficient. To create the critical mass necessary for a president to govern, his votes must be properly distributed. This means he must win states and win states in more than one region of the country.

Under the federal presidential election system, a successful candidate can't simply promise everything to one section of the country and neglect the others. Analogy: Why are professional football teams required to win games in order to get into the playoffs and win the Super Bowl? Why not simply select the teams that scored the most points during the regular season? Any football fan can tell you why. Such a process wouldn't produce the right winner. Teams would run up the score against their weakest opponents, and the best teams in the most competitive divisions would have the least chance to get into the playoffs. Such a system isn't the proper test of the team talent and ability. A nonfederal election is not a proper test of support for the president.

If we abandon the federal principle in presidential elections, we will be abandoning a national consensus building device by allowing candidates to promise everything to the populous Eastern megalopolis, or to promise everything to white Christians, or to suburbanites who are now half of all the voters. These are formulas for inability to govern or even civil war. And a system, like direct popular election, based on raw unstructured numbers alone rather than on the structuring federal principle, would effectively reduce the influence of minorities who often are the swing votes in closely divided states—groups like farmers who are only 2 percent of national population or blacks who are only 12 percent.

We need to remember that when we change the rules, we change the game and the game strategy and the skills needed to win. Under the federal principle successful candidates must have consensus building skills. The goal of politics in this country is harmony—majority rule with minority consent. But when and why would a minority consent to majority rule? The answer is only if the minority can see that on some occasions and on some vital issues it can be part of the majority. It is irrational to consent to a game in which you can never win anything at all. To gain minority consent, the Framers created many devices to allow minorities to be part of the game, devices that give minorities more influence than their raw numbers would warrant including the state equality principle for representation in the Senate and the state distracting principle for the House of Representatives. (The majority party in the House is often "over-represented" if our measure is raw numbers of votes nationally aggregated.) Then, of course, there is the state equality principle in voting on constitutional amendments. And there is the three-fourths requirement for passage of amendments. Such devices are designed to give minorities an influential voice in defining the national interest. The president is a major player in defining the national interest, and therefore it is necessary that the presidency be subjected to the moderating influence of a federal election system.

An equally important outcome of a state based election system is that it serves to balance local and national interests. It is not just racial, religious, ethnic or occupational minorities that must be protected, there are local minorities whose consent must be sought; the people in small states must be protected against misuse of the phrase "the national interest." My favorite example is the problem of nuclear waste which none of us want in our backyards—not in my state. The rest of us can outvote Utah—so let's turn Utah into our national nuclear waste dump. This is majority tyranny in action. Nuclear waste is a national problem and the burden of solving it should not be placed on the people of one state without their consent. Since the president is a major player in making national policy, it is just as important that he be sensitive to balancing

national and local interests, and the federal election system is designed to make it so. The right winner is a presidential candidate who recognizes the necessity and often the justice in balancing national and local interests. As Jefferson said, "the will of the majority to be rightful must be reasonable." The federal principle even and especially in presidential elections is a device for building reasonable majorities.

The opponents of the electoral vote system are head counters who confuse an election with a census. In a census our goal is mere accuracy. We want to know how many people are married or divorced, or have incomes over or under $20,000, or are Catholic or Protestant etc. In short, we want to break down the population into its multiple individual parts. In an election, especially a presidential election, we want to bring the people together. We want to build consensus, to build the support necessary and sufficient for our president to govern.

The proponents of direct national election think their system solves problems, but in fact it creates problems that are addressed or avoided by the federal election system. Presidential elections have multiple goals. Obviously we want to fill the office with someone who can govern, but we also want a swift, sure decision, and we want to reduce the premium on fraud, and most of us want to support the two party system—a major source of national stability and a consensus, coalition-building system.

From this perspective, the current system has been very successful. Since 1836 with the almost universal adoption of the state unit rule, awarding all of a state's electoral votes to the winner of the popular plurality, we have had never had a contingency election. That's a proven record of 160 years. And we know the reason why: the magnifier effect of the state unit rule, a.k.a. the winner-take-all system. The victor in the popular vote contest for president will have a higher percentage of the electoral vote. The Magnifier effect does not exaggerate the mandate—popular vote percentages are widely reported, not electoral vote percentages. The magnifier effect is not like a fisherman's story in which the size of the fish grows with the telling. Rather it is like the strong fishing line that serves to bring the fish, whatever its size, safely to shore. It supports the moderate two-party system, and balances national and state interests. And it makes the general election the only election.

Of course, there would be no magnifier effect under direct non-federal election, and the result is that contingency elections would become the rule. Under one proposal there would be a national run off if no candidate received 50 percent of the popular vote. This provision would turn the general election into a national primary, proliferate candidacies and weaken or destroy the two-party system. It would also increase the potential for fraud and result in contested general elections with every ballot box in the United States having to be reopened and recounted under court supervision. Even the Left-handed Vegetarians Party could bring a court challenge because 1 percent or less of the popular vote could trigger a runoff election. And there would be a reason to challenge. In a runoff election even candidates who are not in the contest can win something by making a deal with one of the remaining two in return for support in the runoff. Not only would this mean an extended period of uncertainty about who the president will be—a temptation to foreign enemies, but also little time for the orderly transfer of power.

Most proponents of direct election, recognizing that to require a majority of the popular votes would produce these problems, suggest a 40 percent instead of a 50 percent runoff rule. The fact that most

supporters of direct election are willing to make this concession indicates the seriousness of the problems attending contingency elections. This is a compromise of their principle—the arithmetical majority principle. Logically, on their principle, whenever no one polls 50 percent plus one vote there should be a runoff election.

And 40 percent is not a magical figure. It could be 42 or 44% with similar result—frequent runoffs. It is true that only one president, Lincoln, (who was not on the ballot in 10 states) failed to reach-the 40 percent plurality figure. However, history under the current system cannot be used to support the 40 percent figure because when you change the rules you change the game. Under the current rules we have had 17 minority presidential terms—presidents who came to the office with less than 50 percent of the popular vote. The last two are Clinton's terms. The list includes some of our best presidents, not only Lincoln, but also Wilson (twice), Polk and Truman. Seventeen minority presidential terms out of 42 presidents! The unit rule magnified their popular pluralities into electoral vote majorities because they won states.

But under direct nonfederal election there would be no magnifier effect. Potential candidates would recognize that multiple entries would be likely to trigger a runoff wherein one losing candidate could win a veto promise, another a Supreme Court nomination and a third a special interest subsidy in return for an endorsement in the runoff. And there is no reason to believe all such deals would be struck in the open. There would be no incentive for coalition building prior to the general election. The two major national parties would lose all control over the presidential nomination process—their lifeblood. Factional candidates, single issue candidates, extremist candidates would serve as spoilers. As one commentator noted, on the day prior to the election, the *New York Times* would have to publish a twenty-page supplement simply to identify all the candidates.

Add to this the second chance psychology that would infect voters, and you have the formula for a national ordeal. Second chance psychology arises from the recognition that a popular vote runoff is a real possibility. Many a voter, thinking he will have another chance to vote in a runoff, will use his general election vote to protest something or other—to send a message.

Recounts would be demanded not only to determine who won, but also whether any candidate actually polled the 40% minimum, and if not which two candidates would be in the runoff—Under the unit rule magnifier effect which discourages multiple candidacies, we have already had five elections in which the popular vote margin was less than one percent. In the 1880 election the margin was one tenth of one percent. If such could happen under the current system where it is unlikely to trigger a runoff, it surely will happen under a 40 percent rule with a hair trigger runoff system. Weeks or months could pass with the outcome in doubt. One candidate could claim victory and start naming his cabinet only to be told some weeks later that he would have to participate in a runoff.

Further, the electorate wearies of prolonged elections. Even in the sports world players as well as teams reach a point where they want an end to it, and so accept sudden death rules. It is so important to fill the office on a timely basis that we have even had one president, Gerald Ford, who was not confirmed by a national election. Ford succeeded to the office on the resignation of his predecessor, Richard Nixon, but unlike vice presidents who had succeeded before him, he had been nominated by Nixon and confirmed by congressional vote under the provisions for filling vice presidential vacancies in the Twenty-fifth Amendment.

No election system is perfect, but the current system has borne the test of time. It has never rejected the winner of a popular vote majority. In every case but one it gave the victory to the winner of the popular plurality. And that one case proves the rule. Cleveland, who lost in the electoral vote, won the popular vote while running a sectional campaign. He did not seek to broaden his support; he focused his message on one section of the country. Unintentionally, he thereby sent a message about the current system to all future presidential candidates: Remember 1888! Don't run a sectional campaign! Further, he won the popular vote by only eight tenths of one percent! This was an election that verged on a tie. Since a timely decision is so important, a reasonable tiebreaker is the win states federal principle.

The proposed amendments would deform not reform the Constitution. It is not just the presidency that is at risk here if the federal principle is illegitimate in presidential elections, why isn't it illegitimate for Senate and House elections? Why should a state with half a million people have the same representation in the Senate as a state with twenty million people? Why should every state have at least one representative in the House? Why shouldn't states with very small populations have to share a representative with folks in another state? And why should each state regardless of its population size have an equal vote on constitutional amendments? The Framers knew the answer to these questions—the federal principle. It is true that the electoral vote system did not work out in precisely the fashion that the Framers anticipated, but it did evolve in conformity to the federal principle and the separation of powers. I have no doubt that they would recognize this if they were here today. It evolved in conformity with the federal spirit of the constitution, the "great discovery," the Framers themselves made.

For this, let us turn to Alexis de Tocqueville, who commenting [in *Democracy in America*, 1835] on the federal principle in the Constitution, called it "a wholly novel theory, which may be considered as a great discovery in modern political science." He goes on to explain that combines the best of both worlds. He says that its advantage is to unite the benefits and avoid the weaknesses of small and large societies. He learned this not only from observation, but also from reading James Madison in *Federalist 39*, who said that our form of government "is, in strictness, neither a national nor a federal Constitution, but a combination of both."

Madison's word "combination" is the key. The federal principle is a "great discovery," because it is a combination like an alloy— my term not his. We create alloys because we want to combine the advantages and avoid the weakness of two different things. We fuse copper and zinc to create brass because brass is harder, more malleable and more ductile than copper. We create steel alloys for the same reason. The federal system is an alloy. It not only makes us strong as a nation, it also allows us to be diverse and flexible, to experiment. It thereby increases our freedom without destroying our national unity. Tocqueville was right; it was a "great discovery" of modern political science. Let us preserve it.

THE CONTINUING DEBATE:
The Electoral College

What Is New

Generally, the country reacted mildly to the oddities of the 2000 election. A few proposals to abolish the Electoral College were introduced in Congress, but they died in committee. Nor did the public react strongly. When one poll pointed out the popular vote/electoral vote mismatch and asked Americans about their reaction, 51% said the outcome was "fair," 46% thought it "unfair," and 3% were unsure. Yet, numerous polls also found about 60% of respondents in favor of instituting direct popular election of the president. Interestingly, these results are fairly consistent with other opinion surveys going back as far as 1948. Thus Americans were willing to abide by the rules as they stood but also favored changing those rules. One has to wonder, though, if most people understand the implications of such a change. One poll that asked respondents if they clearly understood the Electoral College found that 69% said they did, just 27% said they did not, and 4% were uncertain. Yet when another poll asked people what the Electoral College did (correct answer: elect the president), only 20% gave the right answer, 35% gave an incorrect answer, and 46% confessed they did not know.

Where to Find More

An edited book in which contributors discuss various alternatives to the Electoral College and the implications of each is Paul D. Schumaker and, Burdett A. Loomis, *Choosing a President: The Electoral College and Beyond* (Chatham House, 2002). For a defense of the Electoral College, read Gary L. Gregg's edited volume, *Securing Democracy: Why We Have an Electoral College* (Westview, 2001). A valuable Web site for further research is that of the Office of the Federal Register in the National Archives at http://www.archives.gov/federal_register/. The site even has an interactive function that you can use to try to predict the electoral vote count in the next presidential election. Also excellent is the information on the Electoral College on the site of the Federal Election Commission at: http://www.fec.gov/elections.html.

What More to Do

Calculate your state's percentage of the national population and its percentage of the electoral vote. Based on this equation, would your state gain or lose political advantage if the Electoral College were to be abolished?

In addition to debating the future of the Electoral College, it is important to consider the alternatives. If the Electoral College were abolished, how would you determine who is on the ballot? That is now governed by state law, and the candidates vary from state to state. In 2000, there were 16 candidates on one or more state ballots. Some were one-state candidates, such as the Prohibition Party's Earl Dodge, who received 208 votes in Colorado. A national ballot qualifying procedure that was too difficult would restrict democratic choice. A standard that was too easy might replicate the gubernatorial recall election in California in 2003, with 135 candidates on the ballot. Then there is the question of what to do in races with three or more contenders. Does the candidate with the most votes win, even if that is less than 50.1%, or should there be a run-off system to eventually achieve a majority vote? Just since World War II, no presidential candidate has received a majority in 6 (1948, 1960, 1968, 1992, 1996, 2000) of the 14 presidential elections. So, if not the Electoral College, then what?

11

CONGRESS

CONGRESSIONAL TERM LIMITS:
Promoting Choice *or* Restricting Choice?

PROMOTING CHOICE

ADVOCATE: Paul Jacob, Executive Director, U.S. Term Limits

SOURCE: Testimony during hearings on "Limiting Terms of Office for Members of the U.S. Senate and U.S. House of Representatives," U.S. House of Representatives, Committee on the Judiciary, Subcommittee on the Constitution, January 22, 1997

RESTRICTING CHOICE

ADVOCATE: John R. Hibbing, Professor of Political Science, University of Nebraska

SOURCE: Testimony during hearings on "Limiting Terms of Office for Members of the U.S. Senate and U.S. House of Representatives," U.S. House of Representatives, Committee on the Judiciary, Subcommittee on the Constitution, January 22, 1997

One way this debate could have been entitled was with a riddle: "When Does Restricting Voter Choice Improve Democracy?" An alternative riddle/title might have been, "When Does Unrestricted Voter Choice Diminish Democracy?" Those who advocate limiting the number of terms members of Congress may serve argue that incumbents have advantages that make it nearly impossible for challengers to unseat them, thereby limiting the "real" choice of voters. Opponents counter that, among other drawbacks, term limits abridge the voters' democratic right to choose whomever they wish to represent them for as long as they wish.

Statistically, once someone gets elected to Congress they have an extraordinarily good chance of being reelected again. For example, during elections between 1980 and 2002, about 90% of all incumbent members of Congress sought another term, and of those who did, voters returned 93% of the representatives and 89% of the senators. Moreover, incumbents in House races received an average of 71% of the vote in 2002. The senators in office in 2003 had amassed an average 62% of the vote in their previous election. Also indisputable is the fact that the average number of years a person spends in Congress has increased over time. During the 1800s only 3% of representatives and 11% of senators served more than 12 years. Those figures jumped to 27% and 32% during the 1900s, and since 1947 to 35% and 41% respectively.

There are numerous reasons why incumbents have an advantage, which, in sum, create a positive view by most people of their individual members of Congress. One survey found that 62% of respondents approved of the job their members of Congress were doing, only 17% disapproved, and 21% were not sure. This is remarkable given that only 43% of those respondents approved of the job Congress as an institution was doing, with 33% disapproving and 24% unsure.

Term limits have long applied to the tenure of many chief executives. The presidency had a two-term tradition until Franklin Roosevelt sought and won four terms. Soon thereafter, the Twenty-Second Amendment (1951) made the two-term limit mandatory. Additionally, 36 states have term limits for governor. Recently, the idea of also limiting the terms of state and national legislators began to become prominent. California and Oklahoma passed the first such legislation in 1990. It was an idea whose time had come, and soon 20 other states followed suit. Most of these restrictions were enacted by direct democracy techniques, including initiatives and referendums.

Opponents of term limits quickly challenged their constitutionality. In 1995 by a 6 to 3 vote in *U.S. Term Limits, Inc. v. Thornton*, the U.S. Supreme Court struck down the limits that Arkansas (and by implication all other states) had placed on terms in the U.S. Congress. Term limits on state legislatures, by contrast, are matters primarily of state constitutional law, and in this realm, the federal courts and most state courts have upheld term limits.

The Supreme Court decision means that it would be necessary to amend the Constitution in order to limit the number of terms that members of the U.S. Senate and House of Representatives can serve. Part of the "Contract with America" put forth by the successful Republican congressional campaign in 1994 was a pledge to work for such a constitutional amendment, with a limit of two terms (12 years) for senators and 6 terms (12 years) for members of the House. Numerous such proposals were introduced in Congress in 1995, and others have been submitted since then. But none have gathered sufficient support. The "hot topic" of the 1990s faded somewhat in face of the daunting prospect of getting two-thirds of each of the two houses to pass a constitutional amendment and thereby truncate their own political careers. This fate has, among other things, increased the calls to adopt national direct democracy procedures (see Debate 19) and to amend the Constitution so that states can initiate amendments to the U.S. Constriction (see Debate 20). What many see as the problem of entrenched legislators remains, however. The senior senator in the 108th Congress, Robert Byrd, has held his seat since 1959 when Dwight D. Eisenhower was president, and the dean of the House, John Dingle, began his tenure four years before that in 1955 when the current president, George W. Bush was nine years old. As a historical note, the record for the longest combined service in Congress (57 years) is held by Carl Hayden, who served in the House from the time of Arizona's admission to the union in 1912 to 1927, then was in the Senate until 1969. The oldest member ever of Congress was South Carolina Strom Thurmond, who retired at age 100 in 2003 after 48 years in the Senate.

POINTS TO PONDER

➤ Would term limits enhance or diminish Congress' power compared to the president?

➤ John Hibbing notes that senior members of Congress are often more effective in terms of getting legislation passed. Is this because they gain expertise or because they use the power structure to limit the role of junior members?

➤ What impact do you think term limits would have on the proportion of under-represented groups (such as women and racial and ethnic minorities) in Congress?

Congressional Term Limits:
Promoting Choice

PAUL JACOB

America has one clear and decisive advantage over the rest of the world: Our political system.

Our system is unique a democratic republic with constitutional limits on the federal government. It's a system designed to maximize individual freedom and citizen control of government at all levels. Our forebears not only set up this system of protected freedoms, but also recognized the need for change, for continual reform, and for constitutional amendment in order to preserve and enhance our freedom.

George Washington said in his farewell address, "The basis of our political systems is the right of the people to make and alter their constitutions of government." President [Abraham] Lincoln explained: "The country, with its institutions, belongs to the people who inhabit it. Whenever they shall grow weary of the existing government, they can exercise their Constitutional right of amending it." As Thomas Jefferson said to those who object to amending the Constitution, "We might as well require a man to wear still the coat which fitted him when a boy."

The vast majority of Americans today want to amend their Constitution. They want congressional term limits of three terms for House members and two terms for Senators.

EXPERIENCE WITH TERM LIMITS

Term limits is not a new idea. Democracy as far back as Aristotle has known term limits, or rotation in office. Certainly our Founders appreciated rotation in office. John Adams, Ben Franklin, Thomas Jefferson all spoke

to the need for limited tenure in public office. Today, term limits are the law of the land for the President, 40 state governors, 20 state legislatures and thousands of local elected officials including many large cities most notably New York and Los Angeles. Americans support congressional term limits not only for what they hope it will do to the culture in Congress, but for what it has already done at other levels of government.

According to Jody Newman, former head of the National Women's Political Caucus, "Our political system is tremendously biased in favor of incumbents." While this has slowed the progress of women and minorities into elected office, term limits are helping to bring more women, minorities and people from all walks of life into politics. This has been the case in cities like New Orleans and Kansas City where record numbers of minorities now hold office as well as the legislature in California which, according to the *Los Angeles Times*, now includes "a former U.S. Air Force fighter pilot, a former sheriff-coroner, a paralegal, a retired teacher, a video store owner, a businesswoman-homemaker, a children's advocate, an interior designer...and a number of businessmen."

Term limits are bringing more competition, and arguably fairer competition. A recent study by Kermit Daniel of the University of Pennsylvania and Joan R. Lott of the University of Chicago concluded: "California's legislative term limits have dramatically reduced campaign expenditures, while at the same time that more candidates are running for office and races are becoming more competitive. The changes are so large that more incumbents are being defeated, races are closer, more candidates are running, and there are fewer single candidate races than at any other time in our sample."

In Ohio, state legislative term limits were credited with helping pass serious ethics reform. "Term limits established a kind of public-interest momentum" according to Ohio Common Cause executive director Janet Lewis, whose group had led the fight against term limits. Robert McCord, a columnist with the *Arkansas Times* declared "the Arkansas House of Representatives has been reborn" after the state's voters enacted a six-year House limit and representatives were quick to dismantle the seniority system.

Anecdotal and empirical evidence abounds that term limits have reduced partisanship, gridlock, and special interest influence. At the same time, more people are running for office, additional reforms are following in the term limits wake, and the disastrous predictions of opponents are being quietly forgotten.

Unfortunately, Congress continues to be locked in partisan warfare, ethics problems, and largely uncompetitive elections. Congress needs term limits.

CONGRESS HAS A CONFLICT OF INTEREST

When the amendment process of the Constitution was originally debated [in 1787], delegate George Byron of Pennsylvania had tremendous vision. He saw the potential of a congressional conflict of interest and warned, "We shall never find two-thirds of a Congress voting for anything which shall derogate from their own authority and importance."

Even with consistent and overwhelming public support, about three out of four Americans believe Congress will refuse to propose a constitutional amendment for term limits. Why? Because Congress has a clear conflict of interest. Term limits is about limiting your personal power and the power of any individual who takes your place in our system.

Most members of Congress do support the concept of term limits and have for some time. After all, Congress voted by two-thirds of both Houses to propose the Twenty-Second Amendment limiting the President to two terms, eight years, in office. More recently (in the 104th Congress) [1995–1996], 355 members of the House voted to limit committee chairs to three terms. Yet, while supporting and imposing the concept on others, many members do not want limits to apply to them personally.

The congressional conflict of interest results in many members of Congress favoring limits twice as generous as most voters, that is, if they favor any limits at all. Congress has also shown a tremendous ability for political maneuvering on the issue.

Last Congress, the House of Representatives failed to represent their constituents as term limits were defeated by outright opponents and "loved to death" by some questionable friends. The three-term House limit enacted by 15 states and supported by gigantic percentages of voters was opposed by a majority of Republicans, as well as Democrats. Only the freshman Republicans were in sync with the wishes of the American people 72 percent voting for a three-term limit, a constitutional majority itself demonstrating the benefit of regular rotation in office.

This conflict also can be found in some members' demand that Congress, rather than the voters, set the limits. As David Mason of the Heritage Foundation wrote, "At a February 28 [1995] House Judiciary Committee mark-up session on these proposals, a coalition of opponents and wavering supporters amended the McCollum bill, so that it...explicitly would preempt state term limit laws (the original bill was silent on state powers)." What Mr. Mason didn't report was Representative McCollum proposed this amendment to his own bill that would have specifically struck down the shorter term limit imposed on him by the voters of Florida. That the House GOP's point-man on the issue would seek to preempt his own state's term limit law passed by a 77 percent vote is a striking example of his conflict of interest.

The commitment of the House Republican Leadership, especially Speaker Newt Gingrich, has been the subject of much doubt. Television producer Brian Boyer, who spent a great deal of time with Gingrich while filming a 1995 documentary, said, "It was very surprising, and this was, remember, from very long conversations with Gingrich, to learn that he personally is not in favor of term limits." Gingrich's spokesperson Tony Blankley told the *American Spectator* in July of 1994 that term limits was "something conceptually [Newt] doesn't like." Columnist Robert Novak wrote in the *Washington Post*, "Republican leaders profess to want 12 years, but it is clear they prefer no limits at all."

A number of Republicans in the leadership voted against every term limit bill as did five committee chairs. Only one member of the leadership, Majority Leader Dick Armey, and only one committee chair voted for the three-term House limit passed by most states. Yet while Mr. Armey said he would have stripped a member of a committee chairmanship had they like Senator Mark Hatfield voted against the Balanced Budget Amendment, there was no such pressure brought to bear for term limits.

Freshman Michael Forbes of New York told the *New York Times* after the failed House vote, "Candidly, this leadership didn't want [term limits] anymore than the old leadership did." But the American people were not fooled—a *Washington Post*/ABC News poll found close to two-thirds believe neither Republicans nor Democrats in Congress really tried to pass term limits.

THREE TERMS VS. SIX TERMS

The question as to the proper length of the term limits is not merely: What should the limits be? Rather, the essential question is: Who should set the limits? U.S. Term Limits is dedicated to the proposition that the people, not Congress, should set the limits.

Some observers of the battle in Congress over whether House terms should be limited to three terms or six terms have posited that the term limits movement is split. This is simply not the case. The term limits movement is strongly united behind three terms. Only in Congress (and especially among longtime members whose support for any limit whatsoever is questionable) is there significant approval of six terms and fierce opposition to three terms.

Throughout the rest of America, support for three terms far surpasses support for six terms. The American people, pro-limits scholars and virtually every state term limit group in the country supports a three-term limit in the House and a two-term limit in the Senate. Poll after poll demonstrates public support for three terms over six. A 1996 Fabrizio-McLaughlin poll of 1,000 adults nationally found supporters favored three terms 81 percent to 16 percent over six terms.

Not surprisingly, election results bear this out. In every head to head vote three terms has won over six terms. Colorado voters went to the polls in 1994 and voted to lower their limits from six terms to three terms. The arguments in favor of a six-term House limit are so barren, that one such Beltway advocate brazenly and erroneously claims this is "compelling" evidence of support for the longer limit.

ONLY IN WASHINGTON

South Dakota has voted on both a 12-year House limit and a 6-year House limit in separate elections where one would not replace the other. The 6-year limit received 68 percent of the vote to 63 percent for the 12-year limit. After the Wyoming legislature voted to double its state House limits from three terms to six, voters said keep the three-term limit 54 to 46 percent. This even after the sitting governor and three former governors came out in favor of the longer limits.

In fact, the latest trend for politicians opposed to term limits is to pretend to favor term limits, but only longer ones like 12 Years. In New York City, Peter Vallone, Council President and adamant term-limit opponent, was unsuccessful in his attempt to defeat term limits in 1993. Just this past election, he sought to extend the limits from eight years to twelve years. Even with a purposely slanted and misleading ballot title, the voters saw through the council's scheme and rejected this term extension. The same effort to claim support for the term limits concept in order to extend the limits has been and is being repeated in many cities and states with term limits. The voters continue to oppose these term extensions.

The intellectual support for a shorter House limit is also very substantial. A working group of 31 scholars formed by Empower America in December of 1994 studied the term limits issue and concluded, "We put term limits on our agenda, and would even go so far as to favor the specific proposal to limit terms to 6 years in the House and 12 in the Senate."

Mark Petracca, a professor at the University of California-Irvine and a leading scholar on limits, told Congress "my preference is strongly for a limit less expansive than 12 years or 6 terms in the House....A six-term or 12-year limit in the House...won't do much to deprofessionalize the House. Neither may it do much to remedy the other exigencies driving the term limits movement."

David M. Mason of the Heritage Foundation points to "Senate-envy" as the number one reason House members favor the much longer six-term limit and reminds us, "The incumbents' plea for experience only echoes arguments of term limits opponents."

Senator Fred Thompson of Tennessee pointed out one of the reasons people oppose a six-term limit and support three terms. In his 1995 House and Senate testimony, he stated, "Limiting House Members to six terms, instead of the three terms as I have proposed, would leave the seniority system intact and do little to level a playing field that has huge advantages for incumbents." Missouri Senator John Ashcroft recognizes a three-term limit would reduce the incentive for gerrymandering congressional districts for the benefit of incumbents, stating, "it would be one of several benefits exclusive to the 3/2 term proposal..."

Of the major Republican candidates for president in 1996, Lamar Alexander, Pat Buchanan, Steve Forbes, Phil Gramm, and Alan Keyes all supported a limit of three House terms. As Pat Buchanan told the Senate, "Now, what about this 12-year proposal? Well, let me associate myself with what...Lamar Alexander...said. I am unalterably opposed to 12 years. I am for 6 years and out. I know that folks say let's treat both Houses the same way. But the Founding Fathers did not treat both Houses the same way."

There are a plethora of other important policy reasons for enacting a three-term limit as opposed to six terms. Three-term limits will mean greater turnover, more competitive elections, more and quicker campaign reform, and a larger dose of fiscal sanity.

The "Legislative Backgrounder" attached as an appendix to this testimony details further evidence of the public policy benefits associated with a three-term rather than six-term limit.

In reality, many in Congress supposedly favoring a six-term limit appear to not support term limits at all. Representative Bill Barrett of Nebraska has supported the six-term McCollum bill, but wrote in 1995, "I understand voters are frustrated and dissatisfied with the performance of Congress, but I doubt term limits are the answer." Another cosponsor of the McCollum bill is Representative David Camp of Michigan who like Barrett voted against the three-term limits passed in his state. Camp told the *Michigan Midland Daily News* [May 23, 1995], "Voters understand that if they want to limit a member of Congress' term, they can vote for the opponent." These are not the statements of term limit enthusiasts.

In the face of popular and intellectual reasons that three-term limits are superior, the main argument advanced by the longer limit advocates in Congress is that they will simply refuse to support any limits shorter than 6 terms regardless of any support or rationale evidenced against them. This is presented as realism and practicality, but at its core it's the intellectual integrity of a hijacker. Congress in such a case is saying, "The people may have right on their side, but we have the power to ignore them."

INFORMED VOTER LAWS

Nobel prize-winning economist Milton Friedman recognizes the congressional conflict, but also appreciates the ingenuity of the American people in declaring, "Congress is never, not in a million years, going to impose term limits on itself unless it has to."

After the vote in the House in 1995, the American people understood they would have to take matters into their own hands, and they did. The result? In 1996, nine states passed Informed Voter Laws sometimes called Term Limits Accountability

Laws. These states are Alaska, Arkansas, Colorado, Idaho, Maine, Missouri, Nebraska, Nevada and South Dakota.

The laws are very simple. First, they instruct members of Congress to support a specific 3/2 term limits amendment written precisely in the initiative. With differing opinions among members of Congress in the past, and the built-in conflict of interest, the voters of these states seek to make the term limits amendment they want explicitly clear.

Secondly, these laws create a procedure for informing the voters if their instructions on term limits are simply disregarded. If members from these states fail to support the 3/2 amendment or attempt to enact watered-down limits longer than 3/2, the Secretary of State will inform the voters by printing "DISREGARDED VOTER INSTRUCTION ON TERM LIMITS" next to the incumbents' names on the ballot.

Candidates who are not incumbents are allowed to sign a pledge to abide by the voters' instructions when they file for the office. If they do not so pledge, the voters will again be informed by the Secretary of State printing "DECLINED TO PLEDGE TO SUPPORT TERM LIMITS" next to their name on the ballot.

Some will argue these laws are unconstitutional. The opponents of term limits have long used the lawsuit as their primary weapon. Already the voters are being sued by special interests and politicians in a number of states trying to overturn the people's vote. But let me suggest the courts will not save politician-kind this time.

Prior to the 1996 election, the Arkansas Supreme Court declared the state's Informed Voter Initiative unconstitutional and removed it from the ballot. The state court argued the measure would cause "potential political deaths" if elected officials did not heed the instructions of an informed public. To this end, I can only say I certainly hope so. But the U.S. Supreme Court did not allow the Arkansas court to deny the people a vote on this measure. In a highly unusual move, the High Court 7 to 2 issued an emergency stay of the state court decision and the voters got their opportunity to cast ballots for or against the Informed Voter Law.

On November 5, more than 60 percent of Arkansans voted to add the Term Limits Informed Voter amendment to their state constitution. Now the U.S. Supreme Court has been petitioned to take the case, and we believe the people of Arkansas will prevail on the merits.

The response to these Informed Voter Laws has been universal shock and horror from the political establishment. What is there to cause such objection? These laws offer congressmen non-binding instructions from the people they work for and are charged with representing. The republican right of instruction is nothing new and surely no elected official could object to his or her constituents making their desires known regarding their government and their very own representative.

The informational aspect of the initiative has been attacked as the Scarlet Letter. Yet term limit enemies do not argue the information is anything but accurate. Their claims that such an "instruct and inform" tactic is coercive are all predicated on their understanding that the public deeply favors term limits and will likely use the accurate information to oppose those not representing their position. Do incumbents have a right to block truthful information harmful to them from the voting public? If citizens are free to make their instructions known, are they to be denied any knowledge as to how their elected representatives have acted? There is no public good in promoting public ignorance on term limits.

Some have argued that the voters will demand similar information on a whole host of issues. They imagine ballot information such as "VOTED TO RAISE TAXES" or "SUPPORTED CONGRESSIONAL PAY RAISE" next to candidates' names. What if it were so? Isn't public education a good thing? If the voters want more information, then they should have it. Yet, similar voter instructions were given and ballot notations used 90 years ago by the Progressives in pursuit of the Seventeenth Amendment for popular election of U.S. Senators and not until now on term limits have citizens returned to this device. The reasons are obvious. Voters understand they must call the tune if they can hope to overcome the political self-interest of members on the issue.

Harry Truman was called "Give 'em Hell Harry." But Truman remarked, "I never did give anybody hell. I just told the truth and they thought it was hell." These Informed Voter Laws likewise only tell the truth, and while they have popular support, term limits opponents will think they're hell. With public knowledge, politicians lose their wiggle-room on an issue that truly matters to voters.

The American people want a constitutional amendment for a three-term limit in the House and a two-term limit in the Senate. The sooner this body proposes such an amendment, the sooner Congress can be reconnected to this great country. For as the great Englishman Edmund Burke said: "In all forms of Government the people [are] the true legislator."

I ask you to put aside all political games and offer a proposal the American people have endorsed. If this Congress chooses to vote it down, so be it. At least the people will have a clean vote on real term limits.

Congressional Term Limits:
Restricting Choice

JOHN R. HIBBING

I urge you to do what you can to keep the terms of members of Congress from being limited to a set number. I will organize my case against term limits around three points: the value of congressional experience, the uncertain consequences of term limits for representation, and the inability of term limits to improve the public's opinion of Congress.

CONGRESSIONAL EXPERIENCE

The term limit movement believes it is important to have a constant infusion of "new blood" in Congress lest the body become stale and set in its ways. Opponents of term limits worry that too much new blood would lead to a decrease in both legislative quality and institutional memory as inexperienced members wrestle with devilishly complex issues. Which side is correct? What is the optimal level of membership turnover for an institution like Congress? Most of the debate on these questions has proceeded without any firm evidence for the value of congressional experience. I would like to interject some evidence now.

About 10 years ago, I attempted to determine the manner in which members of this house changed as their careers in Congress unfolded. I found that, with a few exceptions of course, most members did not change much ideologically. Liberals stayed liberal and conservatives stayed conservative. Early career roll call patterns were good predictors of late career roll call patterns. Surprisingly, perhaps, early career electoral results were also good predictors of late career electoral results. It is not the case

that many members transform marginal seats into safe seats. The chances of losing office because of an election are nearly as great for senior members as they are for junior members. Attention to the district, as measured by the number of trips home, diminishes with increasing tenure but only by a little. Most senior members work quite hard at maintaining a presence in the district. Finally, the odds of a member being involved in some type of scandalous behavior do not increase with tenure. Junior members are just as likely as senior members to be scandal-ridden. The popular vision of an inert, uncaring, corrupt, and electorally unchallengeable senior member is simply inaccurate. On each of these counts, senior members are almost no different from junior members.

This statement does not apply, however, when attention shifts to legislative activity, that is, actually formulating and passing legislation. Here I found substantial differences between junior and senior members. Senior members, it turns out, are the heart and the soul of the legislative process. They are more active on legislation (giving speeches, offering amendments, and sponsoring bills), they are more specialized (a greater portion of their legislative attention goes to a focused substantive area), and they are more efficient (a greater percentage of their legislation becomes law). These patterns, I might add, persist even when senior members do not become leaders on committees or subcommittees, so it is not just that member activity reflects the positions of power that some senior members hold. The reasons for altered legislative contributions are broader than that and have to do, simply, with increased legislative experience.

Now, I will be the first to admit that many of these indicators of legislative involvement are badly flawed. It is impossible to measure quantitatively a representative's overall legislative contribution. As members know better than anyone, the legislative process is too rich and subtle to be captured by counting speeches or calculating legislative batting averages. But we must try to understand the relative contributions of senior members if we are to know the consequences of statutorily prohibiting the service of senior members, and here it can be said with some confidence that senior members have more active, focused, and successful legislative agendas. Junior members tend to introduce bills on topics about which they know very little. The subject matter of these bills is all over the map and the bills have precious little chance of making it out of committee let alone becoming law. These are empirical facts. We need more senior members; not fewer.

UNCERTAINTY ABOUT CONSEQUENCES

Many people support the term limit movement because they believe it would make members more responsive to the people. The argument is that Congress has grown out of touch and that if members served only short time periods, along the lines of the citizen legislatures of old, they would be more in touch with the needs and concerns of ordinary people. But there are others who support the term limit movement for exactly the opposite reason. [Columnist] George Will is probably the best-known proponent of the position that term limits should be enacted in order to make Congress less sensitive to the desires of ordinary people. Will and others believe that mandatory term limits would embolden representatives, giving them the nerve to go against public opinion. Only when members know their stint in Congress will soon end, the argument is, will members stop pandering to unrealistic public demands for both lower taxes and more government services. I do not know which side is correct about the consequences of term limits for the proximity of Congress to the people but I do know that the inability of those in the term limit movement to agree amongst themselves on whether Congress is too close or not close enough to the people together with their inability to know whether term limits would in actuality reduce or increase the distance between the people and their Congress should give us pause. Before we enshrine a reform in the Constitution of the United States, should we not at least expect the champions of that reform to know what they want to accomplish?

Public Opinion of Congress

My current research interests have to do with the reasons the public tends to be displeased with Congress. People believe Congress has been captured by special interests, extremist parties, and professionalized politicians and that ordinary folks have been lost in the shuffle. They want changes that would restore the public's role in the process. The only way we can restore public confidence in Congress, some reformers argue, is to enact measures, like term limits, that are central to the public's populist agenda.

It is my belief that term limits would not improve the public's opinion of Congress in the long run. Much public unrest stems from the belief that Congress creates conflict. The common notion is that agreement exists among the masses but that when special interests, parties, and ambitious politicians come together in Congress they manage to construct disagreement where it need not exist. But the truth of the matter is that, while interest groups, parties, and politicians sometimes create conflict, most of the time they only reflect the people's diverse views. Survey research indicates clearly that people are deeply divided over how to solve almost every major societal problem. This disagreement would exist whether or not term limits were enacted. In fact, I contend the public would be even more disillusioned than they are currently once they saw political conflict continuing unabated long after term limits were enacted.

The real solution is to educate people on the extent of their own disagreements and on the difficulties faced by elected officials in moving from these disagreements to responsible, brokered solutions to problems. People harbor beliefs that reforms such as term limits will be able to reduce conflict and the accompanying deliberation (bickering) and compromise (selling out) that they find so objectionable. Nothing could be further from the truth. Rather than pretending there is a magic solution to political conflict, we need to educate the people on the necessity of having learned, experienced legislators who can work their way through the challenging assignment of coming to agreement in the face of public ignorance and uncertainty.

THE CONTINUING DEBATE:
Congressional Term Limits

What Is New

The 2002 elections demonstrated the relative safety of incumbents. Of the 34 senators whose terms were up, 28 sought new terms, and 24 were reelected. There was even less turnover in the House, to which voters returned 88% of the incumbents. Most of the members who did not return left voluntarily; only 11 were actually defeated in a general election or a primary. For the 108th Congress (2003–2005), the average length of service in the House was 9.2 years and the average senator had been serving 10.9 years. If a term limit using the most often discussed parameters (12 years in either chamber) existed, it would mean 163 of 435 members of the House would be barred from seeking reelection in 2004, as would be 70 of 100 senators in their next election.

Since the late 1990s, term-limit advocates have had more defeats than victories. The "informed voter measures" favored by advocate Paul Jacobs did not withstand the test of constitutionality. Those in Missouri were challenged and ruled unconstitutional by the U.S. Supreme Court in *Cook v. Gralike* (2001). As for term limits as such, the Supreme Courts of Massachusetts, Oregon, and Washington struck them down as violating their respective state constitutions. Idaho's legislature repealed limits in 2002, and Utah's legislature followed suit in 2003. The last states to hold a referendum on term limits were Mississippi in 1999 and Nebraska in 2000. In Mississippi, 55% of the voters rejected term limits, making the state the first to do so by direct democracy. Taking the opposite stand, 56% of Nebraska's voters supported term limits. This leaves 16 states with limits in place. A final note is that the concept remains popular with the public. When a 2003 survey asked about term limits, 67% of the respondents said term limits were a "a good idea," 27% thought them a "bad idea," 3% replied "it depends," and 4% were unsure.

Where to Find More

A good new study that presents a series of empirical studies of the impact of term limits on state legislatures is Rick Farmer, John David Rausch, Jr., and John C. Green (eds.), *The Test of Time: Coping with Legislative Term Limits* (Lexington, 2003). U.S. Term Limits, the group represented by advocate Paul Jacob, has a helpful Web site at: http://www.termlimits.org/. You can also find good information on the site of the National Conference of State Legislators at http://www.ncsl.org/programs/legman/about/termlimit.htm.

What More to Do

Think about one or more members of Congress whom you admire or who, because of their seniority, are powerful advocates of positions you support but who, at the end of their current term, will have been in their chamber 12 years or longer. Would you want them to be forced to retire because of term limits?

Consider your two senators and one member of the House. How do they stand with the 12-year rule? Also figure out which of the U.S. senators running for the Democratic presidential nomination would have had to retire in 2002 or before if the 12-year rule had been in place and, thus, probably would have faded politically and not been a candidate. Would term limits affect the quality of future presidents?

12 PRESIDENCY

PRESIDENTIAL WAR POWERS AND TERRORISM:
Unilateral Authority *or* Constitutional Constraints?

UNILATERAL AUTHORITY

ADVOCATE: Douglas Kmiec, Dean of the Columbus School of Law, The Catholic University of America

SOURCE: Testimony during hearings on "Applying the War Powers Resolution to the War on Terrorism," before the U.S. Senate Committee on the Judiciary, April 17, 2002

CONSTITUTIONAL CONSTRAINTS

ADVOCATE: Jane Stromseth, Professor of Law, Georgetown University Law Center

SOURCE: Testimony during hearings on "Applying the War Powers Resolution to the War on Terrorism," before the U.S. Senate Committee on the Judiciary, April 17, 2002

"We're going to find out who did this, and we're going to kick their asses," President George Bush vowed angrily to Vice President Richard Cheney on September 11, 2001. Soon thereafter, Bush asked Congress for a resolution supporting action against terrorism in Afghanistan and elsewhere. But in doing so he claimed the right to act without legislative support, "pursuant to my constitutional authority to conduct U.S. foreign relations as Commander in Chief and Chief Executive." In other words, the support of Congress would be nice, but was not necessary.

The immediate debate here is whether in this case the president had the unilateral war powers authority he claimed. This question is part of the larger issue about when presidents may use military force without congressional authorization. It is a dispute that begins with two clauses in the Constitution. Article I empowers Congress "to declare war." Article II designates the president as "commander in chief" of the military. It is clear that the framers of the Constitution believed that the president should be able to act unilaterally in some but not all circumstances. As one framer, Roger Sherman put it, the president should "be able to repel and not commence war." The question is where one begins and the other ends.

There is a long history of the use of the president's war powers, but the matter did not become a central concern until after World War II. Two things changed. First, the United States became a superpower, deployed its forces around the world, and used them often. Second, presidents for the first time asserted broad powers as commander in chief. In the Korean War (1950–1953), the Truman administration argued that it could act alone because, "the president, as commander in chief of the armed forces,…has full control over the use thereof."

This self-proclaimed authority prevailed unchallenged until the trauma of the Vietnam War led Congress to try to rein in the president's war powers. Over a presidential veto, Congress in 1973 enacted the War Powers Resolution (WPR). Unfortunately, the terms of WPR are open to dispute. Section 2c specifies that the authority of the president "to introduce [U.S. forces] into hostilities, or into [so-called harm's way] situations where imminent involvement in hostilities is [likely] are properly" exercised only pursuant to (1) a declaration of war, (2) specific statutory authorization, or (3) a national emergency created by attack upon the United States, its territories or possessions, or its armed forces. Note that this language includes the president putting the military in "harm's way," as well as actual combat use. What causes confusion is section 5b's stipulation that when the president has ordered troops into combat or deployed them in harm's way, then "Within sixty…days…the president shall terminate [military action]…unless the Congress (1) has declared war or has enacted a specific authorization…[or], (2) has extended [the] period." Some read this to mean that the president has unilateral authority for 60 days. Others take the language to mean that the 60 days apples only to the three circumstances indicated in section 2c and that, in other cases, the president must get prior authority from Congress to act.

For all the controversy over the meaning of the WPR, it must also be said that its relevancy is limited by the fact that all presidents since its passage have asserted that the measure violates their authority as commander in chief. Moreover, despite several challenges to "presidential war" in recent years, the Supreme Court has refused to hear such cases, leaving the matter in legal limbo. As a result, whatever relevancy the WPR does have comes from the fact that presidents, despite their claims of constitutional authority, have usually found it politically wise to seek support from Congress. As President Bush explained his appeal for support for the war on terrorism, "I am a product of the Vietnam era. I remember presidents trying to wage war that were very unpopular, and the nation split."

It is also a matter of politics that many members of Congress, even if they oppose the president's policy, are reluctant to deny him authority to act because doing so will seem like not supporting the troops. Some members were worried after 9/11 when Congress considered a resolution giving the president broad authority "to use all necessary and appropriate force…to prevent any future acts of international terrorism against the United States." The fear was the president could use the language to justify action against any county in the world that he determined was aiding terrorism. Yet despite the misgivings of many in Congress about the resolution, it passed by votes of 98 to 0 in the Senate and 420 to 1 in the House (the lone dissenter: Barbara Lee, D-CA).

POINTS TO PONDER

➢ Distinguish between your view about whether a particular military action is wise policy and the constitutional process by which that decision should be made.

➢ Given that President George H. W. Bush acted as commander in chief in 1990 to deploy U.S. forces to protect Saudi Arabia from attack by Iraq even though there was no attack on or threat against the United States nor an alliance with the Saudis, ask your self under what circumstances the president may not unilaterally use force?

➢ Think about what, if any, should be the limits on the authority of the president to deploy military force in harm's way or to order them into combat.

Presidential War Power and Terrorism: Unilateral Authority

Douglas Kmiec

The President is constitutionally authorized as Commander in Chief to introduce troops into hostilities without prior congressional enactment. No President has ever conceded otherwise; no Congress has ever disputed this point, as even the highly controverted (and largely admonitory) War Powers Resolution necessarily concedes the President's constitutional assignment. Today, there are unprecedented terrorist dangers aimed directly at the civilian populations of our Nation and its allies. Congress shares this concern, rightly so. However, a shared concern must not become an occasion to undermine the well-settled constitutional responsibility of the President. Rather, with great respect for the important deliberations of this body, Congress should direct its legislative efforts at determining how best the President can be supported with the people's resources; not how cleverly the President's military judgment can be second-guessed or hampered.

The power to declare war is not a condition predicate to the duties of military self-defense imposed by the Constitution upon the President. No President from [George] Washington onward has ever construed it to be so, and it is largely modern academic commentary that has obscured or misstated this crucial aspect of constitutional understanding. Rather, the purpose of a declaration of war is to define the international effect of military actions undertaken by direction of the President.

In the present War, the Congress by joint resolution has confirmed the President's constitutional authority. That resolution, when construed together with the President's Article II power, is ample and plenary, allowing the President, together with his military, national security and homeland defense advisors, to determine the timing, scope, and appropriateness for military intervention.

Congress's role is one of material support, not tactical judgment. As the representative of the people, Congress is obliged to provide this support if it determines that our lives, safety and security justify the actions being taken by the President. Of course, this appropriations-related authority is a well-considered check upon presidential action. Prudentially and practically, both the President and Congress must necessarily collaborate if wartime efforts are to succeed. No Congress should give a blank check to a President, nor is it constitutionally obligated to do so, and no President should expect one. That said, Congress oversteps its constitutionally determined role if it uses monetary conditions to usurp or impede the tactical decisions that only the President can make.

The President has determined that terrorism is worldwide. It exists in networks or cells of individuals driven by religious or political fanaticism and supported by an international network of drug dealers and other shadowy criminal enterprises, not infrequently disguised as NGOs [non-governmental organizations: private group with multinational memberships] and charities. Unfortunately, no credible intelligence suggests that the War is confined to one nefarious leader or a single country. The successful military campaign in Afghanistan is a start, not a finish of this War. Congress, of course, has the formal power—as the holder of the Nation's purse—to refuse to adequately support the further military efforts to confront what the President has properly called an "axis of evil." It can discount the noncompliance of Iraq with UN sanction and its willingness to use biological weapons on its own people; it can turn a blind eye to the terrorist renegades in Somalia and the Philippines. At the farthest extreme, the legislature is constitutionally empowered even to defend our military and intelligence communities. I doubt that few Americans would think the exercise of congressional powers in this peremptory way to be responsible. In doing so, Congress will have indulged a calculus or risk assessment far different from the President, and perhaps, saved money. In the President's judgment, the Congress very likely will not have saved lives.

Ultimately in our democratic republic, it is the people who either affirm or dispute the policy choices made by their President and the Congress. It will then be up to the people to decide which was the better course—that of the sword aimed at those who hate the responsible exercise of freedom or that of the purse aimed at restraining the sword in this mission. Neither the President nor the Congress can avoid making its respective judgments. Certainly, neither can (or should) use the Constitution as a cover plane for its failure to decide.

The actions being taken by President [George H. W.] Bush are well within the parameters of the authority given to him by the Constitution. I am confident that the U.S. Supreme Court would not say otherwise. Congress may decide not to support these actions with the people's money. That is its prerogative, and it is one for which it will be held accountable.

THE PRESIDENT'S ROLE

The President's power to use military force to respond to terrorist and other attack is clear. Article II, Section 2 provides that the "President shall be Commander in Chief of the Army and Navy of the Unites States, and of the Militia of the several States, when called into actual Service of the United States." Beyond this, the President is fully vested with all executive power and the authority to "take care" that the laws are faithfully executed.

Constitutional practice dating to our first president removes any doubt that wars were, and can be, fought without congressional authorization. During the first five years of his administration, Washington engaged in a prolonged Indian war in the Ohio Valley. This was not a small skirmish, as President Washington himself proclaimed, "We are involved in an actual war!"—one, by the way, that went badly initially for the standing army in 1791. Similarly, John Adams fought a naval war with France, known as the Quasi-War that erupted in 1798 out of France's interference with our commercial relations with Britain. Congress provided the funding, and set the rules for naval engagement, but did not declare war, even as the historical record demonstrates that one was being fought.

Many cases affirm the scope of the President's war power, but it is particularly well affirmed in *The Prize Cases* [1863], where the Supreme Court opined that it was for Abraham Lincoln, as Commander in Chief to determine what necessary means could be used to respond to belligerents, for such questions under the Constitution, are "to be decided by [the President]." In this century, Attorney General [1940–1941] (later [Supreme Court] Justice) Robert Jackson put the matter equally forcefully:

> [The President] shall be Commander in Chief....By virtue of this constitutional office he has supreme command over the land and naval forces of the country and may order them to perform such military

duties as, in his opinion, are necessary or appropriate for the defense of the United States. These powers exist in times of peace as well as in time of war.... [T]his authority undoubtedly includes the power to dispose of troops and equipment in such manner and on such duties as best to promote the safety of the country.

In writing in these terms, Attorney General Jackson was reflecting an unbroken line of undisturbed federal interpretation that properly places both the burden and authority upon the President to preserve "our territorial integrity and the protection of our foreign interests as a matter of constitutional provision, [and not] the enforcement of specific acts of Congress."

The framers justified this grant of authority to the President by the need for military and executive action to be taken with "secrecy and dispatch." Without the quality of what Hamilton referred to as "energy in the executive," the community would be unable to protect itself "against foreign attacks." These were not merely the sentiments of those who favored a strong national government. Thomas Jefferson, serving as George Washington's Secretary of State, observed that "[t]he transactions of business with foreign nations is executive altogether; it belongs, then, to the head of that department, except as to such portions of it as are specially submitted to the senate. [And what's more] [e]xceptions are to be construed strictly."

This exercise of presidential power has been bi-partisan. For example, on August 20, 1998, President [Bill] Clinton launched an air strike against terrorist activity (the African embassy bombings) traced to Osama bin Laden. The President acted without congressional authorization, and he did so for reasons that are directly applicable and similar to the present War on Terrorism: intelligence information that traced the bombings to terrorist groups that have acted against U.S. interests in the past, and suggested planning for additional attacks in the future. These groups were employing or seeking weapons of mass destruction, including chemical and dangerous weapons.

As scholars have pointed out, President Clinton's actions have much in common with President [Ronald] Reagan's April 14, 1986, air strike against Libya in response to that nation's involvement with the killing of Americans and others in Berlin. Like the Clinton actions, the Reagan strike was necessary not only in retaliation, but also as a defensive and preventative response to a terrorist attack on U.S. military personnel and her citizens.

The Congress' Power to Declare War

The Congress' power to declare war is not the power to make war, as should be obvious to every American who has lived through both Pearl Harbor and September 11. War can be made upon us. As was noted expressly in the Constitutional convention, the executive must have the power to repel sudden attacks without prior Congressional authorization. The drafters of our Constitution knew how to use precise language, and indeed, as careful scholarship has since pointed out, "[if] the Framers had wanted to require congressional consent before the initiation of military hostilities, they would have used such language."

The power to declare war, rather than the power to initiate one, was a power to confirm—for international and domestic law purposes—the existence of hostilities between two sovereigns. This was how Blackstone understood the phraseology, and in historical context, how it was understood by the framers as well. In the decades leading up to constitutional drafting and ratification, declaring war meant not authorizing a proper executive response to attack, but to defining the relationship between the citizens of warring nations as to, for example, the seizure or expropriation, of assets. Even the use of the word "declare" in the context of the framing suggests not authorization, but recognition of that which pre-exists. This, for example, is the usage in the Declaration of Independence, recognizing rights that are not created by the government, but pre-exist by virtue of human creation. Professor John Yoo (now of the Office of Legal Counsel) has ably canvassed this area writing that the declare war clause was meant largely to bolster the exclusion of the individual states from the question. He summarizes the historical evidence this way: "a declaration of war was understood as what its name suggests: a declaration. Like a declaratory judgment, a declaration of war represented the judgment of Congress, acting in a [quasi-]judicial capacity (as it does in impeachments), that a state of war existed between the United States and another nation. Such a declaration could take place either before or after hostilities had commenced."

If military activity could only occur upon congressional declaration, this proposition would leave most of American history unexplained, such as American intervention in Korea, Vietnam, Iran, Grenada, Libya, and Panama. Congress has declared war only five times: the War of 1812; the Mexican American War of 1848, the Spanish-American War of 1898, and World War I (1914) and World War II (1941).

Some have disputed this account of the declare war clause, arguing in support of a congressional pre-condition by reference to Article I, Section 8, Clause 11 which gives Congress the power to "grant Letters of Marque and Reprisal,..." This somewhat arcane aspect of constitutional text, however, cannot bear the weight of the claim. Letters of Marque and Reprisal are grants of authority from Congress to private citizens, not the President. Their purpose is to expressly authorize seizure and forfeiture of goods by such citizens in the context of undeclared hostilities. Without such authorization, the citizen could be treated under international law as a pirate. Occasions where one's citizens undertake hostile activity can often entangle the larger sovereignty, and therefore, it was sensible for Congress to desire to have a regulatory check upon it. Authorizing Congress to moderate or oversee private action, however, says absolutely nothing about the President's responsibilities under the Constitution.

The drafters of the American Constitution knew how to express themselves. They were familiar with state constitutional provisions, such as that in South Carolina, which directly stated that the "governor and commander-in-chief shall have no power to commence war, or conclude peace" without legislative approval. Article I, Section 10 expressly prohibits states, without the consent of Congress, from keeping troops or ships of war in time of peace, or engaging in war, unless actually invaded, or in such imminent danger that delay would not be warranted. There is no parallel provision reciting that the President as commander in chief shall not, without the Consent of Congress, exercise his military responsibility.

That the power to declare war is not a power of prior authorization does not leave Congress without check upon executive abuse. That check, however, is anchored in Congress' control of the purse, and, of course, impeachment. When challenged by the anti-federalists, most notably Patrick Henry, to explain how tyranny would not result unless the sword and purse were held by different governments, Madison responded that no efficient government could exist without both, but security is to be found in "that the sword and purse are not to be given to the same member." No reference was made to the declare war clause or marque and reprisal letters.

How great a role can Congress play in the funding process? Here, the historical record would suggest that Congress is as free as the people they represent. It may explore and evaluate the military mission as the President has outlined it. Congress can refuse to fund the continuation of tactical decisions that it believes unsound; Congress, however, cannot dictate a particular course of engagement or so fetter the President's judgment as to preclude its exercise.

THE WAR POWERS ACT

It is facetious to suggest that the War Powers Act or Resolution [WPR] limits constitutional authority, something which it expressly proclaims not to do. (Section 8(d) of the WPR states that "nothing in the Resolution is intended to alter the constitutional authority of either the Congress or the President.") In any event, insofar as the WPR presumes to limit the extent of operations already undertaken by a president, it "makes sense only if the President may introduce troops into hostilities or potential hostilities without prior authorization by the Congress." After surveying comprehensively the large number of occasions where the President has deployed troops without legislative involvement, the Office of Legal Counsel concluded:

> Our history is replete with instances of presidential uses of military force abroad in the absence of prior congressional approval....Thus, constitutional practice over two centuries, supported by the nature of the functions exercised and by the few legal benchmarks that exist, evidences the existence of broad constitutional power.

Even if the WPR could be construed to statutorily amend constitutional text (which it cannot), by its express terms the WPR acknowledges presidential power to introduce Armed Forces into hostilities as a result of an "attack upon the United States, its ter-

ritories or possessions, or its armed forces." Certainly, that was September 11th. In any event, no president has ever accepted the limiting provisions of the WPR.

No president has ever formally complied with the WPR, even as Presidents have used the vehicle to accomplish consultation with Congress. For example, both the first President Bush and President Clinton sent reports to Congress that were described carefully as "consistent with the Resolution," but not pursuant to, or required by, the WPR. Congress has not sought to use the enforcement mechanism under the WPR, though it has occasionally been referenced or advocated by individual members.

Of course, proponents of the WPR take a different view; a view that posits the need for specific authorization. As mentioned, this view is contrary to constitutional text, history and practice, but in the present circumstance, even this objection is superceded by Congress' own legislative action.

The Effect of the Joint Resolution

If presidential power apart from congressional authorization was somehow questionable as a general matter, it is not open to doubt in the present War on Terrorism which Congress has specifically authorized (S.J. Res. 25) [hereinafter "force resolution"]. The force resolution recites that "the President has authority under the Constitution to take action to deter and prevent acts of international terrorism." While this recital might be argued to concede that the force resolution, itself, was unnecessary, the better construction is one that the force resolution acknowledges the contending views over the legality of the WPR and removes all doubt in the present instance. The President thus has full legal authority with respect to either responding with "all necessary and appropriate force against those nations, organizations, or persons [the President] determines planned, authorized, committed or aided the terrorist attacks that occurred on September 11, 2001, or harbored such organizations or persons," and with respect to the steps necessary "to prevent any future acts of international terrorism against the United States by such nations, organizations or persons."

In my judgment, the force resolution must be read consistently with the President's authority. Some have commented that it relates only to "individuals, groups or states that [are] determined to have links to the September 11 attacks." Yet, Congress clearly intended to authorize the President to address terrorist threats of the future, and therefore, it is highly reasonable to construe the linkage to "nations, organizations, or persons" broadly, especially as we are practically discovering that the terrorist network has manifold capacity to direct and aid cells in multiple guises and distant parts of the world.

WHETHER A WAR IS PROPERLY WAGED IS NOT FOR THE COURTS

The Supreme Court has consistently avoided passing upon the legality of particular military engagements, such as Vietnam and Korea. Lower federal courts have also regularly dismissed these matters as political questions and non-justiciable. The Persian Gulf War yielded two variants on this theme in *Dellums v. Bush* and *Ange v. Bush*. Unusually, in Dellums, the trial court decided that Congress possessed sole authority to declare war, and that troop movements authorized without congressional approval by the first President Bush might be challenged if a majority of Congress or the Congress in its entirety joined the litigation. That was not to be, and the suit was dismissed as unripe. By contrast, and far more in keeping with past decision, Judge Lamberth decided in Ange, the parallel case brought by a deployed member of the military, that determining whether the President had exceeded either his constitutional authority or violated the WPR was a nonjusticiable political question.

The judicial branch has consistently found any disagreement between the President and Congress to be a political question, not susceptible to judicial resolution. Common sense and the absence of public measures or standards of judgment readily explains why courts would abstain. Neither the President nor Congress have that luxury. Both must make their constitutionally separate choices. A President who endangers the lives of his military unnecessarily (or for a purpose that is contrary to the first principles in the Declaration of Independence and implemented by the Constitution) or a Congress that obdurately refuses to support those engaged in necessary combat will be accountable to the people.

CONCLUSION—DOES THE WAR ON TERRORISM CHANGE THE CONSTITUTIONAL ORDER?

The short answer is, no. Yet, as General Joulwan, the former NATO Supreme Allied Commander, reflected before the Senate Foreign Relations Committee (February 7, 2002):

> We are at war. But it is a different war than those we fought in the past. There are no front lines. The enemy is dispersed and operates in small cells. The underpinnings of this threat are in its religious radicalism and its hatred of the United States and the civilization that embraces freedom, tolerance and human dignity. It is an enemy willing to commit suicide of its young to achieve its aims and with little regard for human life. While the enemy may be small in number it would be wrong to underestimate the threat—or the depth of their convictions.

Samuel Berger, former National Security Advisor, echoed the same sentiment at the same hearing:

> We must continue to take down al Qaeda cells, and hunt down al Qaeda operatives elsewhere—in Asia,

Europe, Africa, here and elsewhere in this Hemisphere. Disruption will be an ongoing enterprise—a priority that will require international intelligence, law enforcement and military cooperation for the foreseeable future. These cells of fanatics will reconstitute themselves. We must treat this as a chronic illness that must be aggressively managed, while never assuming it has been completely cured.

A dispersed enemy needing to be constantly addressed and combated is ill-met by a historically mistaken, if mistakenly commonplace, understanding of the declare war clause. Our national interests are equally ill-served by a wooden interpretation of a likely unconstitutional war powers resolution that even when enacted largely accommodated conventional warfare or deployments on the scale of World War II, rather than the needed (and often covert) responses to the smaller, yet more insidious and diffused nature of modern terrorism.

From 1975 through October 2001, Presidents—without conceding the constitutional validity of the WPR—submitted some 92 reports under the Resolution. In the same period, there were no declarations of war. One can argue that the resolution has fostered dialogue between the legislative and executive departments. So long as that dialog did not compromise classified information or strategy and facilitated Congress' appropriations role in war making, constitutional purposes were well served. Yet, the primary infirmity of the resolution lies in its faulty assumption: namely, that the Constitution envisions a "collective judgment" on the introduction of armed forces. It does not. It envisions a President capable of responding with energy and dispatch to immediate threat, and a Congress that can deliberate on the actions already taken, and through judicious resource choices, influence others. Congress, itself, recognized this in Section 3, when it modified the statutory consultation to "in every possible instance" and in Section 4 when it admits the possibility of presidential deployment without advance reporting and only reporting "within 48 hours, in the absence of a declaration of war or congressional authorization."

Wisely, Congress by its September 2001 force resolution has authorized the President to respond to the terrorist threat, as it exists—dispersed, chronic and global. In my judgment, the force resolution fully satisfies Section 5(b)(1) of the WPR and therefore exempts the President's deployment from termination by Congress under the controversial time clock set-out in the WPR. Section 5(c)'s provision for termination by concurrent resolution is also unconstitutional under Supreme Court precedent [set in] *INS v. Chadha* [1983]. While Congress has attempted to address the gap created by the decision in Chadha which held legislative veto devices to be unconstitutional, other far more serious constitutional questions would be raised if the subsequent 1983 amendment to section 601(b) of the International Security and Arms Control Act of 1976 (P.L. 94–329) fixing the WPR legislative veto failing is construed to empower Congress to countermand the President's military judgment and "direct" the withdrawal of troops. As suggested above, Congress properly speaks in its allocation of funds; the Constitution does not envision that Congress would determine the deployment of troops or related law enforcement and intelligence personnel—that is for the President.

Presidential War Power and Terrorism: Constitutional Constraints

Jane Stromseth

The September 11th attacks pose unprecedented challenges for our Nation. We were attacked by a global network that was able to inflict massive casualties upon innocent civilians and would do so again, possibly with greater effect, if given the opportunity. Under such circumstances, we have begun to mobilize a broad range of military, diplomatic, intelligence, law enforcement, economic, and financial tools in order to wage this global war on terrorism. This campaign is likely to be long-term and open-ended, with conflict potentially on multiple fronts; and, in contrast to more conventional operations, it will be much harder to determine when or if the war is over or what constitutes victory.

Despite these complexities, indeed, in fact because of them, I will argue here that the basic principles of our Constitution regarding war powers remain as vital and relevant as ever—indeed even more so—in the fight against global terrorism. I will also argue that Congress's post-September 11th authorization of force correctly recognized that both Congress and the President have a vital constitutional role to play in prosecuting the global war on terrorism; that meaningful high-level consultations are essential as the campaign against terrorists with global reach and their state sponsors unfolds; and that additional congressional authorization may be constitutionally required in some situations in the future.

THE CONSTITUTION'S ALLOCATION OF WAR POWERS

Our Constitution deliberately divided war powers between the Congress and the President. In making this choice, the framers sought to create an effective national government capable of protecting and defending the country while also remaining accountable to the American people. The Constitution's provisions concerning war powers—like those concerning other aspects of governance—reflect a structural system of checks and balances designed to protect liberty by guarding against the concentration of power. In a deliberate break with British precedent, the Constitution gave Congress the power to declare war because the founders believed such a significant decision should be made not by one person, but by the legislature as a whole, to ensure careful deliberation by the people's elected representatives and broad national support before the country embarked on a course so full of risks. Reflecting on this allocation of power, James Madison wrote: "In no part of the constitution is more wisdom to be found, than in the clause which confides the question of war or peace to the legislature, and not to the executive department."

At the same time, the framers wanted a strong Executive who could "repel sudden attacks" and act with efficiency and dispatch in protecting the interests of the United States in a dangerous world. By making the President Commander in Chief, moreover, they sought to ensure effective, unified command over U.S. forces and civilian accountability. The Constitution's division of war powers between the President and the Congress has led inevitably to tension between the branches—and to an enduring tug of war over war powers—even as the participation of both branches clearly is essential in protecting our country and advancing American interests.

There is a huge scholarly literature about the Framers' intentions with respect to constitutional war powers and about whether historical practices in the two centuries since the Constitution was ratified should alter how we should understand these authorities today. It is impractical for me to offer a detailed and comprehensive discussion here, but let me instead highlight four propositions from the historical record that, in my estimation, are central for understanding the constitutional roles of Congress and the President today.

First, the power to "declare war" vested in Congress was intended by the Framers to be a power to decide, to make a choice, about whether the United States should go to war; it was not a formalistic power to simply validate that a legal state of war existed. On the contrary, Congress was given the power to determine whether the United States should initiate war in order to ensure that the decision to expose the country to such risks and sacrifices reflected the deliberation and judgment of the legislature—the branch most directly representative of the American people, whose lives and resources will be placed on the line—and to ensure broad national support for such a course of action. This interpretation is further validated by the Constitution's grant of authority to Congress to authorize reprisals, or acts of limited war, that could lead to a wider war, which clearly indicated a broader understanding of Congress's war-commencing role than simply a formal declaration that a state of war existed.

Second, the Chief Executive's authority to repel sudden attacks by force is incontestable. The founders expected the President, as Chief Executive and Commander in Chief, to protect the United States by repelling actual or imminent attacks against the United States, its vessels,

and its armed forces. Moreover, if another nation effectively placed the United States in a state of war—by declaring or openly making war upon the United States—the President as Commander in Chief was expected to exercise the nation's fundamental right of self-defense. However, if an enemy engaged in limited attacks that did not rise to the level of war, the founders expected the President to repel those attacks but not to go beyond this authority and change the state of the nation from peace to war without congressional authorization.

Third, Congress's power of purse, though critically important, is not a substitute for congressional authorization of war before it is commenced. The founders understood that the British monarch's power to go to war was qualified to a substantial degree by the Parliament's power of the purse and its control over military supplies. In giving Congress the power of the purse, including the power of appropriating money to "raise and support Armies" and to "provide and maintain a navy," the Constitution continued this important legislative check. But the Constitution did not stop here. The Constitution also gave Congress the power to declare war and authorize reprisals, so that congressional deliberation would occur before war was commenced. Reliance on the power of the purse alone as a check on executive war powers, moreover, can be an overly blunt and sometimes ineffective tool for expressing the will of Congress. Limiting or cutting off funds after forces have already been committed is problematic because it undercuts both troops in the field and America's credibility with her allies. Restricting funds in advance is often undesirable as well because it can harm the President's ability to carry out effective diplomacy. In short, as important as Congress's power of the purse is, it is not a substitute for Congress's power to authorize war.

Fourth, historical practice has not fundamentally altered how we should understand the Constitution's allocation of war powers today. Practice, of course, cannot supplant or override the clear requirements of the Constitution, which gives the power to declare war to Congress. Furthermore, of the dozen major wars in American history, five were formally declared by Congress and six were authorized by other legislative measures. There is, to be sure, a pattern of practice involving more limited presidential uses of force falling short of major national conflicts, a substantial number of which involved the protection or rescue of U.S. nationals caught up in harm's way. For example, of the 200 or so cases sometimes cited as examples of unilateral commitments of force by the President, nearly 70 involved the protection or rescue of U.S. nationals, actions far short of deliberate war against foreign countries and reasonably covered by the President's authority to respond to sudden threats. A number of other operations were interventions or peace enforcement actions that aimed at limited goals. Others involved more far-reaching objectives, however, even if the risks were relatively low. In some of these cases, like Haiti, for instance, Congress protested unilateral actions taken by the President and made clear its view that its authorization should have been sought in advance. My basic point is this: one must be very cautious in drawing broad conclusions about presidential power from a numerical list of cases. These instances each have to be examined carefully, and the authority claimed by the President and Congress's reaction fully assessed. Ultimately, however, whatever conclusions one comes to concerning the constitutional implications of small-scale presidential actions undertaken without congressional authorization, the fact remains that major wars have been authorized by Congress.

Where exactly does a global war on terrorism fall on the spectrum between major war and smaller scale military actions? If it were purely a police action against hostile non-state actors, akin to operations against pirates or to other small-scale operations with limited objectives, a case can be made that historical practice indicates a record of presidential deployments without advance congressional authorization. The President, after all, clearly possesses authority to repel and to forestall terrorist attacks against the United States, its forces, and citizens.

Yet, this global campaign is much more ambitious than apprehending terrorists. It aims to destroy a multi-state terrorist infrastructure and potentially defeat or overthrow sponsoring regimes. While military force is not the only, or even indeed the main, instrument for waging this war, the range of military activities that we have mounted to date is very diverse—combat operations, continuous air patrols, maritime interception of shipping, the training and equipping of foreign militaries for combat operations, operational assistance to post-conflict stability operations, just to name a few. Given that the current campaign is focused against a global terrorist network that is based in over sixty countries, that has the capacity to inflict massive casualties, and that requires or depends upon the sponsorship or acquiescence of various countries for its training and safe-harbors, the scope and complexities of this military campaign would appear to defy any commonsense notion of a limited police action.

CONGRESS'S POST-SEPTEMBER 11 AUTHORIZATION OF FORCE: SCOPE AND LIMITS

Congress's authorization for the use of force against those responsible for the attacks of September 11 is an express recognition that Congress and the President both have a critical constitutional role to play in the war on terrorism. Mindful of the centrality of congressional war powers in a campaign against terrorism that will be long-term and far-reaching, Congress sought to craft an authorization that both allowed for appropriate executive flexibility but at the same time is not a blank check.

Though not restricted geographically, Congress's post-September 11 authorization does contain some clear limits. The Joint Resolution authorizes the President:

> to use all necessary and appropriate force against those nations, organizations, or persons he determines planned, authorized, committed, or aided the terrorist attacks that occurred on September 11, 2001, or harbored such organizations or persons, in order to prevent any future acts of international terrorism against the United States by such nations, organizations or persons.

The joint resolution, in essence, authorizes (a) necessary and appropriate force, against those states, organizations, or persons who (b) planned, authorized, committed, or aided the September 11th attacks, or (c) harbored such organizations or persons, (d) in order to prevent future acts of international terrorism against the United States by such nations, organizations or persons. Thus, the force must be directed against those responsible in some way for the September 11th attacks, or those who harbored such organizations or persons; and the purpose of using force is focused and future-oriented: to prevent additional terrorist acts against the United States by the states, organizations, or persons responsible for the September 11th attacks or who harbored those responsible. The President determines whether the necessary link to the September 11th attacks is established, and presumably Congress expected he would make his determination

and the basis for it known to Congress in some fashion, perhaps through a war powers report or through briefings, e.g., to the intelligence committees. Moreover, in signing the Joint Resolution, President Bush made clear that he would consult closely with Congress as the United States responds to terrorism.

Congress' post-September 11th resolution was an unambiguous decision to authorize force. Like the Gulf War authorization in 1991, the authorization explicitly affirms that it "is intended to constitute specific statutory authorization within the meaning of section 5(b) of the War Powers Resolution." This removes any actions that fall within the scope of the authorization from the War Powers Resolution's 60-day time-clock provision. At the same time, Congress made clear that the requirements of the War Powers Resolution otherwise remain applicable.

THE WAR POWERS RESOLUTION AND THE WAR AGAINST TERRORISM

For all the controversy it has spurred, key elements of the War Powers Resolution are constitutionally compelling and warrant broad support. First, its overriding purpose is to "insure that the collective judgment of both the Congress and the President" applies to the introduction of U.S. forces into hostilities and to the continued use of those forces. Second, it seeks to enable Congress to better fulfill its constitutional responsibilities by requiring the President "in every possible instance" to "consult with Congress before introducing" U.S. armed forces into hostilities or imminent hostilities and to continue to "consult regularly" with the Congress while U.S. forces are in those situations. Moreover, the legislative history of the War Powers Resolution makes clear that Congress expected consultations to be meaningful:

Rejected was the notion that consultation should be synonymous with merely being informed. Rather, consultation in this provision means that a decision is pending on a problem and that Members of Congress are being asked by the President for their advice and opinions, and in appropriate circumstances, their approval of action contemplated. Furthermore, for consultation to be meaningful, the President himself must participate and all information relevant to the situation must be made available.

Third, under the War Powers Resolution, the President is required to report to Congress within 48 hours in designated situations, and to make periodic reports to Congress at least once every six months if U.S. forces remain in hostilities or imminent hostilities.

Whatever conclusions one reaches about the more controversial provisions of the War Powers Resolution, such as the 60-day time clock, the consultation provisions are sound and reasonable efforts to ensure that both the President and the Congress fulfill their constitutional responsibilities concerning the commitment of U.S. forces abroad. Moreover, even when Congress has authorized the use of force, as it did after September 11, regular, meaningful consultations between Congress and the President remain vital in the ongoing war on terrorism. Such consultations are imperative to ensure that there is a frank exchange of views and a shared understanding between Congress and the President on future directions in the war on terrorism and broad support for the steps ahead. To give a counterexample: The experience in Somalia is a cautionary reminder that congressional authorization and support in the early phases of an operation does not replace the need for continued dialogue about the goals and risks of a changing mission. We cannot afford to make the same mistakes in the current context.

CONSULTATIONS

How should a system of regular, meaningful consultations between Congress and the Administration be structured as the country faces up to what will likely be a long, complex campaign against terrorism? Clearly, a commitment by the President to hold regular consultations with the bipartisan congressional leadership would be invaluable. Second, as the War Powers Resolution expressly provides in section 4(b), Congress should request that a broader range of information be included in the periodic war powers reports provided by the Administration. Those reports, which have generally been perfunctory since the War Powers Resolution was first enacted, should, in the context of the war on terrorism, include a fuller discussion of the objectives and effectiveness of U.S. action, including our efforts to work closely with allies on multiple fronts. Congress may also wish to request that the reports be made more frequently, say every three months, and, in any event, invite Cabinet officials to testify on the state of the war on terrorism when those reports are submitted. The combination of fuller reports and high-level testimony could, in conjunction with meaningful consultations, make for a more significant and effective dialogue between Congress and the Administration regarding future goals and strategies in the war on terrorism.

FUTURE AUTHORIZATION

As important as consultations are, however, they are not a substitute for congressional authorization if military action is contemplated that clearly implicates Congress's war powers. While the post-September 11 authorization is broad, it does contain limits, most notably the requirement of a clear link to the attacks of September 11. Other threats to U.S. security unrelated to those attacks may exist or arise in the future, and various military options may be considered, including options that go beyond measures to prevent future acts of terrorism by those responsible for the September 11th attacks. Whether and when additional congressional authorization is constitutionally required will depend on the facts of the situation and on the nature and objectives of the military action contemplated.

Constitutionally, the President clearly possesses the power to repel attacks and to forestall imminent attacks against the United States and its armed forces, and to protect Americans in imminent danger abroad. But the decision to go beyond this and commence a war belongs to Congress. Major military action with far-reaching objectives such as regime change is precisely the kind of action that constitution-ally should be debated and authorized by Congress in advance. The Constitution's "wisdom" on this point is compelling: Authorization, if provided by Congress, ensures that the risks and implications of any such action have been fully considered and that a national consensus to proceed exists. Congressional authorization also ensures American combat forces that the country is behind them, and conveys America's resolve and unity to allies as well as adversaries.

The war against terrorism will, unfortunately, be with us for a long time. However, as our nation moves ahead on various fronts, using a variety of tools and means, our response will be more effective and more sustainable if the Congress and the President continue to work together in the best tradition of our great Constitution.

THE CONTINUING DEBATE:
Presidential War Powers and Terrorism

What Is New

The decision for war against Iraq in 2003 followed a familiar scenario. Some Bush administration officials opposed asking for a congressional resolution. "We don't want to be in the legal position of asking Congress to authorize the use of force when the president already has that full authority," said one such official. In the end though, Bush was mindful of polls showing, in one survey, that 80% of Americans wanted him to get authorization from Congress before launching an attack, while only 17% thought that an unnecessary step, and 3% were unsure. This and the urge to demonstrate broad support led Bush in October 2002 to seek a resolution, even while maintaining that legally he did not need one. And as has also usually been true, Congress complied by large majorities: in this case, 296 to 133 in the House and 77 to 23 in the Senate. Even in signing the joint resolution, though, Bush asserted his unilateral authority. In his words, "While I appreciate receiving…support, my request for it did not, and my signing this resolution does not, constitute any change in the long-standing positions of the executive branch on either the president's constitutional authority to use force to deter, prevent, or respond to aggression or other threats to U.S. interests or on the [un]constitutionality of the War Powers Resolution."

As has occurred during many recent U.S. conflicts, there was a legal challenge. Six members of Congress and the families of several soldiers being sent to Iraq filed a suit charging that the congressional resolution was an unconstitutional delegation of the authority by Congress to declare war to the president. And, following the established pattern, a federal judge dismissed the suit on the grounds that the lawsuit engaged "political questions in the legal sense that are beyond the jurisdiction of the court."

Where to Find More

One recent study is Ryan C. Hendrickson, The *Clinton Wars: The Constitution, Congress, and War Powers* (Vanderbilt University Press, 2002). An article that advocates repealing the WPR on the grounds that its 60-day provision gives the president too much power is Louis Fisher and David Gray Adler, "The War Powers Resolution: Time to Say Goodbye," *Political Science Quarterly* (Spring 1998). To find a copy of the War Powers Resolution go to the Web site of Yale Law School's Avalon Project at: http://www.yale.edu/lawweb/avalon/warpower.htm. For background on the use of the War Powers Resolution, see the Congressional Research Service report, "The War Power Resolution: Presidential Compliance," March 24, 2003 on the State Department Web site at: http://fpc.state.gov/documents/organization/19134.pdf. Also good is the CRS report, "Response to Terrorism: Legal Aspects of the Military Use of Force," September 13, 2001 at: http://fpc.state.gov/documents/organization/6217.pdf.

What More to Do

Clear up the confusion about Congress' authority to declare war and the president's authority as commander in chief. Write and debate in class an amendment to the Constitution that will specify when (if ever) presidents can use military force or send U.S. forces into harm's way on their own authority and when (if ever) doing so would require a declaration of war or other form of congressional authorization.

13 BUREAUCRACY

THE DEPARTMENT OF EDUCATION AND TITLE IX:
Champion of Equality *or* Overzealous Crusader?

CHAMPION OF EQUALITY

ADVOCATE: Judith Sweet, Vice-President for Championships and Senior
  Women Administrator, National Collegiate Athletic Association

SOURCE: U.S. Department of Education, Secretary's Commission on
  Opportunity in Athletics, Hearings, August 27, 2002

OVERZEALOUS CRUSADER

ADVOCATE: Amanda Ross-Edwards, Visiting Professor of Political Science,
  Fairfield University

SOURCE: "The Department of Education and Title IX: Flawed
  Interpretation and Implementation," an essay written especially for this
  volume, October 2003

We tend to think that elected representatives serving in Congress and, to a degree, the elected president, make federal rules. However, in terms of sheer volume, non-elected agency officials make most government rules. Off these functionaries, the president appoints about 600, with career civil servants making up the rest of the 2.8 million civilian federal employees.

One measure of the deluge of bureaucratic rules is the *Federal Register*, the annual compilation of new rules, rule changes, and other authoritative bureaucratic actions. Just for 2002, the *Federal Register* was an immense 80,332 pages of regulations addressing almost every conceivable subject. So great is the impact of the rule-making and implementation authority of the bureaucracy that some analysts refer to it as the fourth branch of government.

Administrators make binding rules in two ways. One is by issuing regulations that, in theory, simply add detail to the general intent of laws passed by Congress. In practice, many analysts say, agency-made rules take laws in a direction that Congress did not anticipate or even want. The second way that bureaucrats make rules is by how they implement the law. As with regulations, implementation is supposed to follow the intent of the law, but whether that is true is sometimes controversial. You will see presently that advocate Amanda Ross-Edwards charges that the Department of Education has both formulated rules and implemented them in a manner that has subverted Congress' original intent when it enacted Title IX of the Education Amendments (Act) in 1972. This legislation declared that no one "shall, on the basis of sex, be...subjected to discrimination under any education program or activity receiving Federal financial assistance." It is language that covers most activities at all levels of education, although here we will focus on athletics in higher education.

The legislation also, as most acts do, authorized and directed agencies "to effectuate the provisions of [this act]...by issuing rules, regulations, or orders of general applicability which shall be consistent with achievement of the objectives of the statute."

What is not in dispute here is the value of the basic law. It was enacted to protect girls and women from discrimination by schools and colleges, which was widespread as late as the 1960s. For example, after Luci Baines Johnson, the daughter of President Lyndon Johnson, married in 1966, Georgetown University's nursing school denied her re-admission on the grounds that school regulations barred married women (but not married men) from being students. And it was not until 1970 and a federal court order that the University of Virginia even admitted undergraduate women, much less let them play sports.

There can also be no argument that since the passage of Title IX there has been a dramatic increase in the number of women participating college sports and in the percentage of student athletes who are women. Judith Sweet attributes these changes to the enforcement of Title IX, but Amanda Ross-Edward contends that the expansion of women's athletics was already underway and that the changes reflect social norms more than the legislation.

What is very much in dispute here is whether, the Department of Education's Office for Civil Rights, which since 1994 has been responsible for enforcing Title IX, has followed congressional intent when interpreting the law and formulating regulations and policies. Also at issue, albeit less directly so, is the matter of how equal opportunity should be measured. In this sense, this debate is distinctly related to Debate 17 on education policy and affirmative action admissions. Critics of both the way that Title IX has been enforced and many aspects of affirmative action charge that numerical quotas are used overtly or covertly and that they are neither legal nor just.

POINTS TO PONDER

➤ Amanda Ross-Edwards argues men are being subjected to reverse discrimination. What is the basis of the charge, and do you agree?

➤ Currently, only 45.8% of college students are men. Should this mean that 54.2% of all college scholarship athletes should be women?

➤ If not by proportionality, how would you evaluate a school's compliance with Title IX?

The Department of Education and Title IX:
Champion of Equality

JUDITH SWEET

I've loved sports all my life. As a young girl I dreamt of representing my high school and college on a sport team. I never had that opportunity because there were no teams at either the high school or college level.

While I would welcome the opportunity to share my perspective based on those life and campus experiences that Cynthia alluded to, my remarks today will focus on the NCAA.

On behalf of the National Collegiate Athletic Association and its more than 1200 member colleges, universities, conferences, and affiliated organizations, I'm pleased to have the opportunity to provide the Commission with comments about the impact of Title IX on intercollegiate athletics from the Association's perspective.

For those of you who may not be as familiar with the NCAA as others of you are, allow me to briefly note that the NCAA is a membership driven association. The NCAA derives its authority, including all national policy, entirely from the will of the membership through the vote of institutional or conference representatives.

The vast majority of decisions regarding athletics programs, including which sports to sponsor or to cease sponsoring, are made at the campus level. Member institutions have complete autonomy over their programs except where the broader membership has set standards through national policy.

Allow me also briefly to describe the role of intercollegiate athletics for women 30 years ago when Title IX was signed into law. There were no college athletic scholarships to speak of for women, no NCAA championships for women, and very few opportunities for competition.

In 1971/72 a survey of the NCAA member institutions showed that only 29,977 women were participating in sports and recreational programs compared to over 170,000 men, more than five times as many men as women.

The athletics opportunities for women were few, and the prospects for growth were dismal. With numbers like that, it might be fair to wonder what college woman would show any interest at all in athletics.

What a difference 30 years of legislative impetus, opportunity and support make. Today nearly 150,000 women are competing in sports at NCAA member schools.

While some individuals suggest that women do not have a strong interest in sports participation, the numbers prove otherwise. In the last ten years alone female NCAA participants have increased by more than 55,000. The number of collegiate women's soccer teams has grown from 80 in 1982 to 824 in 2002.

The number of girls participating in sports at the high school level exceeds 2.7 million. As opportunity has increased, interest has increased. Of the 87 championships in 22 sports conducted by the NCAA, 43 are exclusively for women, and bowling will be added to the women's championship in 2003/04.

And...the Committee on Women's Athletics has also indicated that they will look at the number of scholarships being provided in all of our sports. The NCAA membership has demonstrated a commitment to both men's and women's Olympic sports through legislation that allows the continuation of championships in Olympic sports even if the number of sponsoring institutions does not meet minimum requirements for championship events.

Clearly Title IX has promoted opportunities for female athletes over the last 30 years, but there is much more still to be done to ensure that men and women who attend NCAA member schools have equitable access to athletics participation.

Although women comprise 54 percent of the undergraduate student population at NCAA member schools on average, as you have heard, they account for only 4 percent of the athletics participants. They receive only 40 percent of the scholarships; they receive only 36 percent of the operating dollars, and have only 32 percent for recruiting budgets.

Like any social legislation designed to change the deeply imbedded status quo, Title IX has had and still has its critics. Over the last 30 years the voices of dissent have been less strident regarding the law itself and have grown more concerned with the standards used to measure compliance.

The Department of Education standards consider an athletics program to be in compliance with Title IX if its student athletes by gender are in proportion to the make-up of the undergraduate student body or if the program can demonstrate a history of expanding its program to meet the needs of the underrepresented gender or if the program can demonstrate that it has fully and effectively accommodated interests and abilities of the underrepresented gender.

Critics argue that the focus of courts and the Office of Civil Rights has been on a proportionality test and that it has become the de facto single test used to determine compliance. The unintended consequence of Title IX they say has been the cutting of the so-called nonrevenue men's sports in order to get the number of athletics participants

for an institution more in line with the undergraduate population by gender.

Others have claimed that increased expenses in providing opportunities for women to comply with Title IX have resulted in a reduction of spending for men's sports. In fact, financial reports from 1972 to 1993 show that in Division 1-A for every new dollar spent on women's sports, three new dollars were spent on men's sports.

Before I discuss the findings of the report on this issue from the United States GAO [General•Accounting Office, an investigate agency of Congress] in March 2001, allow me to share with you a message from the NCAA executive committee, one of the primary decision making bodies within the government structure and comprised of university Presidents and Chancellors.

In a discussion about the work of the Commission at their meetings earlier this month, the President spoke strongly of the value of Title IX and urged the Office of Civil Rights to apply consistent Title IX enforcement and interpretations in all regions of the country.

Regarding decisions by member institutions to cut men's sports, this group of college and university CEOs noted that institutions have dropped sports for various reasons, such as institutional philosophy, program priorities, finances, infractions, safety, lack of conference opportunities, inadequate facilities, insurance costs, and others, but the single most important message that they wanted me to deliver on their behalf was this: Don't blame Title IX for institutional decisions to cut programs.

The President's position is supported by findings of the GAO report. The United States Congress included provisions in the higher education amendments of 1998 that required the GAO to study participation in athletics, including schools' decisions to add or discontinue sports teams. They examined the membership of both the NCAA and the NAIA. Among the GAO's findings are these: Athletics participation for both men and women have increased since 1981. The total number of teams has increased for both men and women.

Since 1992, 963 schools added teams and 30 discontinued teams. Most were able to add teams, usually women's teams, without discontinuing any teams.

The report found that the level of student interest was the factor schools cited most often as greatly or very greatly influencing their decisions to add or discontinue both men's and women's teams.

The conclusions are clear. The decisions to discontinue specific sports are made at the institutional level for a variety of reasons.

If the decision is made to eliminate sports for gender-equity reasons, it is because institutions have chosen this path rather than pursuing other options, not because Title IX dictates such action.

The task before the Commission is an important one. In a perfect world Title IX would not be necessary. There would be enough resources and the will to do the right thing and thus meet everyone's needs. Social legislation exists, of course, because we do not live in that perfect world.

In the charge to this commission the Department of Education acknowledges that extraordinary progress has resulted from the passage of Title IX. While we like to think that this progress would have taken place without Title IX because it was the right thing to do, the fact is that opportunities and support for girls and women in athletics are still not equitable with those provided for men, even though it was 30 years since the law was passed.

Your charge appears to bear more on the federal standards for measure of compliance than on the necessity for the law. The degree to which the Commission can give direction to colleges and universities in achieving compliance with Title IX, emphasizing application of any of the three prongs, would remove the misunderstanding that proportionality is the only way to comply. The law is clear; the intent is to correct inequities.

The NCAA stands ready to assist the Commission any way it can as you deliberate. The ultimate test for compliance with Title IX may have been summed up best by an NCAA gender-equity task force in 1992. It defined gender equity in the following manner: An athletics program can be considered gender equitable when the participants in both men's and women's programs would accept as fair and equitable the overall program of the other gender. No individual should be discriminated against on the basis of gender, institutionally or nationally, in intercollegiate athletics.

As I conclude my comments, I urge you to consider the following: Would participants in both our men's and women's programs accept as fair and equitable 40 percent of the participation opportunities, 36 percent of the operating dollars, and 32 percent of the recruiting dollars? Would we expect that of them?

The Department of Education and Title IX: Overzealous Crusader

AMANDA ROSS-EDWARDS

In 1973, one year after passage of Title IX, tennis professional Billie Jean King received a congratulatory call from President Nixon for being the first female athlete to win one hundred thousand dollars in prize money in a single year. In 2003, Justine Henin-Hardenne received one million dollars in prize money for winning a single event, the U.S. Open in Women's Tennis. It is clear that women's opportunities in sports have increased in the 31 years since Title IX was enacted. It is also clear that in the past ten years Title IX's interpretation and implementation have become flawed. Contrary to Title IX's original aim of equal opportunity for women in education, the courts and the Office for Civil Rights at the Department of Education have equated equal outcomes in the form of statistical proportionality as their primary means of measuring compliance with Title IX statute.

Title IX prohibits sex discrimination in education by institutions that receive federal funding. Although Title IX passed in 1972, it was not until 1975 that the Department of Health, Education and Welfare published implementing regulations. These regulations, however, were vague and thus provided very little guidance on how schools should enforce the law against sex discrimination in athletics. It was not until 1979 that the department's Office of Civil Rights (OCR) established its Title IX Athletics Policy Interpretation. According to Jessica Gavora, a senior policy advisor at the Department of Justice, "although this interpretation lacks the legal status of an official government regulation, it has been treated by succeeding adminis-

trations and by the courts as the government's final word on implementing Title IX in athletics." This document declares that schools may comply with Title IX in one of three ways: 1) proportionality; 2) showing a recent history of adding women's athletic teams; or 3) proving that the interests of the student body were being met. Gavora notes in her book, *Tilting the Playing Field*, that "Officials in the OCR insist that the three-part test is progressive; compliance they say, is measured in stages. If a school is unable to comply under the first test, it may do so under the second and, failing there, it has a final opportunity under the third test. In any case, a school need pass only one of the three tests to be in compliance with the law." Historical evidence, however, demonstrates that this isn't true; statistical proportionality has become a requirement for compliance under Title IX statute.

The Office for Civil Rights has never explicitly defined proportionality; however, the courts have generally agreed at this point that proportionality is an athletics participation rate that is within plus or minus five percent of the sex ratio of the student body. Proportionality, thus, does not count the number of opportunities available to men and women, but rather the actual number of individual men and women competing in sports. In order to comply under the proportionality rule, the percentage of women participating in athletic programs should be proportional to the percentage of women enrolled in the college or university. If 51 percent of the student body is made up of women, but only 45 percent of the athletes are women, then the college or university would not be in compliance with Title IX.

As noted, in theory a school must only meet one of the three prongs. In practice, however, as the result of significant court cases and executive interpretation, the proportionality rule has become a "safe harbor" for a school's compliance with Title IX. In 1991, Brown University cut two women's teams and two men's teams for budgetary reasons. At the time, Brown University had 15 sports teams for women, compared to the average 8.3 for other NCAA Division I schools. In fact, the number of women's varsity teams at Brown outnumbered the men's. Only Harvard had a broader and more generous women's athletic program.

Despite Brown's exemplary program of women's athletics, Amy Cohen, along with seven other women from the teams that had been cut, filed a lawsuit against Brown charging non-compliance with Title IX. They argued that the proportion of women participating in sports at Brown was less then the proportion of female students. At the time the lawsuit was filed, 51 percent of Brown students were women, while only 39 percent of Brown's athletes were women. According to the plaintiffs, if 61 percent of the athletes at Brown were male, then cutting two men's teams and two women's teams merely perpetuated a preexisting inequality.

The relevance of this case is the context within which it was decided and the impact of its outcome on the future actions of other schools regarding men and women and sports. In 1992, the Supreme Court decided the case of *Franklin v. Gwinnett County Public Schools*, which involved Christine Franklin's claim that the Gwinnett County Public School district owed her punitive damages for not protecting her from her teacher's repeated harassing behavior even after she reported the incidents. The Supreme Court ruled in her favor and thus

set precedent for women to receive monetary compensation for Title IX violations.

By the time the Brown case arose, lawyers, such as Arthur Bryant, executive director of the Trial Lawyers for Public Justice (TLPJ), had fully recognized the possibilities associated with Title IX statute. In the early 1990's, Bryant and TLPJ had filed a number of successful Title IX actions against colleges and universities. Their strategy involved filing a case against a university or college that had cut a women's team and demanding that the team be reinstated. The case usually never made it to court because college administrators wanted to avoid the publicity and the legal costs. The women's teams were thus reinstated and Bryant received his attorney's fees.

Aside from the issue that a primary motive behind these cases was monetary gain for Bryant, there is also the question of how Bryant found out about these cases. In the Brown case, a woman named Kathryn Reith, a Brown alumna and director of advocacy for the Women's Sports Foundation, was responsible for creating the case. As a representative of an interest group interested in women's athletics, she wanted female athletes to file federal complaints under Title IX. It was not until the Franklin decision that money provided the needed added incentive for individuals to file complaints. Reith and Bryant thus looked for the ideal client in the Brown University case and chose Amy Cohen, the former captain of the Brown gymnastics team. In the Brown case, therefore, it was not female athletes pressuring the school and the government for more opportunities; instead it was pressure group incentive and monetary interest that led to the creation of this case. Women were not demanding more athletic opportunity; money and organized interests motivated policy reinterpretation.

Unlike the other suits filed by Bryant, Brown University administrator Vartan

Gregorian refused to settle. In court, Cohen's lawyers argued that Brown could correct the discrimination against women by refunding the women's gymnastics and volleyball teams and continuing to create teams for women until proportionality was reached. Brown's lawyers responded that this was a complete misapplication of the law. The three prong test was clearly a misrepresentation of congressional intent. The authors of Title IX legislation stated clearly in the congressional record that Title IX did not mean quotas. Furthermore, athletics is only one part of Title IX's larger applicability to the academic realm. For instance, dance programs have proportionately more women than men, and engineering programs have proportionately more men than women. So why is disproportionate involvement in sports targeted as an indication of discrimination?

In 1995, the lower courts found in favor of Amy Cohen. Brown University immediately filed an appeal. In January 1996, while waiting for the decision of the first circuit of the U.S. Court of Appeals, Norma Cantu, head of the Office of Civil Rights (OCR), issued a clarification of the three part test in which she reinterpreted the third prong. Appointed as President Clinton's Chief Title IX enforcer, Cantu had established a proactive approach to Title IX enforcement. According to Gavora, within the first nineteen months of Cantu's tenure, "OCR began 240 reviews of schools from which no civil rights complaints had been filed." This was in sharp contrast to the Reagan and Bush administrations that waited to initiate investigations until complaints were filed against schools and universities.

Prior to Cantu's reinterpretation, schools were required to meet the interests and abilities of women only to the same degree as they met the interests and abilities of men. Cantu's directive instructed that the interests of only the underrepresented sex be fully accommodated. This reinterpretation served as an indication that compliance with Title IX required more than the provision of equal opportunity for women in athletics; it required remedial action. Cantu also put both the NCAA and its member institutions on notice that the federal government backed the Title IX compliance evolving in the courts. Ten months later, the First Circuit of the U.S. Court of Appeals confirmed the lower courts decision and in April 1997, the Supreme Court denied review thereby letting the lower court's ruling stand. The message was not lost on other schools and their lawyers. Since then, the safest and surest way to comply with Title IX has been by ensuring that statistical quotas are met.

As a result, colleges have proceeded to cut men's teams as the surest means of complying with Title IX. For instance, in the hearings before the U.S. Department of Education, Secretary's Commission on Opportunity in Athletics, Christine Stolba, a senior Fellow with the Independent Women's Forum, testified that between 1993 and 1999, 53 men's golf teams, 39 men's track teams, 43 wrestling teams and baseball teams have been eliminated. The University of Miami's diving team, which had produced 15 Olympic athletes, has also been eliminated. Furthermore, in 2001, the General Accounting Office, reported that between 1981 and 1999, 171 men's wrestling programs, 83 men's tennis teams and 56 men's gymnastics teams, had been eliminated.

These men, whose opportunities to play sports are being denied, have a valid argument that they are victims of reverse discrimination. Men's teams are being cut and opportunities to play are being denied in order to create the required number of male and female athletes. Not only is this inequitable, but it may also have an impact on the Olympic movement in the United States. College athletics is a primary source for our nation's Olympic athletes; therefore, as the number of men's teams is reduced, the number of potential Olympic athletes is also reduced.

Some argue that this is a spending choice. Colleges and universities facing budget cuts choose to cut men's teams rather than cut money and players to sports like football that bring revenue and name recognition to the school. On the one hand, large division 1-A football programs could do a lot to alleviate some of the division between the two sides of this debate by curbing some of the excesses in their programs. On the other hand, division 1-A football programs are more of an exception to the rule. According to Bill Curry, a former college football coach and ESPN game analyst, in 2002, only 17.2% of college football teams were Division 1-A. These are the teams that need the large number of scholarships to field championship teams. Two-thirds of these programs produce revenue for their universities.

When it comes to complying with Title IX under the proportionality rule, however, it is not a budget issue; it is a Title IX issue. Money is beside the point; Title IX deals with the number of bodies on the playing field. As an example, in 1994, Marquette University cut its men's wrestling team. There was no budget issue. At the time, it was the alumni who funded the wrestling team. The real issue was that the number of male wrestlers, more than 30, skewed the overall number of male-to-female athletes at Marquette. Women made up 54% of Marquette's student body compared to only 46% of its student athletes. Marquette University, thus, dropped wrestling in order to comply with Title IX and remain NCAA certified. Furthermore, Marquette University does not have a football team, so football cannot be blamed as a blanket issue.

Also relevant is the number of male versus female walk-on athletes. Studies show that men's team rosters are bigger than women's because more men walk-on than women. If it was really about budget issues then schools wouldn't be turning away non-scholarship, walk-on athletes who don't cost the school very much. Cost has nothing to do with it. Instead, it has to do with a quota over which men's participation cannot go and under which women's participation cannot go. Why should men be penalized because they walk on and women don't?

In response, supporters of the current method of implementation argue that women's demonstrated interest in sports is not a true measure of equality because it fails to consider the potential for female athletic participation. They contend that women turn out to play sports at a lower rate than men as a result of past discrimination against female athletes. It is true that, culturally, in the past women were not encouraged to play sports. Only recently have women athletes become truly accepted role models for future generations. The UCONN women's basketball team, for instance, only began charging for its games in 1993. By the late 90's, every game was sold out. According to this argument, therefore, Title IX needs to ensure that the opportunity exists for women to achieve their full athletic potential. If the opportunities are created, women will want to play these sports. In other words, if you build it, they will come.

Congress, however, did not pass a law thirty years ago that said it was the responsibility of colleges and universities to create interest in athletics. It passed a law that barred discrimination based on sex. The point is not whether or not making sure women reach their full athletic potential is a good idea or not. It's about interpreting the law correctly. If we want schools and universities to create athletic opportunities for women then we need to pass a law for that purpose. Title IX isn't that law. Furthermore, Congress has never amended Title IX in the years since 1972; instead, the executive branch has progressively changed Title IX's meaning through successive reinterpretations of its implementation policy. The eventual consequence of the U.S. Department of Education's Secretary's Commission on Opportunity in Athletics will be further development in Title IX's meaning.

Those who oppose changing the current interpretation of Title IX, such as Judith Sweet, argue that Title IX policy has been directly responsible for changing women's opportunities in education and sport. Title IX's compliance standards should, therefore, not be changed because athletic opportunities for girls and women in athletics are not yet equitable. Evidence suggests, however, that by the time Title IX passed in 1972 the revolution in women's sport had already begun. Women's participation in sport began to increase significantly before Title IX's passage in 1972 and well before the executive enacted Title IX's final policy interpretation in 1979 which established

Title IX's enforcement guidelines. For instance, according to Gavora, "between 1971 and 1972, the number of girls playing high school sports jumped almost threefold, from 294,015 to 817,073." Furthermore, the number of women participating in intercollegiate athletics doubled in the five years *before* Title IX from around 15,000 to 30,000. Although it was the government that created the statute and regulations to enforce the principal of not using the people's money to deny access, it was the changing social environment that led women to seek such access in the first place.

It is clear that Title IX is still needed as a means of ensuring equal opportunities for women in education and athletics. There must be, however, a better way of implementing this law. If courts and policy makers recognize that Title IX guarantees equal opportunity, but does not necessarily guarantee equal outcomes, then they can return to the original intent of Title IX and restore the integrity of this policy's interpretation and implementation.

THE CONTINUING DEBATE:
The Department of Education and Title IX

What Is New

In June 2002, the ongoing uproar over the application of Title IX prompted Secretary of Education Secretary Roderick Paige to create the Commission on Opportunity in Athletics to examine the implementation of Title IX. The 18-member panel was divided evenly between men and women and included individuals with backgrounds in government, academia, and athletics. On February 26, 2003, the Commission submitted several recommendations to Paige, two of which were highly controversial. These drew furious dissent from some of the commissioners, numerous interest groups, and several prominent members of Congress, both Democrat and Republican. One was that the Secretary of Education be allowed to formulate a "reasonable variance" from existing Title IX standards to measure compliance. Opponents of this change argued that "close enough" was not a satisfactory benchmark. The second controversial recommendation was to authorize the secretary to establish "additional ways of demonstrating equity." Proponents of Title IX fretted this vaguely worded standard could be used to gut enforcement. Whether he agreed with these criticisms or was averse to a political donnybrook, Paige announced in July 2003 that he would not act on either of the controversial recommendations.

Where to Find More

Information about Title IX and the Commission on Opportunity in Athletics is available on the Department of Education site: http://www.ed.gov/about/bdscomm/list/athletics/qsandas.html. Two articles that take opposing views on Title IX are Michael Lynch, "Title IX's Pyrrhic Victory," *Reason*, April 2001 (http://reason.com/0104/fe.ml.title.shtml); and Mariah Burton Nelson, "And Now They Tell Us Women Don't Really Like Sports?" *Ms. Magazine*, January 2003 (http://www.mariahburton-nelson.com/WomenSportsMsTitleIX.html). For a group that criticizes Title IX, go to the Web site of the Independent Women's Forum at http://www.iwf.org/issues/titleix/index.shtml. The opposite stance is taken by the National Women's Law Center. Among other things, its Web site (http://www.nwlc.org/) lists 30 colleges which it charges are not in compliance with Title IX.

What More to Do

One thing to do is to visit the Web site of the National Women's Law Center to see if your school is on the list of 30 colleges the Center says are in particular violation of Title IX. Look at the data provided at the site. Assuming it is true, do you agree with the Center? You can also contact the office of your school's athletic department to get comparable data for your college. How does it stand? Also, you can help Secretary of Education Paige come up with Title IX enforcement standards with which everyone can agree. Draft a department regulation detailing how compliance will be measured.

14   JUDICIARY

LEGAL PHILOSOPHY AS A QUALIFICATION FOR THE BENCH:
Judicious Standard *or* Obstructionist Barrier?

JUDICIOUS STANDARD

ADVOCATE: Laurence H. Tribe, Professor, Harvard Law School

SOURCE: Testimony during hearings on "Judicial Nominations, Filibusters, and the Constitution: When a Majority Is Denied Its Right to Consent," before U.S. Senate Committee on the Judiciary, May 6, 2002

OBSTRUCTIONIST BARRIER

ADVOCATE: Todd F. Gaziano, Senior Fellow in Legal Studies and Director, Center for Legal and Judicial Studies, The Heritage Foundation

SOURCE: Testimony during hearings on "A Judiciary Diminished Is Justice Denied: The Constitution, the Senate, and the Vacancy Crisis in the Federal Judiciary" before U.S. House of Representatives, Committee on the Judiciary, Subcommittee on the Constitution, October 10, 2002

The power of federal judges to make policy underlies this debate. As Supreme Court Chief Justice Charles Evans Hughes once put it, "We are under a Constitution, but the Constitution is what the judges say it is." This ability to make policy has two sources. One is the power of interpretation, the ability to find meaning in the words of the Constitution and legislative acts. There is considerable controversy about whether judges should follow "original intent," but many judges adhere to the alternative philosophy of Justice Oliver Wendell Holmes, Jr. that the Constitution should be interpreted "in the light of our whole experience and not merely in that of what was said a hundred years ago."

The courts also make policy through the power of judicial review, the determination of whether state and federal laws and actions taken by officials are constitutional. The policy implications of this power are evident in the cases of *Plessy v. Ferguson* (1896), in which the Supreme Court ruled that separate but equal racial accommodations (in this case in railroad cars) was constitutional, and *Brown v. Board of Education* (1954), in which the court reversed itself and ruled that separate but equal accommodations (in this case in schools) was unconstitutional. U.S. policy changed because nine justices in 1954 saw things differently than nine justices had in 1896.

The powers of judicial review and interpretation that federal judges, particularly Supreme Court justices, possess means that their appointments have important policy ramifications. This is intensified by the rarity of Supreme Court vacancies. Since 1789, there have been 44 presidents but only 18 chief justices, and there have been nearly 12,000 members of Congress, compared to 108 chief and associate justices.

Historically, the willingness of the Senate to usually confirm Supreme Court nominees Court has ebbed and flowed. At first, legislative challenges were common.

From 1789 to 1900, the Senate did not confirm 23 individuals, or about one-third of all nominees to the Supreme Court. Partisanship was often the reason. For example, George Washington's nomination in 1795 of John Rutledge as chief justice was defeated by Federalist Party senators who were offended that Rutledge had opposed the Jay Treaty with Great Britain.

By contrast, during the first half of the 20th century, senators rejected only one nominee to the high court. Many nominees, including Earl Warren, did not even appear before the Senate Judiciary Committee. This was changed by the surprisingly liberal record established as chief justice by Warren, a Republican governor of California appointed by Republican President Dwight Eisenhower. Since 1955, all nominees have testified during the confirmation process. Moreover, the process has become more contentious, with six Supreme Court nominees rejected since 1968. Especially during the terms of Bill Clinton and George W. Bush, resistance to appointments has also increasingly affected nominations to lower courts.

It is important to point out that the issue is not simply presidents appointing members of their own party to the bench. That has been the overwhelming historical norm, which only makes sense given the data that shows, among recent appointments, Democratic judges tend to take liberal positions and Republican judges are more apt to take conservative positions in their rulings.

Compounding the debate, there is controversy over the process. Particularly contentious is the practice in the Senate of members sometimes using a filibuster (a tactic of halting business by speaking continuously) to block confirmation. A filibuster can be halted by a cloture vote, but that is difficult to actuate because it takes 60 votes to pass.

POINTS TO PONDER

➤ Laurence Tribe explains why he opposed the nomination to the Supreme Court of Robert Bork, a nominee of impressive experience (judge of the U.S. Circuit Court of Appeals, Yale law professor, Solicitor General, Acting U.S. attorney general). What is Tribe's reasoning? Do you agree?

➤ Todd F. Gaziano argues "the confirmation process...needs to be fixed somehow." Why does he think it is broken? Who does he hold responsible?

➤ Can the inherently political nomination and confirmation process be expected to create a neutral, apolitical judiciary?

Legal Philosophy as a Qualification for the Bench: Judicious Standard

Laurence H. Tribe

I am honored to have been invited...to shed whatever light I can on the extremely important, and hopefully not too timely, topic of the Senate's role in the consideration of presidential nominations to the Supreme Court of the United States. I say "hopefully not too timely" because I think it wise of the Senate...to focus its attention now—not when a vacancy arises or a name is put forward—on the criteria to be applied in the confirmation process, and particularly on the role of ideology in that process.—

There is a difficult trade-off here, to be sure. In Washington, as elsewhere, the squeaky wheel gets the grease. Focusing meaningful attention on an issue before it becomes a problem, much less a crisis, is difficult in the best of circumstances. Doing so when the issue is as abstract and complex as that of confirmation criteria for Supreme Court Justices is more difficult still. Yet waiting until the matter is upon us, complete with a name or a short list of names, with interest groups and spinmeisters formidably arrayed on both sides, assures that the discussion will resemble a shouting match more than a civil conversation, and that every remark will be filtered through agenda detectors tuned to the highest pitch. On balance, I believe that addressing the question of the Senate's proper role under a veil of ignorance—ignorance as to precisely when a vacancy will first arise, which of the sitting justices will be the first to depart, and which name or names will be brought forth by The White House—seems likeliest to lead to fruitful reflection on how to

proceed when the veil is lifted and we are all confronted with the stark reality of specific names and all that they might portend for the republic.

It is understandable that, partly because of the seemingly abstract and speculative character of such a discussion in the absence of any actual nominee, and partly because the more immediate question actually facing the Senate Judiciary Committee is how best to evaluate a group of nominees already put forward by the President to fill various vacancies in the federal courts of appeals, [you have] chosen to cast its inquiry more broadly than a focus on Supreme Court nominations would indicate and has decided to include in its charge the question of what role ideology should play in considering federal judicial nominations generally. For that reason, at the conclusion of my observations about my principal topic that of Supreme Court nominations I will offer a few thoughts about the broader question....But because I want to preserve to the degree possible the distinct advantages of separating the general question of criteria from any particular nominee or set of nominees, I will carefully avoid saying anything about any pending nomination and will, until the end of my remarks, discuss only the matter of nominations to the Supreme Court.

When my book *God Save This Honorable Court* was published in 1985 defending an active role for the Senate in the appointment of Supreme Court Justices, the Court was delicately balanced, with liberals like William Brennan and Thurgood Marshall offsetting conservatives like William Rehnquist and Antonin Scalia.

Yet, on the inevitable book tour, I found quite a few otherwise well-informed people wondering why the composition of the Supreme Court was all that big a deal, and why it shouldn't suffice for the Senate simply to make sure that the President wasn't packing the Court with cronies and with mediocrities. Having satisfied itself of the professional qualifications and character of the President's nominee, some people wondered, why should the Senate be concerned with that nominee's philosophical leanings or ideological predispositions?

People seemed to view things differently when they were exposed to the historical background showing that the Framers contemplated a much more central role for the Senate in this process, and when they learned that it was mostly the unwieldiness of having a collective body like the Senate make the initial nomination that led the Framers [of the Constitution], at the last minute in the drafting process, to entrust the nomination to the President and to leave the Senate with the task of deciding whether to confirm or reject; that, even in the final version of the Constitution as ratified in 1789, the Senate's task was not left wholly passive (deciding between a thumbs-up and a thumbs-down) but was cast as the role of giving its "advice and consent;" and that, with the exception of an uncharacteristic lull in the last century, the Senate has traditionally exercised its advice and consent function with respect to the Supreme Court in a lively and engaged manner, concerning itself not simply with the intellect and integrity of the nominee but with the nominee's overall approach to the task of judging, and often with the nominee's substantive views on the burning legal and constitutional issues of the day. Those who initially assumed the Senate need not concern itself with a nominee's ideology tended to view the matter in a new light when reminded that, both in the formative days of our nation's history, under presidents as early as George Washington, and in recent decades, there has been a venerable tradition in which the Senate has played anything but a deferential role on Supreme Court nominations.

All of that registered with people back in 1985, but it wasn't until the 1987 resignation of [Justice] Lewis Powell and the confirmation battle later that year over Robert Bork that the concrete stakes in this otherwise abstract controversy came to life for the great majority of the American public. In retrospect, although one can lament the ways in which some interest groups and politicians—on both sides of the question, frankly—exaggerated the record bearing on Judge Bork's views and bearing on what kind of Supreme Court Justice he would have made, the fact is that his confirmation hearings represented an important education for large segments of the public on such fundamental matters as the meaning of the due process and liberty guarantees of the Fifth and Fourteenth Amendments to the Constitution, the relevance and limits of the Ninth Amendment's reference to unenumerated rights, the connection between various ways of approaching the Constitution's text and history and such particular unenumerated rights as personal privacy and reproductive freedom, the relationship between a tightly constrained and literalist reading of the Constitution in matters of personal rights and a more open-textured and fluid reading of the Constitution in matters bearing on state's rights, and a host of other topics of enduring significance.

For my own part, as one of the expert witnesses called to testify about Judge Bork's constitutional philosophy and about the consequences for the nation were he to gain an opportunity to implement that philosophy as a Supreme Court

Justice, I make no apology for anything I said at the time. Knowing full well that my testimony would put me on the enemies' lists of some extremely powerful people with very long memories, I felt it my duty to testify to the truth as I understood it. I would do the same thing again today. When the Senate finally rejected the nomination of Robert Bork, many of his allies cried "foul" and have since practiced decades of payback politics. Indeed, they have even succeeded, with the aid of some revisionist history, in adding to the vocabulary the highly misleading new verb, "to Bork"—meaning, "to smear a nominee with distorted accusations about his or her record and views"—as though the predictions of the sort of justice Robert Bork would have become were in some way misleading or otherwise unfair.

But the truth, as Judge Bork's post-rejection writings made amply clear, was just as his critics had indicated. Unless being confirmed would have caused him to undergo a radical conversion—something on which the nation has a right not to gamble—his rejection, and the subsequent confirmation of Justice Kennedy in his stead, meant one less member on the far right wing of the Court and left Justice Scalia (later with Justice Thomas) holding down the starboard alone. The nation had held a referendum on the Borkian approach to reading the Constitution of the United States, and the Borkian approach had decisively lost. And, lest it be supposed that I review this history simply to reprise a political episode that was painful for all concerned, I should make plain that my purpose is altogether different. It is to remove the fangs from the verb "to Bork" and to restore some perspective, lest anyone be misled into beginning the debate over the Senate's proper role with the erroneous premise that the Senate should be less than proud of the last

instance in which it rejected a Supreme Court nominee on ideological grounds.

Today, it takes very little effort to persuade any informed citizen that the identity of who serves on the Supreme Court of the United States matters enormously— matters not simply to the resolution of these large questions of how the Constitution is to be approached and how its multiple ambiguities are to be addressed, but as well in the disposition of the most mundane, and yet basic, questions of how we lead our lives as Americans. Whether laws enacted for the benefit of the elderly or the disabled are to be rendered virtually unenforceable in circumstances where the violator is a state agency and the victim cannot obtain meaningful redress without going to federal court; whether people stopped in their cars for minor offenses like failing to have a seatbelt properly attached to a child's car seat may be handcuffed and taken by force to the police station where they are arrested and booked and held overnight; whether police may use sense-enhancing technologies like special heat detectors to peer through the walls of our homes in order to detect the details of what we do there; whether, having recognized that everything we do in the privacy of our homes counts as an intimate detail when it comes to protecting us from various kinds of search and surveillance, judges will nonetheless continue to let state legislatures regulate the most intimate sexual details of what we do behind closed doors with those we love; whether government may forbid the kind of research that might prove essential to the prevention and cure of devastating degenerative diseases whenever that research uses stem cells or other tissues from embryos created in clinics for infertile couples—embryos that would otherwise be discarded without making such life-generating new knowledge possible; what kinds of campaign finance restrictions are to be permitted when the broad values of democracy seem pitted against the specific rights of individuals and corporations to use their wealth to purchase as much media time as money can buy; who is to be the next President of the United States—these are just some of the questions whose answers have come to turn on a single vote of a single Supreme Court Justice.

The battle that was fought over the nomination of Judge Bork to become Justice Bork was fought because the general approach to constitutional interpretation that he seemed to represent attracted him to some but frightened an even larger number. Most dramatic among the anticipated consequences of his confirmation would have been the addition of his vote and voice to the far right wing of the Court on such issues as reproductive freedom, which the Constitution of course never mentions in so many words. His confirmation, people came to recognize despite his avowals of open-mindedness on all such matters, would have meant the certain demise of *Roe v. Wade* [1973, permitting abortions], a decision whose most recent application, in last year's "partial birth abortion" case from Nebraska, was, after all these years, still 5 to 4—as are a large number of crucial decisions about personal privacy, gender discrimination, sexual orientation, race-based affirmative action, legislative apportionment, church-state separation, police behavior, and a host of other basic issues.

After the Supreme Court's highly controversial and I believe profoundly misguided performance last December in the case of *Bush v. Gore* [2000, regarding the Florida electoral vote]—in which I should acknowledge I played a role as author of the briefs for Vice President Gore and as oral advocate in the first of the two Supreme Court arguments in the case—it's difficult to find anyone who any longer

questions why it matters so much who serves on the court. The significance of *Bush v. Gore* in this setting doesn't depend on anybody's prediction of who would have won the vote-count in Florida had the counting gone on without the Supreme Court's dramatic and sudden interruption on December 9, 2000, or of who would have been chosen the next President by Congress this January 6 if the Supreme Court had let the constitutional processes operate as designed and if competing electoral slates had been sent from Tallahassee, Florida to Washington, D.C. The great significance of the case is to underscore that, by a margin of a single vote, the branch of our government that is least politically accountable—wisely and designedly so, when matters of individual and minority rights or of basic government structure are at stake—treated the American electorate and the electoral process with a disdain that a differently composed Court would have found unthinkable. So it was that, when push came to shove, and the Supreme Court's faith in democracy was tested, the Supreme Court blinked. It distrusted the people who were doing the counting, it distrusted the state judges, it distrusted the members of Congress to whom the dispute might have been thrown if it hadn't pulled down the curtain. And the Court could get away with it, partly because nobody in the House or Senate, to be brutally honest, relished the thought of discharging the constitutional responsibility of deciding which electoral votes to count and then facing his or her own constituents—and because the people were growing weary of the no longer very sexy or novel topic of dimpled ballots and hanging chads, and Christmas was just around the corner, and, after all, everyone knew that the election was basically too close to call anyway. Lost for some in all of that realism, I fear, was the high price our democracy paid for the convenience of a Court that was willing—no, not just willing, positively eager—to take those burdens from our shoulders and simply decree a result. Among the results is an unprecedented degree of political polarization in the Court's favorability rating with the public—a rating that now stands roughly twice as high among Republicans as among Democrats, surely an ominous gap for the one institution to which we look for action transcending politics.

This isn't the time or place to debate the details of *Bush v. Gore*, a subject about which I have written elsewhere; I stress the case because it shows at least as dramatically as any case possibly could just how much may depend on the composition of the Court; how basic are the questions that the Court at times decides by the closest possible margins; and how absurd are the pretensions and slogans of those who have for years gotten away with saying, and perhaps have deceived even themselves by saying, that the kinds of judges they want on the Court, the "restrained" rather than "activist" kinds of judges, the kinds of judges who don't "legislate from the bench," are the kinds exemplified by today's supposedly "conservative" wing of the Court, led by Chief Justice Rehnquist and supported in area after area by Justices O'Connor, Scalia, Kennedy, and Thomas. Those are, of course, the five justices who decided the presidential election of 2000. They are, as well, the five justices who have struck down one act of Congress after another—invalidating federal legislation at a faster clip than has any other Supreme Court since before the New Deal—on the basis that the Court and the Court alone is entitled to decide what kinds of state action might threaten religious liberty, might discriminate invidiously against the elderly or the disabled, or might otherwise warrant action by Congress in the discharge of its solemn constitutional power under Section 5 of the Fourteenth Amendment to determine what legislation is necessary and appropriate to protect liberty and equality in America.

Some might be tempted, after watching the Court perform so poorly in the pit of presidential politics, and after witnessing it substitute its policy judgments for those of Congress in one legislative arena after another, to imagine that, if we could only wave a magic wand and remove all ideological considerations from judicial selection—both on the part of the President in making nominations and on the part of the Senate in the confirmation process—somehow the Olympian ideal of a federal judiciary once again above politics and beyond partisan reproach could be restored. For several reasons, that is a dangerous illusion. First, there's no way for the Senate to prevent the President from doing what Presidents from the beginning of the republic have asserted the right to do, and what some Presidents have done more successfully than others: pick nominees who will mirror the President's preferred approach to the Constitution's vast areas of ambiguity. Second, in dealing with those areas of ambiguity, there may or may not be any right answers, but there most assuredly are no unique or uncontroversial answers; invariably, in choosing one Supreme Court nominee rather than another, one is making a choice among those answers, and among the approaches that generate them. And third, with a Supreme Court that is already so dramatically tilted in a rightward direction, anything less than a concerted effort to set the balance straight would mean perpetuating the imbalance that gave us not only *Bush v. Gore* but the myriad decisions in the preceding half-dozen years in which the

Court thumbed its nose at Congress and thus at the American people.

In an accompanying memorandum that I prepared for distribution this April to a number of members of the Senate, I explore in greater detail how these recent Supreme Court encroachments on congressional authority have come about and what they signify. For purposes of my statement today, suffice it to say that such encroachments are the antithesis of judicial restraint or modesty; that the justices who have engineered them are the most activist in our history; that holding them up as exemplars of jurists who would never dream of "legislating from the bench" is, to put it mildly, an exercise in dramatic license; and that the judgments the Senate will have to make about the inclinations and proclivities of prospective members of the Supreme Court must be considerably more nuanced than the stereotypical slogans and bumper stickers about activism vs. restraint, and even liberalism vs. conservatism, can possibly accommodate.

Some scholars, including most prominently University of Chicago Law Professor Cass Sunstein,...have powerfully argued that an active, nondeferential, role for the Senate in evaluating Supreme Court nominees is called for, quite independent of *Bush v. Gore*, by the way in which the federal judiciary in general, and the Supreme Court in particular, have been systematically stacked over the past few decades in a particular ideological direction—a direction hostile, for example, to the enactment of protective congressional legislation under Section 5 of the Fourteenth Amendment, and hostile as well to other ostensibly "liberal" or "progressive" judicial positions, on topics ranging from privacy to affirmative action, from states' rights to law enforcement. For Professor Sunstein,...the active role the Senate ought to play is exactly as

it would have been had *Bush v. Gore* never been decided.

Other scholars, most prominently Yale University Law Professor Bruce Ackerman, argue that *Bush v. Gore* has thrown the process of judicial appointment into what Professor Ackerman calls "constitutional disequilibrium," so that, instead of two independent structural checks on a necessarily unrepresentative and politically unaccountable Supreme Court, we are now down to just one. Because, in his view, the current Court must be acknowledged to have "mediated" the "President's relationship to the citizenry"—by helping put him in office by a 5 to 4 vote—"only the Senate retains a normal connection to the electorate," and this demands of that body, as Professor Ackerman sees it, that it shoulder an unusually heavy share of the burden of democratic control, by the people acting through the political branches, of the judicial branch to which we ordinarily look to hold the balance true. Translated into an operational prescription, the Ackerman position would recommend that the Senate simply refuse to confirm any new justices to the Court before President Bush, as Professor Ackerman puts it, "win[s] the 2004 election fair and square, without the Court's help." As a fallback, Professor Ackerman would urge the Senate to consider any nominations President Bush might make to the Court during his current term on their own merits, but without what Ackerman describes as "the deference accorded ordinary presidents."

Although I am intrigued by Professor Ackerman's suggestion, it seems to me the wrong way to go, either in its strongest form or in its fallback version. The strongest form would make sense, I think, only if we were convinced that the justices who voted with the majority in *Bush v. Gore* acted in a manner so corrupt and illegitimate, so devoid of legal justification, that one could say they essentially installed George W. Bush as president in a bloodless but lawless coup. But if we believed that, then the remedy of not letting the leaders of that coup profit from their own wrong of denying them the solace of like-minded successors as they depart the scene— would be far too mild. If we thought the Bush majority guilty of a coup, we should have to conclude that they were guilty of treason to the Constitution, and that they should be impeached, convicted, and removed from office.

Believing that what the *Bush v. Gore* majority did was gravely wrong but not that it amounted to a coup or indeed anything like it— believing that the majority justices acted not to install their favorite candidate but out of a misguided sense that the nation was in grave and imminent peril unless they stopped the election at once—one would have to look to the Ackerman fallback position. But all it tells us is something that I argued was the case anyway as early as 1985— that the Senate should not accord any special deference to nominations made by any President to the Supreme Court. Indeed, I go further than does Professor Sunstein in this respect. As I understand his position, he would have the Senate withhold such deference for reasons peculiar to the recent history of the nation and of appointments to the federal bench and especially to the Supreme Court over the past few decades. Had we not lived through a time of Republican Presidents insistent on, and adept at, naming justices who would carry on their ideological program in judicial form, sandwiching Democratic Presidents uninterested in, or inept at, naming justices similarly attuned to their substantive missions, Professor Sunstein would apparently urge that the Senate give the President his head in these matters and serve only in a backseat capacity, to pre-

vent rogues and fools, more or less, from being elevated to the High Court.

In a world in which each position on the Supreme Court might be given to some idealized version of the wisest lawyer in the land—the most far-sighted and scholarly, the most capable of clearly explaining the Constitution's language and mission, the most adept at generating consensus in support of originally unpopular positions that come to be seen as crucial to the defense of human rights—perhaps we could afford in normal times to accept a posture of Senatorial deference, with exceptions made in special historical periods of the sort some believe we have been living through. But if we ever lived in a world where such a universal paragon of justice could be imagined, and in which the kinds of issues resolved by Supreme Court Justices were not invariably contested, often bitterly so, between competing visions of the right, that day has long since passed.

Today, regardless of whether past Presidents have acted or failed to act so as to produce a Supreme Court bench leaning lopsidedly in a rightward direction, and regardless of whether a majority of the current Court has acted in such a way as to render the President whom it helped to elect less entitled to deference than usual in naming the successors of the Court's current members, the inescapable fact is that the President will name prospective justices about whom he knows a great deal more than the Senate can hope to learn—justices whose paper trail, if the President is skillful about it, will reveal much less to the Senate than the President thinks he knows. Given his allies and those to whom he owes his political victory, as well as those on whom he will need to depend for his re-election, the incumbent President, if those constituencies expect him to leave his mark and therefore theirs upon the Court, will try to name justices who will fulfill the agenda of those constituencies—in the case of President Bush, the agenda of the right—without seeming by their published statements or their records as jurists to be as committed to that agenda as the President will privately believe them to be. Presumably, the incumbent President will look for such nominees among the ranks of Hispanic jurists, or women, or both, in order to distract the opposition and make resistance more painful. And certainly this President, like any other in modern times, will select nominees who have already mastered or can be coached in the none too difficult game of answering questions thoughtfully and without overt deception but in ways calculated to offend no-one and reveal nothing.

In this circumstance, to say that the burden is on those who hold the power of advice and consent to show that there is something disqualifying about the nominee, that there is a smoking gun in the record or a wildly intemperate publication in the bibliography or some other fatal flaw that can justify a rallying cry of opposition, is to guarantee that the President will have the Court of his dreams without the Senate playing any meaningful role whatsoever. Therefore, if the Senate's role is to be what the Framers contemplated, what history confirms, and what a sound appreciation for the realities of American politics demands, the burden must instead be on the nominee and, indeed, on the President. That burden must be to persuade each Senator—for, in the end, this is a duty each Senator must discharge in accord with his or her own conscience— that the nominee's experience, writings, speeches, decisions, and actions affirmatively demonstrate not only the exceptional intellect and wisdom and integrity that greatness as a judge demands but also the understanding of and commitment to those constitutional rights and values and ideals that the Senator regards as important for the republic to uphold.

On this standard, stealth nominees should have a particularly hard time winning confirmation. For proving on the basis of a blank slate the kinds of qualities that the Senate ought to demand, with a record that is unblemished because it is without content, ought to be exceedingly difficult. Testimony alone, however eloquent and reassuring, ought rarely to suffice where its genuineness is not confirmed by a history of action in accord with the beliefs professed. And testimony, in any event, is bound to be clouded by understandable reservations about compromising judicial independence by asking the nominee to commit himself or herself too specifically in advance to how he or she would vote on particular cases that might, in one variant or another, come before the Court. Interestingly, we do not regard sitting justices as having compromised their independence by having written about, and voted on, many of the issues they must confront year in and year out; the talk about compromising judicial independence by asking about such issues sometimes reflects unthinking reflex more than considered judgment. But on the assumption that old habits die hard, and that members of the Senate Judiciary Committee will continue to be rather easily cowed into backing away from asking probing questions about specific issues that might arise during the nominee's service on the Court, it should still be possible to formulate questions for any nominee, including tough follow-up questions, at a level of generality just high enough so that the easy retreat into "I'm sorry, Senator, I can't answer that question because the matter might come before me," will be unavailing. And, to the extent such slightly more general questions yield information too meager for informed judgment, the burden must be on the nominee to satisfy his or her interlocutors that the concern underlying the thwarted line of questioning is one that ought not to disturb the Senator. That satisfaction can be provided only from a life lived in the law that exemplifies, rather than eschewing, a real engagement with problems of justice, with challenges of human rights, and with the practical realities of making law relevant to people's needs. When a nominee cannot provide that satisfaction—when the nominee is but a fancy resume in an empty suit or a vacant dress, perhaps adorned with a touching story of a hard-luck background or of ethnic roots—any Senator who takes his or her oath of office as seriously as I know, deep down, all of you do, should simply say, "No thanks, Mr. President. Send us another nominee."

What this adds up to is, of course, a substantial role for ideology in the consideration of any Supreme Court nominee. It would be naive to the point of foolhardiness to imagine that the President will be tone-deaf to signals of ideological compatibility or incompatibility with his view of the ideal Supreme Court justice; ideology will invariably matter to any President and must therefore matter to any Senator who is not willing simply to hand over to The White House his or her proxy for the discharge of the solemn duty to offer advice and consent.

As a postscript on the distinct subject of circuit court nominees, it seems worth noting that, although such nominees are of course strictly bound by Supreme Court precedents and remain subject to correction by that Court, and although there might therefore seem to be much less reason for the Senate to be ideologically vigilant than in the case of the Supreme Court, three factors militate in favor of at least a degree of ideological oversight even at the circuit court level.

First, well under 1% of the decisions of the circuit courts are actually reviewed by the Supreme Court, which avowedly declines to review even clearly erroneous decisions unless they present some special circumstance such as a circuit conflict. Especially if the circuit courts tend toward a homogeneity that mirrors the ideological complexion of the Supreme Court, that tribunal is exceedingly unlikely to use its discretionary power of review on certiorari to police lower federal courts that stray from the reservation in one direction or another; it will instead focus its firepower on bringing the state courts into line and resolving intolerable conflicts among the lower courts, state and federal.

Second, there are a great many gray areas in which Supreme Court precedents leave the circuit courts a wide berth within which to maneuver without straying into a danger zone wherein further review becomes a likely prospect. Even though no individual circuit court judge is very likely to use that elbow room in order to move the law significantly in one direction or another without a check from the Supreme Court, the overall balance and composition of the circuit court bench can have a considerable effect, in momentum if nothing else, on the options realistically open to the Supreme Court and thus to the country.

Third, in the past few decades, the circuit courts have increasingly served as a kind of "farm team" for Supreme Court nominations. On the Court that decided *Brown v. Board of Education* in 1954 there sat not a single justice who, prior to his appointment to the Supreme Court, had ever served in a judicial capacity. Governors, Senators, distinguished members of the bar, but no former judges. Today, however, rare is the nominee who has not previously served in a judicial capacity, most frequently on a federal circuit court. On the current Court, only the

Chief Justice lacked prior judicial experience when he was first named a justice; and, of the other eight justices, all except Justice O'Connor, who had served as a state court judge, were serving on federal circuit courts when appointed to the Court. The reasons for this change are many; they include, most prominently, the growing recognition that ideology matters and that service on a lower court may be one way of detecting a prospective nominee's particular ideological leanings. Whatever the reasons, the reality has independent significance, for it means that any time the Senate confirms someone to serve on a circuit court, it may be making a record that, in the event the judge should later be nominated to the Supreme Court, will come back to haunt it. "But you had no trouble confirming Judge X to the court of appeals for the Y circuit," supporters of Supreme Court nominee X are likely to intone. Keeping that in mind will require the Senate to give fuller consideration to matters of ideology at the circuit court level than it otherwise might.

The primary ideological issue at the circuit court level, however, should probably remain the overall tilt of the federal bench rather than the particular leanings of any given nominee viewed in isolation. In a bench already tilted overwhelmingly in one direction—today, the right—a group of nominees whose ideological center of gravity is such as to exacerbate rather than correct that tilt should be a matter of concern to any Senator who does not regard the existing tilt as altogether healthy.

And one needn't be particularly liberal to have concerns about the existing tilt. Just as a liberal who recognizes that people who share his views might not have all the right answers ought to be distressed by a federal bench composed overwhelmingly of jurists reminiscent of William J. Brennan, Jr. or William O. Douglas—or

even by a federal bench composed almost entirely of liberals and moderates and few conservatives—and just as such a liberal should doubt the wisdom, in confronting such a bench, of adding a group of judges who would essentially replicate that slant, so too a conservative who is humble enough to recognize that people who share her views might not have a lock on the truth should feel dismayed by a federal bench composed overwhelmingly of jurists in the mold of Antonin Scalia or Clarence Thomas—or even by a federal bench composed almost entirely of conservatives and moderates and few liberals—and ought to doubt the wisdom, in dealing with such a bench, of adding many more judges cut from that same cloth. The fundamental truth that ought to unite people across the ideological spectrum, and that only those who are far too sure of themselves to be comfortable in a democracy should find difficult to accept, is that the federal judiciary in general, and the Supreme Court in particular, ought in principle to reflect and represent a wide range of viewpoints and perspectives rather than being clustered toward any single point on the ideological spectrum.

Indeed, even those who feel utterly persuaded of the rightness of their own particular point of view should, in the end, recognize that their arguments can only be sharpened and strengthened by being tested against the strongest of opposing views. Liberals and conservatives alike can be lulled into sloppy and slothful smugness and self-satisfaction unless they are fairly matched on the bench by the worthiest of opponents. It may even be that the astonishing weakness and vulnerability of the Court's majority opinion in *Bush v. Gore*, and of the majority opinions in a number of the other democracy-defying decisions in whose mold it was cast, are functions in part of the uniquely narrow spectrum of views—narrower, I think, than at any other time in our history—covered by the membership of the current Court—a spectrum which, on most issues, essentially runs the gamut from A through C. On a Court with four justices distinctly on the right, two moderate conservatives, a conservative moderate, two moderates, and no liberals, it's easy for the dominant faction to grow lazy and to issue opinions that, preaching solely to the converted, ring hollow to a degree that ill serves both the Court as an institution and the legal system it is supposed to lead. It is thus in the vital interest of the nation as a whole, and not simply in the interest of those values that liberals and progressives hold dear, that the ideological imbalance of the current Supreme Court and of the federal bench as a whole not be permitted to persist, and that the Senate take ideology intelligently into account throughout the judicial confirmation process with a view to gradually redressing what all should come to see as a genuinely dangerous disequilibrium.

Legal Philosophy as a Qualification for the Bench:
Obstructionist Barrier

TODD F. GAZIANO

A DIMINISHED JUDICIARY: CAUSES AND EFFECTS OF THE SUSTAINED HIGH VACANCY RATES IN THE FEDERAL COURTS

The topic of today's hearing is certainly worthy of this Committee's attention. That you took the time to conduct this hearing so soon before you must recess for the election is further proof that the subject matter is important....

I concur in the statement contained in the hearing title, "A Judiciary Diminished is Justice Denied: the Constitution, the Senate, and the Vacancy Crisis in the Federal Judiciary." Nevertheless, the situation in the federal courts is uneven. There is not yet a crisis across-the-board, even though judicial emergencies have been declared for many courts. On close examination, the consequences of the high vacancy rate are partially ameliorated by the hard work of the judicial branch itself. That said, many federal appellate circuits have had such sustained high vacancy rates that it is straining the justice system mightily and has contributed to at least the perception of judicial manipulation in some very important cases.

The obvious cause of the vacancy crisis is the U.S. Senate's conscious refusal to act in a timely manner on many of the President's judicial nominations. The near complete breakdown in the judicial confirmation process as it relates to United States court of appeals nominees is worthy of special attention and concern. It is simply not possible to justify the stonewalling and other improper committee action on the grounds of payback or any other excuse. In 1997, when the vacancy rate on the appellate courts was less than half of what it is now, the current Chairman of the Senate Judiciary Committee, Patrick Leahy [D-VT], said the situation was a "crisis" that interfered with the administration of justice. The current state is nothing less than a dramatic failure of the Senate's constitutional duty to provide its advice and consent to presidential appointments. It is also a violation of the Senate's obligation of comity to the executive and judicial branches of government, which is a vital aspect of the separation of powers.

The result is not just limited to shame on the Senate, however. The Senate's actions have begun to impair the judicial branch's ability to perform its constitutional functions. That impairment is limited at this point, but the impairment grows steadily as the period of sustained judicial vacancies is extended. The House Constitution Subcommittee is right to explore the implications of the Senate's failure.

THE CONSTITUTIONAL FRAMEWORK OF ANALYSIS

The United States Constitution provides that the President "shall nominate, and by and with the Advice and Consent of the Senate, shall appoint...Judges of the Supreme Court, and all other [Principal] Officers of the United States, whose Appointments are not herein otherwise provided for." That clause further provides that "Congress may by Law vest the Appointment of such inferior Officers, as they think proper, in the President alone, in the Courts of Law, or in the Heads of

Departments." All federal judges below the Supreme Court are inferior in the judicial sense.

Lower court judges might also be "inferior Officers" for Appointments Clause purposes for whom Congress could vest the appointment in either the President or the Supreme Court alone. But Congress (or the Senate) has chosen to retain its power to pass on all judicial nominations. That is its prerogative. Yet, that choice underscores the Senate's duty, which extends to the other two branches of government and to the citizens who rely on the justice system, to provide its advice and consent in good faith and in a timely manner.

Scholars of the founding period have examined the historical record to illuminate some issues that I will only briefly address here. For example, there is evidence [in Federalist Nos. 76–77] that the framers of the Constitution expected every presidential nominee to be voted on by the entire Senate and feared the arbitrary exercise of appointment power by a small committee. That seems clear, but I am unsure whether the text of the Appointments Clause, which confers the advice and consent role to the entire Senate, requires the Senate to act on every nomination. Those I respect have opined that the Constitution does not permit a committee of the Senate to block a nomination, but I am still dubious of that proposition. The Rules Clause that allows the Senate to make its own rules of procedure may permit the entire Senate to delegate its agenda-setting function to a committee.

Others have interpreted the Senate Rules to require a full-Senate vote on presidential nominations regardless of what the relevant committee recommends. In my view, Senate Rule XXXI is ambiguous. It requires referral of all presidential nominations to "appropriate committees," and it further states that "the final question on

every nomination shall be, 'Will the Senate advise and consent to this nomination?'" Does that simply specify what the final question shall be on "every nomination" that is referred back to the full Senate or does it imply that the final question must be asked for "every nomination?" The Senate parliamentarians have given it the first construction.

I have not studied in depth either the constitutional question or the related question regarding the Senate rules in part because there is ultimately no remedy— apart from shame—for the violation of such a requirement. Assuming a disappointed nominee with standing filed a suit to force a full-Senate vote on his nomination, the courts would almost surely rule that the case presented a "political question" and decline to rule on the matter under its "political questions" doctrine. As for the tactic of urging shame, many other aspects of the confirmation process should have generated more shame. But it is still appropriate for citizens to add their voice to the chorus.

In that vein, the full Senate ought to vote on each one of the President's nominees to high office. The Senate should do so as a matter of prudence and in keeping with the comity that is required of each branch of government to the others, whether the Constitution or the Senate's current rules require such a vote or not. This is particularly true for those who have been nominated for a lifetime post in the judicial branch. The procedures the Senate adopts for such nominations affect more than just the business of the Senate; they also touch on the constitutional obligations of both other branches of government. The President has the obligation to nominate and appoint judges to fill up vacancies in the federal courts, and confirmed judges are the only individuals who can exercise the power conferred in Article III of the Constitution.

A full-Senate vote is even more appropriate where it is fairly clear that a majority of the Senate would vote to confirm the nominees, which is still the case with Charles Pickering and Pricilla Owen [both nominated by President George W. Bush to the Fifth Circuit Court of Appeals]. Both Pickering and Owen received well-qualified ratings from the American Bar Association (ABA) review panel. In April 2001, Senator Leahy described a positive rating by the ABA as the "gold standard." Gold does not tarnish, so it is unclear why Senator Leahy and other Democrats on his committee have now abandoned their high regard for the ABA review panel.

No Republican senator announced opposition to either Pickering or Owen, and at least one senator from the majority [Democrats] announced support for both of them. Democratic senators who expressed their support for Pickering and Owen are not on the Judiciary Committee, but they sought the opportunity to vote on the nominations. Yet, the Senate Judiciary Committee [at that point controlled by the Democrats] refuses to forward these nominations to the full Senate—even with a negative recommendation, and Majority Leader Tom Daschle [D-SD] does nothing to bring the nominations to the Senate floor. Whether or not the Constitution or the Senate rules require such a full-Senate vote, it is still undemocratic for the current Senate leadership to block a presidential nomination from even being debated on the Senate floor. Ten senators are currently dictating the composition of the federal bench. Even a filibuster by a minority of the Senate would be less cowardly than the current practice.

THE CAUSE OF SUSTAINED HIGH VACANCIES IN THE FEDERAL COURTS

The most serious problem with the confirmation process is not the Senate Judiciary Committee's refusal to forward nominations that it has acted on to the full Senate, but its refusal to complete its action on most court of appeals nominations. Over the past several decades, the Senate sometimes has slowed down the confirmation process toward the end of a presidential term if the President and Senate majority are from different parties. Although some of President Clinton's judicial nominations were confirmed at the end of the 106th Congress [1999–2000], a slow-down in the last few months and the October adjournment of the 106th Congress contributed to a slightly higher than normal vacancy rate at the beginning of President George W. Bush's administration. (An even more severe slowdown took place at the end of President George H.W. Bush's administration.)

There is always some delay in the judicial nomination process at the start of a new presidential administration. The President possibly could have begun sending judicial nominations to the Senate in March of 2001, but the delayed transition period for President Bush pushed back the normal FBI background check and clearance process for cabinet and sub-cabinet nominees. Some of these officials also help vet potential judges. The pace of President Bush's judicial nominations since early May of 2001 was record setting. Within a year of announcing his first nominees, the President had sent more than 100 judicial nominations to the Senate. The ABA completed its review and supplied its recommendation within about three weeks of each nomination. With one exception, so far the ABA has rated every one of President Bush's nominees either qualified or well-qualified.

Two judges who had received an earlier appointment from President Bill Clinton and a sitting district judge who was acceptable to Louisiana's Democratic senators were promptly confirmed for life-time seats on the appellate courts. Almost all of the remaining nominations languished in the Senate without hearings even being scheduled. For months, the rate of confirmation of all federal judges barely kept pace with retirements. The pace of confirmation of federal district judges has picked up in the past year, but the confirmation process for court of appeals nominees has been set at a glacial pace.

1. THE VACANCY STATISTICS AND PERIODS OF UNREASONABLE DELAY BY THE SENATE

In the past, confirmation battles were waged over certain Supreme Court nominees and a very few lower court nominees. As mentioned above, the Senate sometimes slowed down the confirmation process toward the end of a presidential term, but this slowdown was the exception rather than the rule. What's dramatically different now is the systematic refusal to act on many of President Bush's initial nominees, particularly his appellate court nominees. The number of vacancies on the federal courts has actually increased by about fifteen percent since the end of the last Congress. And during this Congress, most of President Bush's initial group of judicial nominees have been waiting for more than 17 months without so much as a hearing and a committee vote.

Based on the practice of many federal judges in announcing their retirement in advance and my review of recent confirmation statistics, I believe that a vacancy rate of about three to four percent represents the "full employment" level (to borrow a term from economists) for the federal judiciary. Yet, the Senate Judiciary Committee's inaction and the Senate's overall slow pace on most of the President's appellate court nominees have resulted in much higher vacancy rates. On the federal district courts, 50 of

665 judge seats (or 7.5%) are vacant. On the federal appellate courts, 27 of 179 judgeships (or 15.1%) are vacant.

Retired Judge (and former U.S. Senator) James Buckley [R-NY] concluded [in a newspaper op-ed piece] that "the Senate's willful failure to act upon a president's judicial nominees can only be described as an obstruction of justice." Judge Buckley pointed out that, when he was a senator, nominees of the caliber nominated by President George W. Bush "would have been confirmed within weeks after their names had been submitted." Yet, it appears that a majority of President Bush's first eleven court of appeals nominees will not even have a committee vote 20 months after they were nominated.

Whether they all deserve to be confirmed or not (and the ABA thinks they are deserving), the Senate's conscious refusal to schedule hearings for most appellate court nominees is a shocking dereliction of duty. There may not be a committee vote by the end of this year for such distinguished professors, Supreme Court advocates, and judges as Deborah Cook, John Roberts, Jeff Sutton, Michael McConnell, Miguel Estrada, Terrence Boyle, and Timothy Tymkovich. That's inexcusable. Moreover, the two who did receive a hearing this fall (Michael McConnell and Miguel Estrada) may have to start the process all over again in 2003 if the full Senate does not vote on their nominations before the end of the current Congress. [The need to start again is because all pending business dies at the end of each two year Congress.]

With regard to court of appeals nominees, the delays are many times worse than at any recent time. These delays strain the judiciary and are unfair to individual nominees. To the extent that an intentionally prolonged delay can damage a law practice and keep individual nominees in professional and personal limbo, it becomes cruel. As explained further below, those who rely on the federal justice system may suffer as well.

The American Bar Association (ABA) has consistently urged the Senate to act promptly to confirm judicial nominees. In August of 2002, however, the ABA House of Delegates approved an especially strong statement that for the first time specifically identified the Senate Judiciary Committee as a "cause of blockage in the confirmation process" and urged the Committee to take prompt action on nominations. The ABA said that: "The notion that the Committee, by the simple expedient of refusing to hold timely hearings may avoid confirmation proceedings in the full Senate, is simply unacceptable to our notion of an appropriate and constitutional nomination process."

A persistent but low vacancy rate is unavoidable, reflecting a small number of vacancies that are promptly filled. Most federal judges are appointed at the prime of their professional career, or slightly later. Statutes provide comfortable benefits for federal judges who assume a semi-retirement status at age 65 (and after they have served 15 years). Most judges assume this "senior status" soon after they become eligible. Some judges announce their retirement date (colloquially, it is referred to as "going senior") with enough advance notice to allow the President time to nominate a replacement, but other judges do not. Serious illness, death, and other unanticipated events cause some vacancies to arise without notice. Accordingly, there will always be some vacancies in the federal courts.

In recent decades, when the confirmation process is running smoothly, the vacancy rate has dropped to around five percent. Chief Justice William Rehnquist has still admonished past Presidents and past Senates to act more expeditiously in nominating, confirming, and appointing judges to fill anticipated or actual vacancies. By comparison, a congressional seat is not left vacant for long before a special election is held (in the case of a House seat) or a temporary appointment is made (in the case of a Senate seat). When government officials are willing to spend a lot of time and money for a special election to fill 1/435th of the seats in the U.S. House of Representatives, Congress should make more of an effort to promptly fill numerous vacancies in the federal judiciary.

There were 67 judicial vacancies at the end of the 106th Congress and 77 now near the end of the 107th Congress, proving that the Senate is not even keeping pace with new retirements. Dueling statistics have unfortunately become commonplace in this debate, but there is one set of statistics that simply cannot be explained away. The stalling is undeniable when you consider the court of appeals nominations by themselves. The chart below shows the average number of days the first eleven circuit court nominees had to wait for final Senate action, and the respective confirmation rate by President.

President	Average Number of Days Initial 11 Court of Appeals Nominees Waited for Final Senate Action	Court of Appeals Confirmation Rate
Reagan	39	100%
G.H.W. Bush	95	100%
Clinton	115	100%
G.W. Bush	approx. 400 (and counting)	27% (thus far)

If you eliminate the judges nominated by President George W. Bush who were first appointed by President Clinton, the picture looks even worse. Only one of the nine non-Clinton judges has been confirmed, a total of 11%. The average wait approaches 500 days for the remaining nine nominees, and is in excess of 500 days for eight of them. As this testimony is being prepared, seven of them have not had a committee vote and four have not even had a hearing.

Recently, Judge Buckley urged that the Senate rules be changed to allow the Judiciary Committee a few months to review the qualifications of judicial nominees and make its recommendation. Judge Buckley argued that the full Senate should vote after a few months whether or not the committee had acted. The current Chairman of the Senate Judiciary Committee, Patrick Leahy, proposed similar procedures just a few years earlier. Senator Leahy sponsored a bill in 1998 that would have required the Senate to act on all nominations pending for more than 60 days before it took a ten-day or longer recess.

Pursuant to his own legislative plan, Senator Leahy should at least have finished committee action on Miguel Estrada, Deborah Cook, John Roberts, Jeff Sutton, Michael McConnell, Dennis Shedd, Terrence Boyle, Timothy Tymkovich, Charles Pickering, and Priscilla Owen before the Senate took its August recess in 2001. Each of the nominees received a well-qualified rating from the ABA. Each of their nominations had been pending in his committee for over 60 days by then, most for over 80 days. But Leahy did not complete committee action on any of the above nominees by the August 2001 recess. Of those listed above, only Pickering, Owen, and Shedd were given hearings by the August 2002 recess—one year later. Many other court of appeals candidates nominated during the summer of 2001 have not had a committee hearing either.

Although the federal courts of appeals have an overall vacancy rate of over fifteen percent, some circuits have had a sustained vacancy rate of between thirty and fifty percent. The situation in the U.S. Sixth Circuit Court of Appeals is the most dramatic. During the Clinton Administration, the Chief Judge of the Sixth Circuit wrote to the Senate Judiciary Committee to express his deep concern regarding four vacancies in the sixteen-member court. He wrote that his court was "hurting badly" and that the situation was "rapidly deteriorating due to the fact that 25% of the judgeships are vacant."

The Sixth Circuit was operating for most of this past year with only half of its authorized judges. It still has seven vacant positions today, a 44% vacancy rate. President Bush made seven nominations to that court in 2001, two of whom were in the very first batch sent to the Senate on May 9, 2001. (President Bush sent an additional nomination a few months ago.) But Senator Leahy has held a hearing on just two of them, and only one has been confirmed. As explained below, the Senate's complete inaction on the circuit with the highest vacancy rate has caused some particular hardships and led to some questionable judicial practices.

2. THE SENATE JUDICIARY COMMITTEE IS NOT PROVIDING ITS ADVICE AND CONSENT IN A MANNER CONSISTENT WITH THE CONSTITUTION OR THE RULE OF LAW

In addition to the intentionally prolonged delay in voting on most of the President's judicial nominations, several of the hearings that were conducted by the Senate Judiciary Committee were not only irrelevant to the merits of individual nominees, they instead attempted to lay the predicate for improper questioning at later confirmation hearings. In keeping with this agenda, hearings that were conducted for appellate court nominees during this Congress have been intentionally confrontational and focused on matters that are not properly the subject of such a hearing.

The few hearings that were conducted for appellate court nominees focused on a nominee's supposed political beliefs rather than his or her qualifications or philosophy of judging. Texas Supreme Court Justice Priscilla Owen was cross examined for seven hours in one hearing this past July, despite her obvious qualifications to join the U.S. Fifth Circuit Court of Appeals. Justice Owen received a unanimous well-qualified rating from the ABA. Justice Owen's reelection to the Texas Supreme Court in 2000 was endorsed by every major newspaper in Texas, and Owen won the support of a record number of voters in Texas. Yet, on a party-line vote, the Senate Judiciary Committee voted in early September to block her confirmation based on supposed ideological concerns. Last month, committee Democrats also tried to discredit and bully Miguel Estrada over his purported personal ideological leanings.

This conduct is based on a fundamental misconception some senators have regarding the proper role of judges and our judicial system. There is a crucial difference between political ideology, which is a set of political beliefs or goals, and a nominee's judicial philosophy, which is a theory of, or approach to, judicial decisionmaking. Political beliefs ought to play no role in a judge's judicial philosophy.

The rule of law is premised on the following bedrock principle: law can be objectively determined and fairly applied to all no matter what judge or other official is in power. The rule of law is an ideal, and every ideal is imperfect. Yet, American school children learn that this is an essential characteristic of our system of government. Ours is a nation of laws and not men, we are told. This is another way of saying that the application of the law does not vary depending on who is in charge. The law can be, and for the most part is, applied consistently and fairly to all. Any deviation from this norm is to be condemned, not encouraged.

Accordingly, the founding generation believed that the federal judiciary would be "the least dangerous" branch—in large part because they understood that the "judiciary power" was fundamentally different than that exercised by the political branches. In *Federalist* 78, [Alexander] Hamilton argued that legal traditions would cabin a judge's role and mode of decisionmaking. A judge, he maintained, would exercise "judgement" not "will." His argument presupposed that such a distinction was intelligible and readily understood. That conception of law—that judges can objectively discern what the law is, rather than what it should be—was the governing orthodoxy for over 130 years.

Rule by the party embodies a different ideal—one practiced by many communist nations. In that system, all judicial rulings are supposed to conform to the then current dictates, plans, agenda, or beliefs of the governing party. What is desired more than anything else in a judge or other government official is the proper political ideology, because that best informs all other action. Since there is thought to be no objective truth, the correctness of a ruling may change if the party line changes. Generally, only long-time party members who have proven their personal allegiance to the party's teachings are entrusted with high government power.

Antecedents of this thinking in America can be found in post-civil war nihilism, but the legal realists of the 1920s were the first to significantly undermine the rule of law. Legal realism, mingled with strains of pragmatism, relativism, and deconstructionist thought, captured the legal academy between the 1920s and 1960s. It began to bear substantial fruit in the courts thereafter. It is an oversimplification, but the orthodox thought of this era—running at least through the mid-1980s—is that law is just politics by another name.

This development is profoundly misguided and destructive. Yet, it is not surprising that its adherents increasingly urged the courts to become instruments of social change in overtly political ways. The courts' rulings ending government discrimination were (and are) necessary, but the tools the courts developed to fight the massive resistance to civil rights were also invoked to promote more amorphous social goals without clear constitutional foundations.

For a judge, such a seductive request is difficult to resist, even more so if the dominant legal culture has eliminated the traditional moral constraints on judging. With differences of style rather than content, the courts began to assume the role of another political branch to which dissatisfied citizens could turn to have their personal preferences, their will, enacted into law.

In this climate, it is easy to see why judicial confirmation battles might develop for Supreme Court justices. Unfortunately, the confirmation battles themselves further politicize the courts and reinforce the caustic notion that the courts are little more than a political plum. This notion was expressly stated by Abner Mikva [former member of Congress and Chief Judge of District of Columbia Circuit of the Court of Appeals] and many liberal academics, who argue that Bush's Presidency is illegitimate. Still brooding about the correct Supreme Court ruling in *Bush* v. *Gore*, Mikva and others who should know better

have urged the Senate to confirm no Bush nominee to the Supreme Court and encourage all means of thwarting his legitimate nominees to the appellate courts.

Hearings conducted by Senator Charles Schumer [D-NY] last fall on "whether ideology matters" in judicial selection and more recently in connection with the D.C. Circuit Court are an outgrowth of that dangerous thinking. Perhaps ideology matters a great deal for a nominee or senator who believes that there is no meaningful difference between law and politics. But that belief would demonstrate to me that the nominee has an unacceptable judicial philosophy. No further inquiry into the nominee's political beliefs is necessary. Testimony offered by President Clinton's former Counsel, Lloyd Cutler, and President George H.W. Bush's former Counsel, C. Boyden Gray, urged the Senate not to focus on political ideology in judicial selection. They both also agreed that extensive partisan inquiry is harmful to an independent judiciary.

A nominee with an appropriate judicial philosophy is one truly dedicated to the rule of law. Senators should be free to probe a nominee's theory of judging, *i.e.,* the methodology he would use when deciding cases, as long as the question does not ask the nominee to take a position on a matter that may come before him. Thus, I do not think that it is always enough for a nominee for a lower court judgeship to simply pledge that he will follow the law as set forth by the higher courts without explaining what that means. A record of scholarship or prior opinions, or a discussion of venerable old cases might help the committee to determine if the nominee appreciates what the rule of law requires.

I also think nominees reasonably could be asked to explain their general theory of various clauses of the Constitution. A competent grasp of the Constitution is necessary for any judge, and a discussion about its provisions might also be a good window on the nominee's approach to law and legal reasoning. Once again, however, senators must be careful not to ask the nominee about a particular subject matter or legal issue that might come before the nominee. Not only does the Code of Judicial Ethics require current and prospective judges to refuse to pledge how they might rule in the future, the American people want independent judges who have not committed themselves to a particular ruling.

Unfortunately, the argument that political ideology should not matter, and that extensive inquiry about it is destructive of an independent judiciary, is based on an understanding of law (i.e., the rule of law) that many senators seem to reject. The prevailing attitude is that the ideological stakes are high, and to the victor go the spoils. Modern-day legal realists, and their judicial activist advisers, desperately want judges who will impose a liberal or progressive will, not law. This is how the political branches were designed to operate, but not the courts.

A senatorial litmus test on an open or evolving legal issue is even more destructive to an independent judiciary than an improper inquiry about the nominee's general political beliefs. Senators who admit that they are applying such a single-issue litmus test know this full well. Their clear purpose is to eliminate any shred of judicial independence with regard to some controversial legal issue like abortion that is largely settled in the law but still permits some limited room for legislative action. Urged on by special interest groups that are influential in their states, these senators want only activist nominees who will strike down legislation that is permissible under Supreme Court cases, such as parental notification statutes with judicial bypass mechanisms.

These same senators express strong opposition to recent Supreme Court decisions (and lower court judges who would follow them) that enforce any limit in the Constitution on Congress's power to legislate. The senators denounce decisions interfering with any law they sponsored on the ground that it was passed with majority support. But requiring parents to be notified when their minor child seeks an abortion (absent special circumstances) is supported by an overwhelming majority of Americans. The difference, which educated senators should know, is that judges sometimes are required to enforce limits on legislative action and sometimes they are forbidden to do so, according to the Constitution. Lower court judges must follow the rulings of the Supreme Court on these matters, but some liberal senators who pretend to stand on principle really just want progressive outcomes: they want judges to ignore liberal legislation that exceeds Congress's authority and strike down other legislation that is permissible but that they, and their interest group supporters, simply don't like.

In contrast, modern-day federalists sincerely want judges who will fight the temptation to act on political biases, and instead, adhere to a mode of judging that minimizes such influences, including careful adherence to the text and the intent of those who enacted the governing text. Some senators and liberal activists may actually believe such a code cannot be followed. To them, nominees who pledge fidelity to the rule of law are, at best, dupes who will not advance the progressive cause. At worse, such nominees are seen as dissemblers who will become "conservative judicial activists" on the court.

Senator Schumer is at least honest about his view and objectives, and there is something to be said for that. If I were a nominee, I think I would probably rather be bullied by senators over my supposed political beliefs than have my character assassinated over some trumped-up offense—as was the case with Brooks Smith and Charles Pickering. Nevertheless, both practices are destructive to the individual nominees, to the confirmation process, and to the rule of law. And both lines of inquiry fuel the tit-for-tat mentality that helps keep the confirmation wars alive.

A significant change in our collective view of the proper role of the courts is desperately needed (which should also lead to contraction in the judiciary's improper exercise of power). As difficult as that may be to foster, the federalist view is steadily gaining ground again and hearings like this one will help educate the general public about what is at stake. Men of good faith on the right and left have spoken out that ideology should not matter.

Even if it is not possible to alter senators' understanding of the proper role of the courts, the confirmation process still needs to be fixed somehow, perhaps as the result of a political truce. In my view, the President has acted with great restraint so far, perhaps too much restraint. He has a lot more tools at his disposal that he has not employed to bring attention to the judicial vacancy crisis. He could communicate to the Senate that he will call the Senate back into special session if they do not act on a sufficient number of his nominees by its next recess. Indeed, I think he should have delivered such a message last fall, when the Senate's plan of obstruction was already clear.

In addition, the President could fill the longest-standing vacancies with recess appointments under the Recess Appointments Clause, which appointments last until the end of the Senate's "next Session." A President must not abuse his power under that clause, but he needs to take some action to help the courts and change the incentives the Senate faces in doing nothing. I would advise the President to give recess appointments to qualified individuals who are not then nominated for the life-time position. This would allow the Senate to displace the recess appointee at any time it acts to confirm a regular appointee. Such action would not interfere with the Senate's deliberations, but it would undermine the liberal activists who urge the Senate majority to inaction.

If nothing changes in the confirmation process, the legal realists' understanding may become more and more of a self-fulfilling prophesy: only those who behave as political ideologues will be appointed. These are the seeds the Senate majority is sowing now.

EFFECTS OF PROLONGED JUDICIAL VACANCIES ON THE COURTS AND THE ADMINISTRATION OF JUSTICE

The sustained number of judicial vacancies, particularly in the federal appellate courts, is straining the judiciary as never before. In short, the political process and partisan delays risk substantial harm to our justice system.

Although the effect of prolonged judicial vacancies on the courts and the administration of justice is obviously related, it is possible in theory for the remaining judges and their staffs to simply work much harder and more efficiently in an attempt to ensure that the administration of justice is not affected by the Senate's bad faith. This is certainly what the courts have attempted to do. Their level of success is hard to evaluate for some reasons that are explained below, but also because there is a qualitative aspect of administration of justice that is exceedingly difficult to measure.

That said, the federal judiciary is a thoroughly professional institution which is supervised by the very able Chief Justice of the United States. It is aided by many career staff attorneys, judicial law clerks, and administrative personnel. The judicial system can adequately handle a relatively low number of vacancies on a circuit court as well as a district court vacancy in a judicial district where there are many other district judges. (A district court vacancy in a one- or two-judge judicial district, however, presents severe problems.) Likewise, the larger district and circuit courts can adequately handle a short period when there are more than a few vacancies.

When vacancy rates increase in a given court, the Judicial Conference of the United States may declare a judicial emergency for that court (based on guidelines it has developed). This has been done increasingly over the past several years. Nearly 40% of the current judicial vacancies have been classified by the Judicial Conference of the United States as "judicial emergencies." Pursuant to court rules in effect in many judicial districts or circuits, this permits certain emergency rules to operate within that court.

For example, an appellate court must generally decide cases in three-judge panels. Most appellate courts sit to hear oral argument once per month for about four days in randomly-shuffled three judge panels. A sixteen member court with only nine judges (as is the case in the Sixth Circuit, which covers all of Michigan, Ohio, Kentucky, and Tennessee) can form only three panels per month instead of five if it sticks to its active judges alone. Court rules normally in effect allow panels to be formed with two active members of the court and one senior or visiting judge— assuming the court can find visiting and senior judges willing to regularly take on that burden. Emergency rules may allow a panel to be formed with only one active judge and two senior or visiting judges.

The Ninth Circuit panel that decided the "Pledge of Allegiance Case," *Newdow* v.

U.S. Congress, (2002), was composed of one active judge and two senior judges. Circuit rules may also allow the senior or visiting judge that sat on the original panel to sit on the "en banc" panel if the entire court reconsiders the decision. In the Ninth Circuit, where the entire court does not sit on "en banc" rehearing panels, this may further skew the jurisprudence of the court.

Another change the emergency rules may allow is for two judges to rule on motions panels and certain types of summary dispositions if they both agree on the result. At first blush, it may not be clear why this presents a problem since two judges can overrule a third judge who might be assigned in the normal course of events. But there is a reason why three judges are on normal motions and summary disposition panels. The third judge may spot an issue that the first two judges may not notice, and he may convince one of them to change his mind or send the case to the oral argument calendar. In the Fifth Circuit, where I served as a law clerk, any one judge on a summary disposition "screening" panel could send the case to the oral argument docket. A third judge obviously increases the likelihood of that happening.

It is impossible to quantify how often the emergency rules might affect the outcome or handling of a case in the federal courts, but several prominent federal judges are concerned about interference with their normal procedures. Chief Judge Douglas Ginsburg of the D.C. Circuit Court of Appeals explained a few months ago that the court's "ability to manage [its] workload in a timely fashion will be seriously compromised" if it has to operate with only eight of its twelve members for much longer. Chief Judge Ginsburg then catalogued the reduced number of oral argument cases that will be heard in the circuit in the 2002–2003 term and the change in composition and duration of emergency panels. He concluded his remarks with a somber note: "[I]t is clear that the delay [in confirmations] has begun to jeopardize the administration of justice in this Circuit."

The Circuit Judge I had the great pleasure to serve early in my career, Edith Jones, recently published a novel type of workload study in the *Texas Tech Law Review* [in 2002] that provides some additional and interesting insights. Judge Jones's study is not intended to catalogue all of the work she did during the study period of three months, because she excludes many categories of work she performs. For this reason, it is not intended to show the total number of hours she worked—as a lawyer does in private practice. Instead, Judge Jones set out to categorize the type of cases she handled during the study period, note the number of cases in each category and relative time she spent on each type (excluding some periods of time such as oral argument). She also explained the methods her circuit has developed to expedite the relatively repetitious or easy cases so that the court could stay on top of its docket.

To her great credit, Judge Jones does not complain about her workload (which she downplays in her article despite the tremendously long hours I know she works), and she believes her court can manage fairly well with at least fifteen active judges on the seventeen-member court. Yet, her article still highlights some problems with the few vacancies on her court and suggests graver problems for other circuits.

For example, Judge Jones confirmed that the average number of oral argument cases heard by each judge in a year has not varied significantly in over fifteen years. That number is approximately 140. These are the hardest cases, or at least those where the judges believe that a lawyer's argument may be critical. Judge Jones confirms that the "lawyers' appearance has

been critical to our decisionmaking" in a significant number of the oral argument cases. Senior judges are used whenever possible in the Fifth Circuit already. So, even with only two vacancies on the court, the total number of cases that can be scheduled for oral argument is substantially decreased. A fair number of those cases decided without oral argument might have been resolved differently.

Judge Jones explained further that "[w]hat has increased phenomenally during [her] tenure is the volume of the summary calendar." The circuit has come up with some novel and interesting ways of expediting these cases that are determined to be less complicated, legally or factually. One method used in several circuits is for the circuit staff attorneys to prepare memos on the cases that appear to them to be routine. Those cases are distributed randomly to different "screening" panels. If the first judge on the distribution list agrees that it is a routine case, she drafts an opinion and presents it to the other judges in turn. The two other judges on that screening panel do the same thing with their third of cases. Any judge on the panel may review the entire record in the case and send it to the oral argument calendar, but that happens with few cases. No doubt this is principally because the circuit staff attorneys and first reviewing judge got it right, but it is probably also due in part to the fact that the cases placed on the screening panels receive less attention.

Given that the average number of oral argument cases per judge is fixed and the volume on the summary calendar has increased phenomenally, that means an increasing percentage of the circuit's caseload is decided on the summary calendar. Academics have criticized many of the case handling techniques like the one described above. Although I believe the academic criticism is largely uniformed, it is hard to deny that less attention is paid to these cases. (We all must prioritize our work, except perhaps in academia. Would the academics prefer the courts to fall further and further behind on their dockets?) Yet, the only way for a circuit to handle the extra workload that additional vacancies pose is to increase even further the percentage of cases disposed of on the summary calendar.

Judge Jones acknowledges this point with a warning:

> [T]he addition or subtraction of a single screening panel affects a large percentage redistribution of the summary calendar among the active judges. Such a redistribution may occur, for good or ill, as a group of Fifth Circuit judges begins to take senior status in the next few years. If replacements are not speedily confirmed, the per-active-judge burden of the summary calendar will escalate and begin seriously to impinge on the time necessary to address the oral argument docket cases.

The situation in other circuits has already passed the point at which oral arguments are canceled and judges must spend less time on those that are held. The D.C. Circuit has a 33% vacancy rate. The Ninth Circuit has an 18% vacancy rate. And the Sixth Circuit has the highest vacancy rate at 44%.

There are approximately 55,000 appeals filed in federal courts of appeals per year, and the circuit courts generally do not have the discretion to refuse to take such cases. Fifteen percent of that total is 8,250. Who will handle those appeals? How will the work get done? Through the increased use of the summary calendar and emergency procedures, a court may attempt to keep up with its normal flow of cases. But sustained periods of high vacancy on some courts overwhelm even the most diligent courts.

One disturbing possibility is that the emergency rules in place in some circuits also permit judicial manipulation of the docket. The emergency rules may bypass the normal random assignment of judges, and often allow the chief judge to assign visiting and senior judges to panels of his choosing. The rules also increase the chance that cases will not be assigned randomly either. There have been questions raised in several circuits regarding possible manipulation of the rules. Even the appearance of judicial manipulation is disturbing.

One judge in the Sixth Circuit took the extraordinary step of questioning the timing of the en banc [the entire court] hearing of the two University of Michigan racial preference cases in an appendix to his dissent in the first of the cases [*Grutter v. Bolligner*] to be decided....The chief judge waited before he circulated the en banc request until two judges who were appointed by Republicans had taken senior status and would be ineligible to sit with the full court. With the circuit court at half its normal complement of judges, the case was then scheduled and heard. It was decided months later while the Senate Judiciary Committee refused to schedule any hearings for the judges who had been nominated to fill the vacancies.

Part of the Sixth Circuit controversy is related to the fact that the court reached a result in the *Grutter* case in conflict with every other circuit. In an extraordinary writ, the students who are challenging the racially preferential admissions policy asked the Supreme Court last week to take the remaining case, *Gratz* v. *Bollinger*, away from the Sixth Circuit and decide both cases without further action by that court. Hopefully, the Supreme Court will hear the two cases and remove the cloud that hangs over the proceedings in the Sixth Circuit.

[These cases were heard by the Supreme Court. See Debate 17.] But the Senate's inaction with regard to the Sixth Circuit has allowed such a cloud to develop. At its worst, the Senate intended this result. At best, the Senate has enabled such a controversy to arise through its sloth or callous refusal to act. Neither indictment is particularly attractive.

CONCLUSION

The judicial confirmation process is at a new and disturbing low. Ten Democrats on the Senate Judiciary Committee and the current Senate leadership are holding numerous judicial nominees hostage in an attempt to undue the consequences of the last presidential election, and apparently, in an attempt to hold vacancies open for liberal judicial activists.

The immediate harm to the administration of justice is hard to quantify, but it is real, and evidence of it is growing as the judicial confirmation delays stretch on. The long-term harm from the politicized confirmation process to the courts as an institution is even more grave. If the rule of law is to survive in its traditional form, the judicial confirmation process must be radically changed.

THE CONTINUING DEBATE:
Legal Philosophy as a Qualification for the Bench

What Is New

The tension between President Bush and Senate Democrats over judicial nominations continues. As the minority party in the Senate, the Democrats have used the filibuster to block a number of the president's nominees. The most well-known of these was Miguel Estrada, who Bush nominated in 2001 for a seat on the District of Columbia Circuit Court of Appeals. What made Estrada a focal point was the widespread speculation that Bush was positioning him to later be the first Latino Justice of the Supreme Court. No one disputed Estrada's solid legal background. An immigrant from Honduras, he graduated from Harvard Law School, clerked for Supreme Court Justice Anthony Kennedy, and was an attorney in the Justice Department under Presidents George H.W. Bush and Bill Clinton. Suspecting that Estrada was very conservative, Democrats pressed Estrada to state his position on controversial issues, such as abortion. He declined to do so on the grounds that each case is different. The Democrats also asked for internal documents on Estrada's views from the Justice Department. President Bush rejected the request as violating the separation of powers. The Democrats then filibustered to block a confirmation vote. Finally, in mid-2003, a frustrated Estrada withdrew his name from consideration.

Where to Find More

The Supreme Court Historical Society at http://www.supremecourthistory.org is a good place to begin. Then turn to Lee Ryan, "United States Supreme Court Research—Getting Started," University of San Francisco Law Library site at: http://www.usfca.edu/law_library/supres.html. Two good studies of the appointment process are David Yalof, *Pursuit of Justices: Presidential Politics and the Selection of Supreme Court Nominees* (University of Chicago Press, 1999) and Joyce A. Baugh, *Supreme Court Justices In The Post-Bork Era: Confirmation Politics and Judicial Performance* (Peter Lang, 2002). For a group that would support the opposition to Miguel Estrada and similar nominees, go to http://www.pfaw.org/pfaw/general/, the site of the People for the American Way. The opposite view is held by the Committee for Justice at http://www.committeeforjustice.org/.

What More to Do

The issues in this debate are apt to become even more intense when the next Supreme Court vacancy occurs. When that happens, decide what you think and get involved by contacting your senators or, even better, by getting active with one of the many groups that will be involved on one side or the other. More immediately, think about whether blocking otherwise qualified (legal training, experience) judicial nominees based on their political philosophy is acceptable. Whatever your view, react to Todd Gaziano's view that "the confirmation process...needs to be fixed somehow." What, if anything, would you do?

15   ECONOMIC POLICY

CONSTITUTIONALLY REQUIRE A BALANCED BUDGET:
Fiscal Sanity *or* Fiscal Irresponsibility?

FISCAL SANITY

ADVOCATE: William Beach, Director, Center for Data Analysis, Heritage
    Foundation

SOURCE: Testimony during hearings on the "Balanced Budget Amendment"
    before the U.S. House of Representatives Committee on the Judiciary,
    Subcommittee on the Constitution, March 6, 2003

FISCAL IRRESPONSIBILITY

ADVOCATE: Richard Kogan, Senior Fellow, Center on Budget and Policy
    Priorities

SOURCE: Testimony during hearings on the "Balanced Budget Amendment"
    before the U.S. House of Representatives Committee on the Judiciary,
    Subcommittee on the Constitution, March 6, 2003

In a moment of candor, U.S. budget director David Stockman confessed in 1981, "None of us really understands what's going on with all these numbers." Today's budgets are even more daunting, given that they are three times larger (revenue: $1.8 trillion; expenditures: $2.1 trillion) than the one that perplexed Stockman. A few questions and answers about the budget will help provide a foundation for thinking about a balanced budget amendment. Unless noted, all data relates to the fiscal year (FY) 2003 budget (October 1, 2002 to September 30, 2003).

How important is the budget to the U.S. economy? It is the most important aspect of the economy. Budget outlays account for 19.5% of the U.S. gross domestic product (GDP, the value of the wealth produced within a country).

How much has the budget grown? The budget has outpaced inflation and the population. At $1.8 trillion, the FY2000 budget outlays were almost 3.5 million times larger than the 1792 budget ($5.2 million). Even controlled for inflation, the FY2000 budget was 1,101 times larger than in 1792. On a per capita basis, and again controlling for inflation, the $6,406 per U.S. resident that the federal government spent in FY2000 was 196 times more than in 1792.

Where does the money come from? Individual income taxes are the biggest source (49%). Other sources are corporate taxes (10%), payroll taxes (*e.g.*, social security and Medicare, 36%), and miscellaneous taxes (5%).

Where does the money go? Human resources (*e.g.,* health, welfare, and social security) consume 65% of the budget. Other outlays are national defense (17%), physical resources (*e.g.*, environment and transportation, 5%), interest on the national debt (8%), and other functions (5%). The most important shift in spending in recent decades has been the relative decrease in defense spending (48% of outlays in FY1963) and increase in human resources spending, (28% that year).

What are some relevant budget concepts? One set is the *discretionary budget* and the *mandatory budget*. The first involves programs that receive specific annual appropriations. The second involves "entitlement" programs funded by a formula (*e.g.*, food stamps) and also expenditures the government is legally obligated to make (*e.g.*, paying interest on the national debt). Discretionary programs make up 37% of expenditures. Note that Congress, at its discretion, can change the formulas and thus the costs of entitlement programs or even abolish them. The second set of concepts is *on-budget* and *off-budget* receipts and expenditures. On-budget accounts are those that flow in and out of the U.S. Treasury. Off-budget accounts either go through special "trust funds," such as the social security account, or through such corporate-like activities as the U.S. Postal Service. On-budget accounts equal 74% of receipts and 83% of expenditures.

What is the history of budget surpluses and deficits? Since 1900, there has been a budget deficit about 70% of the years, including every year since 1970 except FY1998-FY2001. The estimated budget deficit for FY2003 is $304 billion, about $1,050 per U.S. resident.

How does the government fund the deficit? It borrows money. The government borrows some from itself by, for example, dipping into the social security trust fund. The rest it borrows by selling bonds to the public. In late 2001, the national debt was $5.8 trillion ($20,500 per American). Of that the government owed itself $2.5 trillion and the public $3.3 trillion. Interest on the public debt was $108 billion. Foreign investors hold 30% of the bonds. The national debt is 56% of the GDP, the same proportion as in 1960.

What is the history of trying to control the budget? In recent decades, attempts to legislatively control the budget began amid the perennial and mounting deficits between FY1970 and FY1997. They peaked in FY1992 at $290 billion, equal to about 21% of the budget. During these years, Congress passed several budget control acts. Each had some impact on restraining the budget, but none has provided a permanent solution. The surplus achieved during FY 1998-FY2001 was more the result of revenues generated by one of the most prosperous decades in U.S. history than budget control. Attempts to add a balanced budget amendment to the Constitution have failed. The House passed such an amendment in 1997, but it was defeated in the Senate by one vote.

POINTS TO PONDER

➤ Think about who favors and opposes a constitutional balanced budget amendment. Is the idea inherently conservative or liberal?

➤ Compare the dangers William Beach argues result from deficit spending and those Richard Kogan sees if a balanced budget amendment is adopted.

➤ Consider politics and ask yourself why president and Congress have such a difficult time balancing the budget.

Constitutionally Require a Balanced Budget: Fiscal Sanity

WILLIAM BEACH

There are many things that the 108th Congress [2003–2004] can do for the long-term well being of those represented by the members: among them are strengthen our national and domestic security, provide tax relief that yields a stronger economy, and enact needed reforms to key programs that affect the country's neediest citizens. However, this Congress certainly would secure its place in history and fulfill its obligation to govern for the general good if it referred to the states for ratification an amendment to the Constitution that requires the federal government to operate within a balanced budget.

My testimony today is divided among three headings: 1) the constitutional importance of vigorous debate over competing priorities; 2) the statistical evidence that supports a rapid movement toward a balanced budget amendment; and 3) the role that dynamic revenue estimation plays in the process of achieving annual budget balances.

THE PLACE OF SPENDING DEBATES IN THE HEALTH OF THE CONSTITUTION

I know that many fiscal conservatives view the balanced budget amendment as justified principally on financial grounds. It is virtually uncontroversial that governments at all levels should practice the spending disciplines of well-run businesses. This practice is especially important at the federal level, if for no other reason than the enormous influence that federal spending has on other governments and the economy generally. Spending limitations encourage better accounting controls and auditing processes, which assure that the monies allocated to address the priorities of voters are, indeed, well spent.

However, I believe that a larger, constitutional goal is served by amending the constitution to require a balanced budget: representative government works only as well as it allows a full airing of its citizens' divergent views, particularly in open debates over competing public policy priorities. Without a way to limit spending, such debates are unlikely to occur.

Suppose an extreme situation in which there exist no limitations on the ability of the federal government to spend taxpayers' funds except the capacity of taxpayers to produce revenues. In such a world, no one's spending goals would go unachieved in the short run. There would, as a consequence, be no debate over the direction the nation should go in meeting the needs of its elderly citizens, its educational systems, or its national defense. And, without debate and the deep social, economic, and policy inquiry such debate engenders, we would likely be unable to sustain our republican form of government.

Of course, such an extreme world cannot exist for long, if for no other reason than boundless spending by government inevitably destroys the economy out of which revenues flow. The point of this scenario, however, applies equally well to more realistic gradients of the extreme case. The ability of a government to avoid hard decisions about priorities because it can borrow to meet its revenue shortfalls also diminishes debate over competing views of our country's future and current priorities. This borrowing ability may, as well, enable organizations with powerful lobbying capabilities to squeeze millions of dollars in subsidies from Congress and the Administration with the public scrutiny that debate can produce.

ARE THERE REASONS FOR BEING CONCERNED?

These constitutional considerations should be justification enough to adopt a balanced budget amendment, even if reality had yet to catch up with the possibilities outlined above. However, the evidence is mounting that those fiscal disciplines that may once have protected these vital constitutional processes have yielded utterly to growth in spending that far exceeds required levels.

Let me highlight a few facts:

- The outlays of the federal government today are slightly more than 23 times greater than they were in 1960.

- Government spending after adjusting for inflation has increased by nearly five fold since 1960, while the population has grown by a factor of 1.6.

- Per capita federal spending now stands at $7,600. In 1960, per capita federal spending stood at $510.

- Per capita share of publicly held federal debt now stands at $13,720. In 1960, this share stood at $1,310.

- Total publicly held debt in 1960 was about $236.8 billion. In 2003 it equals about $3.88 trillion.

- Worse news on the debt is on the way. By 2020, most of the baby boom generation will be retired and drawing monthly checks from Social Security. By 2030, the total Medicare enrollment will be more than double the current Medicare population. Neither Medicare nor Social Security is expected to survive the onset of the baby boom

without massive infusions of additional cash or major structural reform. The unfunded liabilities of Social Security alone are now in excess of $21 trillion over the next 75 years.

The recent Congresses have shown little will to reverse or even slow this explosion in federal spending. The 107th Congress completed a four-year spending spree that exceeds every other four-year period since the height of World War II. Between 2000 and 2003, federal spending grew by $782 billion. This growth in spending is equivalent to $73,000 in household spending, which, again, was exceeded only during the darkest hours of the Second World War.

If the spending record of the period 1960 through 2000 fails to convince members of Congress that spending growth is beyond their collective abilities to control, the past four years should abundantly make the case.

THE ROLE OF DYNAMIC REVENUE ESTIMATION IN THE BUDGET PROCESS

Exceptionally rapid growth in government spending, such as we've seen in the last four years, bears down heavily on the general economy and, thus, on federal revenue growth. The consumption of goods and services by government generally comes at the expense of consumption and investment by private companies. This redirection of economic resources should be a concern to policy makers because private companies generally use identical resources more productively than government. When government uses economic resources instead of private firms, the growth of the economy slows below its potential, which reduces potential employment and tax revenue growth.

Members of Congress and the general public do, however, change public policy from time to time in order to achieve a specific end, like winning a war or encouraging an expansion of economic activity that call for spending above revenues. When the public and the Congress begin considering these policy changes, a better, more informed debate will be had if those involved in the decision process are able to see estimates of how their proposed changes would affect budget outcomes.

For reasons well beyond this hearing, Congress has resisted the adoption of dynamic tax and budget analysis in the past. However, the 107th Congress made great progress in bringing macroeconomic analysis into the tax policy debate, and a beginning also was made in introducing this analytical discipline into the preparation of the annual budget.

I raise this emerging capability here because it relates directly to the constitutional and fiscal importance of evaluating competing budget priorities. If the budget committees and those other bodies that propose tax policy changes were to use macroeconomic analysis as a routine part of their deliberations, I am confident the Congress would make better decisions between competing budget priorities than they do now.

Let me briefly illustrate how dynamic economic analysis could inform the annual debate over the federal budget. The Center for Data Analysis at The Heritage Foundation recently completed an econometric analysis of President Bush's proposed economic growth plan. This plan contains a number of major changes to current tax law, including the end to the double taxation of dividends. We introduced these tax law changes into a model of the U.S. economy that is widely used by Fortune 500 companies and government agencies to study such changes. Here are few of the interesting effects we found that would likely stem from adopting the President's plan:

- Employment would grow by nearly a million jobs per year over the next ten years, which adds significantly to the tax base of federal and state governments.

- The drop in the unemployment rate reduces government outlays for unemployed workers at all levels of government.

- Investment grows much more strongly under a tax regime without the double taxation of dividends than with such a policy, which expands the growth rate of the general economy, thus offsetting some of the deleterious effects of rapidly growing federal spending.

- The payroll tax revenues grow more rapidly with President Bush's plan than without, thus adding about $60 billion more to the trust funds than currently forecasted.

- Most importantly, the forecasts of fiscal doom made by many of the plan's critics fail to materialize. The additional economic growth produced by the plan reduces the ten-year "cost" to about 45 percent of its static amount.

- This economic feedback also reduces the growth of new publicly held debt that the plan's critics expect. Instead of a trillion dollars in new debt, the economic growth components of the plan produce significantly under 50 percent of that amount. In fact, the plan supports the creation of $3 in after-tax disposable income for every $1 of new debt, while still reducing all publicly held debt by 28 percent between 2004 and 2012.

While this testimony has touched on only a few of the many arguments that can be advanced in support of a balanced budget amendment, I trust that the thrust of my interest in this constitutional outcome is clear. We need the amendment not only to contain the growth in spending (a worthy goal all by itself), but also to protect our constitutional process of vigorous public debate over important policy alternatives. A budget process constrained by a balanced budget amendment and accompanied by the routine use of standard macroeconomic analysis would be more likely to produce the size and quality of government that most Americans desire.

Constitutionally Require a Balanced Budget: Fiscal Irresponsibility

Richard Kogan

The question before us today is whether the Constitution should be amended to require that the federal budget be balanced every year....

First, let me very briefly explain how restrictive the text of the current proposed amendment really is. By requiring that each year's expenditures be covered by that year's income, the amendment would preclude borrowing, even during times of unusual duress, such as wars or recessions; moreover, it would effectively preclude saving for the future, because the money saved in the present *could not be used* to cover future costs.

No state or local government, no family, and no business is required to operate under such restrictions. Every family borrows to finance the purchase of a house—that's what a mortgage is—and many borrow to finance higher education; every state, city, or county borrows to pay for school, road, or hospital construction or parkland acquisition; and most growing businesses borrow to finance new capital construction or acquisition.

Moreover, the amendment would prohibit dipping into past savings, since under the amendment *this* year's costs must be covered entirely by *this* year's income. Yet most families dip into savings to pay for a child's college education and certainly to cover costs during retirement; every state that "balances" its budget in fact can use its rainy day fund to help cover costs during a recession; and businesses often use retained earnings from prior years to finance expansions. This amendment makes saving for the future

pointless because the saved money could never be used: it would be unconstitutional to use rainy day funds, or to use the accumulating assets in the Social Security trust fund to help cover the costs of the baby boomers' retirement. In effect, it would prohibit this generation from building up public savings, or paying down public debt, for the express purpose of providing assets to make the burden on future generations lighter.

Second, such a restrictive amendment is truly inferior economics—it would require the government to reduce consumption during recessions, thus slowing the economy even further, throwing more people out of work, and in some cases running the risk of turning a recession into a full-blown depression. This Administration is exactly right when it says that Congress should not raise taxes during a recession. By the same token, Congress should not cut public spending during a recession. Either action takes purchasing power out of the hands of consumers at exactly the wrong time. In effect, the amendment would ban automatic stabilizers, such as unemployment compensation. Likewise, the amendment would give the seal of approval to over-stimulating the economy during an inflationary boom, risking an acceleration of inflation that could be seriously destabilizing.

Even though the states operate under much less restrictive rules, the actions states are forced to take during the current recession—raising taxes and cutting education, health care, social services, and infrastructure—are harming the economy and slowing the recovery; this fact makes it doubly important to maintain robust automatic stabilizers at the federal level.

Third, the experience of the last twenty years illustrates that setting targets for a budget surplus, or deficit, or balance, is not workable but that limiting the cost of legislation works far better. From the mid 1980s through 2000, three Presidents and many Congresses gradually worked to undo the damage of the first half of the 1980s, mostly by taking hard votes but partly by writing statutory rules or rules of House and Senate procedure providing guidance that Congress very largely followed. Especially after Gramm-Rudman-Hollings I and II were replaced by the far more workable system of appropriations caps and a rule of budget neutrality for tax and entitlement legislation—the so-called PAYGO rule—the budget moved from deficit to surplus. The relative failure of GRH I and II is important because those laws, like the amendment before us, attempted to set a specific fiscal target for the budget. The relative success of caps and the PAYGO rule illustrates that targeting the *cost of legislation*—rather than the overall level of the surplus or deficit—is a far superior road to the desired result. If this subcommittee is truly concerned about future deficits, it should work with the Budget and Rules Committees and the Administration to re-impose reasonable appropriations caps and the rule of budget neutrality. More importantly, Members should eschew any new tax cuts or entitlement increases, such as a pre-scription drug benefit, except to the extent that they are fully offset.

Fourth, almost every state has a political system in which the governor is inherently much more powerful than the legislators, most of whom are part-time legislators with other jobs. This is a logical consequence of allowing governors great freedom to implement or not implement elements of the budget, depending on circumstances, given various state balanced-budget requirements. By analogy, this amendment could lead to a vast strengthening of presidential powers and a weakening of congressional authority. This worries me; Congress is not very efficient, but its very inefficiency was deliberate, to minimize hasty and ill-considered actions. This has worked well for a few centuries, and I see no need to fundamentally change the balance of power.

Fifth, it is possible that power won't be shifted from the Congress to the President, but rather from the Congress and President to the courts. My guess is that the courts would find the amendment unenforceable, making this exercise mere show. But if the courts believed the Constitution prohibited an unbalanced budget except to the extent Congress voted by supermajority to approve it, then the risks of this amendment would be profound. We have absolutely no way of knowing what a court would do to balance the budget when Congress refused, or more likely, when the budget fell out of balance despite Congress' best efforts. I have attached a paper raising many of the legal avenues that can be imagined—court-ordered surtaxes or benefit cuts; court-ordered enactment of tax increases or spending cuts that the President had vetoed; court-ordered enactment of tax increases or benefit cuts that Congress had designed but had been defeated; court-ordered invalidation of appropriations bills, entitlement increases, and tax cuts; or contempt citations.

Sixth, whether the Courts will enforce the balanced budget amendment or not, there are a wide variety of gimmicks Congress can use to evade it. Among these are borrowing by another name, e.g. lease-purchase contracts; paying for costs through contingent liabilities, e.g. loan guarantees or insurance contracts; timing shifts that move costs from the present to the future, e.g. back-loaded IRAs and the new so-called "savings account" proposals; off-loading federal programs onto nominally independent "government-sponsored enterprises" such as REFCORP [Resolution Funding Corporation: an agency created in 1989 to issue bonds needed to raise funds to deal with the crisis caused by the collapse of numerous savings and loan institutions.]; and the perennial favorite, unfunded mandates on states, localities, businesses, and individuals. In fact, if this amendment were enacted, it could ultimately be referred to as the Unfunded Mandates Act of 2003. [Unfunded mandates are requirements to act without providing funding to carry out the mandated actions].

Seventh, let us leave aside the constitutional question for the moment and ask the public policy question. *Should* the Federal Government aim to balance its budgets? Clearly not during a recession, as I have said. How about on average over the business cycle? Even here, I think that a balanced budget would be the wrong general target. A better target would be to run surpluses, not balance, for the remainder of the decade, in an attempt to pay off much or all of the debt before the baby boom generation retires. The purpose, in this case, is to reduce or eliminate future federal payments for interest on the debt and thereby allow future tax revenue to be used entirely to pay for public benefits and needs, such as Social Security or defense. Because the federal government is a major supporter of people in retirement and because there will be a bulge in retirees at the end of the decade, federal costs will inevitably grow starting in about a decade. If we can reduce federal costs for interest at the same time that the federal costs of Social Security and Medicare are growing, we can afford *part* of the increased costs of Social Security and Medicare without having to raise taxes.

Thus, the question is whether we should pay somewhat higher taxes now (when I am paying them) in order to pay off the debt, or wait a decade or more to raise taxes, when I will be retired but my children will be paying taxes. It seems to me only fair that I and my generation be willing to reduce the tax burden on my children and their generation by being willing to pay somewhat higher taxes now so that we can reduce or eliminate the debt before we retire.

In short, if we are discussing budget policy rather than artificial budget rules, we happen to be in one of the rare decades in which surpluses are generally a better goal than balanced budgets. A surplus doesn't mean we are collecting "extra, unneeded" taxes; it merely means that the taxes we are collecting now will be needed for our future retirement.

This policy discussion illustrates one reason the constitutional amendment is a bad idea: circumstances change over time. During some decades, balance might be generally a good goal, but one should also take into account the private saving rate and needs of the future. In the particular circumstance we are in, where we can predict with certainty that the need for public expenditures will increase in the future compared with current needs, it makes sense for the nation to save for the future by paying down debt. Unlike the right to free speech or the right to a lawyer (which can be viewed as a permanent right), the appropriate general target for fiscal policy depends on circumstances, so it is inherently wrong to enact any such target into the Constitution.

Finally, a constitutional balanced budget amendment is fundamentally unworthy of a democracy. Our Constitution currently allows *every* public policy question—war versus peace, the levels and types of taxes, the purposes and amount of public expenditures, what constitutes a federal crime, whether to admit a new state to the Union—to be decided by majority vote. (True, the rights of individual citizens are protected against a majority decision to discriminate, and it takes a 2/3 vote to override a presidential veto. But these aspects of the Constitution do not favor one set of public policy preferences over any other.) Under a constitutional Balanced Budget Amendment, citizens with one preference on public policy (let us say, those who favor a tax cut or an increase in unemployment benefits during a recession, or merely allowing revenues to fall naturally and the normal unemployment compensation law to continue to operate) would have fewer legal rights than citizens with the opposite viewpoints because they would need more votes to win. This is so inherently unfair that it should be rejected out of hand. Equal legal rights, including the right to have our votes count the same amount as anyone else's votes, is fundamental.

THE CONTINUING DEBATE:
Constitutionally Require a Balanced Budget

What Is New

Concern over chronic budget deficits was quieted for a time by the cumulative $558 billion budget surplus of FY1998–FY2001. Then the budget plunged back into deficit spending. Lagging revenue was one cause. Congress enacted significant tax cuts at the request of President Bush. Also, the economy slowed. Rising unemployment decreased income taxes, and the downturn in the stock market cost the government billions of dollars in lost capital gains and dividends taxes. The net result is that revenue for FY2003 was $162 billion less than for FY2000. Increased spending was the other cause of renewed budget deficits. The Bush administration's responses to the September 11, 2001 terrorist attacks added about $100 billion to the budget between FY2000 and FY2003 to increase military and homeland security spending. Human resource outlays also grew during these years, adding $200 billion to the budget. The net result was a return to deficit spending (–$159 billion) in FY 2002. Moreover, current estimates are for deficits at least through FY2008. The administration's Office of Management and Budget (OMB) projects a cumulative deficit for FY2002–FY2008 of $1.6 trillion. For those years, the Congressional Budget Office (CBO) puts the cumulative deficit at $2 trillion.

Where to Find More

Data and commentary about the budget, budget history, and projected budgets are available at the OMB site (http://www.whitehouse.gov/omb/) and the CBO site (http://www.cbo.gov/). To learn the details of the balanced budget amendment introduced in the House of Representatives in 2003, go to Thomas, the Web page of Congress, at http://thomas.loc.gov/, and enter in "HJ Res 22" (House Joint Resolution 22) in the window labeled "Bill Number." Further information is available on the Web sites of the two advocates' centers: Richard Kogan's Center on Budget and Policy Priorities (http://www.cbpp.org/) and William Beach's Center for Data Analysis, Heritage Foundation (http://www.heritage.org/research/).

What More to Do

There are few if any painless budget choices. It is easy to say, "Slash welfare spending and make those people get jobs" or "Vastly increase taxes on those fat-cat rich people and corporations and make them pay their fair share." But such statements do not make real budgets. To "get real," do two things. One, in your class take the FY2003 budget and revise it. If you want to balance it, you will need to hike taxes or cut spending. So decide who gives and who gets. Second, debate and, if you wish, amend House Joint Resolution 22, the proposal in the 108th Congress to add a balanced budget amendment to the Constitution. While you are at it, tell your members of Congress what you think.

16 CRIMINAL JUSTICE POLICY

THE DEATH PENALTY:
Racially Biased *or* Justice Served?

RACIALLY BIASED

ADVOCATE: Julian Bond, Professor of History, University of Virginia and Distinguished Professor-in-Residence, American University.

SOURCE: Testimony during hearings on "Race and the Federal Death Penalty," before the U.S. Senate Committee on the Judiciary, Subcommittee on Constitution, Federalism, and Property Rights, June 13, 2001

JUSTICE SERVED

ADVOCATE: Andrew G. McBride, former U.S. Associate Deputy Attorney General

SOURCE: Testimony during hearings on "Race and the Federal Death Penalty," before the U.S. Senate Committee on the Judiciary, Subcommittee on Constitution, Federalism, and Property Rights, June 13, 2001

Murder and capital punishment share four elements. They are: (1) a planned act (2) to kill (3) a specific person who (4) is not immediately attacking anyone. Should then murder and capital punishment be judged just or unjust by the same standard?

The first question is whether killing is ever justified. The doctrine of most religions contain some variation of the commandment, "Thou shalt not kill." For moral absolutists and pacifists, this prohibition is unbendable. They would not kill another person under any circumstances. Most people, however, are moral relativists who evaluate good and evil within a context. They do not condemn as immoral killing in such circumstances as self-defense and military combat.

What about premeditated acts by individuals? Most societies condemn these as murder even if the other person has harmed you. To see this, assume that a murderer has killed a member of your family. You witnessed it and thus are sure who is guilty. If you track down the murderer and execute him or her, by law now you are also a murderer. Yet 67% of Americans favor capital punishment, which is the state carrying out roughly the same act.

Arguably the difference is the willingness of most people to apply different moral standards to individuals acting privately and society acting through its government. This distinction is an ancient one. For example, God may have commanded "Thou shalt not kill" for individuals (Exodus 20:13), but in the very next chapter God details "ordinances" to Moses, including, "Whosoever strikes a man so that he dies shall be put to death" (Exodus 21:12). The point here is not whether you want to accept the words that Exodus attributes to a deity. After all, just two verses later, God also decrees death to "whoever curses his father or his mother." This would leave few teenagers alive today. Instead, the issue to wrestle with is whether and why it is just or unjust for a government, but not an individual, to commit an act with the four elements noted in the first paragraph. For those who see no moral distinction between actions by individuals and a society, capital punishment is wrong no matter how heinous the crime is, how fair the legal system is, or what the claimed benefits of executing criminals are.

There are others, though, who do not argue that capital punishment is inherently immoral. Their view is that executions have no positive effect. To think about this point, you have to first decide what it is you want capital punishment to accomplish. One possibility is to deter others from committing similar crimes. The other possibility is punishment as a way of expressing the society's outrage at the act. A great deal of the debate at this level is about whether capital punishment is a deterrent. It is beyond the limited space here to take up that debate, but to a degree it misses the point of why most Americans who favor capital punishment do so. When asked in a 2001 poll why they support it, 70% replied it is "a fitting punishment" for convicted murders, while only 25% thought, "the death penalty deters crime," and 4% were unsure.

Yet another line of attack on capital punishment is that the system is flawed. Some contend that mistakes get made, and innocent people are sometimes convicted and executed. Then there is the argument represented in this debate made by Julian Bond and disputed by Andrew McBride that, as conducted in the United States, the process from investigation, through trial and sentencing, to the carrying out of the death penalty is racially tainted. There can be little doubt that the demographic characteristics of those executed are not in proportion to their group's percentage of the society. Between 1977 and 2001, African Americans (about 12% of the population) made up 36% of those executed. Because federal criminal justice statistics classify Latinos as "white," it is hard to find the impact of executions on that group. However, Texas and California give some clues. Combined, the two states' population is 49% white, 9% African American, 28% Latino, and 16% other identifiers. The two states' combined death row population is 37% white, 38% African American, 22% Latino, and 4% others. It must be said that the disproportionate number of blacks executed does not by itself prove racial bias. Fully 98% of all those executed are men, yet there is little to argue the system is biased against males. Instead, consider the arguments of Bond and McBride carefully.

POINTS TO PONDER

➤ What evidence does Julian Bond provide to support his claim that "the death penalty serves as a shield for attitudes on race" in the United States.

➤ Given the disproportionate percentage of blacks executed, how does Andrew McBride justify his argument that "there is no credible statistical evidence of racial bias in the enforcement of the federal death penalty"?

➤ What, if anything, would make you change your view on capital punishment?

The Death Penalty:
Racially Biased

JULIAN BOND

Thank you for inviting me to offer my perspective as Chairman of the Board of the National Association for the Advancement of Colored People (NAACP) and as a member of Citizens for a Moratorium on Federal Executions (CMFE).

The NAACP is the nation's oldest and largest civil rights organization. We have long been opposed to the death penalty and are horrified by its all too frequent and easily documented racially discriminatory application. We do not believe it deters crime. It targets and victimizes those who cannot afford decent legal representation. It is used against the mentally incompetent. It tragically sends the innocent to death.

The death penalty serves as a shield for attitudes on race. It is used most often in states with the largest African-American populations and disproportionately used when the accused is black and the victim is white. In addition to being bad domestic policy, it increasingly alienates the United States from our allies and lessens our voice in the international human rights arena.

I am also a member of Citizens for a Moratorium on Federal Executions (CMFE). CMFE is a coalition of dozens of American public figures who joined together last fall when Juan Raul Garza was scheduled to be the first individual executed by the United States Government in nearly 40 years. Some members of CMFE support the death penalty in specific circumstances; others are unalterably opposed. Nonetheless, we spoke with one voice in urging President Clinton to declare a moratorium on federal executions.

Among the 40 people who signed CMFE's first letter to President [Bill] Clinton, delivered on November 20, 2000, were former high-ranking members of the Justice Department, former Clinton administration officials, the Dean of the Yale Law School, a Nobel Laureate, Congressional Gold Medal and Presidential Medal of Freedom recipients, civil rights, religious and civic leaders, former U.S. Senators, and prominent individuals in the world of arts and entertainment. Since last November, CMFE's roster has expanded to include an even broader spectrum of civil rights and religious leaders, the Founder and President of the Rutherford Institute, the Editor of the *American Spectator*, and a former United States Ambassador.

There can be no question that CMFE was able to assemble this cross-section of prominent U.S. citizens to call for a moratorium on federal executions because the public is prepared to carefully re-examine the use of capital punishment in this nation. At no time since the death penalty was reinstated by the Supreme Court in 1976 have Americans voiced such grave doubts about the fairness and reliability of capital punishment. At the state level, those doubts are reflected in the unprecedented moratorium on executions put into place by Governor Ryan of Illinois, in death penalty moratorium bills introduced and enacted in state legislatures, and in studies commissioned by Governors in other states. At the national level, Senator [Dianne] Feingold [D-CA] has introduced a bill calling for a moratorium on federal executions and Senator [Patrick] Leahy

[D-VT] has introduced legislation that would require greater protections for those prosecuted for capital crimes at the state and federal levels. Professional, community and civil rights organizations, including the League of United Latin American Citizens (LULAC), the National Urban League, the NAACP, the Black Leadership Forum, the Leadership Conference on Civil Rights and the American Bar Association, have called on the Executive Branch to suspend federal executions, and religious organizations have intensified their long-standing calls for a death penalty moratorium.

When CMFE addressed President Clinton on November 20, we were responding to the September 12 release of the Department of Justice survey that documented racial, ethnic and geographic disparities in the charging of federal capital cases. The CMFE wrote: "Unless you take action, executions will begin at a time when your own Attorney General has expressed concern about racial and other disparities in the federal death penalty process. Such a result would be an intolerable affront to the goals of justice and equality for which you have worked during your Presidency. Consequently, we urge you to put in place a moratorium until the Department of Justice completes its review of the federal death penalty process."

As I speak to you today, of course, the first federal execution in almost 40 years has been carried out. The man put to death was not Mr. Garza, who now faces execution in less than a week's time, on June 19 [Garza was executed that day at the U.S. Penitentiary in Terre Haute, Indiana].

Mr. Garza did not precede Timothy McVeigh to the death chamber in Terre Haute because, on December 7, 2000, President Clinton stayed Mr. Garza's execution for six months. While the President announced that he was not prepared to halt all federal executions, he nonetheless told the nation that further examination of possible racial and regional bias in the federal death penalty system "… should be completed before the United States goes forward with an execution in a case that may implicate the very questions raised by the Justice Department's continuing study. In this area there is no room for error."

Nothing has transpired since President Clinton's December 7 statement and grant of reprieve that warrants going forward with Mr. Garza's execution nor with carrying out the death sentence of any of the other 19 individuals on federal death row. We reject any suggestion that the report released by Mr. Ashcroft on June 6 constitutes a reliable or thorough study of possible racial and regional bias in the federal death penalty system. Nor does it answer the troubling questions raised by the Justice Department's September 12 survey.

On December 8, the day following the President's decision to stay Mr. Garza's execution, I was one of several CMFE representatives, who, along with Congressman John Conyers, met with former Attorney General Reno, former Deputy Attorney General Holder and other Justice Department attorneys to discuss President Clinton's announcement and plans for a more comprehensive investigation of the federal death penalty, which would include the participation of outside experts. Members of the Department of Justice acknowledged that this critical task could not be accomplished by the end of April of this year, the timetable set by President Clinton when he announced the December reprieve for Mr. Garza.

The result of that discussion with Attorney General Reno and Deputy Attorney General Holder was memorialized in the CMFE's letter to President Clinton, dated January 4, 2001.

We next learned that on January 10, 2001, the National Institute of Justice assembled a group of experts from within and without the Department of Justice to discuss the parameters of the comprehensive investigation that the Attorney General, Deputy Attorney General and the President had announced was needed.

At his confirmation hearing, then-Attorney General-designate John Ashcroft stated that evidence of racial disparities in the application of the federal death penalty "troubles me deeply." Acknowledging he was "unsure" why more than half the federal capital prosecutions were initiated in less than one-third of the states, the Attorney General asserted that he was also "troubled" by this evidence.

He expressed his approval of a "thorough study of the system," and proclaimed, "Nor should race play any role in determining whether someone is subject to capital punishment."

On June 4, 2001, CMFE wrote to President Bush, reiterating our call for a moratorium on federal executions. We raised the concern that the Attorney General's actions and statements subsequent to his confirmation hearing "cast doubt" on "the Administration's commitment to the principles he set forth at his confirmation hearing." We noted that "[t]here has been no indication that the Department intends to continue the necessary independent investigation of racial and geographic bias in the death penalty, which was to have been administered by the National Institute of Justice. Moreover, Attorney General Ashcroft's statements to members of Congress, including his testimony before the House Appropriations Committee in early May, suggest that even the internal inquiry that the Department of Justice embarked upon will consist of little more than a re-analysis of the same data already examined and found to demonstrate 'troubling' racial and geographic disparities." Just two days later, on June 6

2001, the Department of Justice released a flawed study purporting to demonstrate that federal administration of the death penalty was bias-free.

Now, Attorney General Ashcroft claims that "there is no evidence of favoritism towards white defendants in comparison with minority defendants." But such evidence does exist, and its existence raises serious doubts about fairness in our criminal justice system.

Without guarantees of fairness, there can be no public confidence in the administration of justice.

That lack of confidence is heightened and the guarantees of fairness are lessened by the Department of Justice's recent report on the Federal Death Penalty System.

Evidence of race-of-victim discrimination was ignored. Differences among geographical regions in which the penalty is sought by United States' Attorneys, approved by the Attorney General, and imposed by juries were ignored. Stark racial differences in death-penalty avoidance by whites and minorities who enter a plea to a non-capital charge were not fully examined or explained. The entrance of racial disparities at discrete stages in decision-making was evaded. Arguments for further study by researchers assembled by the Department of Justice were ignored.

Before Tuesday [June 11, 2001, the day Timothy McVeigh was executed], the United States had not executed anyone for nearly 40 years. What is the hurry, especially when life and liberty are at stake? When asked at his confirmation hearing, "Do you agree with President Clinton that there is a need for 'continuing study' of 'possible racial and regional bias' because 'in this area there is no room for error?'" the Attorney General unequivocally answered, "Yes!"

Attorney General Ashcroft has broken his pledge to the United States Senate. There has been no "thorough study of the system." It has fallen to you to assure Americans that, at least when it comes to the ultimate penalty in our federal system, justice is blind to race and ethnicity.

You cannot fix everything that is wrong in our justice system, but you can do this.

The Death Penalty:
Justice Served

ANDREW G. MCBRIDE

INTRODUCTION

I am honored to appear…today on the important subject of the fair and even-handed enforcement of the federal death penalty.…

I believe that the death penalty serves an important role in the spectrum of penalties that the federal criminal justice system has available. Recent studies indicate the death penalty does in fact play a role in the general deterrence of capital crimes. We know the death penalty accomplishes specific deterrence, for it eliminates the possibility that a known-killer will kill again in prison or upon eventual release. The death penalty offers an additional measure of protection for our federal law enforcement officers—who are often faced with the prospect of arresting violent felons who are already facing life imprisonment. Most importantly, the death penalty sends a message of society's outrage and resolve to defend itself against the most heinous of crimes. As we have seen most recently in the [Oklahoma City federal building bomber Timothy] McVeigh case, it gives survivors a sense of justice and closure that even life imprisonment without parole cannot accord. As a former prosecutor who has tried capital cases, and as a citizen, I share the concern [everyone here] that the death penalty be enforced in a fair, even-handed, and race-neutral manner. At the same time, I am wary of the misuse of race and racial statistics as a "stalking horse" for those who are opposed to the death penalty in all circumstances. Honest opposition to capital punishment on moral grounds is

one thing, throwing charges of racism at federal law enforcement officers and federal prosecutors in order to block enforcement of a penalty the Congress has authorized and the American people clearly support, is another. I fear that some of my fellow panelists today have let vehement opposition to all capital punishment blind them to some simple facts about enforcement of the federal death penalty.

THERE IS NO CREDIBLE STATISTICAL EVIDENCE OF RACIAL BIAS IN THE ENFORCEMENT OF THE FEDERAL DEATH PENALTY.

The dangers of statistical analyses are perhaps best captured in the old saying "Figures never lie but liars often figure." [We] should be very wary of the results of regression analysis or other statistical devices applied to capital punishment. No two capital defendants are the same. No two capital crimes are the same. Federal law and the Eighth Amendment require that juries be allowed to consider every aspect of the crime, the background and competence of the defendant, and even impact evidence regarding the victim, in arriving at the correct punishment. Regression analysis posits that each factor relevant to the imposition of the death penalty can be identified and then given an assigned weight, such that very different cases can be meaningfully compared. This premise is simply false. There are literally millions of legitimate variables that a prosecutor or jury could consider in seeking or imposing capital punishment. If we truly believed that they could all be identified and weighted, we would allow computers to deliberate and impose penalty. Instead, we quite properly rely upon human judgment, the judgment of the prosecutor, the death penalty committee in the Department of Justice, the Attorney General, the district court judge, and a fairly-selected jury from the venue where the crime occurred. In my opinion, and in my experience for seven years as a federal prosecutor, I saw no evidence that the race of defendants or victims had any overt or covert influence on this process. I believe the charge is fabricated by those who wish to block enforcement of the federal death penalty for other reasons.

I would ask [you] to keep four points in mind as it evaluates these very serious, but, in my opinion, wholly unsupported charges. First, pointing to statistical disparities between racial percentages of capital defendants and racial percentages in the population at large is utterly specious. The population at large does not commit violent felonies—only a small percentage of both the white and non-white communities are ever involved in violent crime. The sad fact is that non-whites are statistically much more likely to commit certain crimes of violence that might lead to death penalty prosecutions. African Americans make up approximately 13 percent of the nation's population. Yet, according to the FBI's 1999 uniform crime reports, there were 14,112 murder offenders in the United States in 1999, and of those offenders for whom race was known, 50 percent were black. Given that most murders are intra-racial, it is not surprising that of the 12,658 murder victims in 1999, 47 percent were black.

Capital crimes also are more likely to occur in urban areas that are more densely populated and tend to have higher minority populations. According to the FBI data, 43 percent of murders in 1999 were recorded in the South, the most heavily populated area of the country. The same data shows that the Nation's metropolitan areas reported a 1999 murder rate of 6 victims per 100,000 inhabitants, compared to rates of 4 per 100,000 for rural counties and cities outside metropolitan areas.

One cannot simply ignore these facts in evaluating the performance of our criminal justice system. Indeed, if the numbers of federal capital defendants of each race precisely mirrored their representation in society as a whole, that would be truly a cause for alarm. It would suggest real "racial profiling" in the death penalty.

Second, the federal government does not have general jurisdiction over all violent crimes committed within its jurisdiction. From 1988 to 1994, the only federal death available was for murder in relation to certain drug-trafficking crimes. This period coincided with the worst drug epidemic in our Nation's history—the spread of crack cocaine from New York and Los Angeles to all our major urban centers. Most of the participants in the drug organizations that distributed crack cocaine were black, and most of the homicides connected with this drug trade were black-on-black homicides. Approximately half of the defendants presently on federal death row were convicted of a drug-related homicide.

The Department of Justice study released last week indicates that the Eastern District of Virginia [a federal district court area] is a prime example of an area where the type of crime at issue and the needs of state and federal law enforcement have shaped the statistics. I was a prosecutor in that district for a period of seven years, and I can assure [you] that I never saw any racial bias in the investigation or charging stages by federal agents or prosecutors during my tenure there.

Drug-related homicide was a major problem in the urban areas of Richmond, Norfolk, and Virginia Beach. Many of these homicides were unsolved and had in fact been committed by interstate drug gangs with roots as far away as New York, Los Angeles, and even Jamaica. Joint task forces, composed of federal agents, state police, and local detectives investigated these cases under the supervision of federal prosecutors. Local leaders and politicians, including leaders of the African American community, welcomed this effort to focus federal resources on inner-city crimes and the unsolved murders of African-American citizens. These prosecutions were a classic example of the federal government lending support where support was needed and requested and the crimes had a significant interstate element. The results of aggressive federal prosecutions have included cutting the murder rate in Richmond, Virginia in half from its high in the early 1990's.

Third, the available statistical evidence indicates that whites who enter the federal capital system (both pre- and post-1994) are significantly more likely to face the death penalty than minority defendants. Thus, even opponents of the federal death penalty seem to concede that there is no racial bias in the Department of Justice procedures for determining whether or not to seek the death penalty. Instead, they posit racial bias in the decision to make a case federal in the first place. It is obvious that these critics have never served as a state or federal prosecutor. The same federal prosecutors who make the initial intake decision regarding state or federal prosecution also make the initial decision on the death penalty and prepare the recommendation memorandum to the Attorney General's standing committee. The proposition that they are severely racially biased in the former (the intake decision when capital status is unsure) but are not biased in the latter (when the decision to seek the death penalty is actually

made) is absurd. Intake decisions are made by supervisors in the United States Attorney's Offices, who often have fixed protocols with their state counterparts regarding certain crimes. The fact that a group of bank robbers is multi-jurisdictional, or that an organization's trafficking level of cocaine has gone above 10 kilograms of crack are factors likely to result in federal prosecution. Race is never a factor and the notion that federal law enforcement agents are making "racist" intake decisions (by themselves) is a baseless charge that displays a shocking lack of knowledge of how our federal/state criminal justice system actually works.

Fourth, [you] should not place any stock in statistical patterns or comparisons. A "pool" of approximately 700 federal capital cases is too small a cohort for any serious statistician to produce any reliable conclusions. Moreover, all such studies suffer from the flaw noted above—they assume that all the factors that influence capital punishment can be quantified. It is clear that they cannot be. Rather than focus on largely meaningless statistical games, we should focus on continuing and improving the procedures in place at the Department of Justice to ensure that every capital eligible crime is submitted and reviewed, and that every decision to seek the death penalty is fully justified by the facts and circumstances of the case.

CONCLUSION

In my opinion as a former federal prosecutor, there is no racial bias in the federal capital system. The decision to seek federal prosecution itself is made by federal prosecutors based on largely fixed criteria regarding the interstate nature of the crime or other objective, non-racial factors. The decision to actually seek the death penalty for a capital eligible crime has several layers of review and includes a standing committee that ensures fairness and continuity. Statistical evidence is of little or no probative value in this area and is, in my opinion, being manipulated by those who simply oppose the federal death penalty for any crime. The American people overwhelmingly support capital pun- ishment and Congress has made it available for a limited set of federal crimes. I believe that the Department of Justice has enforced these laws in an unbiased manner to date and that it will continue to do so under the leadership of Attorney General [John] Ashcroft.

THE CONTINUING DEBATE:
The Death Penalty

What Is New

Globally, about half the world's countries have a death penalty, and about 40% actually use it. The United States is among the countries most likely to carry out the death penalty. According to Amnesty International, there were 1,526 known executions in 31 countries during 2002. Of these, 81% were carried out in three countries: China (1,060), Iran (113), and the United States (71).

The number of death row inmates in U.S. prisons has grown from 692 in 1980, to 2,346 in 1990, to 3,581 in 2001. Of the condemned, 43% are African Americans. The U.S. Department of Justice continues not to report data for Hispanics.

Where to Find More

To review the legal background of capital punishment, including the U.S. Supreme Court's suspension of the death penalty in *Furman v. Georgia* (1972) and its reinstatement of capital punishment in *Gregg v. Georgia* (1976), go to Cornell University's Legal Information Institute at http://www.law.cornell.edu and enter "death penalty" in the search function. Also read the anti-death penalty article, William S. McFeely, "Trial and Error: Capital Punishment in U.S. History," January 2001 at http://historymatters.gmu.edu/d/5420/; and the more neutral review, Donna Lyons "Capital Punishment on Trial," *State Legislatures* (May 2000) at http://www.ncsl.org/programs/cj/cappun.htm. For a group on each side of the issue, visit the Web sites of Pro-Death Penalty.com at http://www.prodeathpenalty.com/ and the Death Penalty Information Center at: http://www.deathpenaltyinfo.org/. What seems to be a bizarre site, but on further examination is important to visit, lists the last meal requests of the more than 300 prisoners executed in Texas since 1982. What makes the site at http://www.tdcj.state.tx.us/stat/finalmeals.htm worth visiting is that you can hyperlink from the name of each executed individual to a picture, personal information, and a description of the crime each committed. It puts a "face" on the data about both those convicted of murders and the victims.

What More to Do

Discuss all the various permutations of the death penalty debate, including whether it is ever justified under any circumstances and, if so, under what circumstances; whether it is only justified by utilitarianism (if it deters later murders) and/or as punishment per se, and whether the fact that executions are not proportionate among various demographic groups is evidence that capital punishment should be abolished. Also, get active. The federal government and 38 states have death penalty laws on the books; 12 states and the District of Columbia do not. Find out the law in your state and support or oppose it.

17 EDUCATION POLICY

AFFIRMATIVE ACTION ADMISSIONS:
Promoting Equality *or* Unfair Advantage?

PROMOTING EQUALITY

ADVOCATE: 41 College Students and 3 Student Coalitions

SOURCE: Amicus Curiae brief to the U.S. Supreme Court in *Grutter v. Bollinger* (2003)

UNFAIR ADVANTAGE

ADVOCATE: 21 Law Professors

SOURCE: Amicus Curiae brief to the U.S. Supreme Court in *Grutter v. Bollinger* (2003)

Equal opportunity—Surveys show that nearly all Americans support having it, but the data on the circumstances of various groups casts doubt on whether the country has yet to achieve it. Economically, for example, the average household income of non-Hispanic whites (Eurowhites) is 63% greater than that of African Americans and 69% greater than that of Hispanics. The 24% poverty rate among black and Latino households is triple that for Eurowhite households. There are also income gaps for the employed. For every dollar made by the average Eurowhite worker, blacks make 72 cents, and Latinos make 65 cents. As for unemployment, the July 2000 rate of Eurowhite unemployment was about 4%, compared to 11% for blacks and 8% for Latinos. Moreover, significant disparities in poverty, income, and unemployment have persisted as far back as the data goes.

To address such gaps, the federal government began to promote affirmative action in 1961 when President John F. Kennedy issued Executive Order 10925 requiring that federally financed projects "take affirmative action to ensure that hiring and employment practices are free of racial bias."

Later, state and local governments also adopted affirmative action programs, and they and the federal government extended them to education and other areas. Title IX, featured in Debate 16, was part of that effort. Whether because of these policies or more general social changes, the position of women and minorities in education improved somewhat. Women now make up a majority of college undergraduates and 44% of graduate students. Asian Americans are a greater percentage of both undergraduate and graduate students than they are in the general population. However, improvement for blacks and Latinos has been slower. Between 1980 and 2000, African Americans rose from 9.9% to 13.4% of undergraduates, and Latino enrollment went from 3.7% to 8.6%. This enrollment gap has created a large disparity in college graduates, with 28% of Eurowhites over age 25 having a bachelor's degree, compared to 16.5% of African Americans, and 10.6% of Hispanics. At the professional school level, Eurowhite enrollment between 1980 and 2000 dropped from 81% to 73.9%, while black enrollment grew from 5.8% to 7.2%, and Latino enrollment climbed from 3.9% to 4.7%. This leaves minorities particularly underrepresented in law, medicine, and other professions. Among lawyers, 5.4% are blacks, and 3.9% are Latinos. African Americans are 6.3% of the physicians, and Hispanics are 3.4%. As a reference point, the population in 2000 was 69% Eurowhite, 12.3% African American, 12.5% Hispanic, and 3.3% Asian American, with other groups making up the balance. Women were 51.9% of the population.

While Americans strongly support the theory of equal opportunity, many have disagreed with the application of affirmative action programs in education and other areas. As a result, there have been a number of court challenges alleging unconstitutional "reverse discrimination." The first significant education case was *Regents of the University of California* v. *Bakke* (1978), which involved the rejection of a white applicant to medical school that reserved 16% of its places for minority students. In a 5–4 decision, the Supreme Court ruled somewhat confusingly that (a) numerical quotas were not constitutional but that (b) race could legitimately be considered during the admissions process. The following articles trace the legal background more, but the ambiguities in the *Bakke* ruling created disagreements among various Circuit Courts of Appeals over what could and could not be done with respect to affirmative action admissions. This set the groundwork for two "companion" cases involving the University of Michigan. One, *Gratz* v. *Bollinger*, focused on undergraduate admission and involved the university giving minority students 20 points on a 150-point admissions score. The second, *Grutter* v. *Bollinger*, related to law school admissions but did not involve a stated quota or a point scheme, only the goal of achieving a "critical mass" of minority students.

The articles below relate to *Grutter*, although most of its underlying rationale also applied to *Gratz*. The two articles are *amicus curiae* (friend of the court) briefs filed by those who were not direct parties to the case but who the court agreed had an important concern. The first, supporting the university's affirmative action program, was filed by a coalition of three student groups and 41 individual students. The second, opposing the university, was written by 21 law professors.

POINTS TO PONDER

➢ Read the briefs as a Supreme Court justice. What is your decision in *Grutter v. Bollinger* and why?

➢ Assuming the only difference *Gratz v. Bollinger* is the explicit use of a point system, would you make the same decision as in *Grutter* and why?

➢ What should affirmative action mean as a policy directive?

Affirmative Action Admissions:
Promoting Equality

41 COLLEGE STUDENTS AND 3 STUDENT COALITIONS

STATEMENT OF THE CASE

When plaintiff filed suit in *Grutter v. Bollinger* in 1997, 41 individually named black, Latino, Native American, Arab American, Asian Pacific American, other minority and white students and three coalitions—United for Equality and Affirmative Action (UEAA), Law Students for Affirmative Action, and the Coalition to Defend Affirmative Action and Integration & Fight for Equality By Any Means Necessary (BAMN), sought and eventually won the right to present our defense of the Law School's affirmative action plan.

Beginning on the 16th of January 2001, a day after the Martin Luther King holiday, the *Grutter v. Bollinger* case went to trial. One month later, after 15 days of trial, and 24 witnesses, the case concluded. The student intervenors fought for the district court trial in order to disprove the plaintiff's claim of "reverse discrimination" and to lift the profound stigma that the attack on affirmative action has placed on the shoulders of minority students. We presented the overwhelming majority of evidence at trial: 15 of the 24 witnesses were called by us, and we used 28 hours and 48 minutes of the 30-hour limit imposed by the district court.

As the student intervenors will show, the plaintiff has not proved that she has been a victim of discrimination—and the United States has not offered a viable alternative to affirmative action. The facts show that if the plaintiff prevails in this Court, the Law School will quickly and inevitably resegregate. That conclusion is confirmed by the resegregation of the uni-

versities that has resulted from the end of affirmative action in California, Texas, and Florida. If the plaintiff prevails, gains toward integration will be reversed and replaced by a massive return to segregation starting in the most selective universities and spreading throughout higher education and into the society as a whole.

I. RACE AND THE LAW SCHOOL APPLICATION POOL

For two-thirds of black students and 70 percent of Latino students, the path to the future leads through segregated elementary and secondary schools. The worst segregation, which was once in the South, is now in the major industrial states of the Northeast and Midwest. Michigan [has] 83 percent of its black students attending segregated schools. For Latinos, segregation by race and ethnicity is compounded by segregation by language, with 50 percent of the Latinos in California speaking Spanish at home. For Native Americans, over half live in cities where they face segregation like that faced by blacks and Latinos, while just under half remain in impoverished government-run reservations and boarding schools.

The segregation concentrates and compounds the effects of poverty. While poverty disadvantages the poor of all races, poor whites are more dispersed residentially, and their children are far more likely to enroll in schools that have a substantial number of middle-class students. That is far less likely for black, Latino, and Native American students.

Even for black students from middle- and upper-middleclass families, substantial disadvantage exists. For equivalent incomes, black families have less wealth, less education, and fewer relatives who can provide financial and other assistance in times of trouble. Even when middle class black people or Latinos move to nearby suburbs, the suburbs are, or quickly become, segregated and the school systems quickly decline. Even for the very few black families who move to stable white, upper-middleclass suburbs with good school systems, there remain racial isolation, stereotyping, tracking, and stigma.

In testimony at trial [in the Federal District Court] on behalf of the student defendants, Professor Gary Orfield of the Harvard University School of Education summarized the impact of segregation:

> There never was a separate but equal school system. That's because of many things. It's because the poverty levels in segregated schools are much higher....[T]here are fewer minorities in teacher training. There are many fewer teachers who choose to go to work in schools of this sort. Most teachers who start in segregated schools leave faster. The curriculum that is offered is more limited. The probability that the teacher will be trained in their field is much more limited. The level of competition is less. The respect for the institution in the outside world is less. The connections to colleges are less. There are more children with health problems....The population is much more unstable....The kids don't have books....There [are] no facilities....[I]t is like a different planet, a different society.

Segregation—separate and unequal schools—means that there are far fewer black, Latino, and Native American students who graduate from college. The national

pool of students who could apply to a school like Michigan is disproportionately white—and many of the comparatively small number of black, Latino, and Native American students in that pool attended segregated elementary and secondary schools.

II. BIAS IN MICHIGAN'S ADMISSIONS SYSTEM WITHOUT AFFIRMATIVE ACTION

A. A Segregated School in a Segregated Profession

Before the advent of affirmative action, there were very few black students who graduated from college, fewer still who applied to law school, and almost none who were admitted to law school.

In the 1950s and early 1960s, except for the law schools at the historically black colleges and universities, the nation's law schools were essentially all white and all male. In 1960, the nation had 286,000 lawyers, of whom 2180 were black and not more than 25 were Native American. The number of Latinos was not recorded but was unquestionably minuscule. Before 1968, each year there were about 200 black law graduates in the nation.

From 1960 through 1968, the Law School graduated 2687 law students, of whom four were black and none were Latino or Native American.

B. The LSAT

In the early 1960s, the University of Michigan Law School admitted students based on a rigid index that combined undergraduate grades with an LSAT score. At that time, the School was not nearly as selective as it would become. But as more students went to college—and as affirmative action began to open the doors to minorities and to women of all races—the number of applicants to all law schools expanded dramatically. The schools became more selective and the LSAT became far more important.

The plaintiff and the United States call the LSAT "objective"—but they offer no proof to support the claim that it is an "objective" measure of anything important or that it is "race-neutral" in any way. In fact, all the evidence at trial showed the reverse.

The uncontested evidence presented at trial by the student defendants also demonstrated that test scores had little predictive value. In an uncontested study, Professor Richard Lempert, a member of the committee that drafted the 1992 policy, testifying for the students at trial, established that an applicant's LSAT score did not correlate with later success as a lawyer, measured by income, stated satisfaction, or political and community leadership.

C. Undergraduate Grades

The other major "objective" criterion in the traditional Law School admissions system is the undergraduate grade point average (UGPA). While the racial gap on that average is much smaller than the LSAT gap, the gap is still significant when admissions are very competitive, as they have been at the Law School for many years.

The racial segregation in K–12 education causes part of the racial gap in UGPAs; but the conditions on the nation's campuses also contribute to the gap. Black, Latino, and Native American students feel and are isolated; and the cumulative effect of a daily run of slights and profiling takes its toll on black and other minority students. As the district court conceded, while the effect cannot be quantified for each student, racial prejudice depresses the undergraduate grades and overall academic performance of minority students who apply to Law Schools.

The grids prepared by the plaintiff's chief witness, Dr. Kinley Larntz, reflect the gap in test scores and grades and stand as a measure of the cumulative effect of discriminatory tests, segregated education, social inequality, and the depressing effect of racial prejudice on the undergraduate grades and overall academic performance of minority students.

III. THE LAW SCHOOL AFFIRMATIVE ACTION PROGRAM

Under pressure from students on the campus and the civil rights movement, the law faculty began an intense series of debates that stretched from the 1960s through the current date about how to deal with the realities outlined above.

In the course of those debates, faculty members repeatedly recognized that numerical credentials discriminated against black and other minority applicants, "caus[ing] [their] actual potential...to be underestimated, especially when gauged by standard testing procedures...thought to be 'culturally biased.'"

In 1973, the [University of Michigan] Law School graduated 41 black students and its first Latino student. In 1975, it graduated its first two Asian-Americans, followed by its first Native American in 1976. The increasing number of black and other minority students cleared the way for the admission of increasing numbers of women of all races.

After this Court handed down its decision in *Bakke* in June 1978, the faculty formulated a policy to comply with the decision.

In 1992, the faculty adopted the plan that is now in effect. The plan calls for consideration of each applicant as an individual; attempts to seek many forms of diversity; and states the School's commitment to enrolling a "critical mass" of black, Latino, and Native American students, who would not be admitted to the Law School in significant numbers without that commitment.

IV. WHAT ENDING AFFIRMATIVE ACTION WOULD MEAN

In ruling for the plaintiff, the district court conceded that the elimination of affirmative action at the Law School would result in an immediate reduction in underrepresented minority enrollment of over 73 percent. But this would only be the start. The end of affirmative action at selective colleges would dramatically reduce the pool of minority applicants to the Law School, driving the number of minority law students down still further. Within a few years at most, the Law School would again be nearly as segregated as it was in the 1960s.

In 1997, the ban on affirmative action announced by the University of California (UC) Board of Regents went into effect. The following year, only one black student enrolled at Boalt Hall. Minority enrollment at the UCLA School of Law dropped dramatically.

The few black and other minority students who remain at California's most selective campuses have faced increased racism caused by the elimination of affirmative action.

Dr. Eugene Garcia, the Dean of the Graduate School of Education at Berkeley, testified that black, Latino, and Native American students have been forced from the flagship campuses of the UC system onto its two least selective campuses. As the state's population continues to grow, the "cascade" will continue until the vast majority of black, Latino, and Native American students are forced out of the UC system altogether.

The UC faculty and administrations opposed the ban and sought to undo its effects. At Berkeley, the school downplayed the importance of grades and test scores; at UCLA, the school attempted to substitute the consideration of socio-economic status for the consideration of race. Because neither approach could serve as a substitute for affirmative action, both schools found it impossible to enroll a class including more than token numbers of black and other minority students.

SUMMARY OF THE ARGUMENT

In this case, the plaintiff is asking the Court to reinterpret the American Constitution to the dramatic detriment of black, Latino, and other minority people and women of all races. If the Court does what [the] plaintiff asks, it will resegregate, divide, and polarize our country. The authority of the Court would be compromised.

Segregation and inequality are increasing in education. Irrespective of the legal forms used to enforce, to maintain, or passively to justify the separate and unequal condition of education at virtually every level, the fact stands as a profound insult and provocation to the minority youth of America and to the best of the nation's legal and political traditions. Minority children are, in their increasing majority, relegated to second-class, segregated schools—today's version of the back of the bus. The very small handful of black, Mexican American, and Native American students who have made it to the front of America's education bus—institutions like the University of Michigan Law School—are now being told by the plaintiff to get out of their seat and move to the back of the bus.

The demographic fabric of America is changing. By the middle of this century, no racial grouping will be in the majority. America will be a more diverse society; it must not become a more segregated society. We must strive to make equality more, not less, of a reality, or we will surely face renewed social convulsions.

The movement to defend affirmative action and integration has awakened and stirred into action every sector of this society. What unites these many peoples in defense of affirmative action is the conviction that the Constitution's pledge of equality should have meaning and currency in our collective American future. Our progress as a nation depends on the realization of this prospect.

Affirmative Action Admissions: Unfair Advantage

21 LAW PROFESSORS

INTEREST OF *AMICI CURIAE*

Amici curiae are law professors with a professional interest in promoting learning environments free from the taint of racial discrimination. *Amici* are committed to the principles of equality under law embodied in the Constitution, and oppose invidious racial discrimination of any kind. In particular, *amici* oppose as unconstitutional the race-based admissions policies employed by the University of Michigan School of Law and many other institutions of higher learning. A list of the *amici* and their institutional affiliations is provided as an appendix to this brief. The institutional affiliations are for identification purposes only. The views expressed in this brief are those of the individual *amici* and do not necessarily reflect the views of the institutions at which they teach.

SUMMARY OF ARGUMENT

This Court should hold that "diversity" is not a compelling state interest sufficient to justify race-based discrimination. First, "diversity" is employed by universities as a shorthand term for discrimination on the basis of race, is indistinguishable from the use of quotas, and is not a remedial interest. Second, racial "diversity" in the classroom does not constitute academic diversity; to the contrary, it is based on racial stereotyping and fosters stigmatization and hostility. Furthermore, even stereotypically assuming it resulted in a greater diversity of views and information, such a result is not a compelling interest that would outweigh constitutional rights in this or other contexts. Finally, "diversity" is a race-balancing inter-

est that would, by its own terms, require race discrimination for eternity.

ARGUMENT

The Court has held repeatedly that racial classifications are "*presumptively invalid* and can be upheld only upon an extraordinary justification." (*Shaw* v. *Reno*, 1993) Race-based classifications can survive strict scrutiny only if they are narrowly tailored to serve a compelling state interest.

The University of Michigan School of Law ("Michigan") employs race-based classifications in its admissions policies, and race often is the deciding factor between the admission of one applicant and the rejection of another with equal or better qualifications. The questions for this Court, therefore, are whether Michigan's asserted interest is constitutionally "compelling" and whether its admissions program is narrowly tailored to serve that interest.

Amici [we]respectfully submit that this Court should state in words so clear that they cannot be misunderstood by university administrators that the use of racial preferences, classifications, or "pluses" for the purpose of achieving a racially diverse student body is prohibited by the Fourteenth Amendment. The failure of the Court to address the "diversity" question head-on could have devastating consequences for the rights of individuals of all races who participate in the admissions process. Since *Bakke* [*University of California v. Bakke*, 1978], the "diversity" principle in practice has been used to create a loophole through which universities continue to discriminate broadly and openly on the basis of race.

I. MICHIGAN'S DIRECT PURSUIT OF RACIAL DIVERSITY NECESSARILY ENTAILS RACIAL CLASSIFICATIONS

The pursuit of "diversity" in general is a broad and potentially varied exercise that can turn on any number of characteristics or traits. Universities can seek geographic diversity, intellectual diversity, athletic and artistic diversity, and even socio-economic diversity. Those qualities are directly relevant to the educational mission and are not themselves constitutionally suspect. But the direct pursuit of *racial* diversity as an end unto itself, and as a supposed means of creating other types of diversity, is quite different. That pursuit involves taking a single characteristic—race—that the Constitution and this Court have declared unrelated to legitimate bases for distinguishing among individuals, and relying upon it not withstanding such admonitions.

A. Pursuit of "Diversity" Is a Euphemism for Race-Based Decisionmaking

Making disingenuous use of Justice Powell's lone dictum regarding "diversity," [in the *Bakke* decision], universities such as Michigan have adopted the seemingly benign language of pursuing diversity in general as a misleading euphemism for decision-making processes and goals based overtly on race. It is the view and experience of *amici* here that whatever nods of the head universities make toward more general notions of diversity, their affirmative action programs, such as the one in this case, remain targeted at a narrow vision of *racial* diversity *regardless* of the consequences of such programs for other types of diversity.

Numerous experienced law professors, including even those who support racial preferences in admissions, have recognized and acknowledged that the language of educational diversity in the admissions context is generally used as a cover for direct racial decision-making. Such professors speak not merely as academics who have studied the issue, but as first-hand observers within law school communities and administrations, and often as direct participants of the very admissions processes they describe. Professor Alan Dershowitz of Harvard has been forthright about the deceptive use of the "diversity" label in connection with race-driven admissions programs:

> The *raison d'être* for race-specific affirmative action programs has simply never been diversity for the sake of education. The checkered history of "diversity" demonstrates that it was designed largely as a cover to achieve other legally, morally, and politically controversial goals. In recent years, it has been invoked—especially by professional schools—as a clever post facto justification for increasing the number of minority group students in the student body.

Professor Samuel Issacharoff, of Columbia and formerly of Texas, makes a similar point. One of the attorneys who defended the University of Texas School of Law's racedriven admissions policy, has nonetheless has acknowledged that "diversity" is the current jargon for racial discrimination: "[O]ne of the clear legacies of *Bakke* has been to enshrine the term 'diversity' within the legal lexicon to cover everything from curricular enrichments to thinly-veiled set-asides."

Other experienced law professors with diverse views of the affirmative action issue in general have recognized the same truth. Professor Jed Rubenfeld of Yale, who defends "affirmative action" on non-diversity grounds not advanced by Michigan in this case, notes the disingenuousness of the claim that race-driven admissions advance true "diversity" measured by any criteria *other than* race. "[T]he pro-affirmative action crowd needs to own up to the weaknesses of 'diversity' as a defense of most affirmative action plans. Everyone knows that in most cases a true diversity of perspectives and backgrounds is not really being pursued.

In the end, even the proponents of affirmative action, if they are being candid, recognize that the "diversity" pursued by programs such as Michigan's is directly race-based in both its means and its ends, favoring or disfavoring particular races for their own sake without concern for diversity of qualities other than race. While such programs may pay lip-service to intellectual or experiential qualities other than race, they invariably collapse back to using race for its own sake, or as a proxy for other, pertinent, qualities without regard to whether such racial stereotyping is true or permissible.

B. DIRECT PURSUIT OF RACIAL DIVERSITY IS FUNCTIONALLY INDISTINGUISHABLE FROM RACIAL QUOTAS

"Diversity"-based admissions policies such as the one at Michigan necessarily begin and end with some perceived level of optimal diversity among the characteristics— in this case race—that they use to classify candidates. In order to achieve its claimed interest in diversity, Michigan must have at least some sense of what constitutes the proper representation of each race before it can decide that certain racial groups are "under-represented" and the student body thereby insufficiently diverse. Professor Issacharoff candidly acknowledges the point:

The problem with diversity as a justification for a challenged affirmative action program is that it is an almost incoherent concept to opera-

tionalize, unless diversity means a pre-determined number of admittees from a desired group. * * * [S]elective institutions must approach the applicant pool with predetermined notions of what an appropriately balanced incoming class should look like.

The only way to ensure adequate "representation" among the races at the end of the admissions process is to begin with an institutional definition of "diversity" that necessarily produces the desired proportions of racial representation in a class of admitted students. Michigan's "diversity" policy is symbolic of the numbers game that has become synonymous with admissions policies that employ racial preferences. For example, members of Michigan's admissions staff receive "daily reports," which track applicants by race. Dennis Shields, the former director of admissions at Michigan, has acknowledged that "as an admissions season progressed, he would consult the daily reports more and more frequently in order to keep track of the racial and ethnic composition of the class." Mr. Shields said that he did this to ensure that a "critical mass" of minority students were enrolled. "Diversity in education" through race-driven admissions is meaningless without quotas or something constituting the functional equivalent of a quota system.

The district court determined after careful consideration of all of the facts that the "critical mass" concept is functionally equivalent to a quota system. The district court explained:

[O]ver the years, [critical mass] has meant in practice that the law school attempts to enroll an entering class 10% to 17% of which consists of underrepresented minority students. The 10% figure, as a target, has historical roots going back to the late 1960s. Beginning in the 1970s, the law school documents begin referring to 10–12% as the desired percentage. Professor Lempert testified that critical mass lies in the range of 11–17%. Indeed this percentage range appeared in a draft of the 1992 admissions policy, and it was omitted from the final version despite Professor Regan's suggestion that it remain for the sake of "candor."

"Diversity" policies must be described as what they are—means of implementing racial quotas. That such quotas might be informal or hidden under a cloak of rhetoric does not change that essential fact.

C. "Diversity" Is Not a Remedial Interest

Thus far, the only constitutionally compelling interest recognized by this Court as satisfying strict scrutiny for racial classifications is the remediation of the effects of past race discrimination.

Michigan's "diversity" policy is not, and does not purport to be, remedial. The question for this Court then is whether "diversity" should be added as a "compelling," not merely valid or permissible, state interest that can be used to justify direct and intentional racial discrimination.

Because the Court has "strictly" limited the use of racial classifications to the remedial context, respondents must demonstrate that there is something so special, so *compelling*, about marginal differences in the educational experiences of post-secondary students that universities, alone among our government-sponsored institutions, should be allowed to practice what the Constitution prohibit[s]—naked race discrimination. Although the question properly posed seems to answer itself, an examination of the realities of "diversity" in the classroom also leads to the conclusion that this so-called justification for discrimination does not pass constitutional muster.

II. RACIAL "DIVERSITY" IS NOT A COMPELLING INTEREST

Because the pursuit of racial diversity for its own sake is an affront to the Fourteenth Amendment, the defenders of "diversity" ultimately resort to some version of the argument that bringing together persons of different "backgrounds"—as defined by their skin color or national origin—will "enhance" the educational experience of students by creating academic or viewpoint diversity. But Michigan's admissions policy, and other "diversity" policies like it, cannot be defended on the ground that racial diversity promotes academic diversity. The defense of "diversity" programs on the ground that they expose people of different races to one another, thereby facilitating learning, respect and appreciation among the races, does not relate to a true "interest in intellectual diversity—diversity of 'experiences, outlooks and ideas' that would otherwise be left out—but specifically in racial and ethnic diversity as such."

A. Interests in "Diversity" That Assume Stereotyping Cannot Have Compelling Weight

The "diversity" rationale suggests that it is permissible to use race as a proxy for experiences, outlooks or ideas, and that the use of race as a proxy will ensure that different viewpoints are brought to the classroom. But however desirable a diversity of *ideas* may be, there is no basis for categorizing it as "compelling," rather than merely acceptable or substantial for purposes of analyses *other than* strict scrutiny. The abhorrent essential predicate to the interest—governmental stereotyping of different races as to their views—also assures that the interest in racial diversity for its secondary viewpoint effects cannot count as compelling.

Common sense and classroom experiences demonstrate that "viewpoint diversity" and "academic diversity" in the classroom are not affected by the racial composition of a student body. Dean and long-time professor at Michigan, Professor Terrance Sandalow, wrote in the *Michigan Law Review*:

> "My own experience and that of colleagues with whom I have discussed the question, experience that concededly is limited to the classroom setting, is that racial diversity is not responsible for generating ideas unfamiliar to some members of the class. Students do, of course, quite frequently express and develop ideas that others in the class have not previously encountered, but even though the subjects I teach deal extensively with racial issues, I cannot recall an instance in which, for example, ideas were expressed by a black student that have not also been expressed by white students. Black students do, at times, call attention to the racial implications of issues that are not facially concerned with race, but white and Asian-American students are in my experience no less likely to do so."

Racial diversity is not required to foster a full discussion of issues and viewpoints in the classroom. If a white applicant and a black applicant each have the same view on an issue, and their respective race is ignored as it must be under the Constitution, there is no true "intellectual" or "academic" reason for admitting one of the students over the other.

Any "diversity" policy that is premised on the notion that people of different races bring particular viewpoints to the classroom solely because of their race should be struck down. If schools truly think that viewpoint diversity enhances education, they can pursue it directly rather than using race as a proxy.

Apparently realizing the difficulty of defending its admissions policy on the ground that race defines viewpoint, Michigan attempts an alternative claim that racial diversity in the classroom is required to *dismantle* stereotypes.

[The University of] Michigan argues in essence that, because it assumes individuals generally believe that members of a "minority" race all share the same viewpoint on all issues, the educational experiences of members of the benighted majority will be "enhanced" by interaction with a "critical mass" of minority students. This argument merely shifts the stereotyped assumptions over to the majority racial group, but is no less offensive therefore.

Moreover, Michigan hardly needs racial preferences to teach the obvious—that not all members of any given minority think alike. If, miraculously, something more were needed to make this point to students, surely a sufficiently diverse *reading list* would suffice. Michigan's self-contradictory treatment of individuals as members of groups, purportedly in order to demonstrate that individuals are *not* members of groups, is closer to being incredible than it is to being compelling.

B. Discrimination Resulting from Racial Stereotyping Results in Stigmatization and Hostility

Even if one were to hypothesize that a compelled increase in racial diversity would increase educationally valuable viewpoint diversity to some degree, it would also generate educationally detrimental stigma and hostility based on precisely the same type of stereotyping regarding race employed by the University. Indeed, policies that seek diversity through race are [according to one scholar] a "statement by government that certain persons identified by race are in fact being placed in positions they may be presumed not likely to hold but for their race."

"Diversity" admissions programs, such as Michigan's, foster rather than minimize the focus on race. The policy treats preferred minorities as a group, rather than as individuals. Although Michigan purports to consider other types of diversity—such as unusual employment experiences and extracurricular activities—race is the most identifiable diversity factor that separates one applicant from another.

Amici's collective experiences support the conclusion that both students who are admitted, and those who are not admitted, recognize that race indisputably plays an important role in admissions. Applicants from races that do not benefit from Michigan's preferences, who have high LSAT scores and GPAs, but who nonetheless are denied admission, will likely conclude that race determined their fate in the admissions process. Similarly, members of all races who gain admission may believe that their minority classmates would not be their classmates but for their race. Because of the lowered expectations that accompany racial preferences in admissions, members of minority groups are and will be stigmatized—sometimes self-stigmatized—as inferior.

The racial hostility and stigmatization that is bred in universities as a result of racial preferences is felt both in our classrooms and throughout all of society. If not stopped now, the hostility and scarring that can result from racial preferences based on "diversity" could take generations to heal. At a minimum, however, such consequences cut against any claimed benefits and render Michigan's asserted interest in the educational benefits of racial diversity necessarily less than compelling.

C. Government-Defined Viewpoint Diversity Is Not a Compelling Interest

Regardless whether racial classifications generate viewpoint diversity and accepting that viewpoint diversity is, in general, a valuable thing in an educational environment, that does not even remotely satisfy the requirement that it must be a "compelling"

interest sufficient to justify otherwise unconstitutional conduct. The difficulty in too-easy a transition from merely desirable to constitutionally compelling seems apparent: We would not authorize state universities to violate students' right to free speech or free exercise of religion on the ground that doing so would, in the view of academics, create a better educational environment or a greater "diversity" of views.

But if it is a compelling interest to discriminate on the basis of race in order to promote an educational atmosphere with a supposedly more diverse set of student views, then it is unavoidably a compelling interest for all other constitutional purposes. The notion that the government might impose a myriad of speech restrictions and compulsions in the name of "diversity" demonstrates the absurd premise that marginal differences in educational diversity rise to the level of "compelling" state interests.

D. The "Diversity" Rationale Is Limitless

"Diversity" also fails as a "compelling interest" because it has no logical stopping point. The Court has repeatedly rejected alleged "compelling interests" that extend indefinitely into the future.

By definition, a "diversity" interest supports indefinite discrimination on the basis of race in university admissions because there will always be a need to engage in race-based decisionmaking to ensure a "properly diverse" student body. "Diversity"—with its concomitant quotas and careful monitoring of racial admissions—indeed would *require* unending use of race in admissions.

For this reason, and for all of the other reasons set forth above, "diversity" does not constitute an extraordinary justification sufficient to overcome the presumptive invalidity of government-sponsored race discrimination.

THE CONTINUING DEBATE:
Affirmative Action Admissions

What Is New

In 2003, the Supreme Court upheld the University of Michigan's position in *Grutter v. Bollinger* and rejected it in *Gratz v. Bollinger*. By a 5 to 4 vote in *Grutter*, the court permitted the law school's use of race as one factor in determining admissions on the grounds that a "compelling state interest" existed in promoting diversity at all levels of society. But by 6 to 3 in *Gratz*, the justices rejected the undergraduate admission process that gave automatic points to minorities on the admissions scale. These decisions reconfirmed *Bakke*, but thereby also left some of that decision's uncertainties in place about how to judge an affirmative action program without resorting to numbers when establishing goals or monitoring progress.

Perhaps reflecting the fine line the court walked in the two decisions, public opinion about affirmative actions varies with the way the question is asked. For example, consider the wording and results of three polls taken in 2003. The first asked Americans if they "generally favor or oppose affirmative action programs for racial minorities? A plurality (49%) replied, "favor," 43% said "oppose," and 8% were unsure. The second poll introduced a reason for affirmative action, asking, "In order to overcome past discrimination, do you favor or oppose affirmative action programs...[for minorities]?" With that prompt, support for affirmative action was much higher (63% in favor, 29% opposed, 8% unsure). By contrast, support declined to 38% (with 51% opposed, and 10% unsure) in a poll whose question included the word "preferences" ("Do you favor or oppose affirmative action programs that give preferences to...minorities?").

Where to Find More

For an extensive legal and policy review of affirmative action, turn to Samuel Leiter and William M. Leiter, *Affirmative Action in Antidiscrimination Law and Policy: An Overview and Synthesis* (State University of New York Press, 2002). You can read the decisions and the dissents for both *Grutter v. Bollinger* and *Gratz v. Bollinger* by going to the Supreme Court Collection Web page of Cornell University's Legal Information Institute at http://supct.law.cornell.edu/supct/ and entering the case names in the search function. The Web site of the Coalition to Defend Affirmative Action and Integration & Fight for Equality By Any Means Necessary (BAMN), one of the student groups who filed an amicus curiae brief in *Grutter*, is at http://www.bamn.com/. An organization with an opposing point of view is Americans Against Discrimination and Preferences, located on the Web at http://www.aadap.org/Default.shtml.

What More to Do

Write an admission policy for your university that addresses the demographic component. Then find out what your school's written policy is (if any) and interview admissions officials to find out how they implement affirmative action. How does the school's policy compare with your views?

THE BUSH DOCTRINE:
Wisdom *or* Folly?

WISDOM

Advocate: Thomas Donnelly, Resident Fellow, American Enterprise Institute

Source: "The Underpinnings of the Bush Doctrine," *National Security Outlook,* AEI Online, February 1, 2003

FOLLY

Advocate: Todd Gitlin, Professor of Journalism and Sociology, Columbia University.

Source: "America's Age of Empire," *Mother Jones,* January/February 2003

A country so powerful that it alone can dominate its world is a rare actor in world history. In ancient times the Egypt of the pharos, Alexander the Great's Macedonia, and Rome under the caesars were such hegemonic (dominant) powers. More recently the Holy Roman Empire under the Hapsburg dynasty and, later, the British and their empire stood astride much of the world. Now the United States is arguably the latest to be (some would say, aspire to be) the unchallenged hegemonic power. It is not surprising that a conservative analyst like Charles Krauthammer depicted the United States as "the center of world power." But this view is also held by such liberals as scholar Joseph Nye, who observes, "Not since Rome has one nation loomed so large above the others."

Power is a tool, not a policy, and the question for Americans is what to do with their might. President Bush provided his answer in September 2002 when he issued "The National Security Strategy of the United States of America." Dubbed the Bush Doctrine, the report heralded the U.S. "position of unparalleled military strength and great economic and political influence."

The president proposed using U.S. power in several ways. Cautioning, "This position [of power] comes with unparalleled responsibilities, obligations, and opportunities," he went on to argue, "The great strength of this nation must be used to promote a balance of power that favors freedom." What he meant by freedom was clarified in his argument that U.S. strength should be used to advance human rights, democracy, and free economic interchange around the world. As for U.S. military power, Bush not only projected using it to "defend the peace by fighting terrorists and tyrants," he also advocated employing preemptive force to that end. "Given the goals of rogue states and terrorists, the United States can no longer solely rely on a reactive posture," Bush argued. Instead, he pledged, "To forestall or prevent hostile acts by our adversaries, the United States will, if necessary, act preemptively."

The Bush Doctrine was in part a reaction to the 9-11 terrorist attacks and to the increasing number of countries capable of building weapons of mass destruction (biological, chemical, nuclear, and radiological weapons) and delivering them against distant targets by giving WMDs to terrorists or by using missiles. Additionally, the Bush Doctrine's genesis can be traced to the influence of the significant number of neoconservatives (neocons), including Vice President Richard Cheney and Secretary of Defense Donald Rumsfeld, in the administration. These individuals have all been associated with the Project for the New American Century, a think-tank that had long advocated removing Saddam Hussein from power and that, from a wider perspective, believes "American leadership is good both for America and for the world." It is important to see that neocons do not argue that U.S. power should be used only for self-interest. Rather, they believe that U.S. power should establish a Pax Americana, a modern version of the stability that existed two millennia ago under the Pax Romana. As Gary Schmitt, the executive director of PNAC wrote in 2003, "The unavoidable reality is that the exercise of American power is key to maintaining what peace and order there is in the world today." Neocons also argue that U.S. power should be used to enhance the human condition by promoting American ideals in such ways as building a democratic Iraq. As Schmitt put it, "That's a dream only American power can inspire."

The neocon view, which President Bush has clearly adopted in many ways, also argues that the United States must be ready to act unilaterally when necessary. In the Bush Doctrine, the president expressed his intent to cooperate with other "main centers of global power," but he has had perhaps the most unilateralist approach of any president since World War II. For example, despite the objections of many U.S. allies, he rejected U.S. adherence to the Kyoto Protocol to reduce "greenhouse gases," he abrogated the Anti-ballistic Missile Treaty with Russia, and he declined to present the treaty establishing the International Criminal Court to the Senate for ratification. It should be noted that advocate Thomas Donnelly is associated with PNAC, as well as with the American Enterprise Institute under whose auspices he wrote the article. Criticism of the Bush Doctrine came from both liberals and traditional conservatives. Advocate Todd Gitlin provides a liberal critique. An example of the conservative view is listed in Where to Find More on page 266.

POINTS TO PONDER

➤ On what basis does Thomas Donnelly support of the Bush Doctrine?
➤ What are the pitfalls of the Doctrine according to Todd Gitlin?
➤ What are the various aspects of the Bush Doctrine?

The Bush Doctrine:
Wisdom

THOMAS DONNELLY

The Bush Doctrine, which is likely to shape U.S. policy for decades to come, reflects the realities of American power as well as the aspirations of American political principles.

Does the Bush Doctrine represent a new course for American policy or simply an elaborate justification for the administration's actions? Why attack Iraq but not North Korea? What is the real role of preemption? What is wrong with the tried-and-true concepts of deterrence? If nothing else, the Bush Doctrine, articulated by the president over the past eighteen months in a series of speeches and encapsulated in the new National Security Strategy paper released in September [2002], represents a reversal of course from Clinton-era policies in regard to the uses of U.S. power and, especially, military force. So perhaps it is no surprise that many Americans—and others in the rest of the world as well—are struggling to keep up with the changes. Indeed, it often appears that many in the administration cannot keep up with the president. But in fact the Bush Doctrine represents a return to the first principles of American security strategy. The Bush Doctrine also represents the realities of international politics in the post-cold-war, sole-superpower world. Further, the combination of these two factors—America's universal political principles and unprecedented global power and influence—make the Bush Doctrine a whole greater than the sum of its parts; it is likely to remain the basis for U.S. security strategy for decades to come.

This does not mean that American leaders will be freed from the need to make un-pleasant choices; North Korea's recent actions remind us of ways in which the possession by others of nuclear weapons and ballistic missiles places limits on policy options. But the expansion of "the American perimeter"— those parts of the world where a liberal, democratic order is accepted as the norm—is likely to continue, even accelerate; having, at last, determined to reform the politics of the greater Middle East, we will find it difficult and dangerous to stop with half measures. The Bush Doctrine continues a tradition that can be traced to the Monroe and Truman doctrines. It is an attempt, in a new century and under new strategic circumstances, to "foster a world environment where the American system can survive and flourish," as Paul Nitze [Director, Policy Planning Staff, U.S. State Department] put it in 1950, in the famous "NSC 68" memorandum [National Security Council 68, "United States Objective and Programs for National Security, a document often said to have been the foundation of U.S. cold war policy].

A comprehensive history of U.S. national security strategy is well beyond the scope of this article, but let it be stipulated that Americans always have taken an expansive view of their security interests and been more than willing to exercise military power where the correlation of forces is favorable. Blessed now with a global balance heavily weighted in favor of the United States, the Bush administration has declared itself ready to remove the rogue regimes and terrorists it regards as uniquely dangerous. For Americans, normal power calculations of "threats" and "opportunities" have been colored by an abiding faith in a set of political principles believed to have universal application. Americans have come to regard the exercise of their power as not simply a force for national greatness but for human liberty.

THE LOGIC OF AMERICAN PRIMACY

Today, at least four realities argue convincingly for the continued and vigorous exercise of American national power, to include "preemptive" military actions. First of all, the fact of unprecedented American power is hardly in dispute. Those who oppose it find themselves frustrated by the seeming invincibility of American "imperialism." The French, for example, both lament and wonder at American *hyperpuissance.* Even [Yale historian] Paul Kennedy, who famously foresaw American "imperial overstretch," now marvels at the scope of U.S. power. In a recent essay, he confessed to having made some "recalculations" of American power "as measured by the standard social science criteria," and came away with "the overwhelming impression of how far this single nation stood above all possible contenders as the global hegemon." With less than 5 percent of world population, the United States generates about 30 percent of total world economic product, "a percentage that has actually increased in recent years." Indeed, Kennedy wrote, "even more remarkable is the size of the American military preeminence." The campaign in Afghanistan only impressed him further:

> Nothing has ever existed like this disparity of power; nothing....The Pax Britannica was run on the cheap, Britain's army was much smaller than European armies, and even the Royal Navy was equal only to the next two navies—right now all the other navies in the world combined could not dent American maritime supremacy. Charlemagne's empire was merely

western-European in its reach. The Roman Empire stretched farther afield, but there was another great empire in Persia and a larger one in China. There is, therefore, no comparison.

In other words, the fundamental premise of the Bush Doctrine is true: The United States possesses the means—economic, military, diplomatic—to realize its expansive geopolitical purposes. Further, and especially in light of the domestic political reaction to the attacks of September 11, the victory in Afghanistan and the remarkable skill demonstrated by President Bush in focusing national attention, it is equally true that Americans possess the requisite political willpower to pursue an expansive strategy.

Second, the description of the threats to U.S. interests advanced in the National Security Strategy is also an accurate one. America faces no immediate great-power threat, no superpower doppelgänger [a ghostly counterpart of a living person] to replace the Soviet Union. The Russian empire has contracted to a 400-year "low," and Moscow has proven militarily incapable of subduing a single insurrectionist province. More importantly, Russia seems to have lost the appetite for empire, as it has become increasingly democratic and geopolitically inclined toward the West and the United States. The immediate post-cold-war fears of Russian revanche have not been realized.

The two other candidates as great-power balancers to American primacy, the People's Republic of China and the European Union, likewise are not immediately up to the challenge. A few observers believe that, as Europe becomes more politically integrated, it will take issue with American geopolitical leadership. "It is now Europe's turn to ascend and break away from an America that refuses to surrender its privileges of primacy," writes Charles Kupchan, a former Clinton administration official now at Georgetown University. "Europe will inevitably rise up as America's principal competitor." Some regard the defiance of France and Germany over Iraq as an occasion of "soft balancing"—the use of so-called "soft power" to offset American military might, diplomatic determination, and ideological motivation. Yet it does not seem as if the Europeans will be successful in thwarting the Bush administration's march to war. It is far more likely that Europe will remain essentially content with its status as a junior partner in the current Pax Americana, demanding a certain amount of deference—and, after Iraq, perhaps very little deference—but still fundamentally unwilling to forge or employ the tools of "hard power" needed to create a genuinely multipolar international order.

China's economic growth over the past decade has fueled a program of military modernization that poses some particularly severe problems for the United States, such as across the Taiwan Straits. Further, these localized challenges may cause larger problems for a brittle American-led regional order based upon bilateral security partnerships between the United States and its East Asian allies. But Beijing does not yet have the ability to mount a broader regional—let alone global—challenge or lead an anti-American coalition. Moreover, the weakening of communist ideology in China and the advance of capitalism pose an internal problem of legitimacy for a regime in the throes of a generational leadership change. In addition, there may be international consequences for promoting an intense and aggressive Han nationalism as a partial remedy for these domestic problems. Beijing cannot style itself, as the United States reasonably can, as a benign hegemon.

Beyond potential great-power rivals there is good reason for continued concern over "rogue" states such as Iraq, North Korea, and Iran. These are modest powers with outsized ambitions that clearly see weapons of mass destruction as not simply a means to intimidate their immediate neighbors. They understand that, under a global security order headed by the United States, the first hurdle to becoming a regional hegemon is getting America out of the way. Nor are these regimes driven simply by external ambitions. Indeed, these regimes' internal position rests, in some measure, in having created hegemonic national ambitions—and their long-term survival in part rests upon seeming to satisfy them. Whatever the personal desires for glory among Saddam Hussein, Kim Jong Il, or the Iranian mullahs, they can also be driven by domestic political pressures to adopt a more aggressive posture.

Where the immediate opportunity for aggrandizement is limited by American power, these states are increasingly attracted to weapons proliferation and flirtations with international terrorist organizations. What under normal circumstances the United States might simply ignore—and often has ignored, even in the recent past—looms as a greater problem for America, its allies, and the international system. While coalitions of convenience among rogue states and terrorists may have been limited in the past and may carry inherent dangers for leaders of the rogue states themselves, the difficulty of resisting the Pax Americana is likely to mean that cooperation will increase in the future. Indeed, as the Bush Doctrine is further realized in Afghanistan and Iraq, cooperation could become desperation.

Similar concerns add urgency to the "war on terrorism," which is, in truth, not a global war on all terrorist organizations—so far, the FARC [Revolutionary Armed Forces of Colombia, a guerilla group] in Colombia and the Irish Republican Army seemed to have escaped much attention from the Bush administration—but principally upon "Islamism," that violent political movement antipathetic to modernity and to the West, and especially to their expression through American power. The motivating core of this movement appears to be more "Arab" than "pan-Islamic," and often stems from the Saudi-funded spread of Wahhabism [a puritanical Muslim movement]. It is like communism in that it is, in some measure, an ideologically motivated international political movement, though it relies upon the means of military weakness—terrorism—where the Soviet Union deployed great tank armies and nuclear arsenals.

Any comprehensive U.S. "threat assessment" would conclude that the normal constraints of international politics—counterbalancing powers—no longer immediately inhibit the exercise of American might. At the same time, proliferation of weapons of mass destruction promises to upset the "normal" rules of power among nation-states, devaluing the conventional military strength (and other kinds of power, as well) amassed by the United States. This undercuts the general peace won by the victory in the cold war and would complicate any future great-power competition or challenge to the American-led international order. Small "rogue" states and violent, but nevertheless weak, international movements like Islamic radicalism are coming to have a disproportionate "weight" in global security calculations. Moreover Islamism represents a kind of ideological threat to the Western political principles that made the end of the cold war against the Soviet Union also seem like the end of history.

A third reality that argues for assertive U.S. power is that the opportunities to extend a "balance of power that favors freedom"—or, more precisely, a preponderance of American power that favors freedom—

outlined in the Bush Doctrine are genuine. The collapse of the Soviet Union is clearly making for a Europe "whole and free." Democratic practices are taking firmer root in cultures previously thought to be inhospitable, particularly in Asia, where Lee Kwan Yew's [the dominant political leader in Singapore] assertion of an authoritarian streak in "Confucian culture" looks increasingly suspect; Taiwan has spawned an almost raucous multiparty system and seen a peaceful transfer of power within it. In such a context, the Bush Doctrine's promise to liberalize the Islamic world—especially as it remains itself politically fractured—cannot be lightly dismissed, even if it may take many years to fulfill.

The opportunities to expand the Pax Americana also rest upon one of the few solid truths of social science: Democracies rarely war on other democracies. One of the reasons it is so hard to imagine the European Union becoming a genuine competitor to the United States is that there are no serious, direct transatlantic geopolitical disputes. Differences in the Middle East, for example, have no immediate relationship to the power balance between Europe and America—nothing today is analogous to the previous colonial competition. Nor is it easy to imagine a similar future struggle with Japan, Korea, India, or any Asian democracy. Those regions of the world that have, often because of the result of defeats in past wars, been brought into the American system do not require continued, heavy military occupation or imperial government. Pax Americana enjoys a "strategic rear" that is remarkably peaceful, prosperous, and free. What were once feuding great powers have more or less permanently, and apparently quite happily, ceded their security interests to American management.

A thorough "opportunities assessment" would conclude that the prospects for an expanded, American-led liberal international order are clouded by a military balance complicated by weapons proliferation. Nuclear weapons, in particular, now pose a deterrent threat to the United States; hopes for a stable and democratized Islamic world, for example, may be short-lived if Iraq or Iran were to acquire such a capability. We see already how the tiny North Korean arsenal—and its proclivities to proliferate—could confound America's position as the guarantor of East Asian security and democracy.

This suggests a fourth and final factor favoring the continued and vigorous exercise of American power: The realities of primacy, rising threats, and emerging opportunities combine to give the United States a "systemic" responsibility, that is, a responsibility for preserving the viability and legitimacy of the liberal international order of nation-states. A failure to remove Saddam Hussein from power in Baghdad—and indeed, a failure to continue the mission and replace the Ba'ath regime with at least a protodemocratic government—would materially change the global correlation of forces, to use Soviet-speak. Because power is measured everywhere in relation to the United States, regional events have greater global significance, beyond even the linkages supposed between cold war "dominoes."

THE LOGIC OF PREEMPTION

Taken together, American principles, interests, and systemic responsibilities argue strongly in favor of an active and expansive stance of strategic primacy and a continued willingness to employ military force. Within that context, and given the ways in which nuclear weapons and other weapons of mass destruction can distort normal calculations of international power relationships, there is a compelling need to hold open the option of—and indeed, to build forces more capable of—preemptive strike

operations. The United States must take a wider view of the traditional doctrine of "imminent danger," considering how such dangers might threaten not only its direct interests, but its allies, the liberal international order, and the opportunities for greater freedom in the world.

Yet practicalities limit the likelihood for an overly preemptive or "preventive" use of American military power. Despite the energetic rhetoric in the National Security Strategy, the immediate test of the Bush Doctrine's emphasis on preemption is not to be found in today's crises in Iraq and North Korea. The United States has been at war with Saddam Hussein for more than a decade; if an invasion comes it will be a response to past provocations as much as a preemption of future threats. And North Korea represents the nightmare that comes when weak states acquire super-power weapons; even a "regime change" strategy for Pyongyang would prefer other instruments to direct preemption, at least at this point.

Yet it takes little imagination to dream up other scenarios that might call for preemptive military action. Consider the choices for an American president if a radical regime overthrew, or simply defeated at the ballot box, the Musharraf government in Pakistan—would fears about Pakistan's nuclear weapons constitute an imminent danger? What about a massing of Chinese forces across the Taiwan Strait, perhaps preceded by an enlarged "missile embargo" of the sort attempted in 1996? These hypotheticals suggest that the heightened emphasis on preemption is not misplaced.

The preservation of today's Pax Americana rests upon both actual military strength and the perception of strength. The variety of victories scored by U.S. forces since the end of the cold war is testament to both the futility of directly challenging the United States and the desire of its enemies to keep poking and prodding to find a weakness in the American global order. Convincing would-be great powers, rogue states, and terrorists to accept the liberal democratic order—and the challenge to autocratic forms of rule that come with it—requires not only an overwhelming response when the peace is broken, but a willingness to step in when the danger is imminent. The message of the Bush Doctrine—"Don't even think about it!"—rests in part on a logic of preemption that underlies the logic of primacy.

The Bush Doctrine:
Folly

Todd Gitlin

On September 20, the Bush administration published a national security manifesto overturning the established order. Not because it commits the United States to global intervention: We've been there before. Not because it targets terrorism and rogue states: Nothing new there either. No, what's new in this document is that it makes a long-building imperial tendency explicit and permanent. The policy paper, titled "The National Security Strategy of the United States of America,"—call it the Bush Doctrine—is a romantic justification for easy recourse to war whenever and wherever an American president chooses.

This document truly deserves the overused term "revolutionary," but its release was eclipsed by the Iraq debate. Recall the moment. Bush, having just backed away from unilateralism long enough to deliver a speech to the United Nations, was now telling Congress to give him the power to go to war with Iraq whenever and however he liked. Congress, with selective reluctance, was skating sideways toward a qualified endorsement. The administration had fended off doubts from the likes of George Bush Sr.'s national security adviser Brent Scowcroft, and retreated from its maximal designs (at least on Tuesdays and Thursdays), giving doubters, and politicians preoccupied with their reelection, reasons to overcome their doubts and sign on.

The Bush White House chose this moment to put down in black and white its grand strategy—to doctrinize, as it were, its impulse to act alone with the instruments of war. Hitching a ride on Al Qaeda's indisputable threat, the doctrine

generalizes. It is limitless in time and space. It not only commits the United States to dominating the world from now into the distant future, but also advocates what it calls the preemptive use of force: "America will act against emerging threats before they are fully formed."

The United States has many times sent armed forces to take over foreign countries for weeks, years, even decades. But the Bush doctrine is the first to elevate such wars of offense to the status of official policy, and to call "preemptive" (referring to imminent peril) what is actually preventive (referring to longer-term, hypothetical, avoidable peril). This semantic shift is crucial. When prevention of a remote possibility is called preemption, anything goes. CIA caution can be overridden, Al Qaeda connections fabricated, dangers exaggerated—and the United States will have a doctrine to substitute for international law.

The Bush manifesto displays bluster, romance, and illogic in equal measure. Premise: America is fundamentally righteous. "In keeping with our heritage and principles, we do not use our strength to press for unilateral advantage." This will be news to much of the world, but never mind. An imperial strategy is justified because there is in the world but "a single sustainable model for national success: freedom, democracy, and free enterprise"—a model that, surprise, the United States embodies. (As for success without freedom or democracy or free enterprise, what about China? As for free enterprise and democracy of a sort without success, what about Argentina?) Conclusion: Whatever America does will be right—pursuing terrorists, pre-emptive war, free trade, whatever. Nuance be damned. For all the boilerplate about national differences, the doctrine's key concern is clear: If all the world speaks American values (though sometimes in funny local accents), why shouldn't everyone dance to our tune?

Look closer, and even the document's core phrases lose their meaning. Just what is "a balance of power that favors freedom"—a term the authors use no fewer than four times? Perhaps the answer is implicit in the doctrine's insistence that no rivals shall be permitted to exercise power the likes of America's: "Our forces will be strong enough to dissuade potential adversaries from pursuing a military buildup in hopes of surpassing, or equaling, the power of the United States." Balance, indeed.

The doctrine goes beyond the preemption theme sounded by President Bush in a West Point speech [in] June [2001]. Read beneath its kitchen-sink rhetoric and you see, in black and white, Bush codifying the unilateral treaty-busting moves of his first months in office—his rejection of the Kyoto climate-change protocol, his cancellation of the ABM [Antiballistic Missile] accord, his obstruction of the bioweapons treaty, and his flat withdrawal from participation in the International Criminal Court, to name only the most dramatic. Those go-it-alone exercises were not casual or tactical retreats from global cooperation. They were applications of a new policy that had not yet been spelled out. The September manifesto does spell it out: The United States rules.

The core of the National Security Strategy is unilateralist, but it pays tribute to consultations with allies and "good relations among the great powers." It is militarist, though it nods in the direction of democracy and development. Make no mistake: There's no big surge in develop-ment aid forthcoming. Nor, from an oil administration, any recognition that global warming inflicts irrevocable damage and that sustainable energy is a security issue—for us as well as the impoverished nations whose well-being the doctrine purports to care about. In Bush Country, there's no downside to free trade, which it calls "a moral principle," no corporations ravaging forests or pushing peasants off their land. The document does, however, pause to put in a good word for lower tax rates.

It would be easy to dismiss Bush's manifesto on the grounds that it is a thumpingly cliché-ridden monstrosity, a heap of Washington pixels expended because Congress in 1986 mandated periodic reports on national security strategy. The document is meant not so much to be read as to be brandished. This is internationalism imperial-style—as in Rome, when Rome ruled. Its scope is breathtaking. There were large parts of the world that Rome couldn't reach, but the Bush doctrine recognizes no limits.

The government of the United States will ask not so much as a by-your-leave. It will know when threats are emerging, partly formed, and it will not have to say how it knows, or be convincing about what it knows. The doctrine affirms all of the comforts and recognizes none of the dangers of empire. It ignores the costs of unbounded deployment and war. It acknowledges no danger that reckless swashbuckling helps recruit terrorists. It forgets that all empires fall—they cost too much, they incite too many enemies, they inspire contrary empires. The new imperialists think they are different. All empires do.

Robert Jervis, a professor of international politics at Columbia University and a leading foreign-affairs realist in the academy, calls the document's rhetoric "in-

credibly ambitious and incredibly activist." As a declaration of American strategy vis-à-vis the world, it is, Jervis believes,
"the boldest public statement since 1947,"
when containment became policy and the
Truman Doctrine committed the United
States to intervene against Communist in-
surgencies around the world. Like the
Bush doctrine, containment was open-
ended; unlike the new doctrine, it was
predicated on a network of alliances and
multinational organizations, of which
NATO was the most formidable.

Bush now trades in alliances for ad hoc
"coalitions." He makes a pass at disguising
unilateralism as "a distinctly American internationalism that reflects the union of our
values and our national interests."
Interestingly, the doctrine retroactively
downgrades the old threat, characterizing
Soviet Communism as "a generally status
quo, risk-averse adversary." (If only Ronald
Reagan had grasped that before he committed the country to the massive deficits
of the 1980s.) Bush and his allies want their
challenge to surpass all previous challenges,
their terrain to extend beyond all previous
terrains. The whole world is their turf.

Now, some things are true even if
George W. Bush says them. It is true and
important that Al Qaeda and its brethren
are uncontainable and undeterrable. American power does sometimes serve a larger
good—as it would in the Middle East, were
Bush wise enough to exert it on behalf of a
two-state Israel/Palestine solution. But Al
Qaeda is not the Bush doctrine's principal
target, nor does it have more than a few
words to spare about the Middle East.
Terrorism is the occasion for what is really a
doctrinal update. The National Security
Strategy proclaims the virtue of a power
extension—call it regime extension—that
its authors have sought for years.

During his campaign for the presidency, George W. Bush never so much as
hinted at the grandiosity of the vision he
has now loosed upon the world. But don't
think that it erupted out of the blue after
the massacres of September 11. The emphasis on preemption is new, but on the
whole, the National Security Strategy is
the most recent version of a go-for-broke
imperial outlook that has emerged over
the last decade. The first version was
drafted in 1992 by then-Secretary of Defense Dick Cheney's then-subordinate
Paul Wolfowitz; the leaked document was
repudiated by then-President Bush. A successor manifesto was drawn up in 2000
over the names of Wolfowitz and others
who soon thereafter landed high positions
in the administration of George Bush II.
Both documents emphasized pumping up
American military power to such a high
pitch that rivals would opt not to compete. Both emphasized far-flung bases and
unilateralism. The new doctrine thus represents the triumph of the Cheney-Rums-
feld-Wolfowitz group who have sought to
establish an American Millennium ever
since the collapse of the Soviet Union.

If Bush had doubts about regime extension before September 11, he surely
does no longer. The moralism of a president with a mission has now fused with
the parochialism of a man whose well of
world knowledge is filled with oil. He will
take the battle to the enemy, even if the
enemy is far-flung, even if allies are frightened and skeptical, even if the political
and economic costs of war are immense.
(Since the economic costs will fall mainly
on America's poor and middle class and
will have the effect of forestalling any progressive spending initiatives at home, they
do not concern him unduly.) Americans
know fear now, so fear is what he will mobilize. Americans want multilateralism, so
he patches together ad hoc coalitions,
even goes to the United Nations—once he
has already decided on war.

The doctrine is so sweeping that it discredits what might have been, from another hand, more modest imperatives. There is surely (as the U.N. Charter insists) a case to be made for national self-defense as a last resort. There are organizations like Al Qaeda whose purposes can properly be called genocidal, and it is not clear how, in the years to come, they and their purposes are to be coped with. Critics of American bravado are obliged to address the question in earnest. It is mightily worth underscoring that, as the document says, "international obligations are to be taken seriously. They are not to be undertaken symbolically to rally support for an ideal without furthering its attainment."

But the document undermines its own most defensible points because it exudes the spirit of take-it-or-leave-it. It carries out Bush's impulse to rip-roar through obstacles after a bit of small-group communion. It has all the logic of the Republican Supreme Court majority in *Bush v. Gore*, the logic that put W in the White House, the logic that now leads the charmed circle of Bush, Cheney, Rumsfeld, Wolfowitz, and Condoleezza Rice to make enormous decisions behind closed doors without much consultation (except an occasional nod to Colin Powell). It has the bluster of an administration that presses the intelligence agencies to sign onto its view of how things must be, against their better judgment. This is the manifesto of a bully with a ferocious will who fumbles in search of reasons to explain why he does what he feels like doing.

If you thought the promulgation of such a manifesto would be big news, you would be mistaken. On release, the National Security Strategy was jabbed at by a few opposition politicians, picked apart in a handful of newspaper columns, and promptly sank from sight. On television, it hardly even happened. That Democrats paid attention to the Bush doctrine at all is to the credit of Al Gore, who in a September 23 speech in San Francisco said that it conveys "one of the most fateful decisions in our history: a decision to abandon what we have thought was America's mission in the world." He concluded that the new doctrine "destroys the goal of a world in which states consider themselves subject to law" in favor of "the notion that there is no law but the discretion of the President of the United States." No major networks deigned to take more than passing note of his speech.

As a nation, we're still in a trance. The leadership of the most powerful nation-state on earth proceeds to set out its grand strategy, its unified theory of everything, and its prime channels of information don't see fit to let the populace in on the news that their government is hell-bent on empire and has said so in black and white.

Nonetheless, Bush's strategy is now in force. It confirms suspicions and stokes paranoia. In propounding that there are no more than two models for how a society lives in the world, and that those who despise the one must enlist behind the other, it indulges in the same drastic oversimplification that motivates the terrorists. Americans will have to contend with the consequences for generations. This is why the Bush doctrine is dangerous: It's a gift to anti-Americans everywhere.

THE CONTINUING DEBATE:
The Bush Doctrine

What Is New

The invasion of Iraq was the first major application of the Bush Doctrine. It was preemptive, it was largely unilateral, and it seeks to remake Iraq into an American-style democracy. Tension with North Korea and Iran over their nuclear weapons programs and with Syria over its alleged support of terrorism are the most likely issues to lead in the near future to another such action.

There have been barrages of criticism of the war and the administration's policy in post-war Iraq. White House supporters have fired counter-volleys, and the issue will be central to the 2004 presidential campaign. However one evaluates whether or not the war was just, it went well as a military campaign, while the post-war stabilization effort faltered badly. These experiences can be used to evaluate the Bush Doctrine, but it would be too narrow to use them alone to judge the president's vision. Sometimes, good policy is carried out badly; at other times bad policy is carried out well. Therefore consider the Bush Doctrine as a whole and in its constituent parts, and decide whether all or some of it provides a sound basis for American foreign policy.

Where to Find More

Begin by reading the Bush Doctrine, "The National Security Strategy of the United States of America," at: http://www.whitehouse.gov/nsc/nss.html. To learn more about the neoconservative view, visit the Web site of Project for a New American Century (PNAC) at: http://newamericancentury.org. Also, read Elizabeth Drew, "The Neocons in Power," *New York Review of Books*, June 12, 2003 at http://www.nybooks.com/archives. An article favoring President Bush's foreign policy principles is Charles Krauthammer, "The Bush Doctrine: ABM, Kyoto, and the New American Unilateralism," *The Weekly Standard,* June 4, 2001. The journal (edited by William Kristol, who is also chairman of PNAC) is a leading neocon venue. A traditional conservative critique of the Bush Doctrine is Andrew J. Bacevich, "Bush's Grand Strategy," *The American Conservative*, November 4, 2002, at: http://www.amconmag.com/archive.html. The liberal critique can be found in John Steinbruner, "Confusing Ends and Means: The Doctrine of Coercive Pre-emption," *Arms Control Today*, January/February, 2003 at: http://www.armscontrol.org/act/archived.asp.

What More to Do

It is easier to criticize than create, so one thing to do if you disagree with all or any aspect of the Bush Doctrine is to author the _____ Doctrine (fill your surname in the blank space). In it lay out your foreign policy principles. Also, if you do not like the Bush Doctrine, get active to defeat its author in the 2004 election. Or, if you support the doctrine, support the man for reelection.

CREDITS

Amicus Curiae brief to the United States Supreme Court in *Grutter v. Bollinger* (2003).

Aultman, Kathi A. Testimony during hearings on the "Partial-Birth Abortion Ban Act of 2002" before the U.S. Senate Committee on the Judiciary, Subcommittee on the Constitution, July 9, 2002.

Beach, William. Testimony during hearings on the "Balanced Budget Amendment" before the U.S. House of Representatives Committee on the Judiciary, Subcommittee on the Constitution, October 10, 2002.

Best, Judith A. Testimony during hearings on "Proposals for Electoral College Reform: H.J. Res. 28 and J.J. Res. 43" before the U.S. House of Representatives Committee on the Judiciary, Subcommittee on the Constitution, September 4, 1997.

Bond, Julian. Testimony during hearings on "Race and the Federal Death Penalty," before the U.S. Senate Committee on the Judiciary, Subcommittee on Constitution, Federalism, and Property Rights, June 13, 2001.

Cain, Becky. Testimony during hearings on "Proposals for Electoral College Reform: H.J. Res. 28 and J.J. Res. 43" before the U.S. House of Representatives Committee on the Judiciary, Subcommittee on the Constitution, September 4, 1997.

Casse, Daniel. "An Emerging Republican Majority?" Reprinted from *Commentary*, January 2003, by permission of the publisher and the author. All rights reserved.

Center for Reproductive Rights. Excerpt from "Unconstitutional Assault on the Right to Choose: 'Partial-Birth Abortion' Ban Is an Affront to Women and to the U.S. Supreme Court," February 2003. Reprinted by permission of the Center for Reproductive Rights. (www.reproductiverights.org).

Chen, Edward M. Testimony during hearings on "Implications of 'Official English' Legislation," before the United States House of Representatives Committee on Economic and Educational Opportunities, Subcommittee on Early Childhood, Youth, and Families, November 1, 1995.

Donnelly, Thomas. "The Underpinnings of the Bush Doctrine" from *National Security Outlook*, AEI Online, February 1, 2003. Reprinted by permission of the American Enterprise Institute.

Farber, Daniel A. From "Disarmed by Time: The Second Amendment and the Failure of Originalism," *Chicago-Ken Law Review*, Vol. 76, No. 1 (2000). Reprinted by permission of the author.

Friedman, Leon. "Overruling the Court." Reprinted with permission of the publisher and author from *The American Prospect*, Volume 12, Number 15: August 27, 2001. The American Prospect, 5 Broad Street, Boston, MA 02109. All rights reserved

Friedman, Paul. "TV: A Missed Opportunity." Reprinted from *Columbia Journalism Review*, May/June 2003. © 2003 by Columbia Journalism Review. Used by permission of the publisher and Paul Friedman.

Gaziano, Todd F. Testimony during hearings on a "Judiciary Diminished Is Justice Denied: The Constitution, the Senate, and the Vacancy Crisis in the Federal Judiciary," before U.S. House of Representatives, Committee on the Judiciary, Subcommittee on the Constitution, October 10, 2002.

Gitlin, Todd. "America's Age of Empire," *Mother Jones*, January/February 2003. ©2003, Foundation for National Progress. Reprinted by permission.

Hamilton, Marci A. Testimony during hearings before the Senate Committee on the Judiciary on "Narrowing the Nation's Power: The Supreme Court Sides with the States," October 1, 2002.

Hanson, Victor Davis. "I Love Iraq, Bomb Texas." Reprinted from *Commentary*, December 2002, by permission of the publisher and the author. All rights reserved

Hibbing, John R. Testimony during hearings on "Limiting Terms of Office for Members of the U.S. Senate and U.S. House of Representatives," U.S. House of Representatives, Committee on the Judiciary, Subcommittee on the Constitution, January 22, 1997.

Jacob, Paul. Testimony during hearings on "Limiting Terms of Office for Members of the U.S. Senate and U.S. House of Representatives," U.S. House of Representatives, Committee on the Judiciary, Subcommittee on the Constitution, January 22, 1997.

Judis, John B., and Ruy Teixeira. "America's Changing Political Geography: Where Democrats Can Build a Majority," from the September/October 2002 issue of *Blueprint: Ideas for a New Century*, journal of New Democrats Online. http://www.ndol.org/blueprint. Reprinted by permission.

Kmiec, Douglas. Testimony during hearings on "Applying the War Powers Resolution to the War on Terrorism," before the U.S. Senate Committee on the Judiciary, April 17, 2002.

Kogan, Richard. Testimony during hearings on the "Balanced Budget Amendment" before the U.S. House of Representatives Committee on the Judiciary, Subcommittee on the Constitution, October 10, 2002.

Lynch, Timothy. From "Breaking the Vicious Cycle: Preserving Our Liberties While Fighting Terrorism," *Cato Policy Analysis*, No. 443, June 16, 2002. Reprinted by permission of the Cato Institute.

Malcolm, Joyce. "Infringement," *Common-place*, Vol. 2: No. 4, July 2002. www.common-place.org. Copyright © 2002 by Common-place: The Interactive Journal of Early American Life. Reprinted by permission.

McBride, Andrew. Testimony during hearings on "Race and the Federal Death Penalty," before the U.S. Senate Committee on the Judiciary, Subcommittee on Constitution, Federalism, and Property Rights, June 13, 2001.

Mujica, Mauro E. "Statement from the Chairman" and all material from the U.S. ENGLISH Web site is reprinted by permission. © 2003, U.S. ENGLISH, Inc. (http://www.us-english.org/inc).

Ponnuru, Ramesh. "1984 in 2003?" from *National Review*, June 2, 2003, pp. 17–18. © 2003 by National Review, Inc., 215 Lexington Avenue, New York, NY 10016. Reprinted by permission.

Ricchiardi, Sherry. From "Close to the Action," *American Journalism Review*, May 2003. Reprinted by permission of American Journalism Review.

Ross-Edwards, Amanda. "The Department of Education and Title IX: Flawed Interpretation and Implementation," an essay written for this volume, October 2003.

Shain, Yossi. From "For Ethnic Americans, The Old Country Calls," *Foreign Service Journal*, October 2000. Reprinted by permission of Yossi Shain.

Stromseth, Jane. Testimony during hearings on "Applying the War Powers Resolution to the War on Terrorism," before the U.S. Senate Committee on the Judiciary, April 17, 2002.

Sweet, Judith. U.S. Department of Education, Secretary's Commission on Opportunity in Athletics, Hearings, August 27, 2002.

Tribe, Laurence H. Testimony during hearings on "Judicial Nominations, Filibusters, and the Constitution: When a Majority Is Denied Its Right to Consent," before U.S. Senate Committee on the Judiciary, May 6, 2002.

Vidal, Gore. "We Are the Patriots." Originally appeared in *The Nation*, June 2, 2003. Reprinted by permission of the author.

Wheatcroft, Geoffrey. "Hyphenated Americans," *Guardian Unlimited Online*, April 25, 2000. Reprinted by permission of the author.